Maria✝Holic

Volume 5

by Minari Endou

HAMBURG // LONDON // LOS ANGELES // TOKYO

Maria Holic Volume 5
Created by Minari Endou

Translation - Yuko Fukami
English Adaptation - Clint Bickham
Retouch and Lettering - Star Print Brokers
Production Artist - Rui Kyo and Michael Paolilli
Graphic Designer - Christian Lownds

Editor - Hope Donovan
Print Production Manager - Lucas Rivera
Managing Editor - Vy Nguyen
Senior Designer - Louis Csontos
Art Director - Al-Insan Lashley
Director of Sales and Manufacturing - Allyson De Simone
Associate Publisher - Marco F. Pavia
President and C.O.O. - John Parker
C.E.O. and Chief Creative Officer - Stu Levy

A  Manga

TOKYOPOP and  are trademarks or registered trademarks of TOKYOPOP Inc.

TOKYOPOP Inc.
5900 Wilshire Blvd. Suite 2000
Los Angeles, CA 90036

E-mail: info@TOKYOPOP.com
Come visit us online at www.TOKYOPOP.com

© 2009 Minari Endou. First published in Japan in 2009 by MEDIA FACTORY, Inc., Tokyo, Japan. English publication rights arranged through MEDIA FACTORY,Inc. English text copyright © 2010 TOKYOPOP Inc.

All rights reserved. No portion of this book may be reproduced or transmitted in any form or by any means without written permission from the copyright holders. This manga is a work of fiction. Any resemblance to actual events or locales or persons, living or dead, is entirely coincidental.

ISBN: 978-1-4278-1829-4

First TOKYOPOP printing: November 2010
10 9 8 7 6 5 4 3 2 1
Printed in the USA

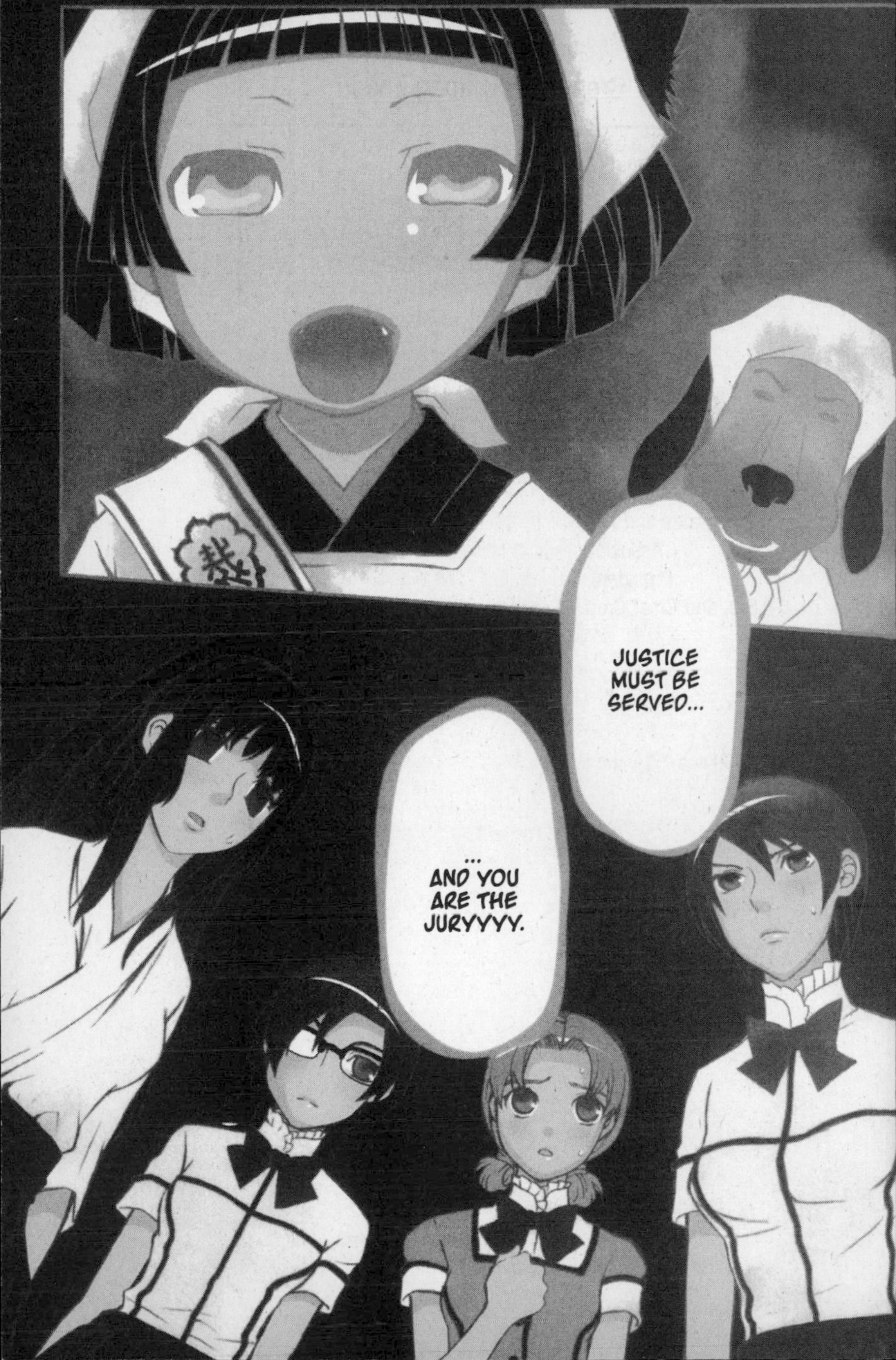
JUSTICE MUST BE SERVED...
... AND YOU ARE THE JURYYYY.

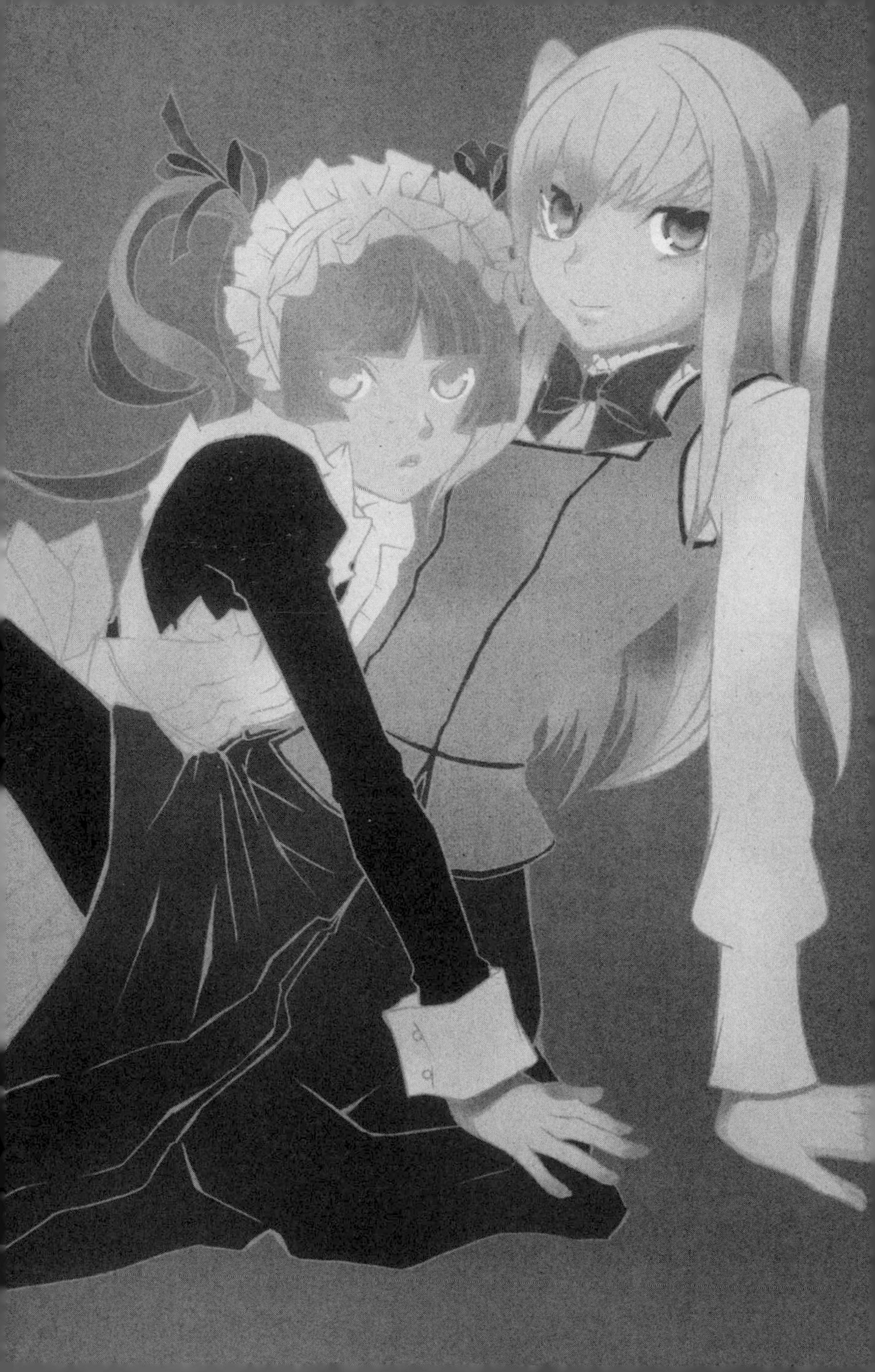

Prayer 25
The Yonakuni Trial ①

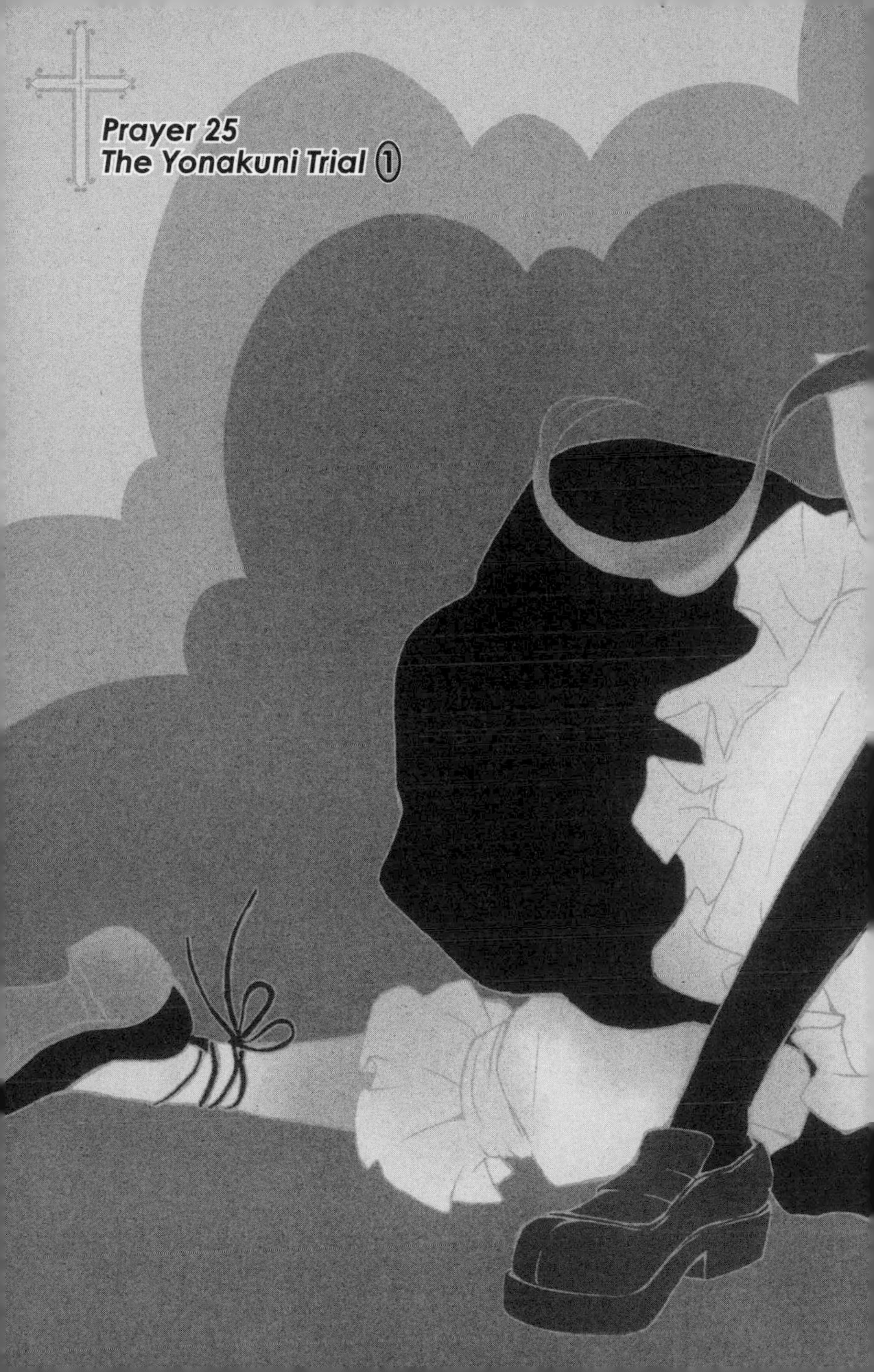

MARIA
HOLIC

5

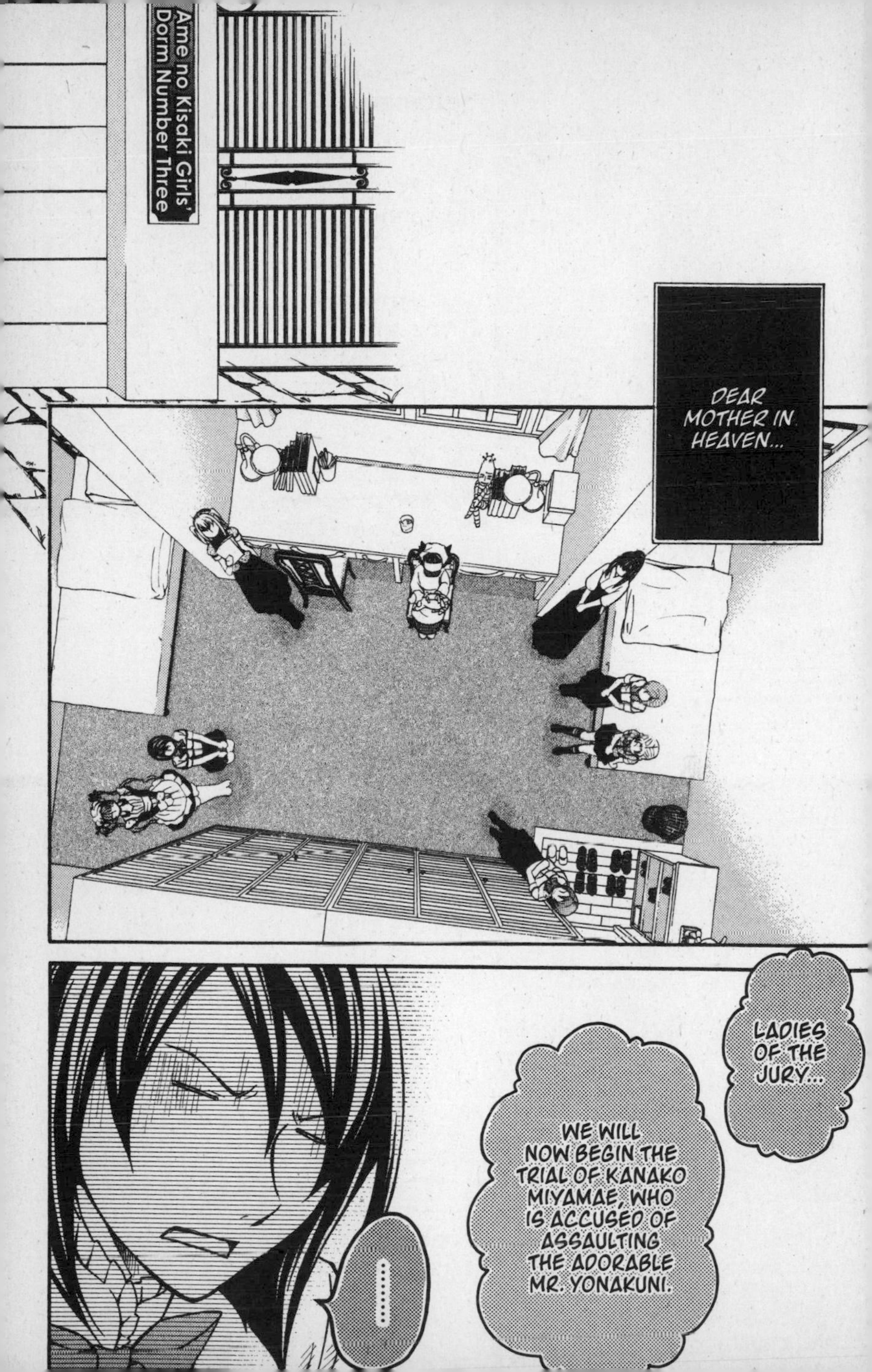
Ame no Kisaki Girls' Dorm Number Three
DEAR MOTHER IN HEAVEN...
LADIES OF THE JURY...
WE WILL NOW BEGIN THE TRIAL OF KANAKO MIYAMAE, WHO IS ACCUSED OF ASSAULTING THE ADORABLE MR. YONAKUNI.
....

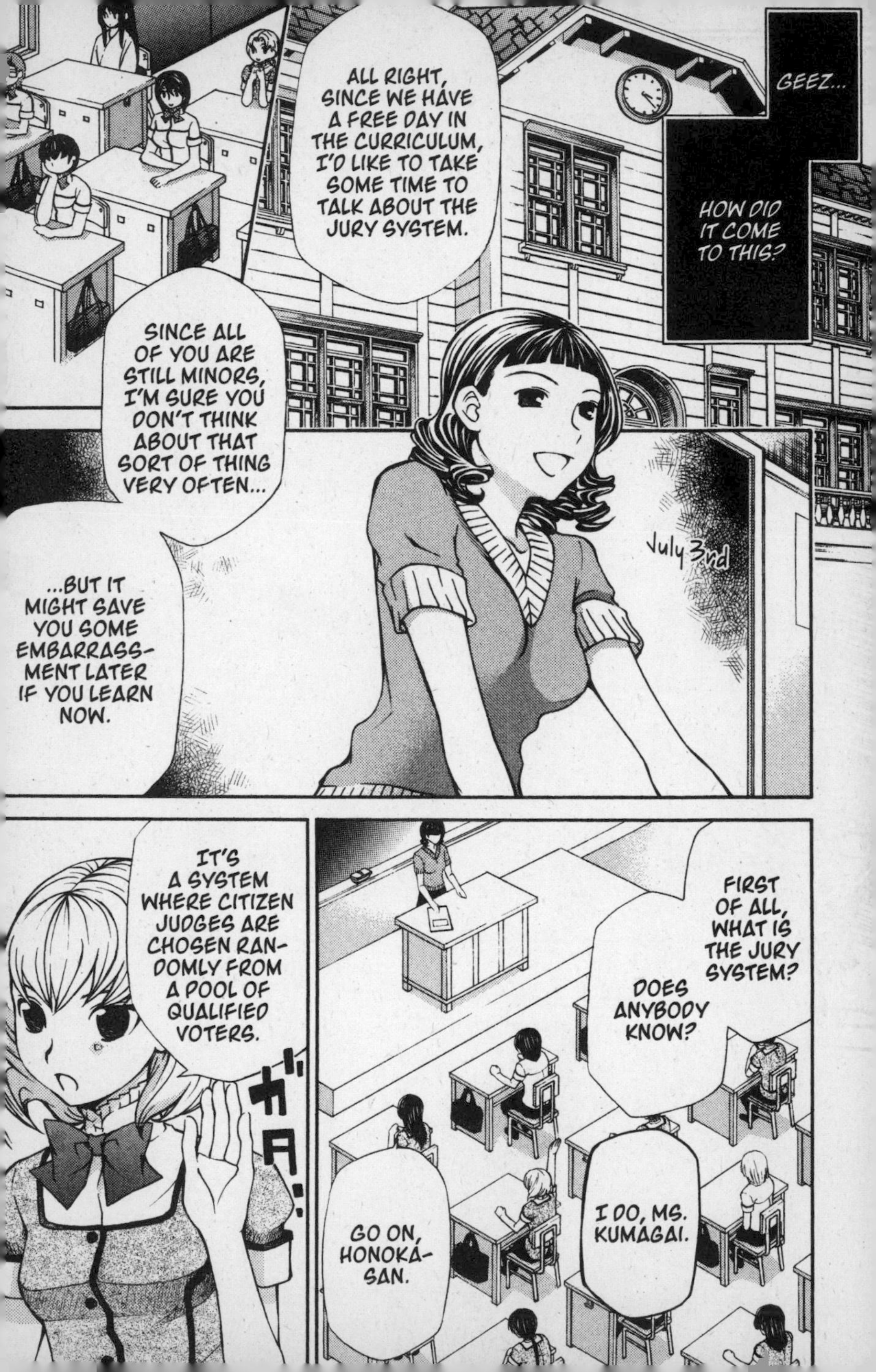
GEEZ...
HOW DID IT COME TO THIS?
ALL RIGHT, SINCE WE HAVE A FREE DAY IN THE CURRICULUM, I'D LIKE TO TAKE SOME TIME TO TALK ABOUT THE JURY SYSTEM.
July 3rd
SINCE ALL OF YOU ARE STILL MINORS, I'M SURE YOU DON'T THINK ABOUT THAT SORT OF THING VERY OFTEN...
...BUT IT MIGHT SAVE YOU SOME EMBARRASS-MENT LATER IF YOU LEARN NOW.
FIRST OF ALL, WHAT IS THE JURY SYSTEM?
DOES ANYBODY KNOW?
I DO, MS. KUMAGAI.
GO ON, HONOKA-SAN.
IT'S A SYSTEM WHERE CITIZEN JUDGES ARE CHOSEN RAN-DOMLY FROM A POOL OF QUALIFIED VOTERS.

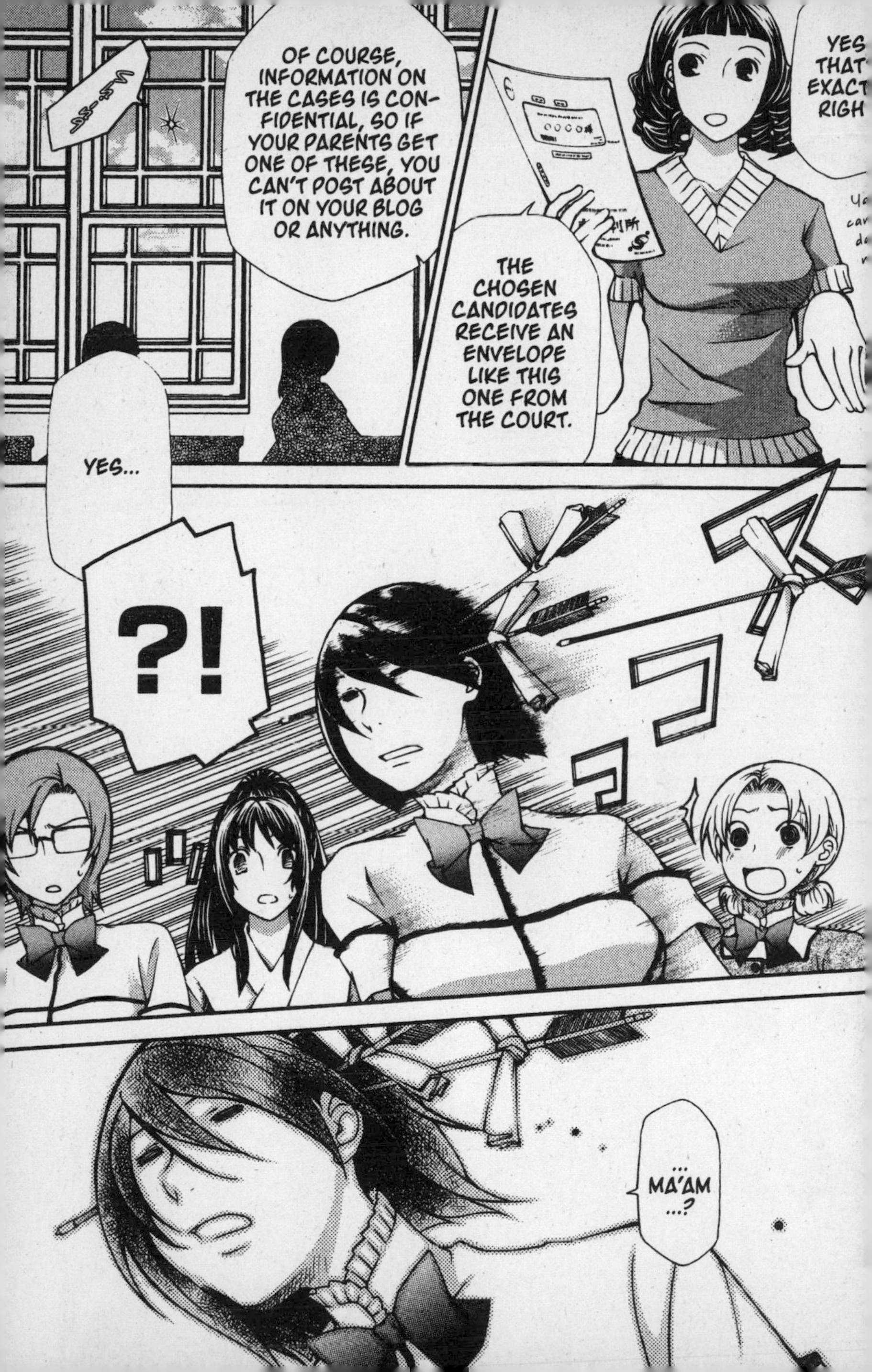

YES THAT EXACT RIGH
THE CHOSEN CANDIDATES RECEIVE AN ENVELOPE LIKE THIS ONE FROM THE COURT.
OF COURSE, INFORMATION ON THE CASES IS CONFIDENTIAL, SO IF YOUR PARENTS GET ONE OF THESE, YOU CAN'T POST ABOUT IT ON YOUR BLOG OR ANYTHING.
YES...
?!
...MA'AM ...?

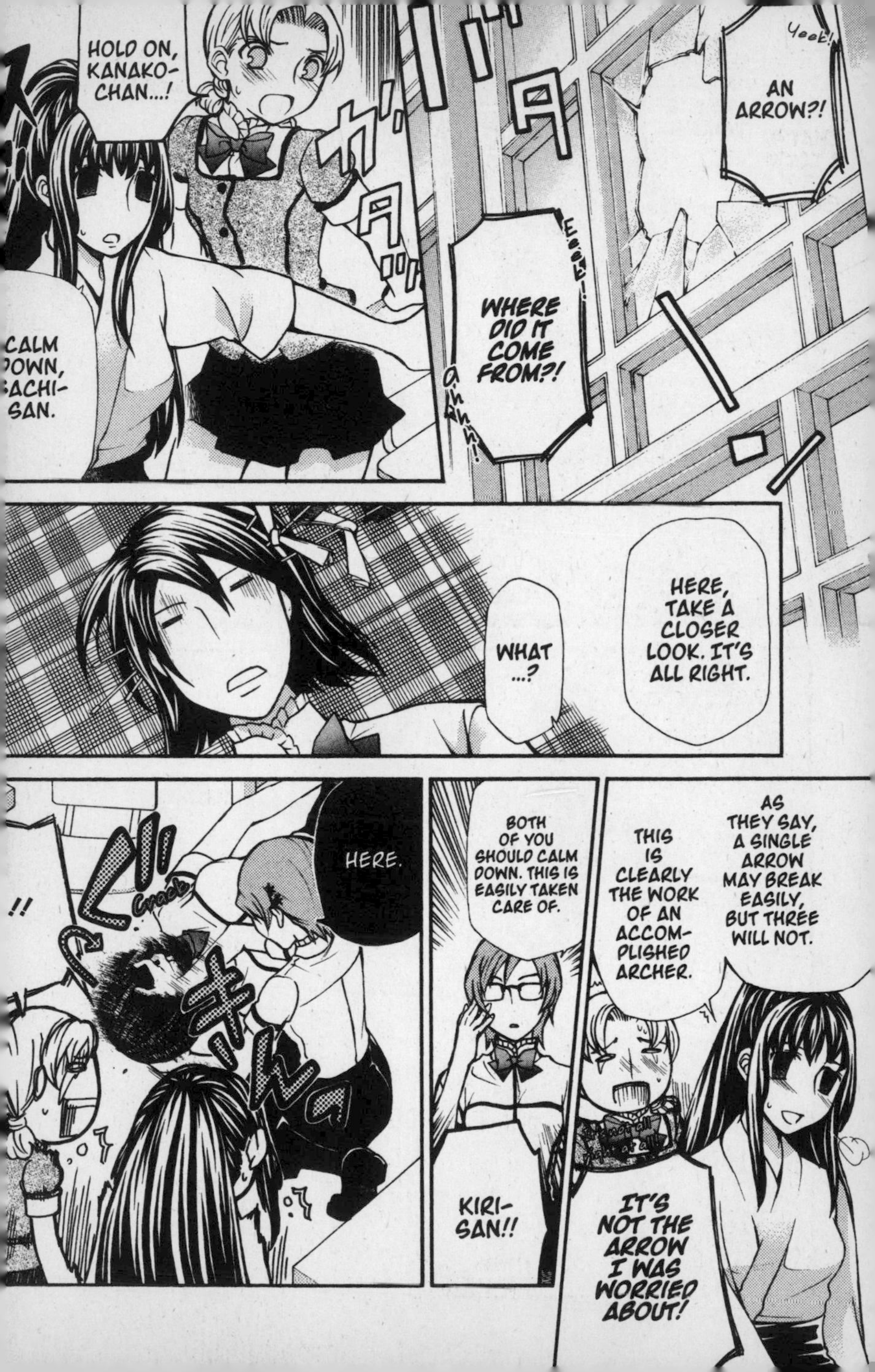
Yeek!
AN ARROW?!
WHERE DID IT COME FROM?!
HOLD ON, KANAKO-CHAN...!
CALM DOWN, SACHI-SAN.
HERE, TAKE A CLOSER LOOK. IT'S ALL RIGHT.
WHAT ...?
AS THEY SAY, A SINGLE ARROW MAY BREAK EASILY, BUT THREE WILL NOT.
THIS IS CLEARLY THE WORK OF AN ACCOMPLISHED ARCHER.
IT'S NOT THE ARROW I WAS WORRIED ABOUT!
BOTH OF YOU SHOULD CALM DOWN. THIS IS EASILY TAKEN CARE OF.
KIRI-SAN!!
HERE.
Grab
!!

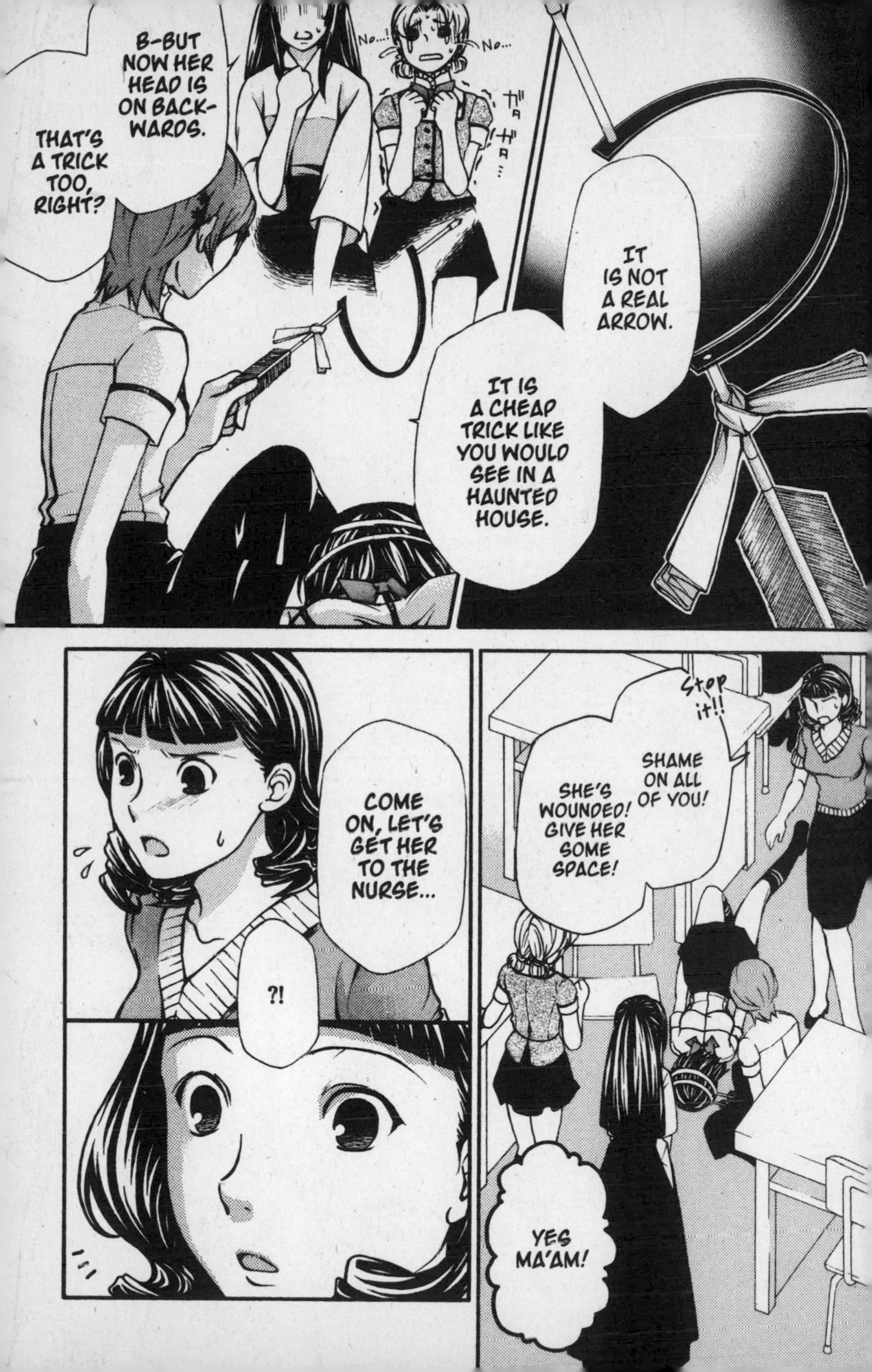
IT IS NOT A REAL ARROW.
IT IS A CHEAP TRICK LIKE YOU WOULD SEE IN A HAUNTED HOUSE.
ガタ ガタ...
No...
No...!
B-BUT NOW HER HEAD IS ON BACK-WARDS.
THAT'S A TRICK TOO, RIGHT?
Stop it!!
SHAME ON ALL OF YOU!
SHE'S WOUNDED! GIVE HER SOME SPACE!
YES MA'AM!
COME ON, LET'S GET HER TO THE NURSE...
?!

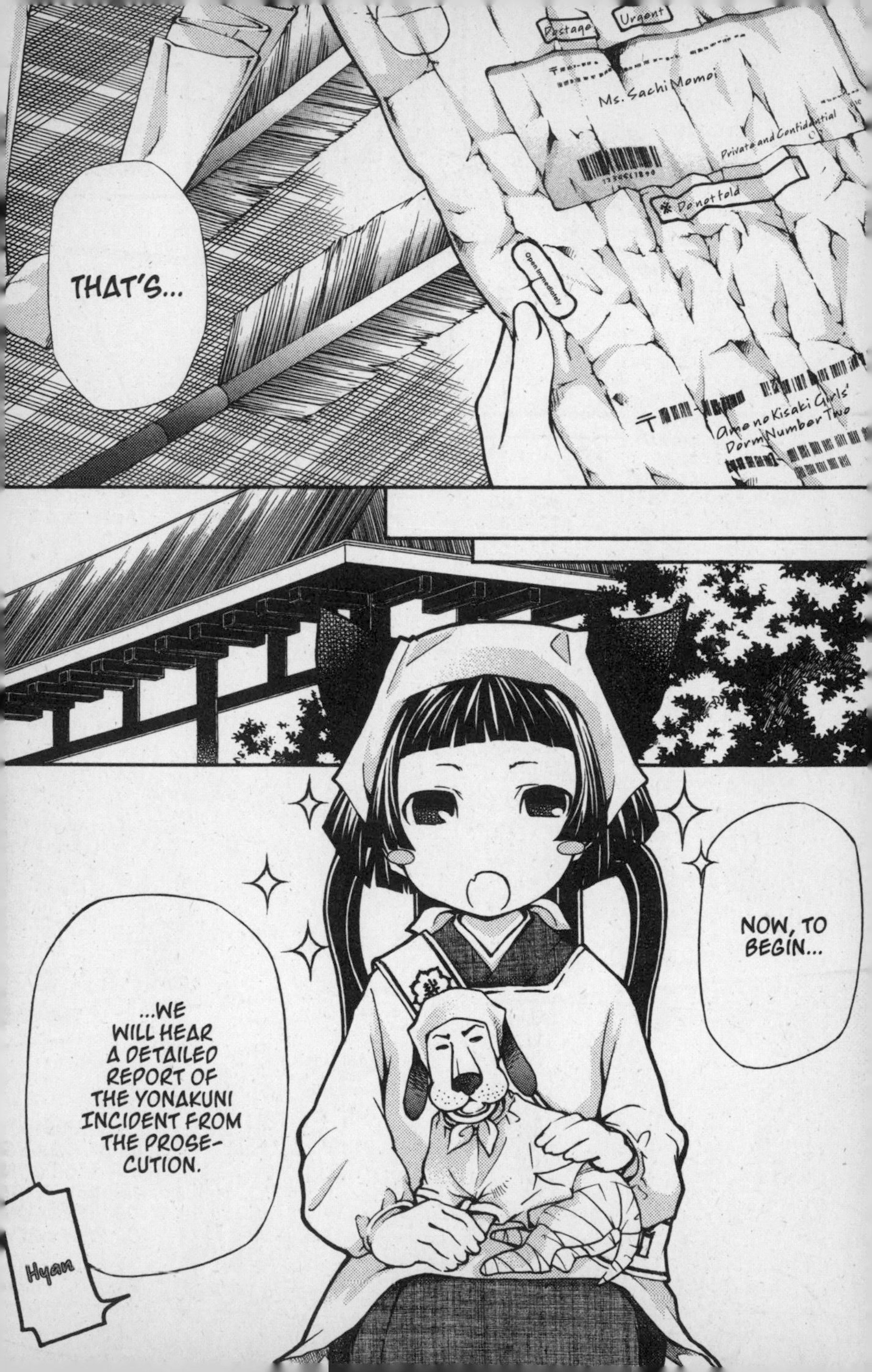
Urgent
Postage
Ms. Sachi Momoi
Private and Confidential
※ Do not fold
Open Immediately
Ame no Kisaki Girls' Dorm Number Two
THAT'S...
NOW, TO BEGIN...
...WE WILL HEAR A DETAILED REPORT OF THE YONAKUNI INCIDENT FROM THE PROSE-CUTION.
Hyan

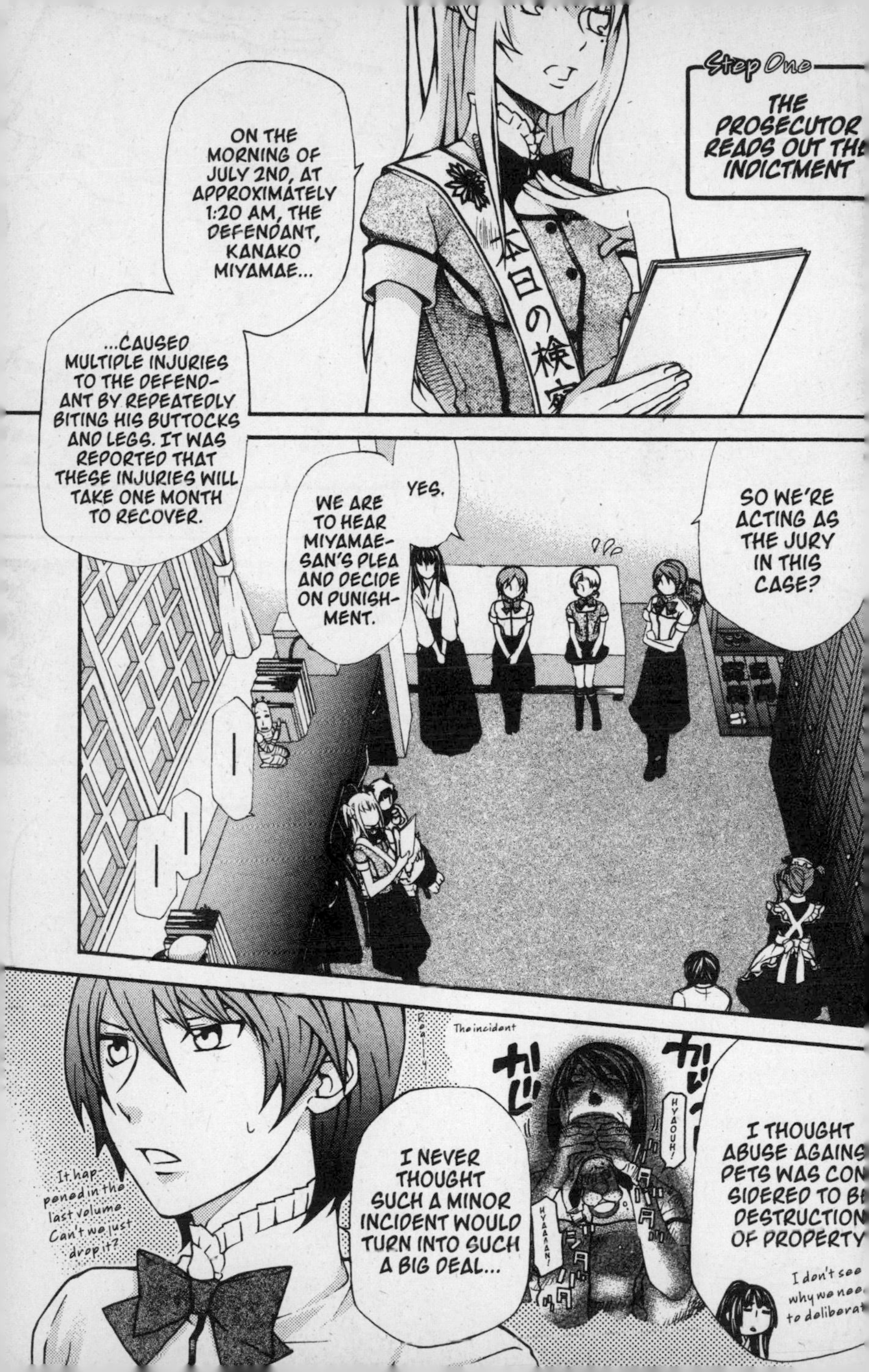
Step One
THE PROSECUTOR READS OUT THE INDICTMENT
ON THE MORNING OF JULY 2ND, AT APPROXIMATELY 1:20 AM, THE DEFENDANT, KANAKO MIYAMAE...
本日の検
...CAUSED MULTIPLE INJURIES TO THE DEFENDANT BY REPEATEDLY BITING HIS BUTTOCKS AND LEGS. IT WAS REPORTED THAT THESE INJURIES WILL TAKE ONE MONTH TO RECOVER.
SO WE'RE ACTING AS THE JURY IN THIS CASE?
YES.
WE ARE TO HEAR MIYAMAE-SAN'S PLEA AND DECIDE ON PUNISHMENT.
I THOUGHT ABUSE AGAINS PETS WAS CON SIDERED TO B DESTRUCTION OF PROPERTY
I don't see why we nee to deliberat
HYAOUH!
HYAAAAN!
The incident
I NEVER THOUGHT SUCH A MINOR INCIDENT WOULD TURN INTO SUCH A BIG DEAL...
Really
It happened in the last volume. Can't we just drop it?

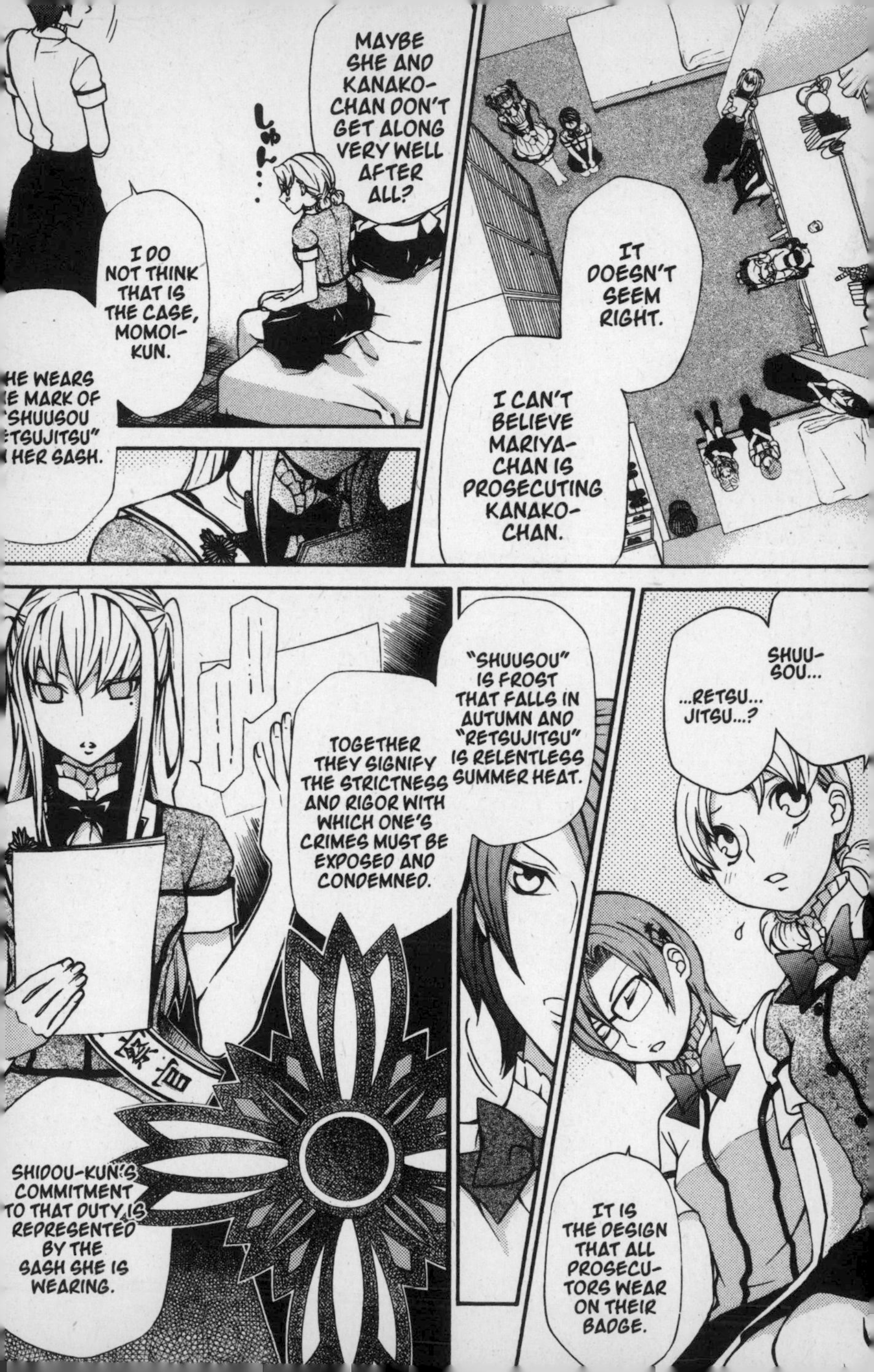
IT DOESN'T SEEM RIGHT.
I CAN'T BELIEVE MARIYA-CHAN IS PROSECUTING KANAKO-CHAN.
MAYBE SHE AND KANAKO-CHAN DON'T GET ALONG VERY WELL AFTER ALL?
しゅん…
I DO NOT THINK THAT IS THE CASE, MOMOI-KUN.
HE WEARS E MARK OF "SHUUSOU ETSUJITSU" HER SASH.
SHUU-SOU...
...RETSU... JITSU...?
IT IS THE DESIGN THAT ALL PROSECUTORS WEAR ON THEIR BADGE.
"SHUUSOU" IS FROST THAT FALLS IN AUTUMN AND "RETSUJITSU" IS RELENTLESS SUMMER HEAT.
TOGETHER THEY SIGNIFY THE STRICTNESS AND RIGOR WITH WHICH ONE'S CRIMES MUST BE EXPOSED AND CONDEMNED.
SHIDOU-KUN'S COMMITMENT TO THAT DUTY IS REPRESENTED BY THE SASH SHE IS WEARING.

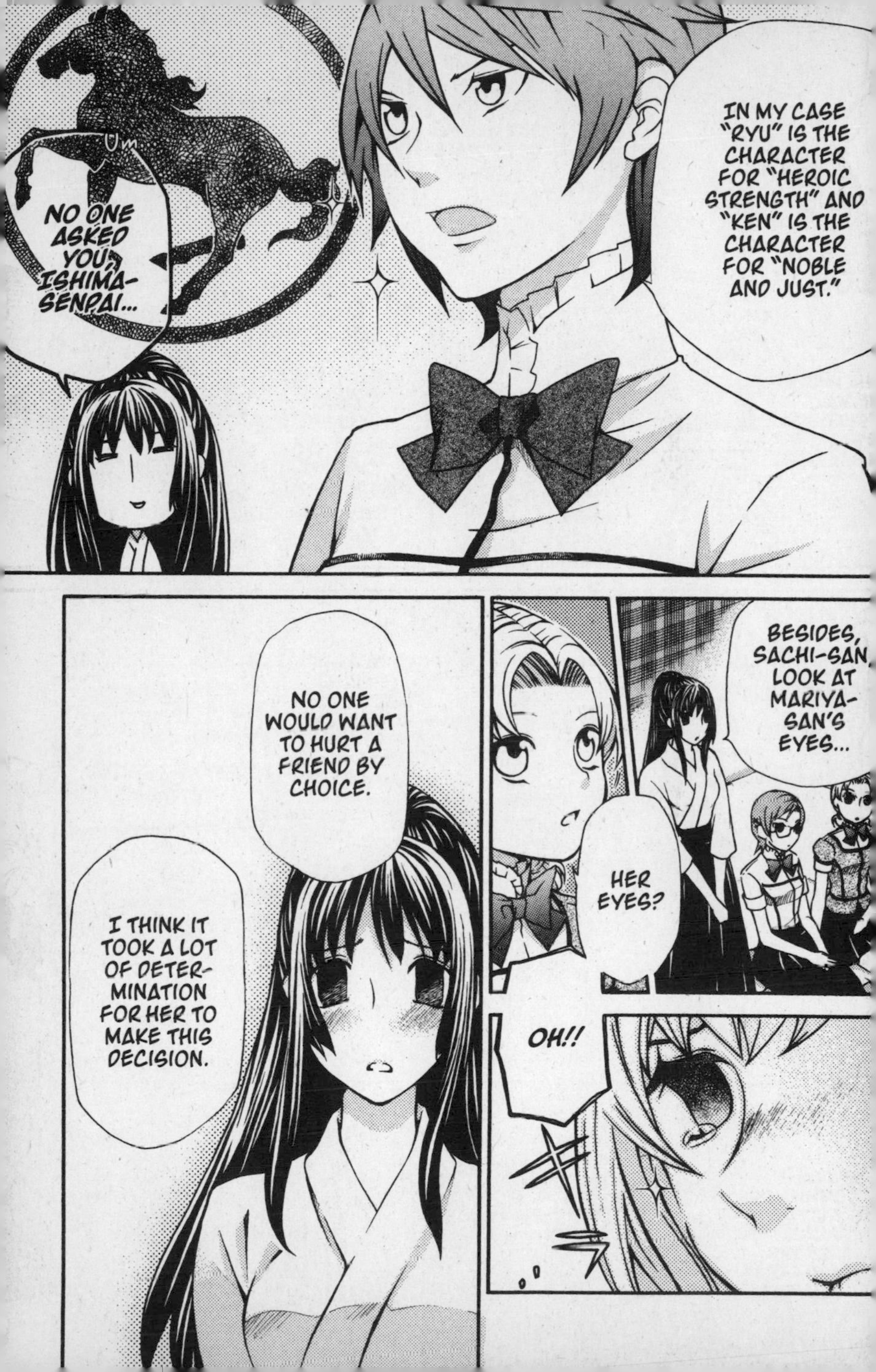
IN MY CASE "RYU" IS THE CHARACTER FOR "HEROIC STRENGTH" AND "KEN" IS THE CHARACTER FOR "NOBLE AND JUST."
NO ONE ASKED YOU, ISHIMA-SENPAI...
BESIDES, SACHI-SAN, LOOK AT MARIYA-SAN'S EYES...
HER EYES?
OH!!
NO ONE WOULD WANT TO HURT A FRIEND BY CHOICE.
I THINK IT TOOK A LOT OF DETERMINATION FOR HER TO MAKE THIS DECISION.

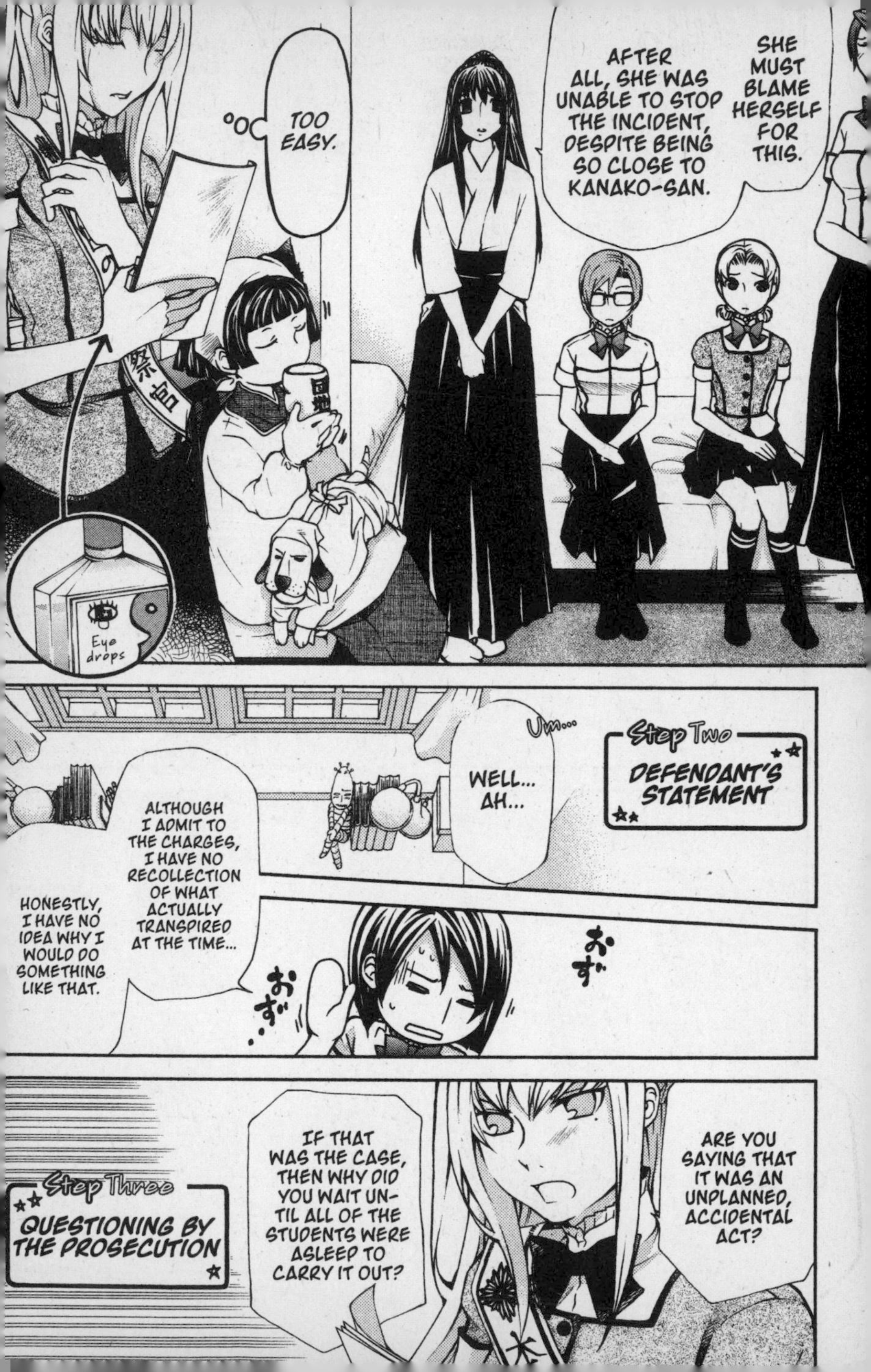
SHE MUST BLAME HERSELF FOR THIS.
AFTER ALL, SHE WAS UNABLE TO STOP THE INCIDENT, DESPITE BEING SO CLOSE TO KANAKO-SAN.
TOO EASY.
Eye drops
Step Two
DEFENDANT'S STATEMENT
Um...
WELL... AH...
ALTHOUGH I ADMIT TO THE CHARGES, I HAVE NO RECOLLECTION OF WHAT ACTUALLY TRANSPIRED AT THE TIME...
HONESTLY, I HAVE NO IDEA WHY I WOULD DO SOMETHING LIKE THAT.
おず
おず
ARE YOU SAYING THAT IT WAS AN UNPLANNED, ACCIDENTAL ACT?
IF THAT WAS THE CASE, THEN WHY DID YOU WAIT UN-TIL ALL OF THE STUDENTS WERE ASLEEP TO CARRY IT OUT?
Step Three
QUESTIONING BY THE PROSECUTION

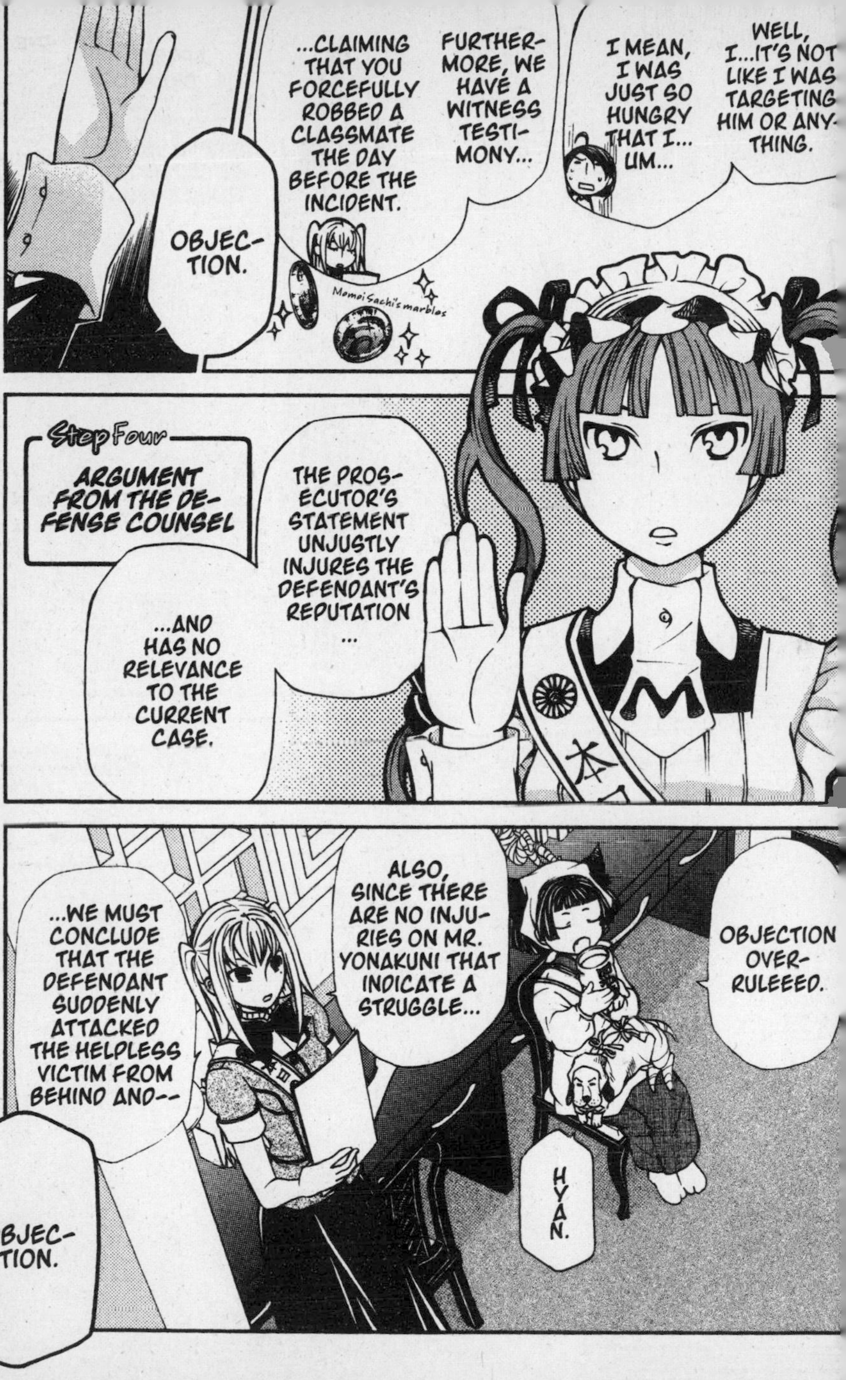
WELL, I...IT'S NOT LIKE I WAS TARGETING HIM OR ANYTHING.
I MEAN, I WAS JUST SO HUNGRY THAT I... UM...
FURTHERMORE, WE HAVE A WITNESS TESTIMONY...
...CLAIMING THAT YOU FORCEFULLY ROBBED A CLASSMATE THE DAY BEFORE THE INCIDENT.
OBJECTION.
Momoi Sachi's marbles
Step Four
ARGUMENT FROM THE DEFENSE COUNSEL
THE PROSECUTOR'S STATEMENT UNJUSTLY INJURES THE DEFENDANT'S REPUTATION ...
...AND HAS NO RELEVANCE TO THE CURRENT CASE.
OBJECTION OVERRULEEED.
HYAN.
ALSO, SINCE THERE ARE NO INJURIES ON MR. YONAKUNI THAT INDICATE A STRUGGLE...
...WE MUST CONCLUDE THAT THE DEFENDANT SUDDENLY ATTACKED THE HELPLESS VICTIM FROM BEHIND AND--
OBJECTION.

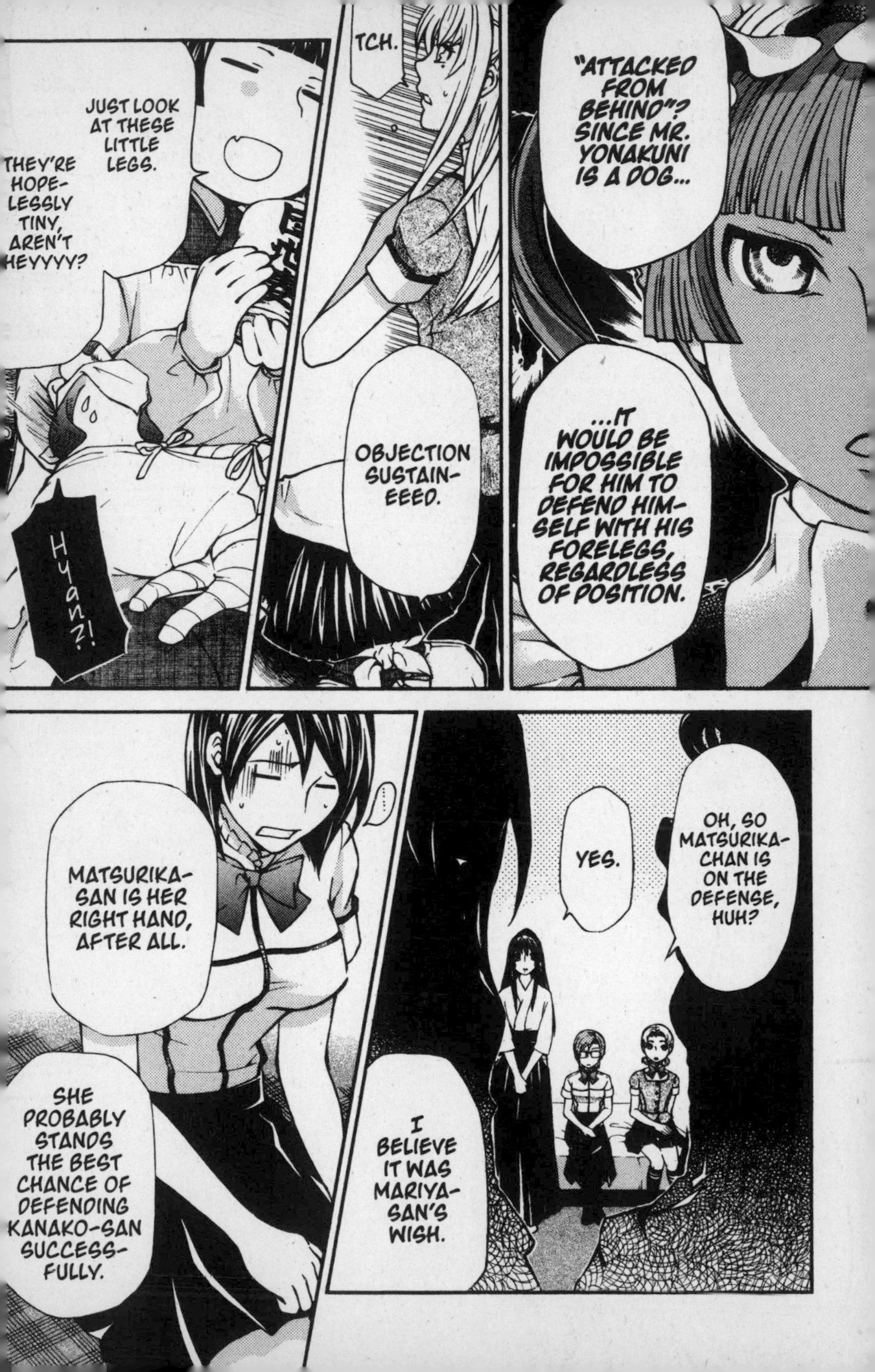
"ATTACKED FROM BEHIND"? SINCE MR. YONAKUNI IS A DOG...
...IT WOULD BE IMPOSSIBLE FOR HIM TO DEFEND HIMSELF WITH HIS FORELEGS, REGARDLESS OF POSITION.
TCH.
OBJECTION SUSTAIN-EEED.
JUST LOOK AT THESE LITTLE LEGS.
THEY'RE HOPE-LESSLY TINY, AREN'T HEYYYY?
Hyan?!
OH, SO MATSURIKA-CHAN IS ON THE DEFENSE, HUH?
YES.
I BELIEVE IT WAS MARIYA-SAN'S WISH.
...
MATSURIKA-SAN IS HER RIGHT HAND, AFTER ALL.
SHE PROBABLY STANDS THE BEST CHANCE OF DEFENDING KANAKO-SAN SUCCESS-FULLY.

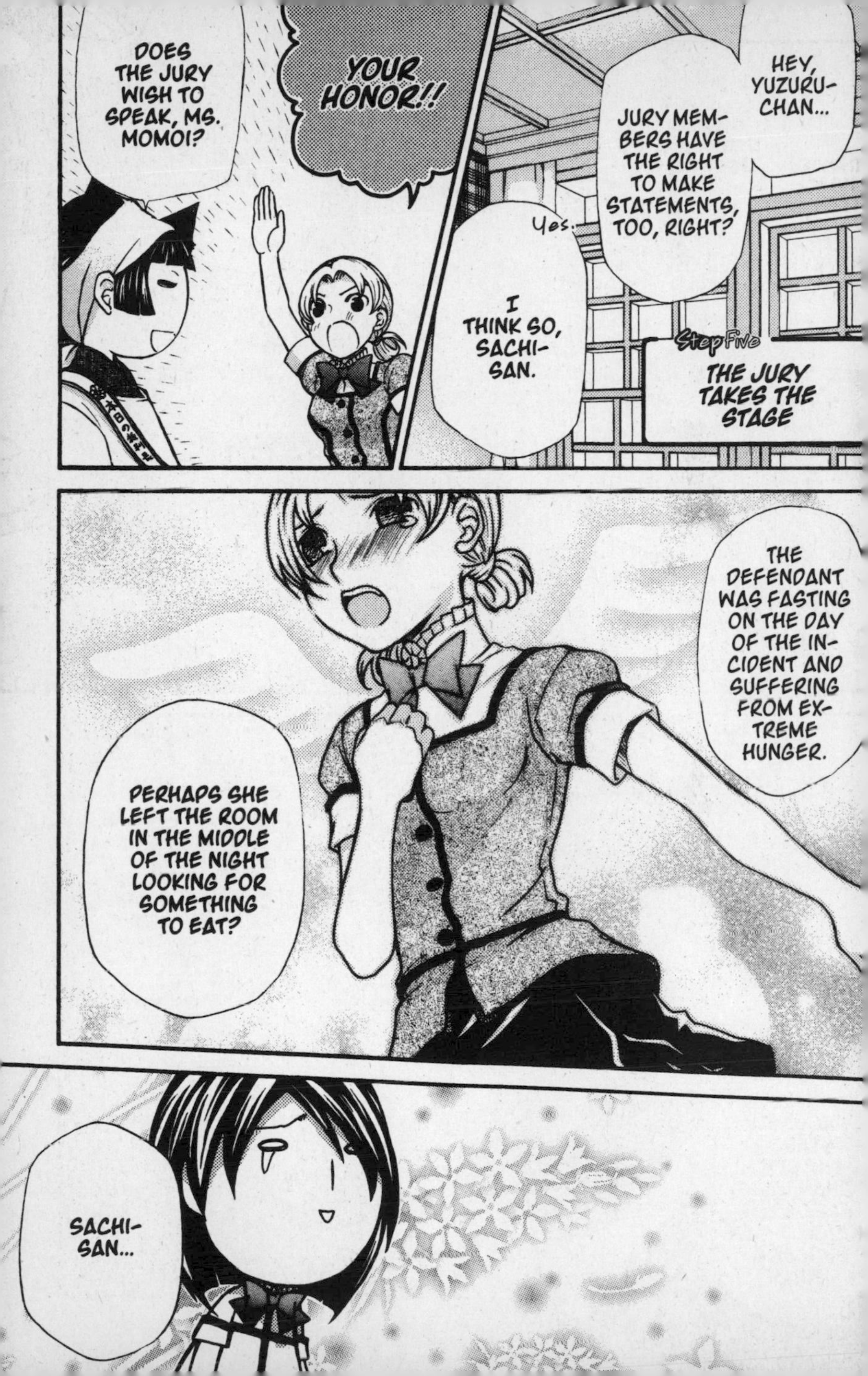
Step Five
THE JURY TAKES THE STAGE
HEY, YUZURU-CHAN...
JURY MEMBERS HAVE THE RIGHT TO MAKE STATEMENTS, TOO, RIGHT?
Yes.
I THINK SO, SACHI-SAN.
YOUR HONOR!!
DOES THE JURY WISH TO SPEAK, MS. MOMOI?
THE DEFENDANT WAS FASTING ON THE DAY OF THE INCIDENT AND SUFFERING FROM EXTREME HUNGER.
PERHAPS SHE LEFT THE ROOM IN THE MIDDLE OF THE NIGHT LOOKING FOR SOMETHING TO EAT?
SACHI-SAN...

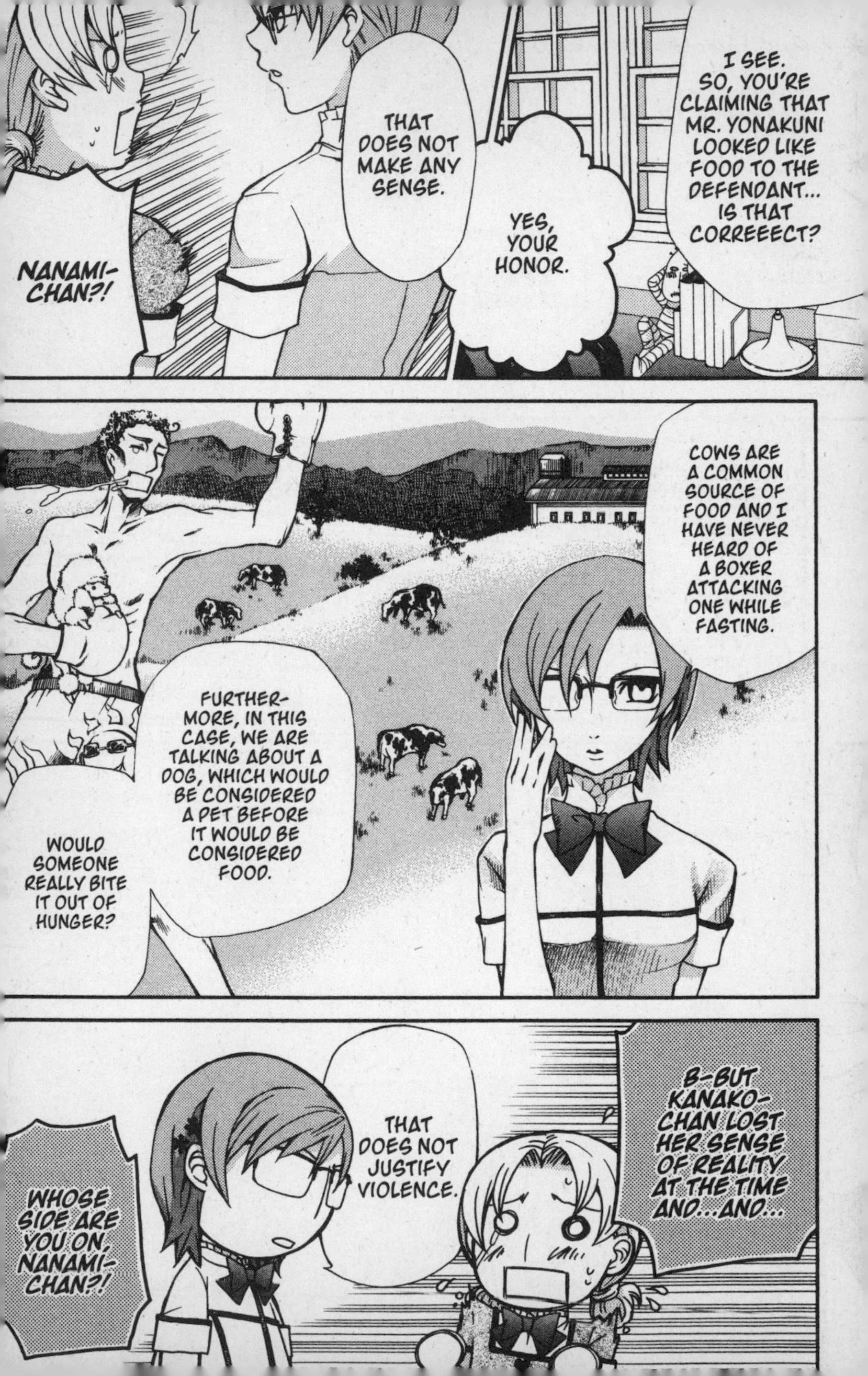
I SEE. SO, YOU'RE CLAIMING THAT MR. YONAKUNI LOOKED LIKE FOOD TO THE DEFENDANT... IS THAT CORREEECT?
YES, YOUR HONOR.
THAT DOES NOT MAKE ANY SENSE.
NANAMI-CHAN?!
COWS ARE A COMMON SOURCE OF FOOD AND I HAVE NEVER HEARD OF A BOXER ATTACKING ONE WHILE FASTING.
FURTHER-MORE, IN THIS CASE, WE ARE TALKING ABOUT A DOG, WHICH WOULD BE CONSIDERED A PET BEFORE IT WOULD BE CONSIDERED FOOD.
WOULD SOMEONE REALLY BITE IT OUT OF HUNGER?
B-BUT KANAKO-CHAN LOST HER SENSE OF REALITY AT THE TIME AND...AND...
THAT DOES NOT JUSTIFY VIOLENCE.
WHOSE SIDE ARE YOU ON, NANAMI-CHAN?!

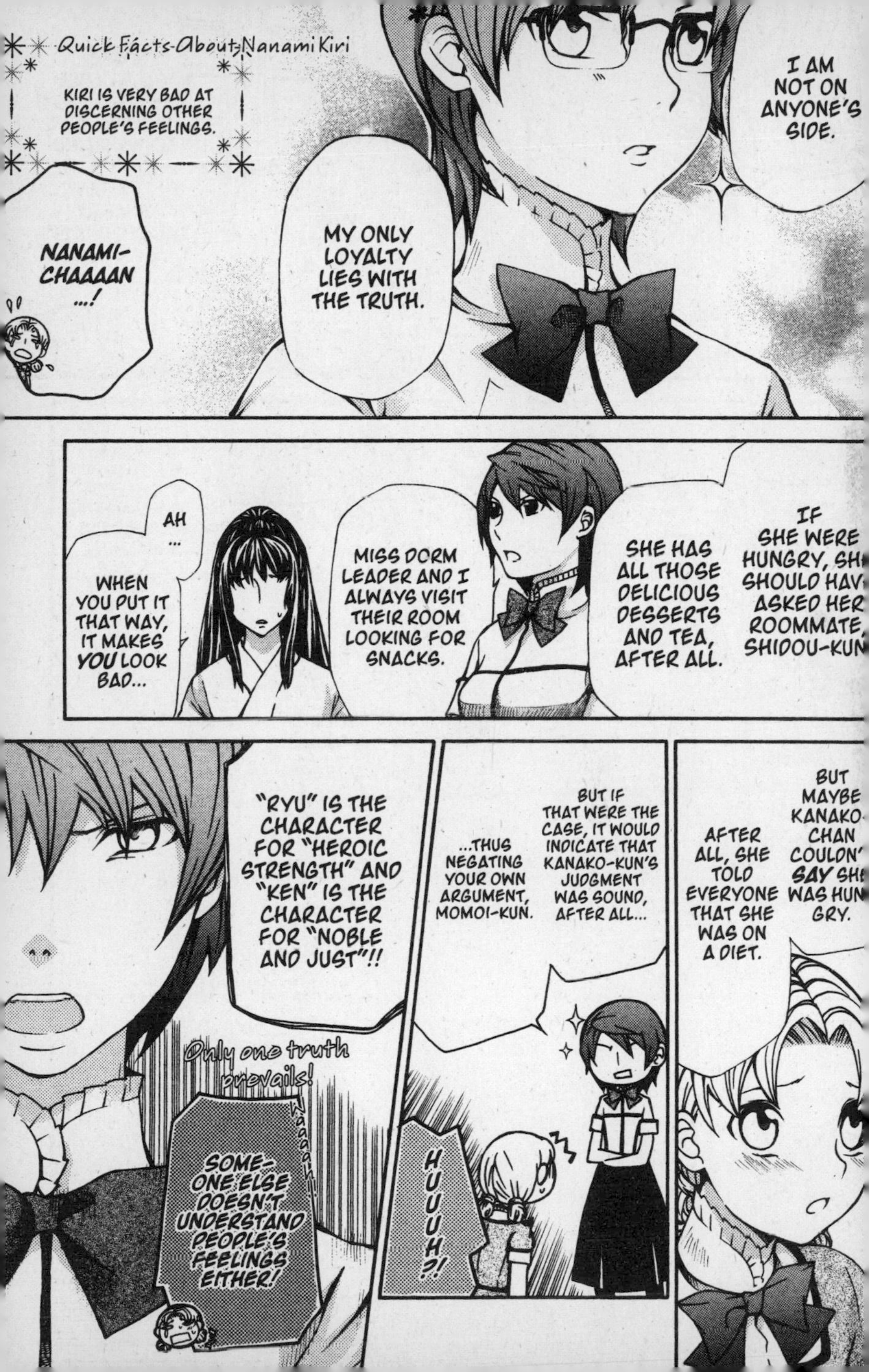
I AM NOT ON ANYONE'S SIDE.
MY ONLY LOYALTY LIES WITH THE TRUTH.
Quick Facts About Nanami Kiri
KIRI IS VERY BAD AT DISCERNING OTHER PEOPLE'S FEELINGS.
NANAMI-CHAAAAN ...!
IF SHE WERE HUNGRY, SH SHOULD HAV ASKED HER ROOMMATE SHIDOU-KUN
SHE HAS ALL THOSE DELICIOUS DESSERTS AND TEA, AFTER ALL.
MISS DORM LEADER AND I ALWAYS VISIT THEIR ROOM LOOKING FOR SNACKS.
AH ...
WHEN YOU PUT IT THAT WAY, IT MAKES YOU LOOK BAD...
BUT MAYBE KANAKO-CHAN COULDN' SAY SH WAS HUN-GRY.
AFTER ALL, SHE TOLD EVERYONE THAT SHE WAS ON A DIET.
BUT IF THAT WERE THE CASE, IT WOULD INDICATE THAT KANAKO-KUN'S JUDGMENT WAS SOUND, AFTER ALL...
...THUS NEGATING YOUR OWN ARGUMENT, MOMOI-KUN.
HUUUH?!
"RYU" IS THE CHARACTER FOR "HEROIC STRENGTH" AND "KEN" IS THE CHARACTER FOR "NOBLE AND JUST"!!
Only one truth prevails!
SOME-ONE ELSE DOESN'T UNDERSTAND PEOPLE'S FEELINGS EITHER!

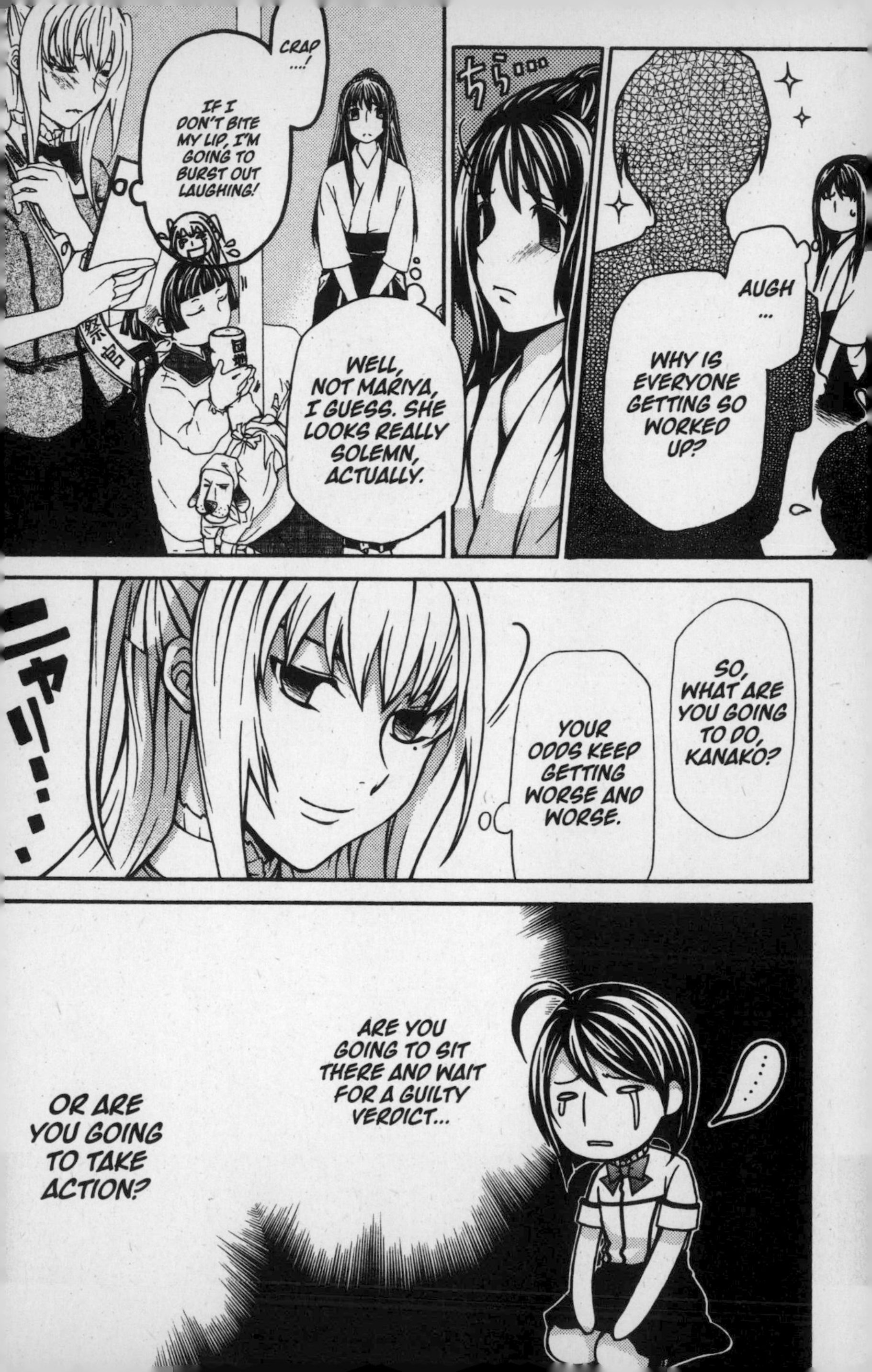
AUGH ...
WHY IS EVERYONE GETTING SO WORKED UP?
ちら...
CRAP ....!
IF I DON'T BITE MY LIP, I'M GOING TO BURST OUT LAUGHING!
WELL, NOT MARIYA, I GUESS. SHE LOOKS REALLY SOLEMN, ACTUALLY.
SO, WHAT ARE YOU GOING TO DO, KANAKO?
YOUR ODDS KEEP GETTING WORSE AND WORSE.
ニヤリ...
......
ARE YOU GOING TO SIT THERE AND WAIT FOR A GUILTY VERDICT...
OR ARE YOU GOING TO TAKE ACTION?

M A R I A H O L I C

Maria Holic

Maria✝Holic

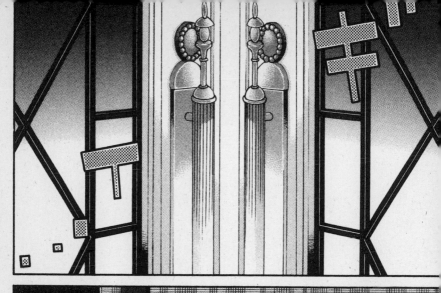

tromp *tromp*

WHAT ?!

OH NO! WHAT'S HE DOING HERE?!

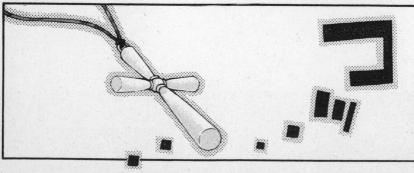

Prayer 26
The Yonakuni Trial ②

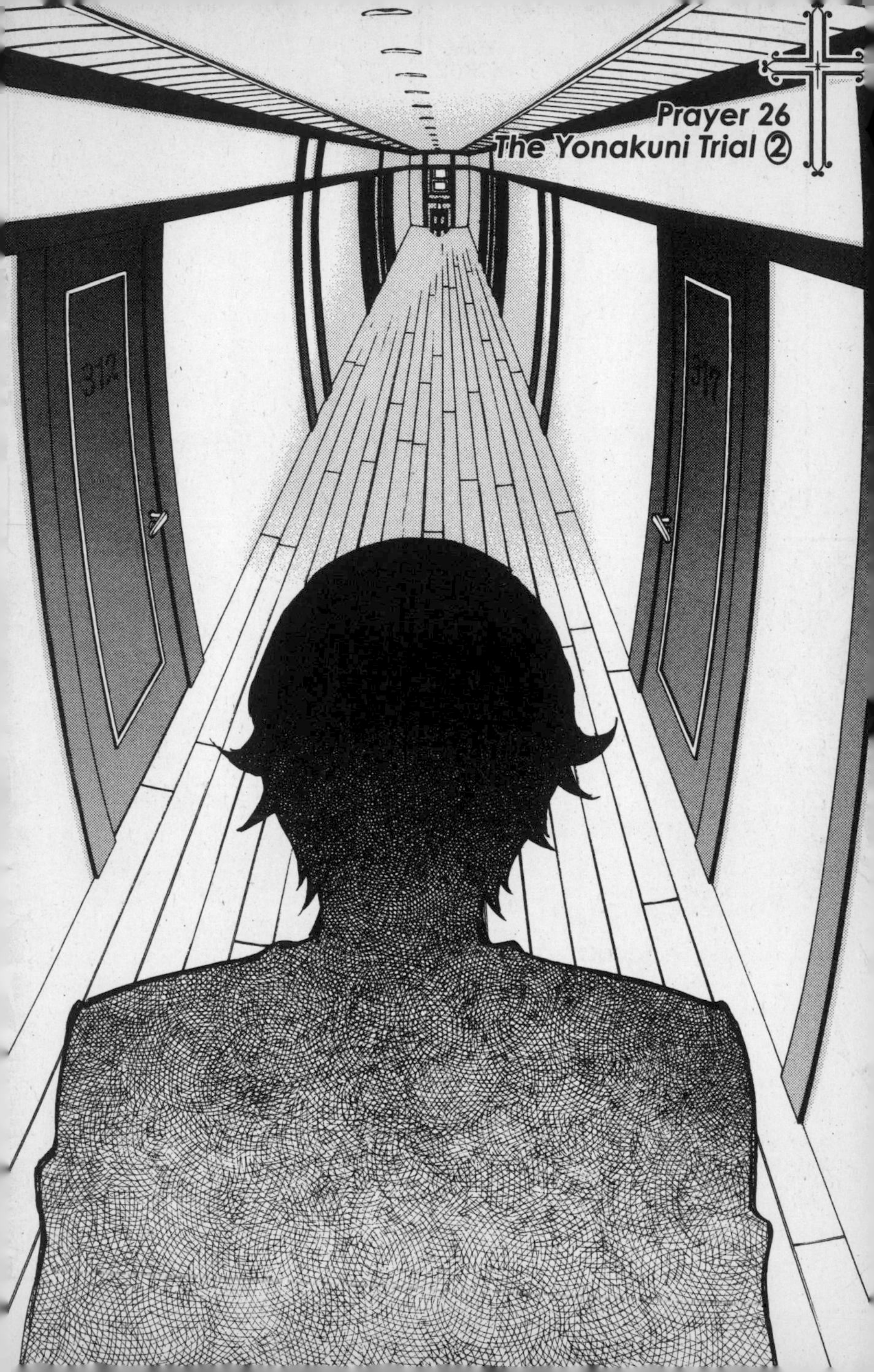

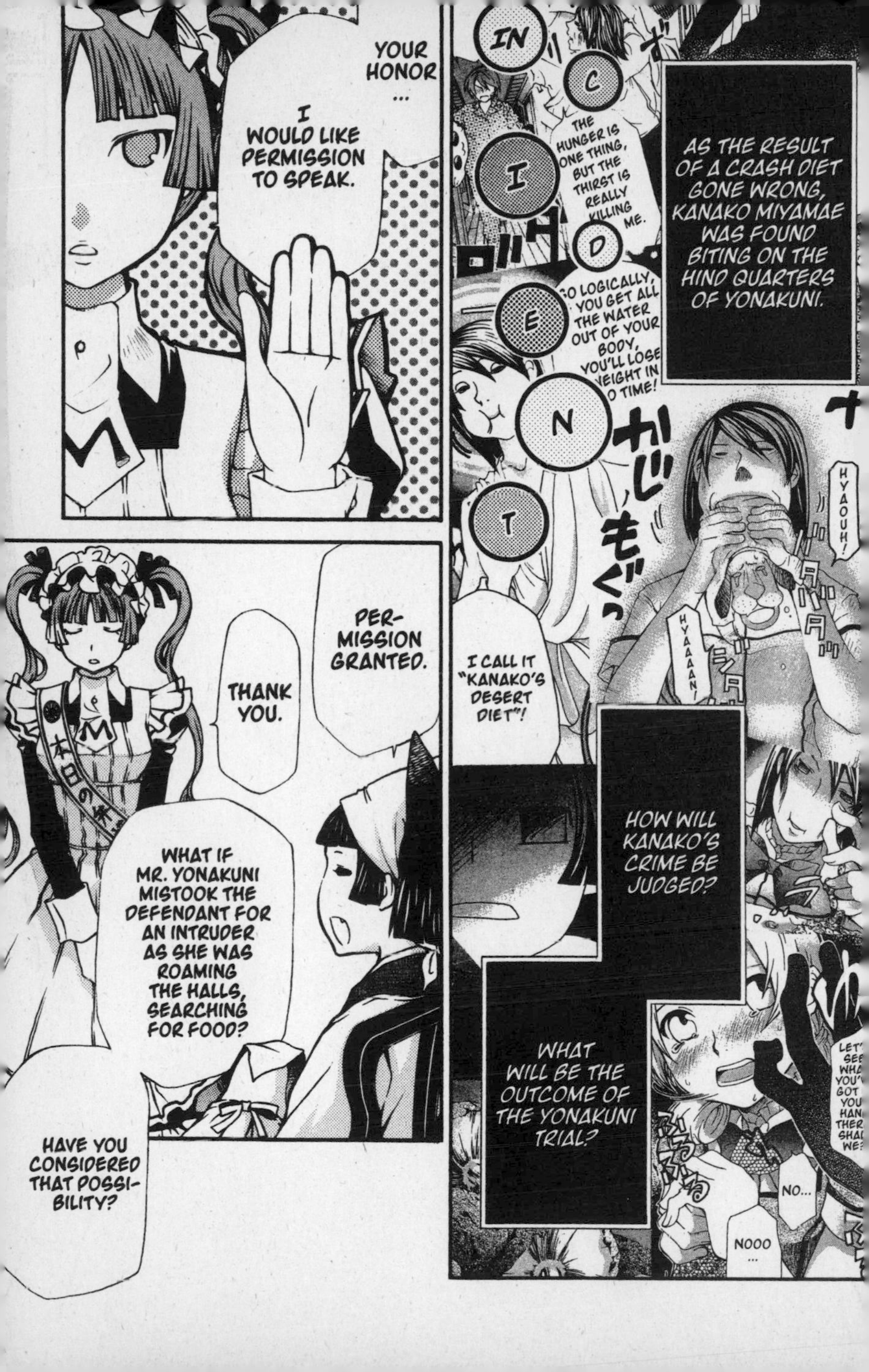

AS THE RESULT OF A CRASH DIET GONE WRONG, KANAKO MIYAMAE WAS FOUND BITING ON THE HIND QUARTERS OF YONAKUNI.
IN C I D E N T
THE HUNGER IS ONE THING, BUT THE THIRST IS REALLY KILLING ME.
SO LOGICALLY, YOU GET ALL THE WATER OUT OF YOUR BODY, YOU'LL LOSE WEIGHT IN NO TIME!
I CALL IT "KANAKO'S DESERT DIET"!
HYAOUH!
HYAAAAN!
HOW WILL KANAKO'S CRIME BE JUDGED?
WHAT WILL BE THE OUTCOME OF THE YONAKUNI TRIAL?
LET'S SEE WHA YOU' GOT YOU HAN THER SHA WE?
NO...
NOOO ...
YOUR HONOR ...
I WOULD LIKE PERMISSION TO SPEAK.
PER-MISSION GRANTED.
THANK YOU.
WHAT IF MR. YONAKUNI MISTOOK THE DEFENDANT FOR AN INTRUDER AS SHE WAS ROAMING THE HALLS, SEARCHING FOR FOOD?
HAVE YOU CONSIDERED THAT POSSI-BILITY?

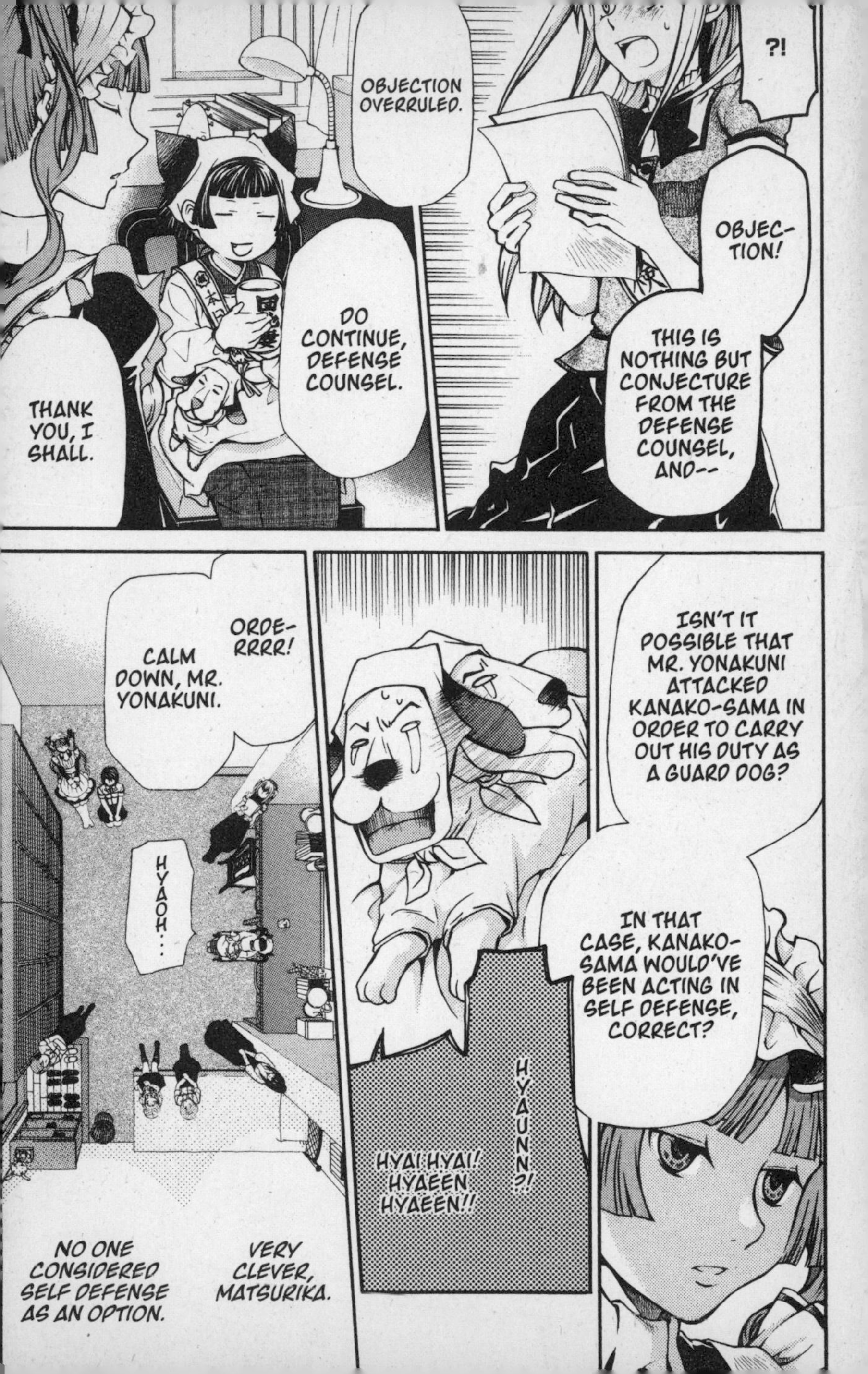
?!
OBJECTION!
THIS IS NOTHING BUT CONJECTURE FROM THE DEFENSE COUNSEL, AND--
OBJECTION OVERRULED.
DO CONTINUE, DEFENSE COUNSEL.
THANK YOU, I SHALL.
ISN'T IT POSSIBLE THAT MR. YONAKUNI ATTACKED KANAKO-SAMA IN ORDER TO CARRY OUT HIS DUTY AS A GUARD DOG?
IN THAT CASE, KANAKO-SAMA WOULD'VE BEEN ACTING IN SELF DEFENSE, CORRECT?
HYAUNN?!
HYAI HYAI! HYAEEN HYAEEN!!
ORDE-RRRR!
CALM DOWN, MR. YONAKUNI.
HYAOH...
VERY CLEVER, MATSURIKA.
NO ONE CONSIDERED SELF DEFENSE AS AN OPTION.

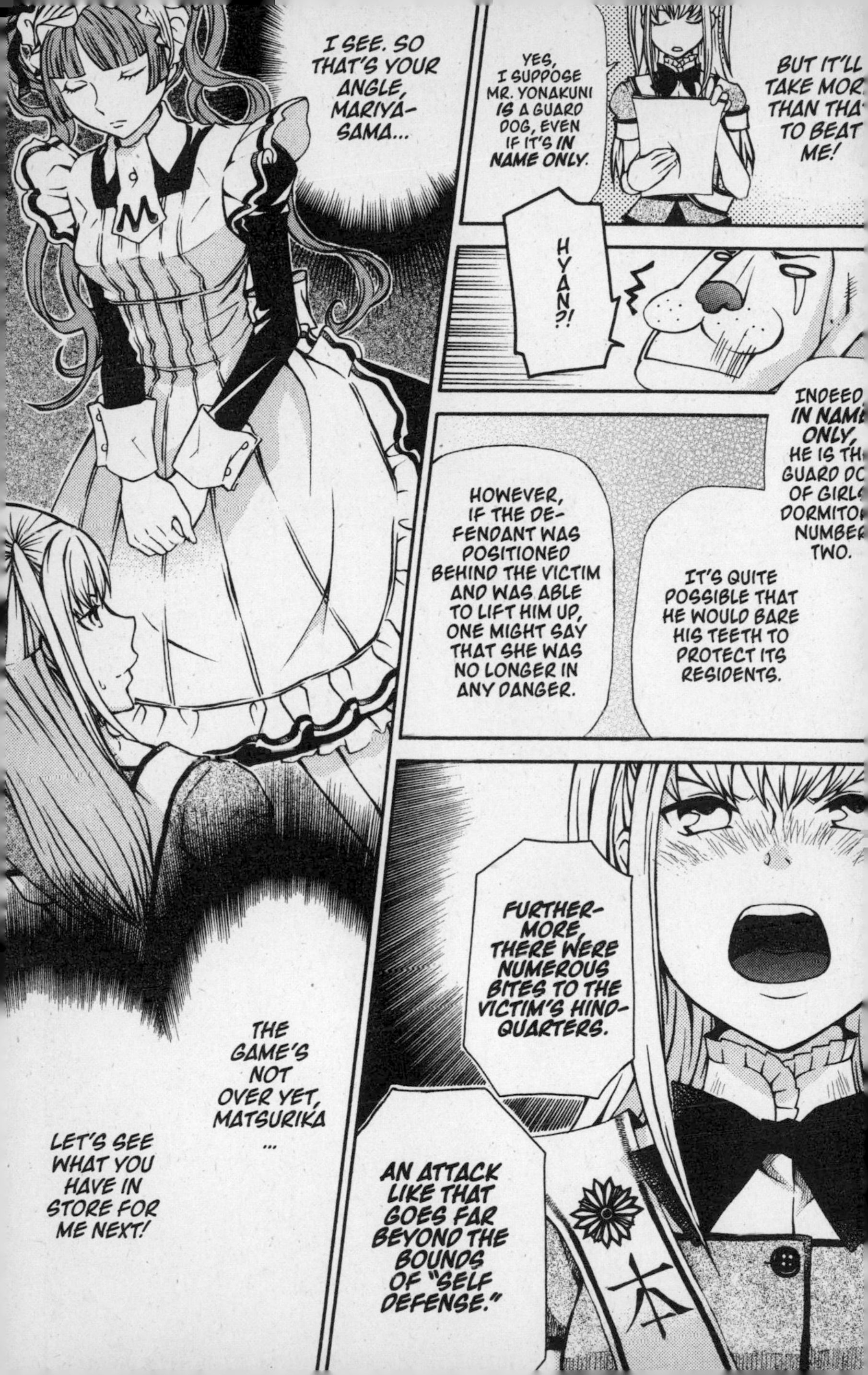
BUT IT'LL TAKE MOR THAN THA TO BEAT ME!
YES, I SUPPOSE MR. YONAKUNI IS A GUARD DOG, EVEN IF IT'S IN NAME ONLY.
HYAN?!
INDEED IN NAM ONLY, HE IS TH GUARD DO OF GIRLS DORMITO NUMBER TWO.
IT'S QUITE POSSIBLE THAT HE WOULD BARE HIS TEETH TO PROTECT ITS RESIDENTS.
HOWEVER, IF THE DE-FENDANT WAS POSITIONED BEHIND THE VICTIM AND WAS ABLE TO LIFT HIM UP, ONE MIGHT SAY THAT SHE WAS NO LONGER IN ANY DANGER.
FURTHER-MORE, THERE WERE NUMEROUS BITES TO THE VICTIM'S HIND-QUARTERS.
AN ATTACK LIKE THAT GOES FAR BEYOND THE BOUNDS OF "SELF DEFENSE."
I SEE. SO THAT'S YOUR ANGLE, MARIYA-SAMA...
THE GAME'S NOT OVER YET, MATSURIKA ...
LET'S SEE WHAT YOU HAVE IN STORE FOR ME NEXT!

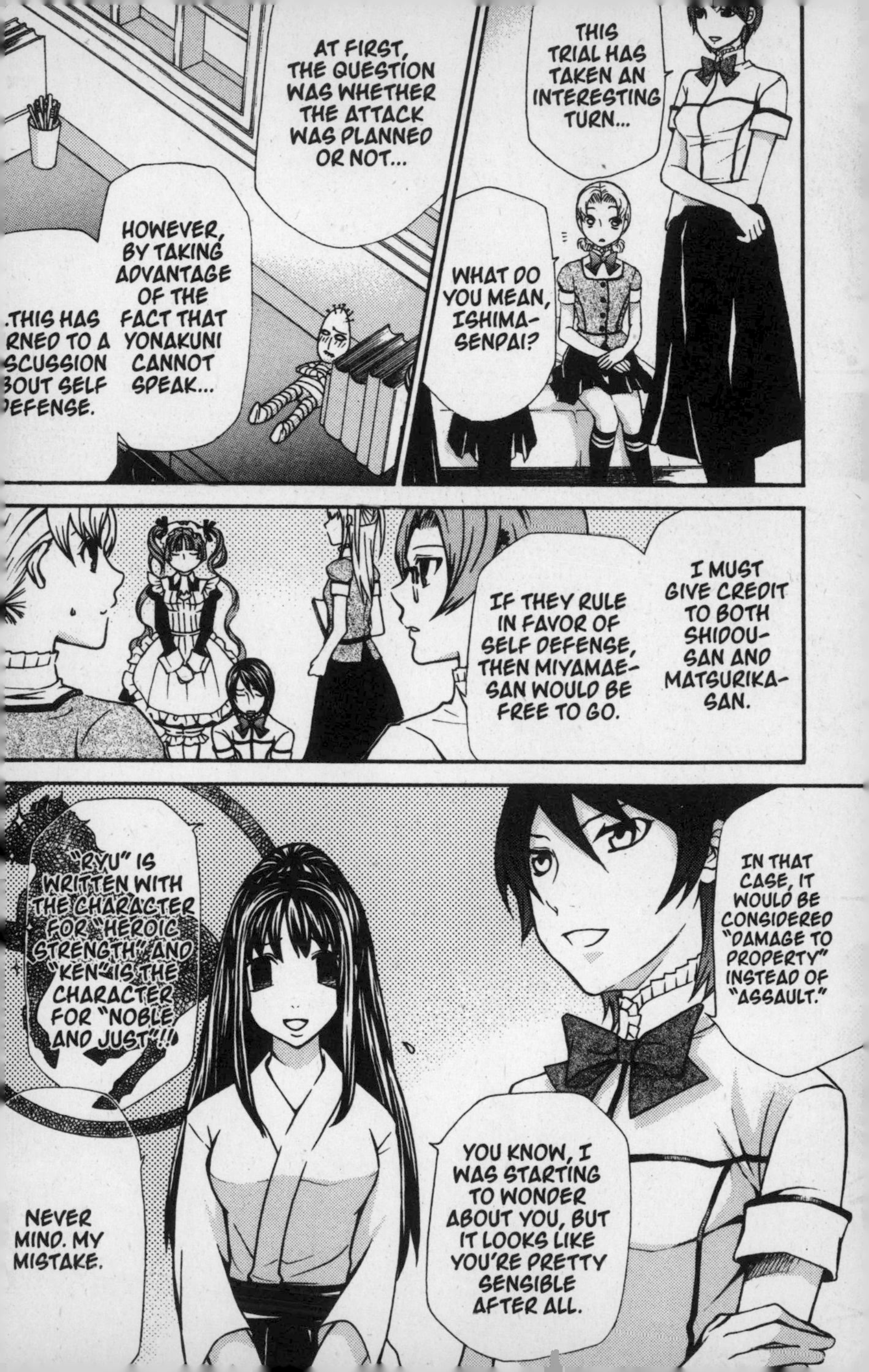
THIS TRIAL HAS TAKEN AN INTERESTING TURN...
WHAT DO YOU MEAN, ISHIMA-SENPAI?
AT FIRST, THE QUESTION WAS WHETHER THE ATTACK WAS PLANNED OR NOT...
HOWEVER, BY TAKING ADVANTAGE OF THE FACT THAT YONAKUNI CANNOT SPEAK...
.THIS HAS RNED TO A SCUSSION BOUT SELF EFENSE.
I MUST GIVE CREDIT TO BOTH SHIDOU-SAN AND MATSURIKA-SAN.
IF THEY RULE IN FAVOR OF SELF DEFENSE, THEN MIYAMAE-SAN WOULD BE FREE TO GO.
IN THAT CASE, IT WOULD BE CONSIDERED "DAMAGE TO PROPERTY" INSTEAD OF "ASSAULT."
"RYU" IS WRITTEN WITH THE CHARACTER FOR "HEROIC STRENGTH" AND "KEN" IS THE CHARACTER FOR "NOBLE AND JUST"!!
YOU KNOW, I WAS STARTING TO WONDER ABOUT YOU, BUT IT LOOKS LIKE YOU'RE PRETTY SENSIBLE AFTER ALL.
NEVER MIND. MY MISTAKE.

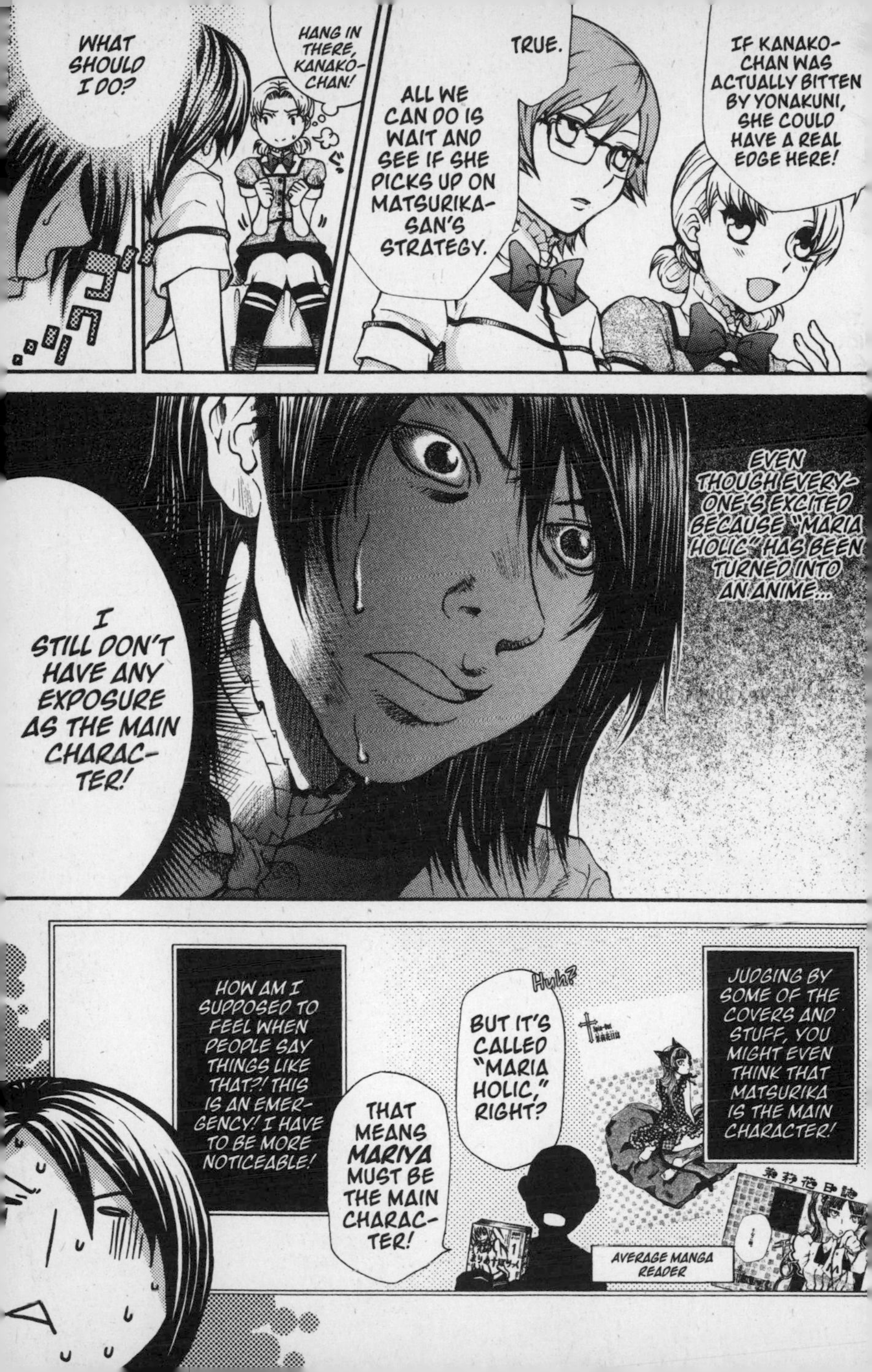
IF KANAKO-CHAN WAS ACTUALLY BITTEN BY YONAKUNI, SHE COULD HAVE A REAL EDGE HERE!
TRUE.
ALL WE CAN DO IS WAIT AND SEE IF SHE PICKS UP ON MATSURIKA-SAN'S STRATEGY.
HANG IN THERE, KANAKO-CHAN!
WHAT SHOULD I DO?
EVEN THOUGH EVERY-ONE'S EXCITED BECAUSE "MARIA HOLIC" HAS BEEN TURNED INTO AN ANIME...
I STILL DON'T HAVE ANY EXPOSURE AS THE MAIN CHARACTER!
JUDGING BY SOME OF THE COVERS AND STUFF, YOU MIGHT EVEN THINK THAT MATSURIKA IS THE MAIN CHARACTER!
Huh?
BUT IT'S CALLED "MARIA HOLIC," RIGHT?
THAT MEANS MARIYA MUST BE THE MAIN CHARACTER!
AVERAGE MANGA READER
HOW AM I SUPPOSED TO FEEL WHEN PEOPLE SAY THINGS LIKE THAT?! THIS IS AN EMERGENCY! I HAVE TO BE MORE NOTICEABLE!

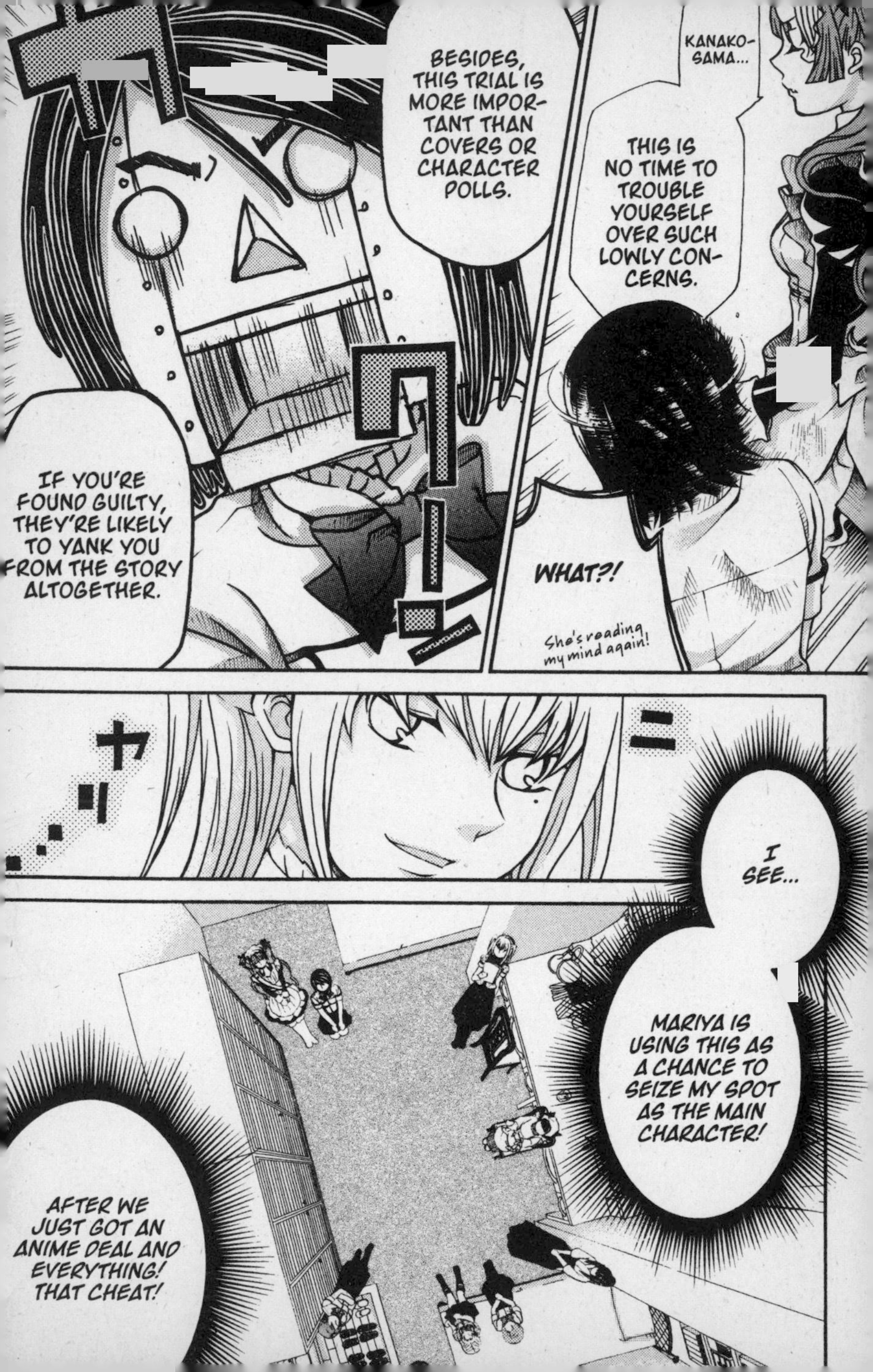
KANAKO-SAMA...
THIS IS NO TIME TO TROUBLE YOURSELF OVER SUCH LOWLY CONCERNS.
WHAT?!
She's reading my mind again!
BESIDES, THIS TRIAL IS MORE IMPORTANT THAN COVERS OR CHARACTER POLLS.
IF YOU'RE FOUND GUILTY, THEY'RE LIKELY TO YANK YOU FROM THE STORY ALTOGETHER.
I SEE...
MARIYA IS USING THIS AS A CHANCE TO SEIZE MY SPOT AS THE MAIN CHARACTER!
AFTER WE JUST GOT AN ANIME DEAL AND EVERYTHING! THAT CHEAT!

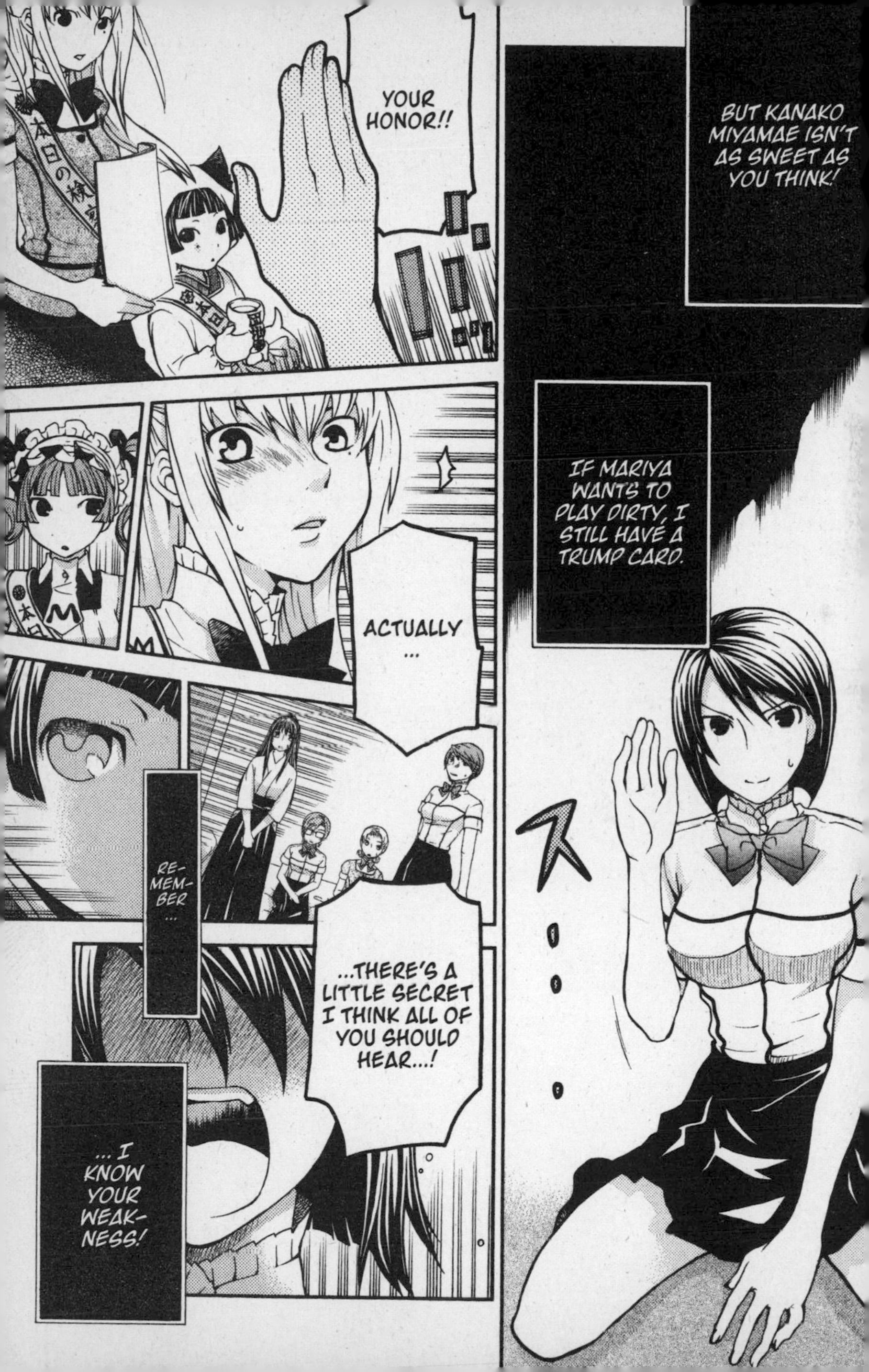
BUT KANAKO MIYAMAE ISN'T AS SWEET AS YOU THINK!
IF MARIYA WANTS TO PLAY DIRTY, I STILL HAVE A TRUMP CARD.
ス
YOUR HONOR!!
ACTUALLY ...
...THERE'S A LITTLE SECRET I THINK ALL OF YOU SHOULD HEAR...!
RE-MEMBER ...
... I KNOW YOUR WEAK-NESS!

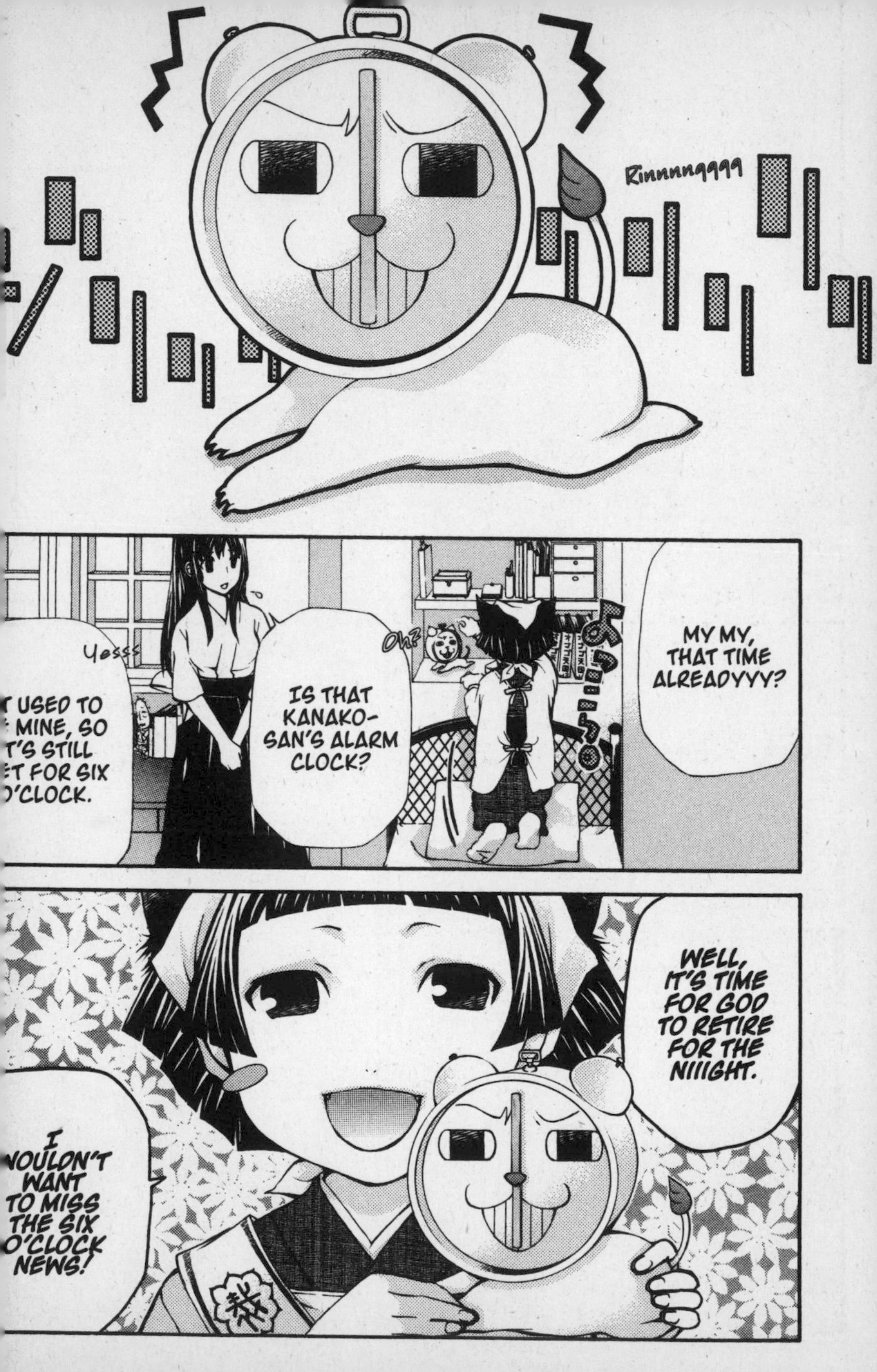
Rinnnnggggg
MY MY, THAT TIME ALREADYYY?
Oh?
IS THAT KANAKO-SAN'S ALARM CLOCK?
Yesss
T USED TO MINE, SO T'S STILL T FOR SIX O'CLOCK.
WELL, IT'S TIME FOR GOD TO RETIRE FOR THE NIIIGHT.
I WOULDN'T WANT TO MISS THE SIX O'CLOCK NEWS!

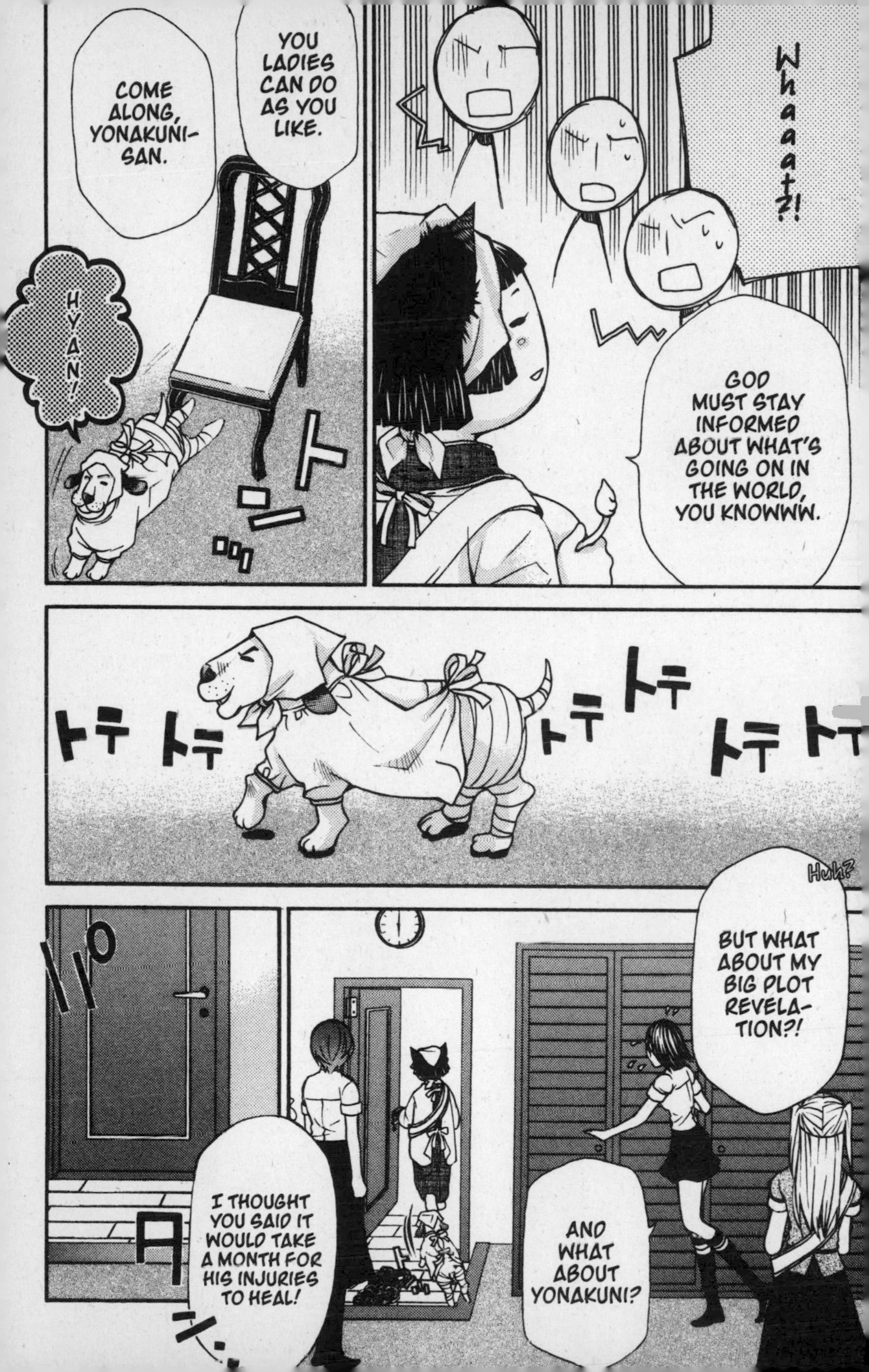
Whaaaat?!
GOD MUST STAY INFORMED ABOUT WHAT'S GOING ON IN THE WORLD, YOU KNOWWW.
YOU LADIES CAN DO AS YOU LIKE.
COME ALONG, YONAKUNI-SAN.
HYAN!
トテ トテ トテ トテ トテ トテ
Huh?
BUT WHAT ABOUT MY BIG PLOT REVELATION?!
AND WHAT ABOUT YONAKUNI?
I THOUGHT YOU SAID IT WOULD TAKE A MONTH FOR HIS INJURIES TO HEAL!

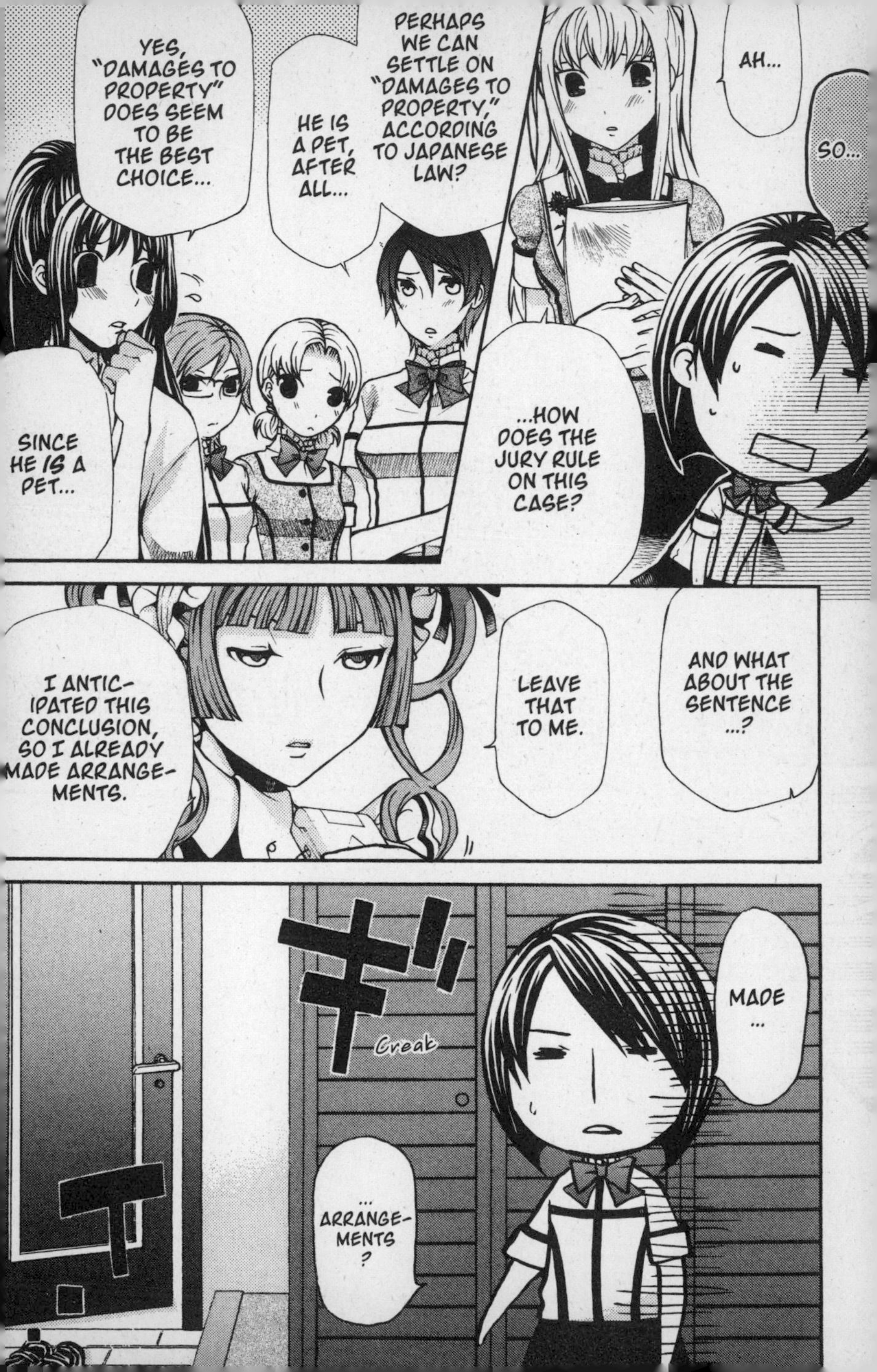
AH...
SO...
...HOW DOES THE JURY RULE ON THIS CASE?
PERHAPS WE CAN SETTLE ON "DAMAGES TO PROPERTY," ACCORDING TO JAPANESE LAW?
HE IS A PET, AFTER ALL...
YES, "DAMAGES TO PROPERTY" DOES SEEM TO BE THE BEST CHOICE...
SINCE HE *IS* A PET...
AND WHAT ABOUT THE SENTENCE ...?
LEAVE THAT TO ME.
I ANTIC-IPATED THIS CONCLUSION, SO I ALREADY MADE ARRANGE-MENTS.
MADE ...
Creak
... ARRANGE-MENTS ?

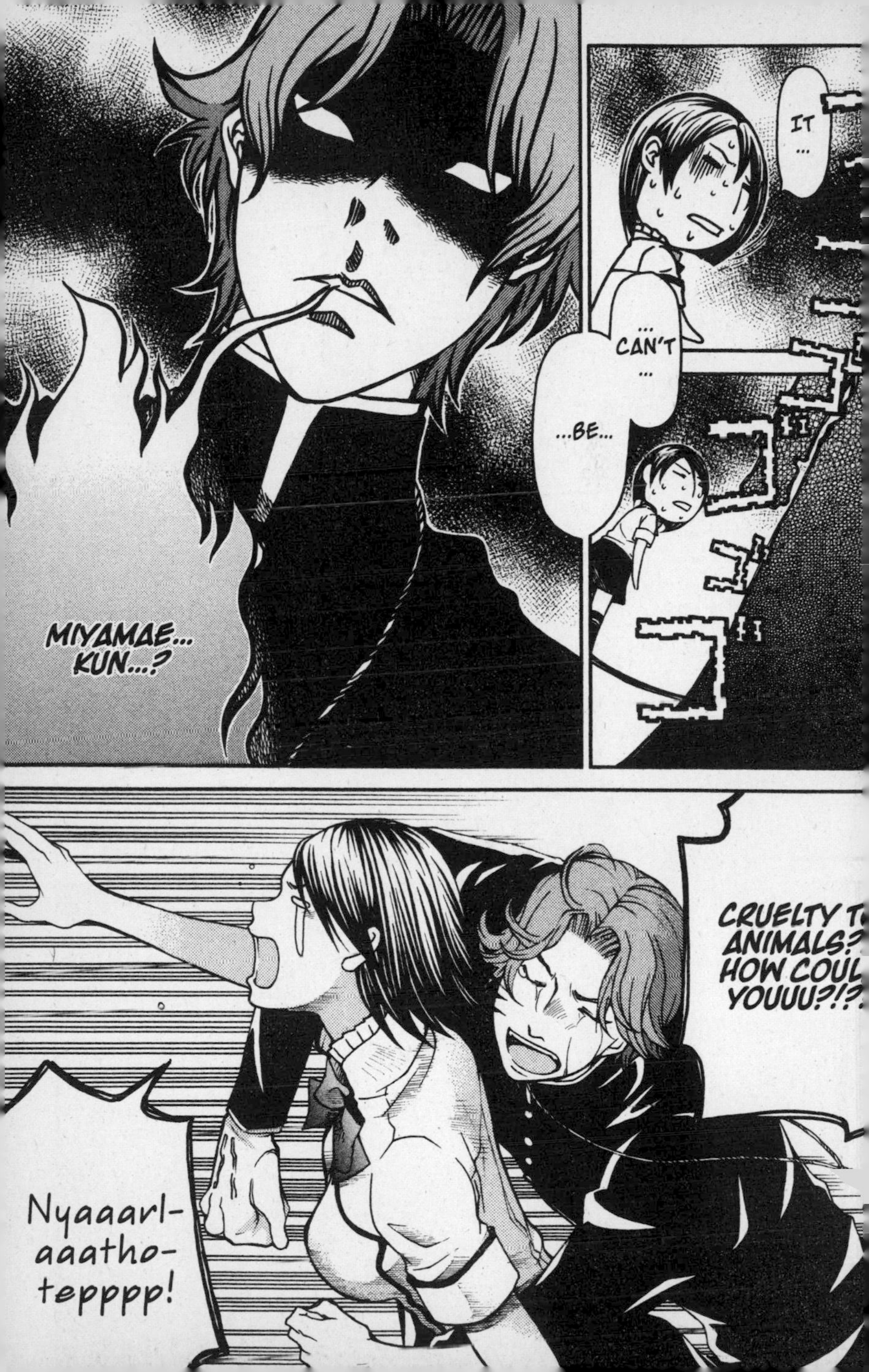
IT ...
... CAN'T ...
...BE...
MIYAMAE... KUN...?
CRUELTY T ANIMALS? HOW COUL YOUUU?!?
Nyaaarl-aaatho-tepppp!

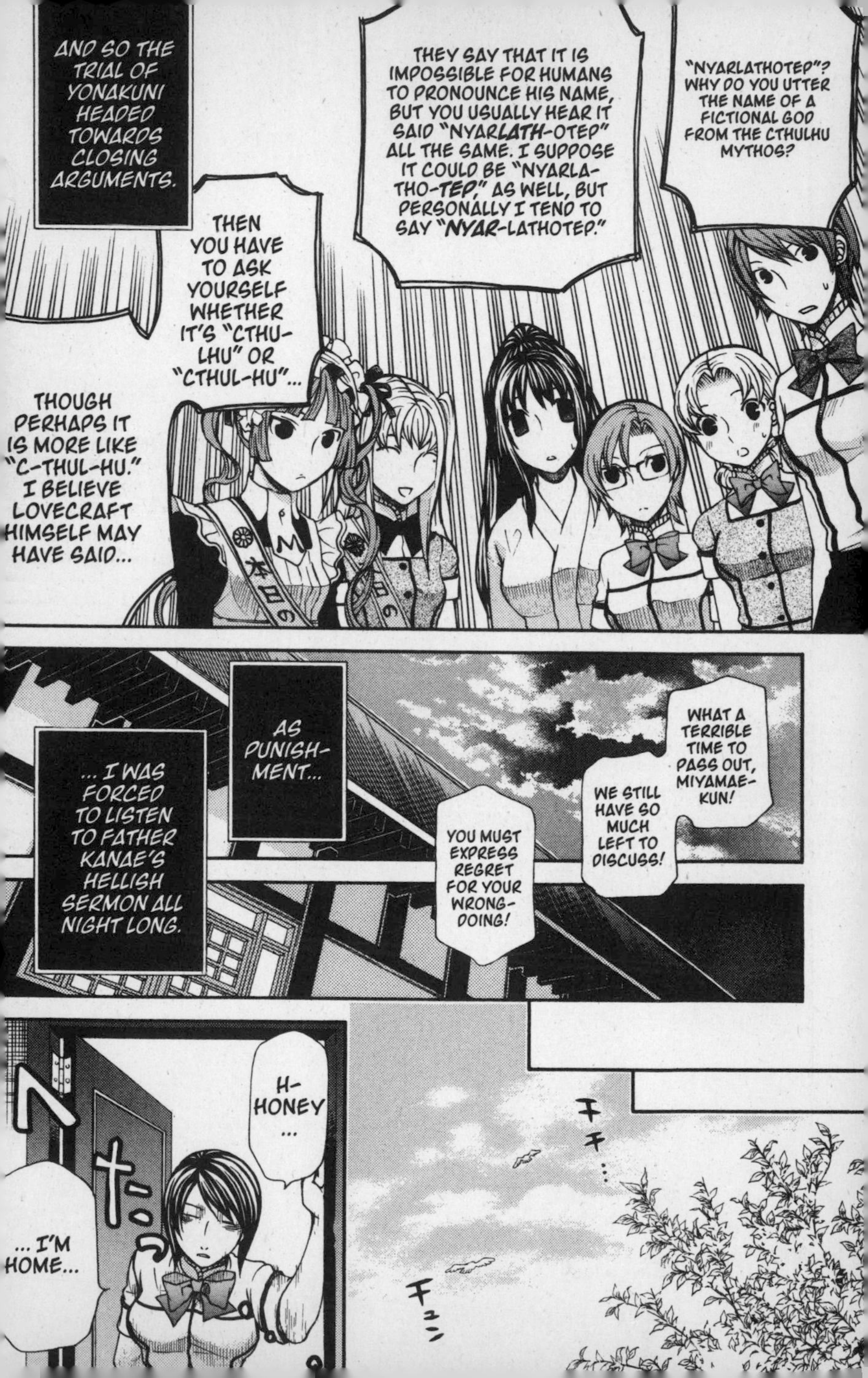
"NYARLATHOTEP"? WHY DO YOU UTTER THE NAME OF A FICTIONAL GOD FROM THE CTHULHU MYTHOS?
THEY SAY THAT IT IS IMPOSSIBLE FOR HUMANS TO PRONOUNCE HIS NAME, BUT YOU USUALLY HEAR IT SAID "NYARLATH-OTEP" ALL THE SAME. I SUPPOSE IT COULD BE "NYARLA-THO-TEP," AS WELL, BUT PERSONALLY I TEND TO SAY "NYAR-LATHOTEP."
AND SO THE TRIAL OF YONAKUNI HEADED TOWARDS CLOSING ARGUMENTS.
THEN YOU HAVE TO ASK YOURSELF WHETHER IT'S "CTHU-LHU" OR "CTHUL-HU"...
THOUGH PERHAPS IT IS MORE LIKE "C-THUL-HU." I BELIEVE LOVECRAFT HIMSELF MAY HAVE SAID...
WHAT A TERRIBLE TIME TO PASS OUT, MIYAMAE-KUN!
WE STILL HAVE SO MUCH LEFT TO DISCUSS!
YOU MUST EXPRESS REGRET FOR YOUR WRONG-DOING!
AS PUNISH-MENT...
... I WAS FORCED TO LISTEN TO FATHER KANAE'S HELLISH SERMON ALL NIGHT LONG.
チチ…
チ
H-HONEY ...
... I'M HOME...

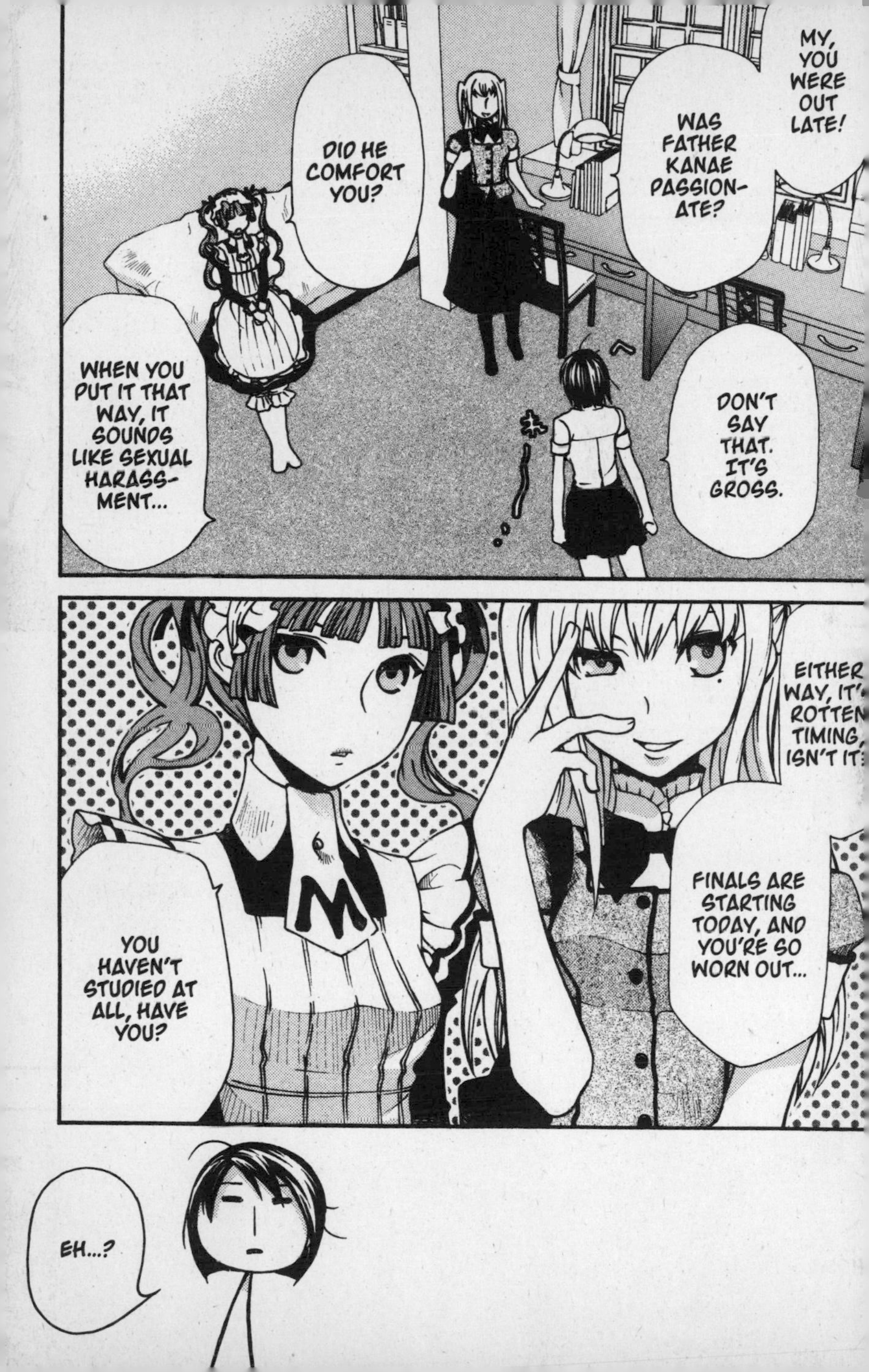
MY, YOU WERE OUT LATE!
WAS FATHER KANAE PASSION-ATE?
DID HE COMFORT YOU?
DON'T SAY THAT. IT'S GROSS.
WHEN YOU PUT IT THAT WAY, IT SOUNDS LIKE SEXUAL HARASS-MENT...
EITHER WAY, IT' ROTTEN TIMING, ISN'T IT
FINALS ARE STARTING TODAY, AND YOU'RE SO WORN OUT...
YOU HAVEN'T STUDIED AT ALL, HAVE YOU?
EH...?

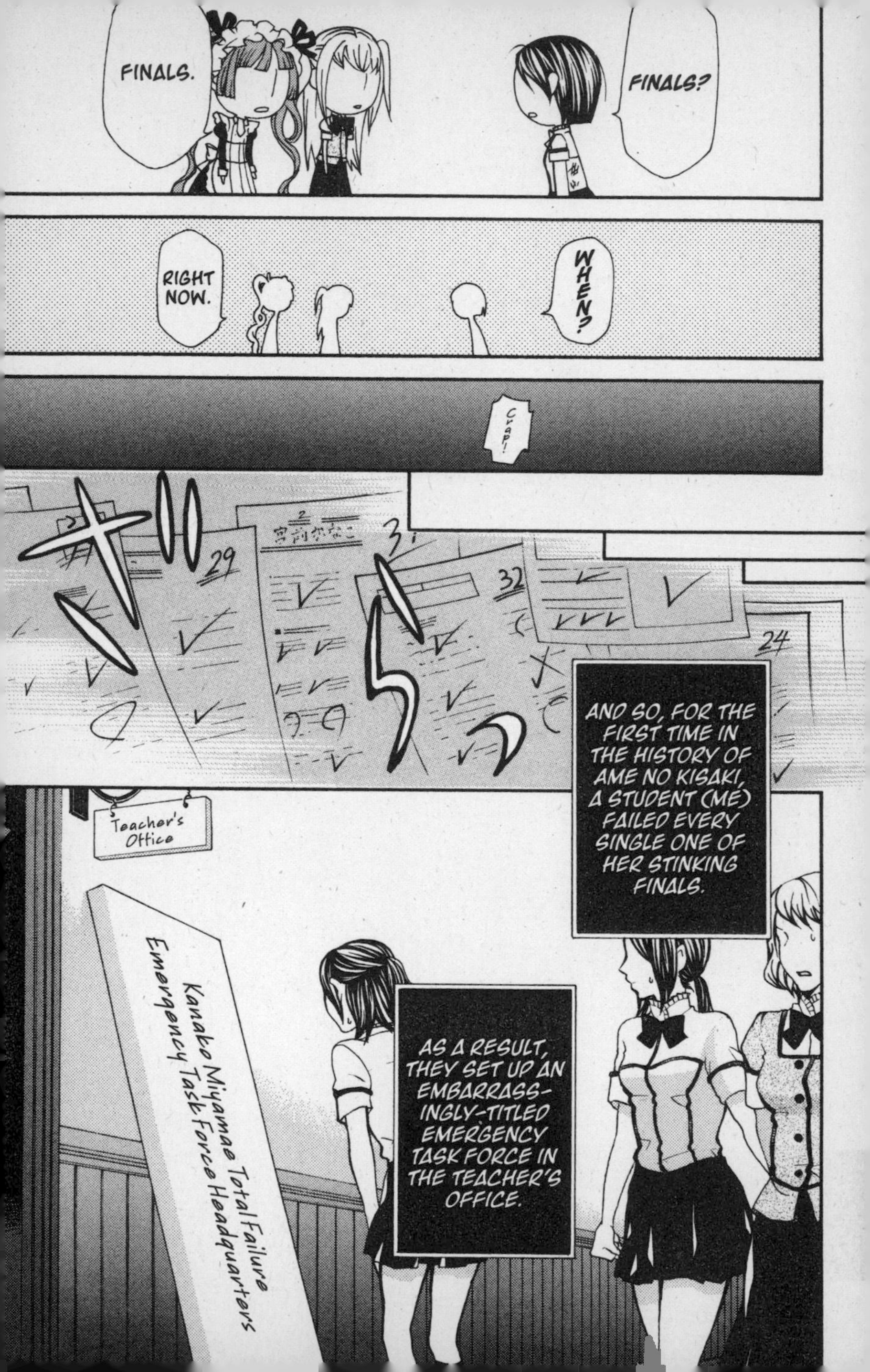
FINALS?
FINALS.
WHEN?
RIGHT NOW.
Crap!
29
32
24
AND SO, FOR THE FIRST TIME IN THE HISTORY OF AME NO KISAKI, A STUDENT (ME) FAILED EVERY SINGLE ONE OF HER STINKING FINALS.
Teacher's Office
AS A RESULT, THEY SET UP AN EMBARRASS-INGLY-TITLED EMERGENCY TASK FORCE IN THE TEACHER'S OFFICE.
Kanako Miyamae Total Failure Emergency Task Force Headquarters

M A R I A H O L I

Maria Holic

Maria†Holic

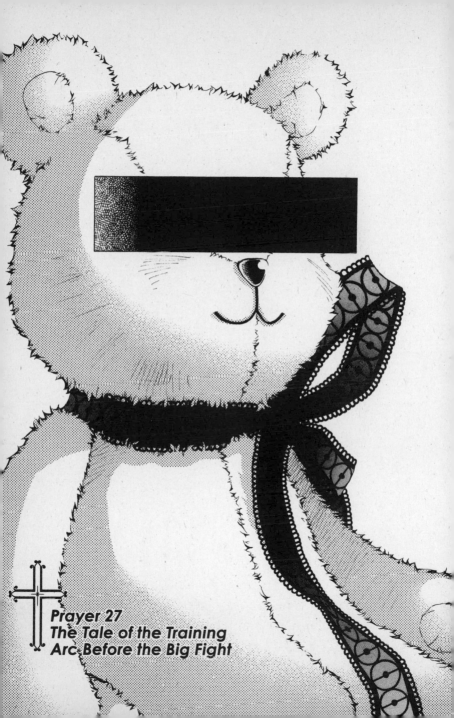

Prayer 27
The Tale of the Training
Arc Before the Big Fight

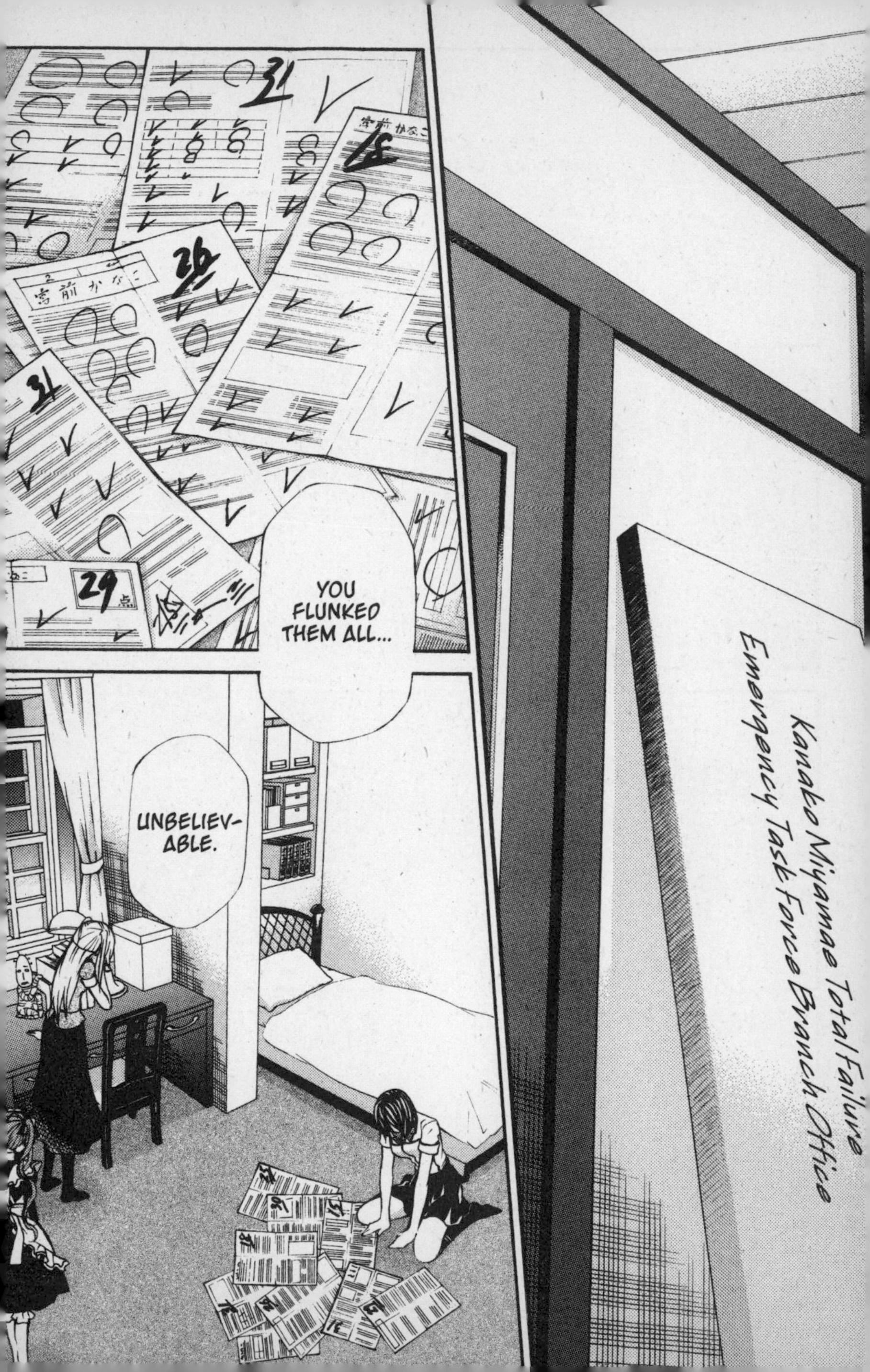
Kanako Miyamae Total Failure
Emergency Task Force Branch Office
YOU FLUNKED THEM ALL...
UNBELIEV-ABLE.

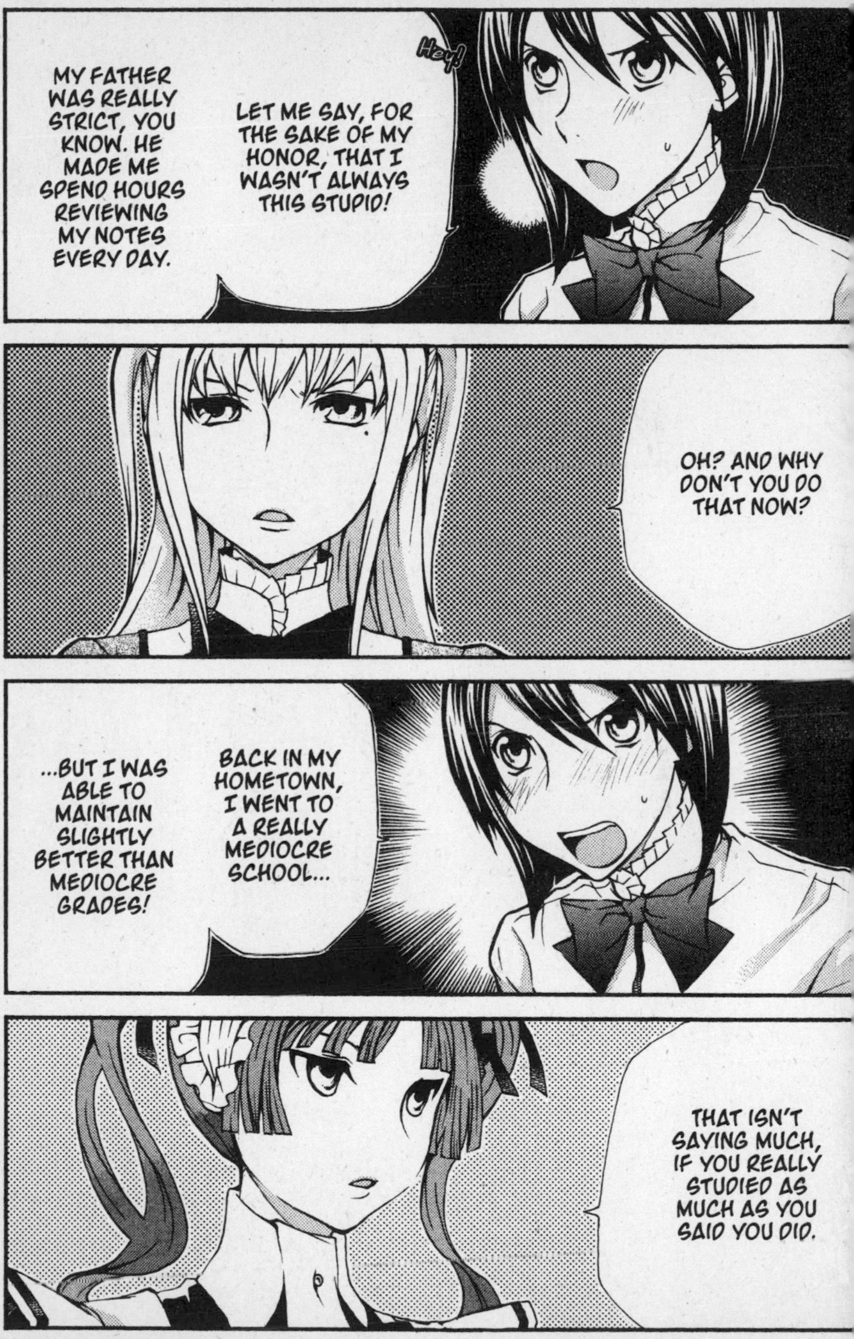
Hey!
LET ME SAY, FOR THE SAKE OF MY HONOR, THAT I WASN'T ALWAYS THIS STUPID!
MY FATHER WAS REALLY STRICT, YOU KNOW. HE MADE ME SPEND HOURS REVIEWING MY NOTES EVERY DAY.
OH? AND WHY DON'T YOU DO THAT NOW?
BACK IN MY HOMETOWN, I WENT TO A REALLY MEDIOCRE SCHOOL...
...BUT I WAS ABLE TO MAINTAIN SLIGHTLY BETTER THAN MEDIOCRE GRADES!
THAT ISN'T SAYING MUCH, IF YOU REALLY STUDIED AS MUCH AS YOU SAID YOU DID.

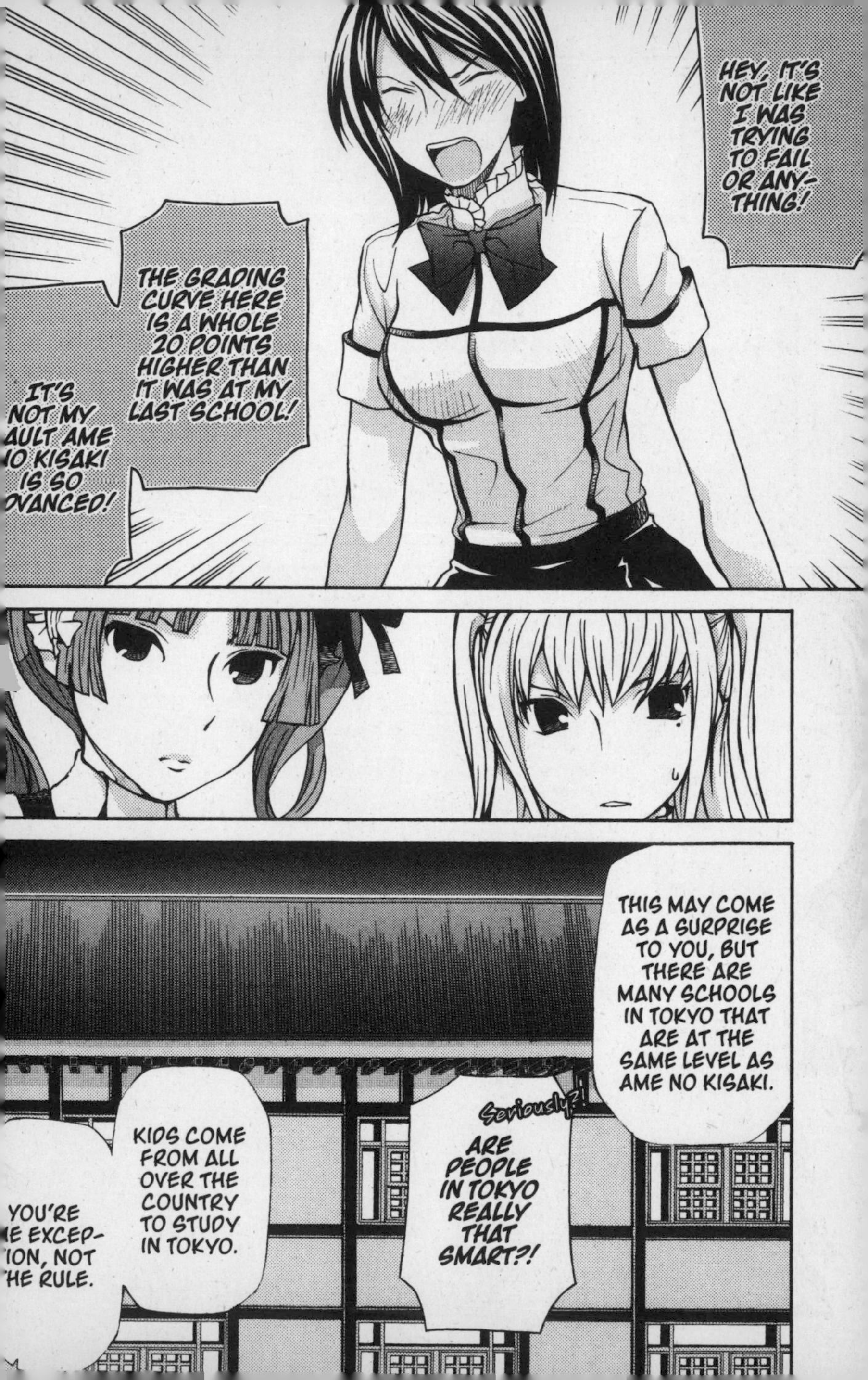
HEY, IT'S NOT LIKE I WAS TRYING TO FAIL OR ANY-THING!
THE GRADING CURVE HERE IS A WHOLE 20 POINTS HIGHER THAN IT WAS AT MY LAST SCHOOL!
IT'S NOT MY AULT AME O KISAKI IS SO DVANCED!
THIS MAY COME AS A SURPRISE TO YOU, BUT THERE ARE MANY SCHOOLS IN TOKYO THAT ARE AT THE SAME LEVEL AS AME NO KISAKI.
Seriously?!
ARE PEOPLE IN TOKYO REALLY THAT SMART?!
KIDS COME FROM ALL OVER THE COUNTRY TO STUDY IN TOKYO.
YOU'RE E EXCEP-ION, NOT HE RULE.

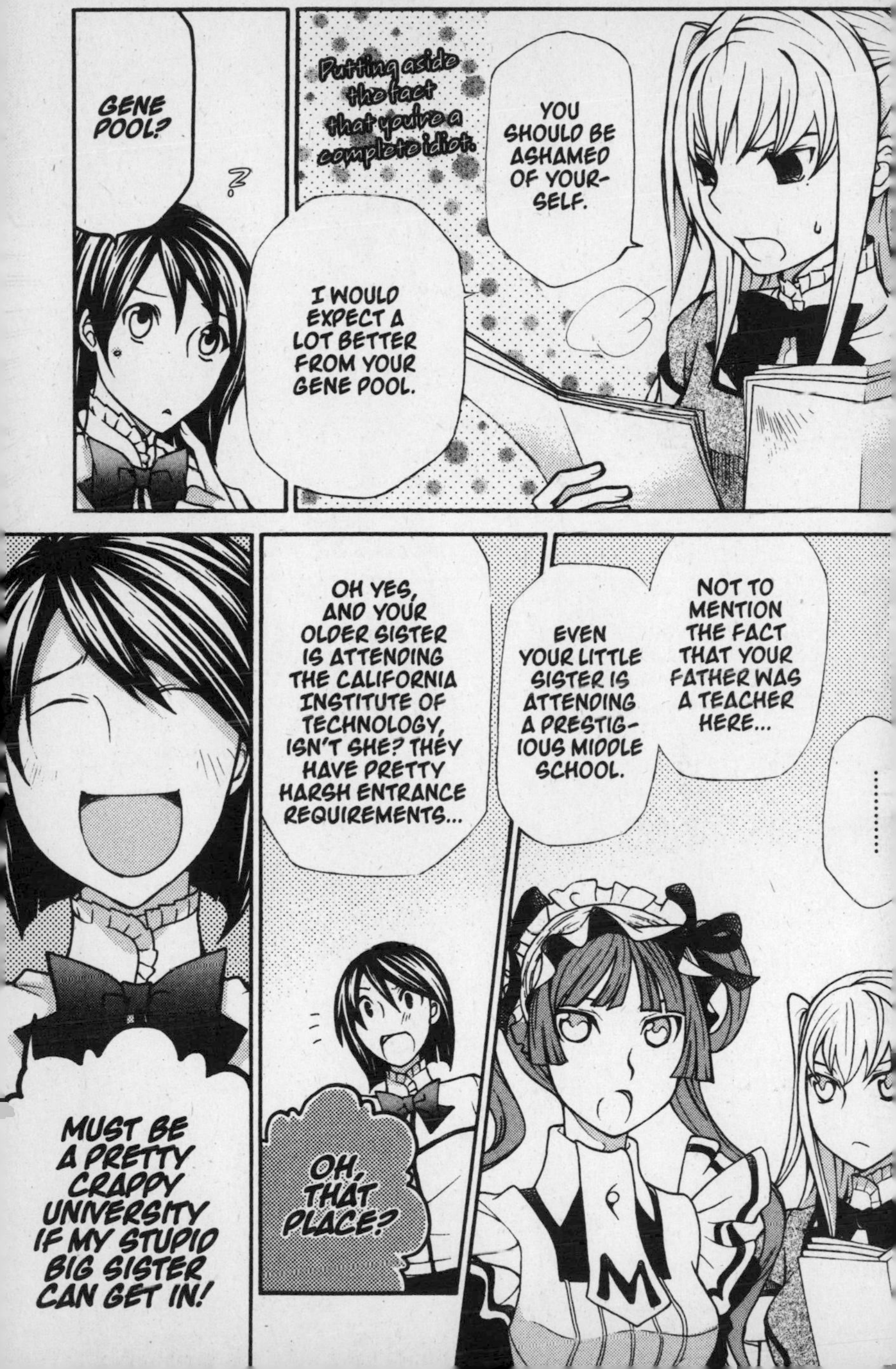
YOU SHOULD BE ASHAMED OF YOURSELF.
Putting aside the fact that you're a complete idiot.
I WOULD EXPECT A LOT BETTER FROM YOUR GENE POOL.
GENE POOL?
?
NOT TO MENTION THE FACT THAT YOUR FATHER WAS A TEACHER HERE...
EVEN YOUR LITTLE SISTER IS ATTENDING A PRESTIGIOUS MIDDLE SCHOOL.
......
OH YES, AND YOUR OLDER SISTER IS ATTENDING THE CALIFORNIA INSTITUTE OF TECHNOLOGY, ISN'T SHE? THEY HAVE PRETTY HARSH ENTRANCE REQUIREMENTS...
OH, THAT PLACE?
MUST BE A PRETTY CRAPPY UNIVERSITY IF MY STUPID BIG SISTER CAN GET IN!

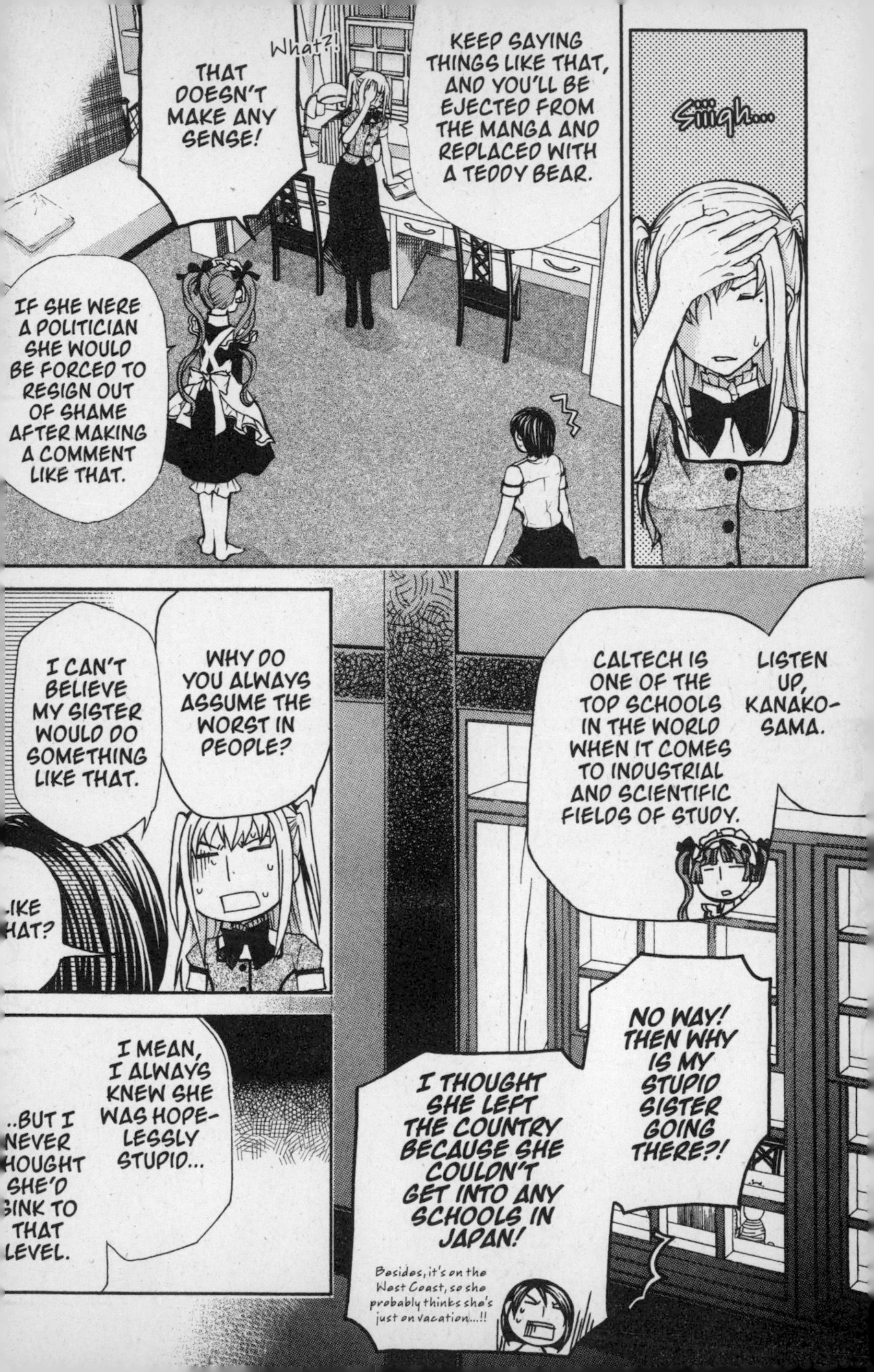
Siiigh...
KEEP SAYING THINGS LIKE THAT, AND YOU'LL BE EJECTED FROM THE MANGA AND REPLACED WITH A TEDDY BEAR.
What?!
THAT DOESN'T MAKE ANY SENSE!
IF SHE WERE A POLITICIAN SHE WOULD BE FORCED TO RESIGN OUT OF SHAME AFTER MAKING A COMMENT LIKE THAT.
LISTEN UP, KANAKO-SAMA.
CALTECH IS ONE OF THE TOP SCHOOLS IN THE WORLD WHEN IT COMES TO INDUSTRIAL AND SCIENTIFIC FIELDS OF STUDY.
NO WAY! THEN WHY IS MY STUPID SISTER GOING THERE?!
I THOUGHT SHE LEFT THE COUNTRY BECAUSE SHE COULDN'T GET INTO ANY SCHOOLS IN JAPAN!
Besides, it's on the West Coast, so she probably thinks she's just on vacation...!!
WHY DO YOU ALWAYS ASSUME THE WORST IN PEOPLE?
I CAN'T BELIEVE MY SISTER WOULD DO SOMETHING LIKE THAT.
IKE HAT?
I MEAN, I ALWAYS KNEW SHE WAS HOPE-LESSLY STUPID...
..BUT I NEVER HOUGHT SHE'D INK TO THAT LEVEL.

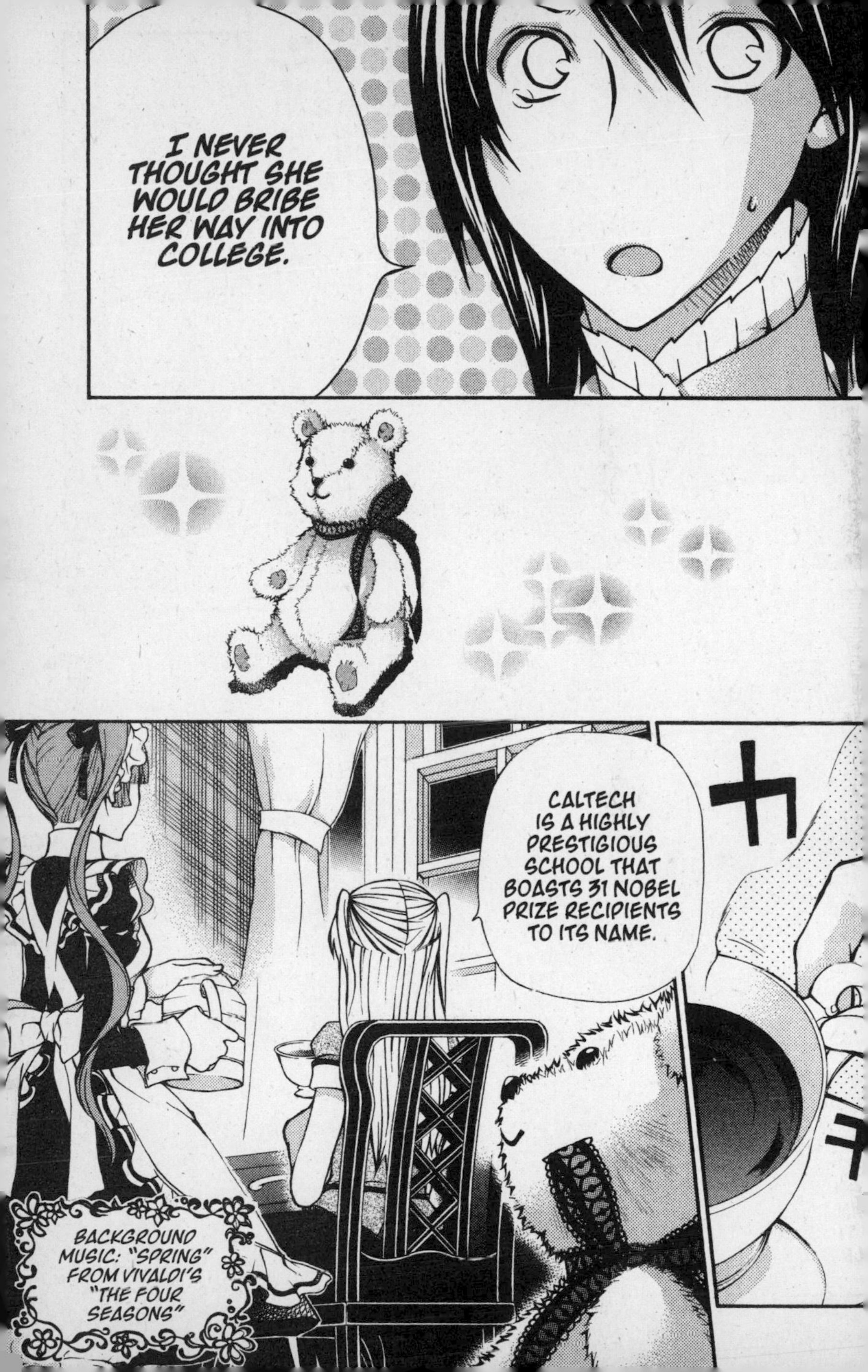
I NEVER THOUGHT SHE WOULD BRIBE HER WAY INTO COLLEGE.
CALTECH IS A HIGHLY PRESTIGIOUS SCHOOL THAT BOASTS 31 NOBEL PRIZE RECIPIENTS TO ITS NAME.
BACKGROUND MUSIC: "SPRING" FROM VIVALDI'S "THE FOUR SEASONS"

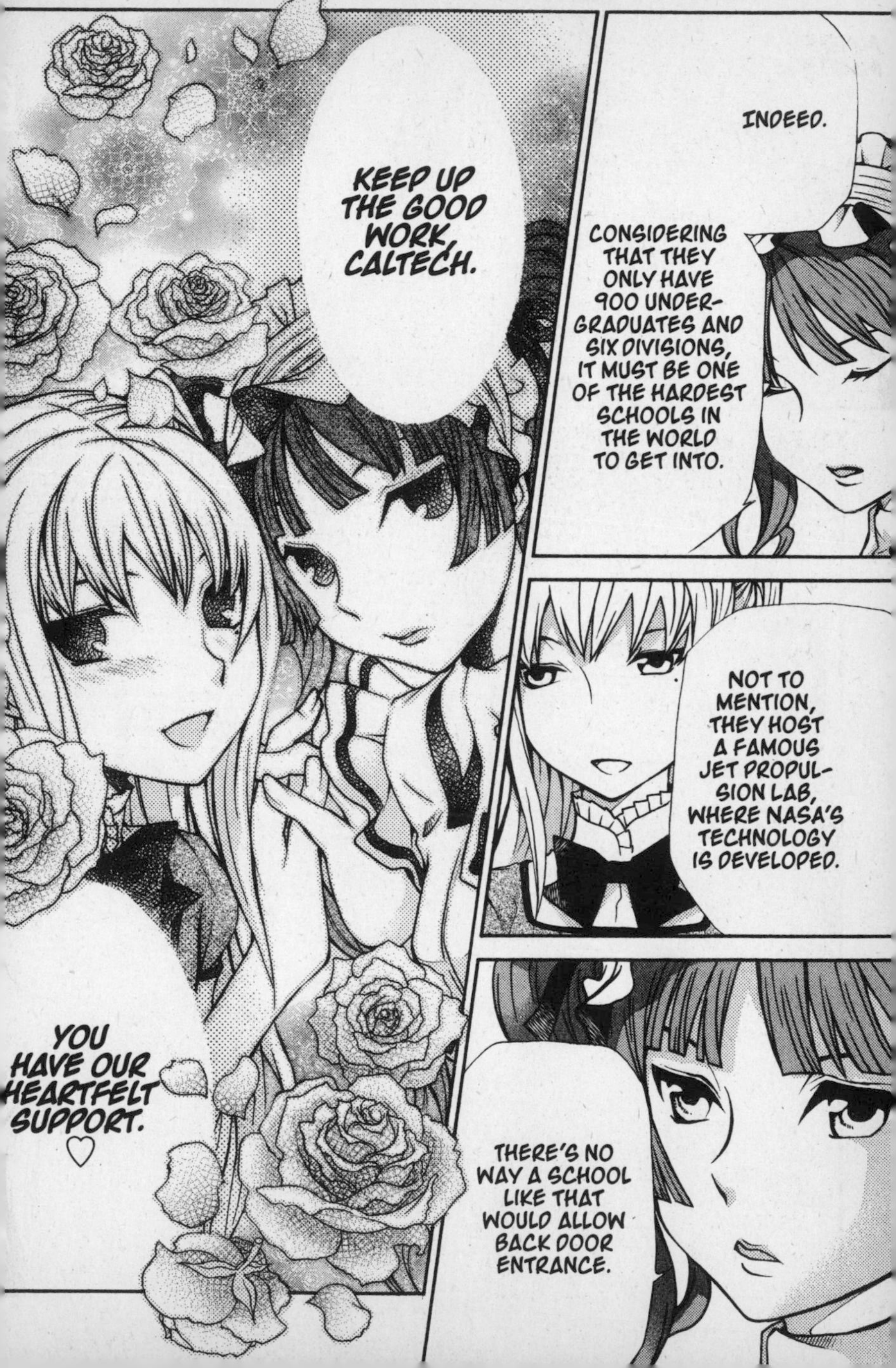
INDEED.
CONSIDERING THAT THEY ONLY HAVE 900 UNDER-GRADUATES AND SIX DIVISIONS, IT MUST BE ONE OF THE HARDEST SCHOOLS IN THE WORLD TO GET INTO.
NOT TO MENTION, THEY HOST A FAMOUS JET PROPUL-SION LAB, WHERE NASA'S TECHNOLOGY IS DEVELOPED.
THERE'S NO WAY A SCHOOL LIKE THAT WOULD ALLOW BACK DOOR ENTRANCE.
KEEP UP THE GOOD WORK, CALTECH.
YOU HAVE OUR HEARTFELT SUPPORT. ♡

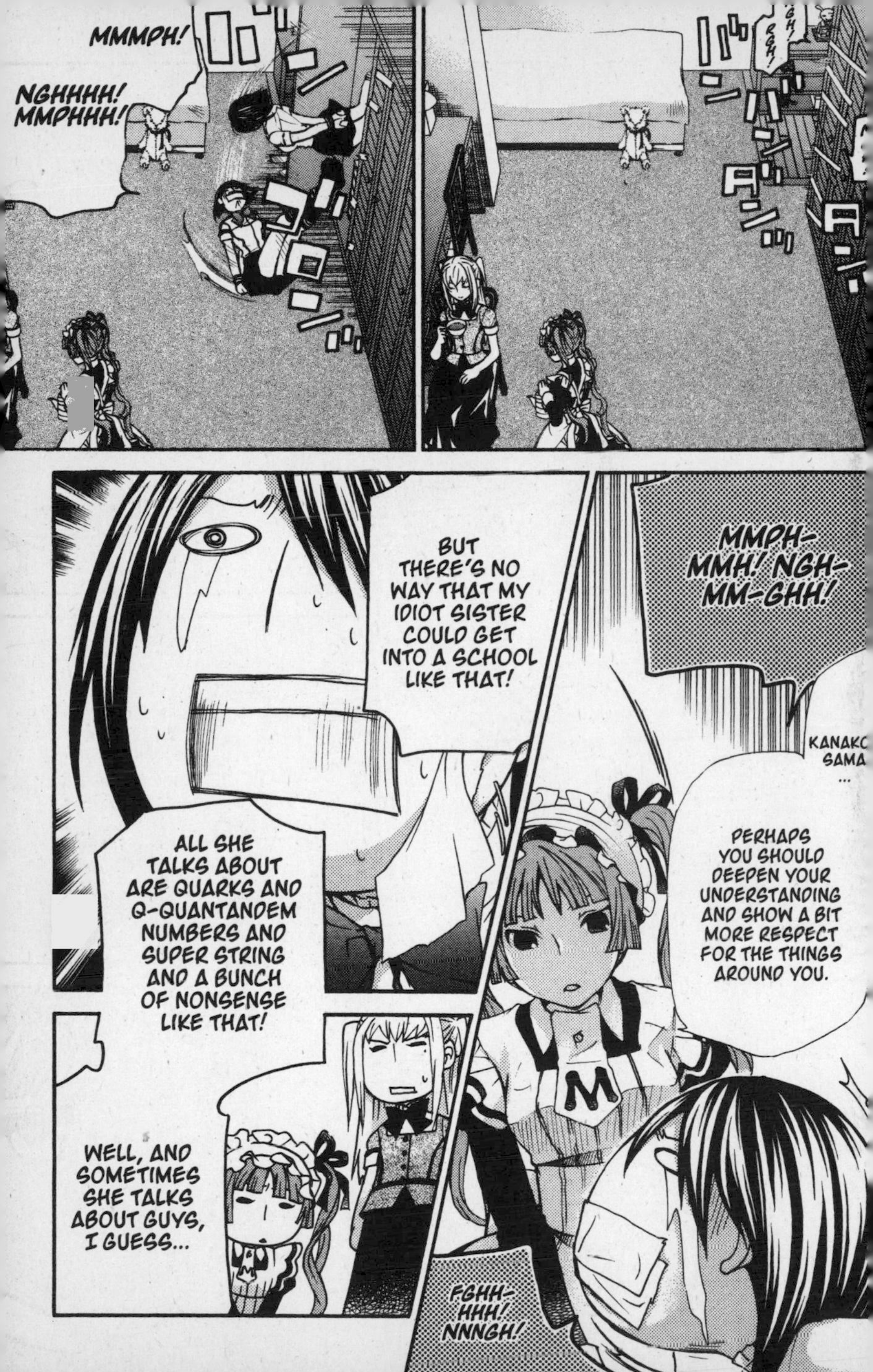
RGH!
MMMPH!
NGHHHH! MMPHHH!
MMPH-MMH! NGH-MM-GHH!
KANAKO-SAMA...
PERHAPS YOU SHOULD DEEPEN YOUR UNDERSTANDING AND SHOW A BIT MORE RESPECT FOR THE THINGS AROUND YOU.
FGHH-HHH! NNNGH!
BUT THERE'S NO WAY THAT MY IDIOT SISTER COULD GET INTO A SCHOOL LIKE THAT!
ALL SHE TALKS ABOUT ARE QUARKS AND Q-QUANTANDEM NUMBERS AND SUPER STRING AND A BUNCH OF NONSENSE LIKE THAT!
WELL, AND SOMETIMES SHE TALKS ABOUT GUYS, I GUESS...

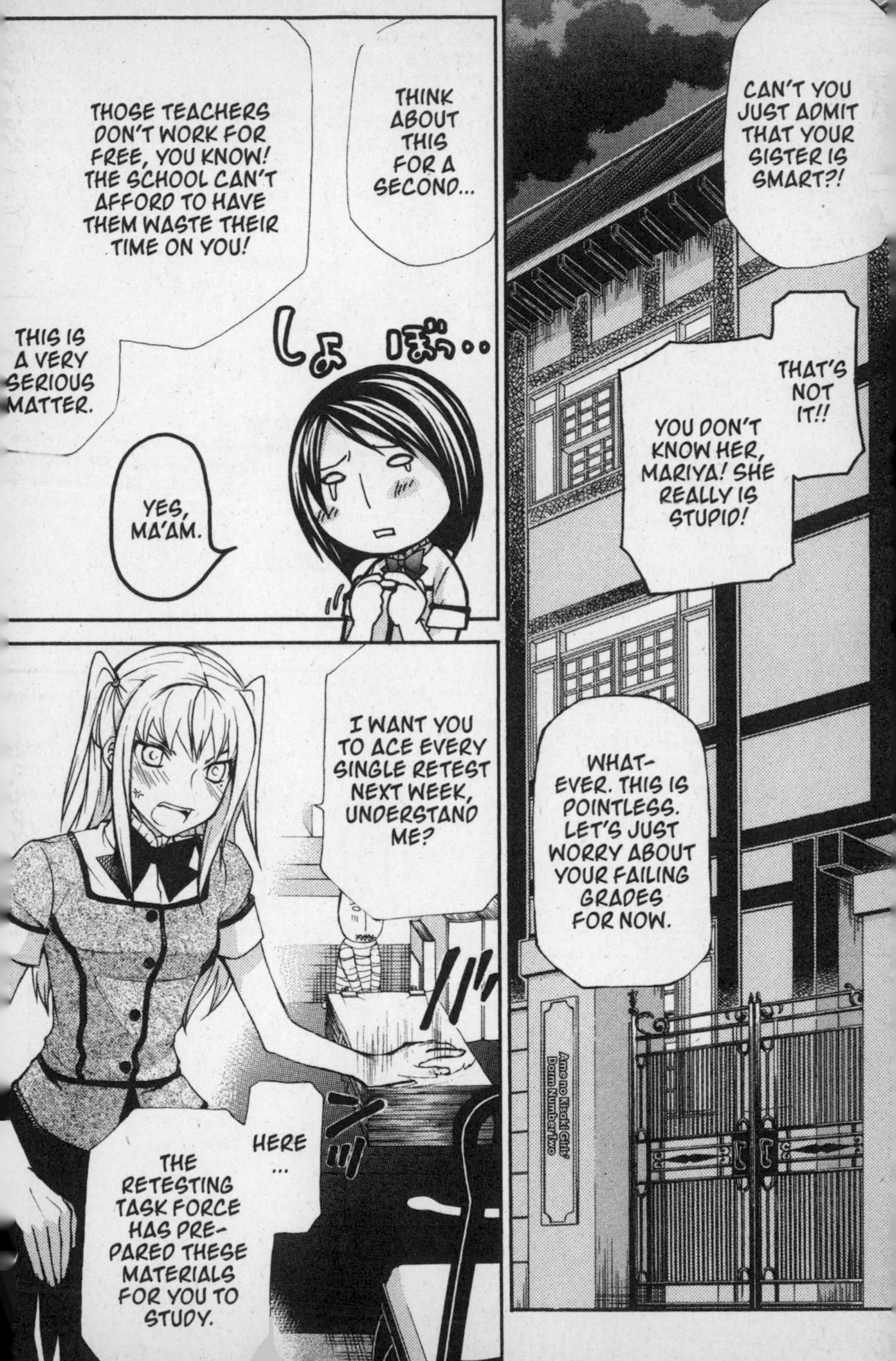
CAN'T YOU JUST ADMIT THAT YOUR SISTER IS SMART?!
THAT'S NOT IT!!
YOU DON'T KNOW HER, MARIYA! SHE REALLY IS STUPID!
WHAT-EVER. THIS IS POINTLESS. LET'S JUST WORRY ABOUT YOUR FAILING GRADES FOR NOW.
Ame no Kisaki Girls' Dorm Number Two
THINK ABOUT THIS FOR A SECOND...
THOSE TEACHERS DON'T WORK FOR FREE, YOU KNOW! THE SCHOOL CAN'T AFFORD TO HAVE THEM WASTE THEIR TIME ON YOU!
THIS IS A VERY SERIOUS MATTER.
しょぼ…
YES, MA'AM.
I WANT YOU TO ACE EVERY SINGLE RETEST NEXT WEEK, UNDERSTAND ME?
HERE...
THE RETESTING TASK FORCE HAS PRE-PARED THESE MATERIALS FOR YOU TO STUDY.

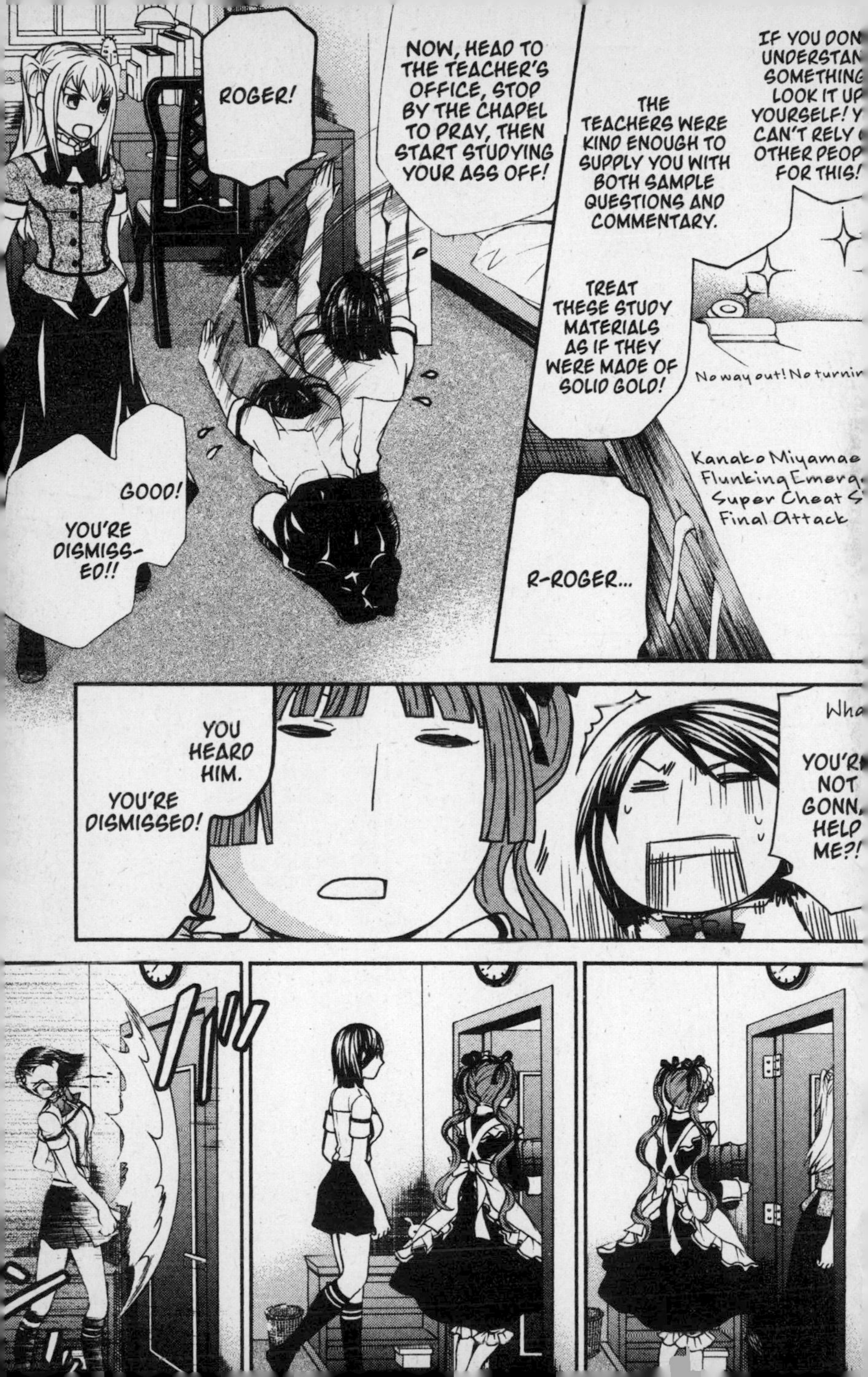

IF YOU DON UNDERSTAN SOMETHING LOOK IT UP YOURSELF! Y CAN'T RELY OTHER PEOP FOR THIS!
THE TEACHERS WERE KIND ENOUGH TO SUPPLY YOU WITH BOTH SAMPLE QUESTIONS AND COMMENTARY.
TREAT THESE STUDY MATERIALS AS IF THEY WERE MADE OF SOLID GOLD!
No way out! No turnin
Kanako Miyamae Flunking Emerg Super Cheat S Final Attack
R-ROGER...
NOW, HEAD TO THE TEACHER'S OFFICE, STOP BY THE CHAPEL TO PRAY, THEN START STUDYING YOUR ASS OFF!
ROGER!
GOOD!
YOU'RE DISMISS-ED!!
Wha
YOU'R NOT GONN HELP ME?!
YOU HEARD HIM.
YOU'RE DISMISSED!

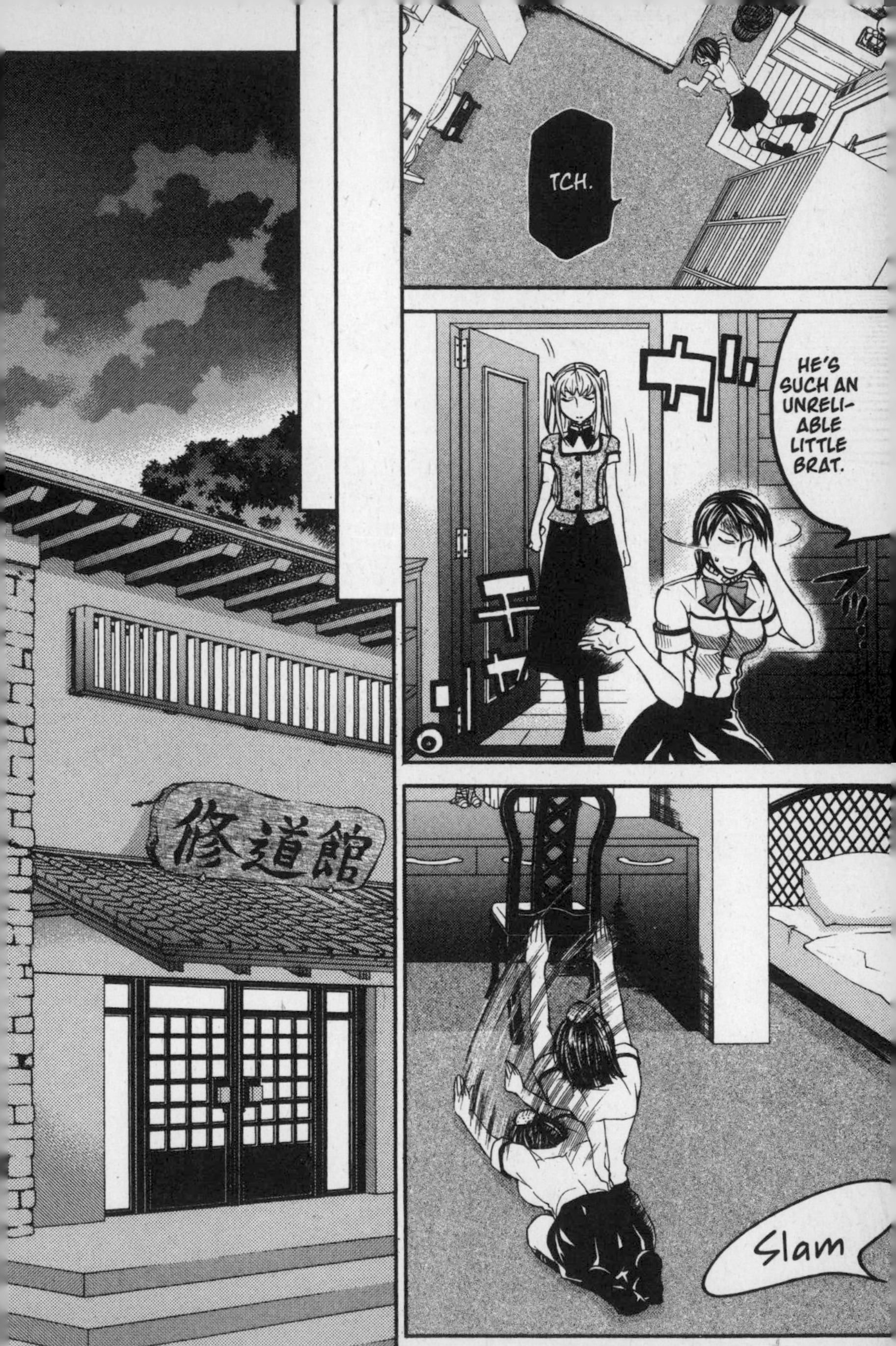
TCH.
HE'S SUCH AN UNRELI-ABLE LITTLE BRAT.
Slam
修道館

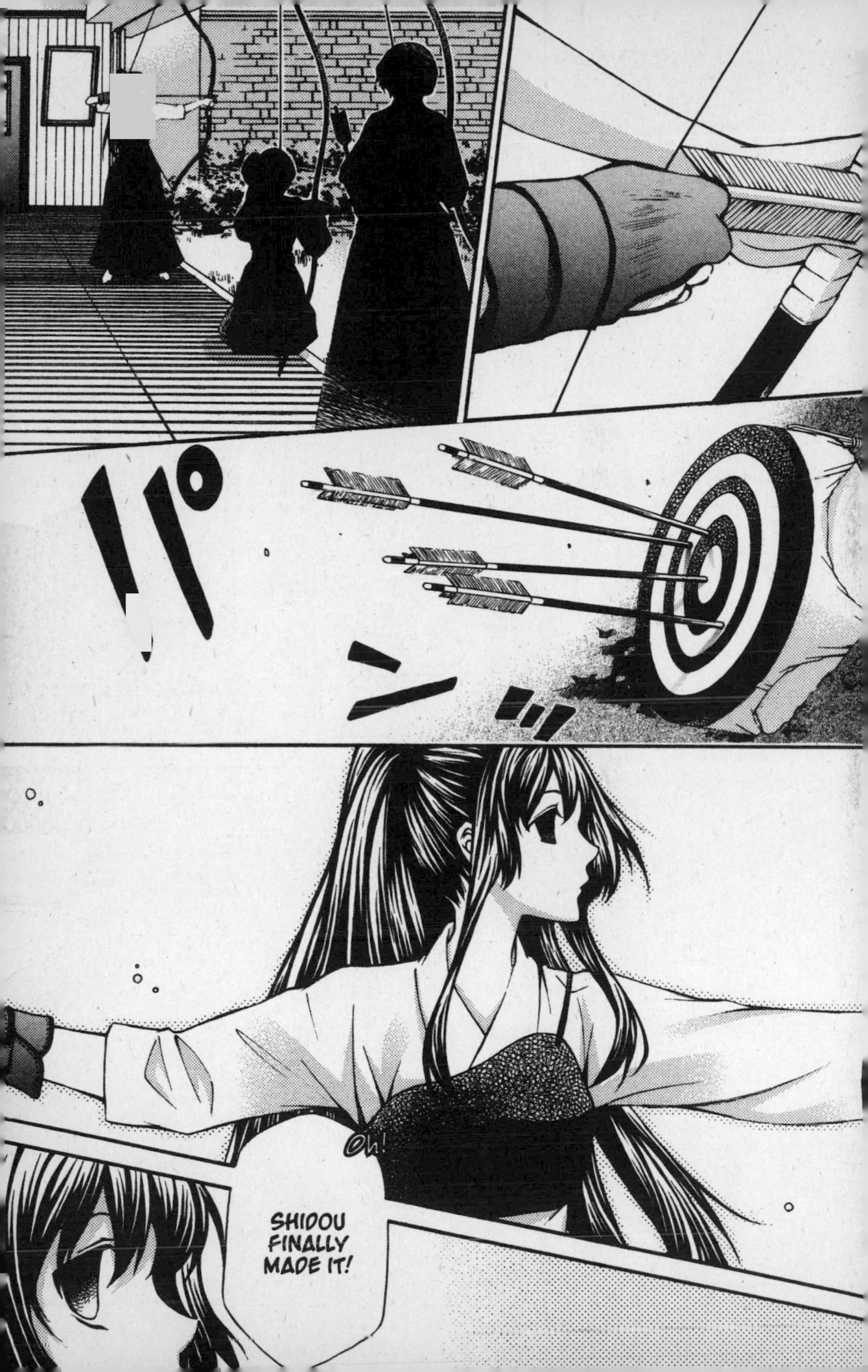
パン…
Oh!
SHIDOU FINALLY MADE IT!

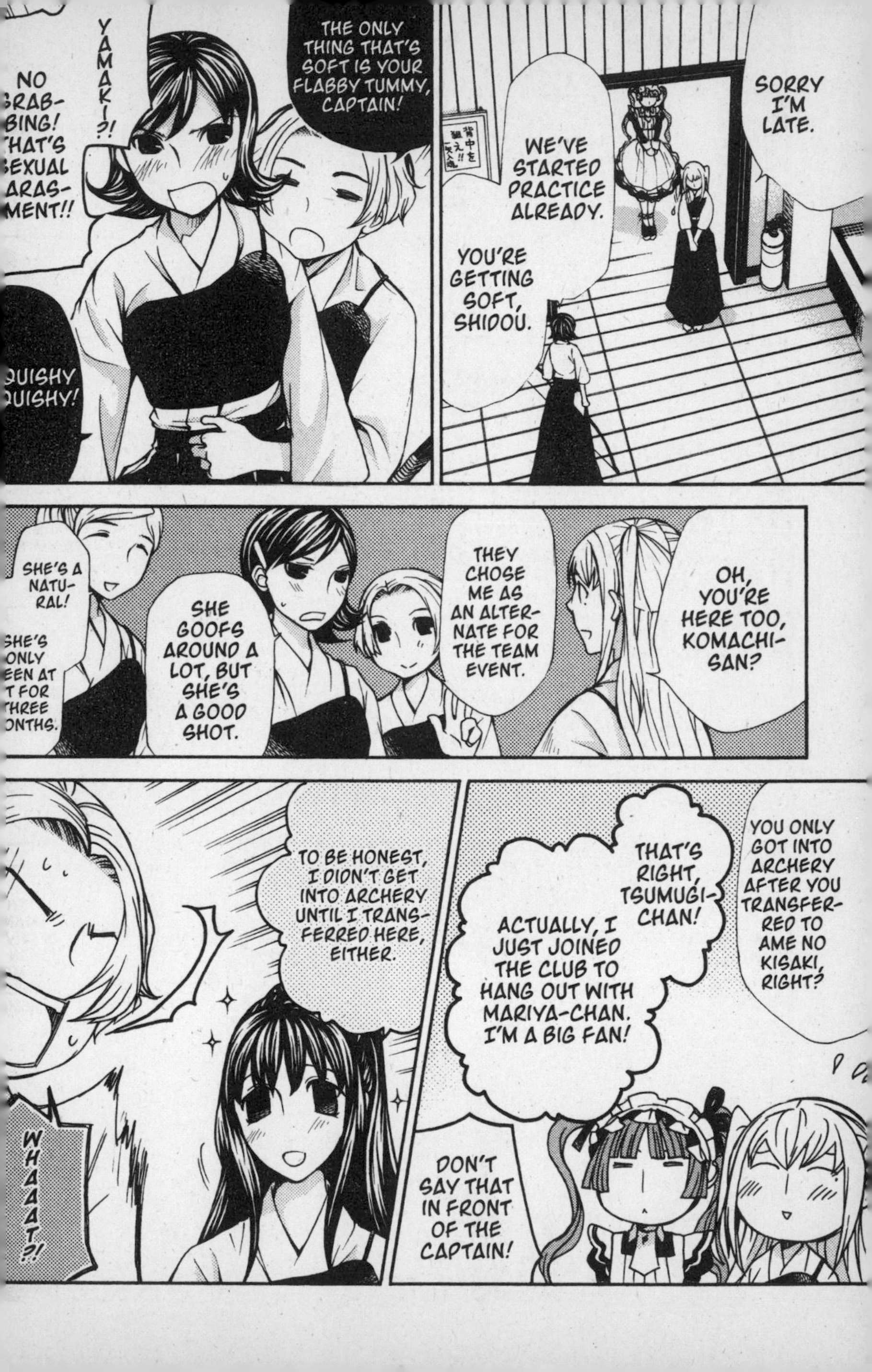
SORRY I'M LATE.
WE'VE STARTED PRACTICE ALREADY.
YOU'RE GETTING SOFT, SHIDOU.
THE ONLY THING THAT'S SOFT IS YOUR FLABBY TUMMY, CAPTAIN!
YAMAKI?!
NO RAB-BING! HAT'S EXUAL ARAS-MENT!!
QUISHY QUISHY!
OH, YOU'RE HERE TOO, KOMACHI-SAN?
THEY CHOSE ME AS AN ALTER-NATE FOR THE TEAM EVENT.
SHE GOOFS AROUND A LOT, BUT SHE'S A GOOD SHOT.
SHE'S A NATU-RAL!
HE'S ONLY EEN AT T FOR THREE ONTHS.
YOU ONLY GOT INTO ARCHERY AFTER YOU TRANSFER-RED TO AME NO KISAKI, RIGHT?
THAT'S RIGHT, TSUMUGI-CHAN!
ACTUALLY, I JUST JOINED THE CLUB TO HANG OUT WITH MARIYA-CHAN. I'M A BIG FAN!
DON'T SAY THAT IN FRONT OF THE CAPTAIN!
TO BE HONEST, I DIDN'T GET INTO ARCHERY UNTIL I TRANS-FERRED HERE, EITHER.
WHAAAAT?!

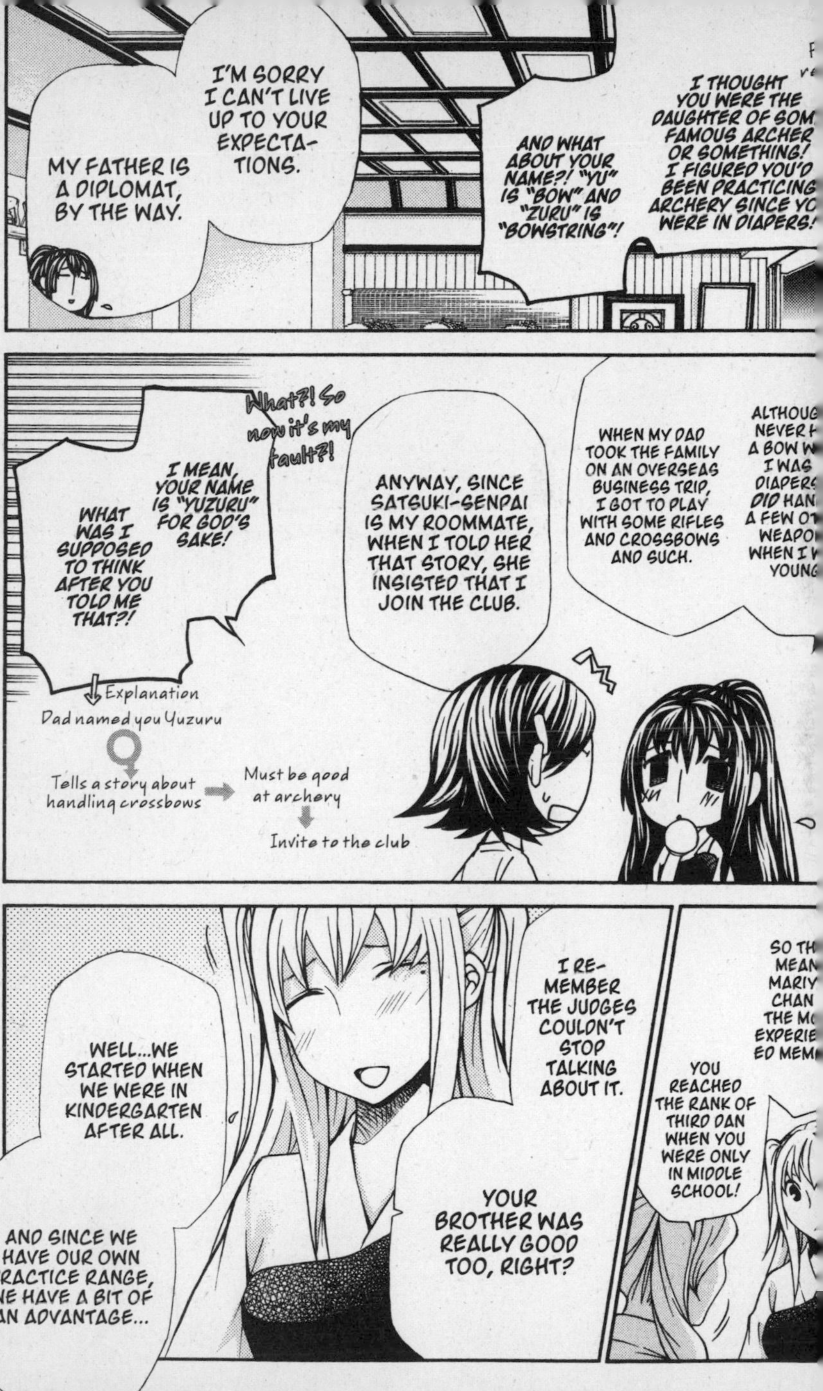
I THOUGHT YOU WERE THE DAUGHTER OF SOM FAMOUS ARCHER OR SOMETHING! I FIGURED YOU'D BEEN PRACTICING ARCHERY SINCE YO WERE IN DIAPERS!
AND WHAT ABOUT YOUR NAME?! "YU" IS "BOW" AND "ZURU" IS "BOWSTRING"!
I'M SORRY I CAN'T LIVE UP TO YOUR EXPECTATIONS.
MY FATHER IS A DIPLOMAT, BY THE WAY.
ALTHOUG NEVER H A BOW W I WAS DIAPERS DID HAN A FEW OT WEAPO WHEN I W YOUNG
WHEN MY DAD TOOK THE FAMILY ON AN OVERSEAS BUSINESS TRIP, I GOT TO PLAY WITH SOME RIFLES AND CROSSBOWS AND SUCH.
ANYWAY, SINCE SATSUKI-SENPAI IS MY ROOMMATE, WHEN I TOLD HER THAT STORY, SHE INSISTED THAT I JOIN THE CLUB.
What?! So now it's my fault?!
I MEAN, YOUR NAME IS "YUZURU" FOR GOD'S SAKE!
WHAT WAS I SUPPOSED TO THINK AFTER YOU TOLD ME THAT?!
Explanation
Dad named you Yuzuru
Tells a story about handling crossbows
Must be good at archery
Invite to the club
SO TH MEAN MARIY CHAN THE MO EXPERIE ED MEM
YOU REACHED THE RANK OF THIRD DAN WHEN YOU WERE ONLY IN MIDDLE SCHOOL!
I REMEMBER THE JUDGES COULDN'T STOP TALKING ABOUT IT.
YOUR BROTHER WAS REALLY GOOD TOO, RIGHT?
WELL...WE STARTED WHEN WE WERE IN KINDERGARTEN AFTER ALL.
AND SINCE WE HAVE OUR OWN PRACTICE RANGE, WE HAVE A BIT OF AN ADVANTAGE...

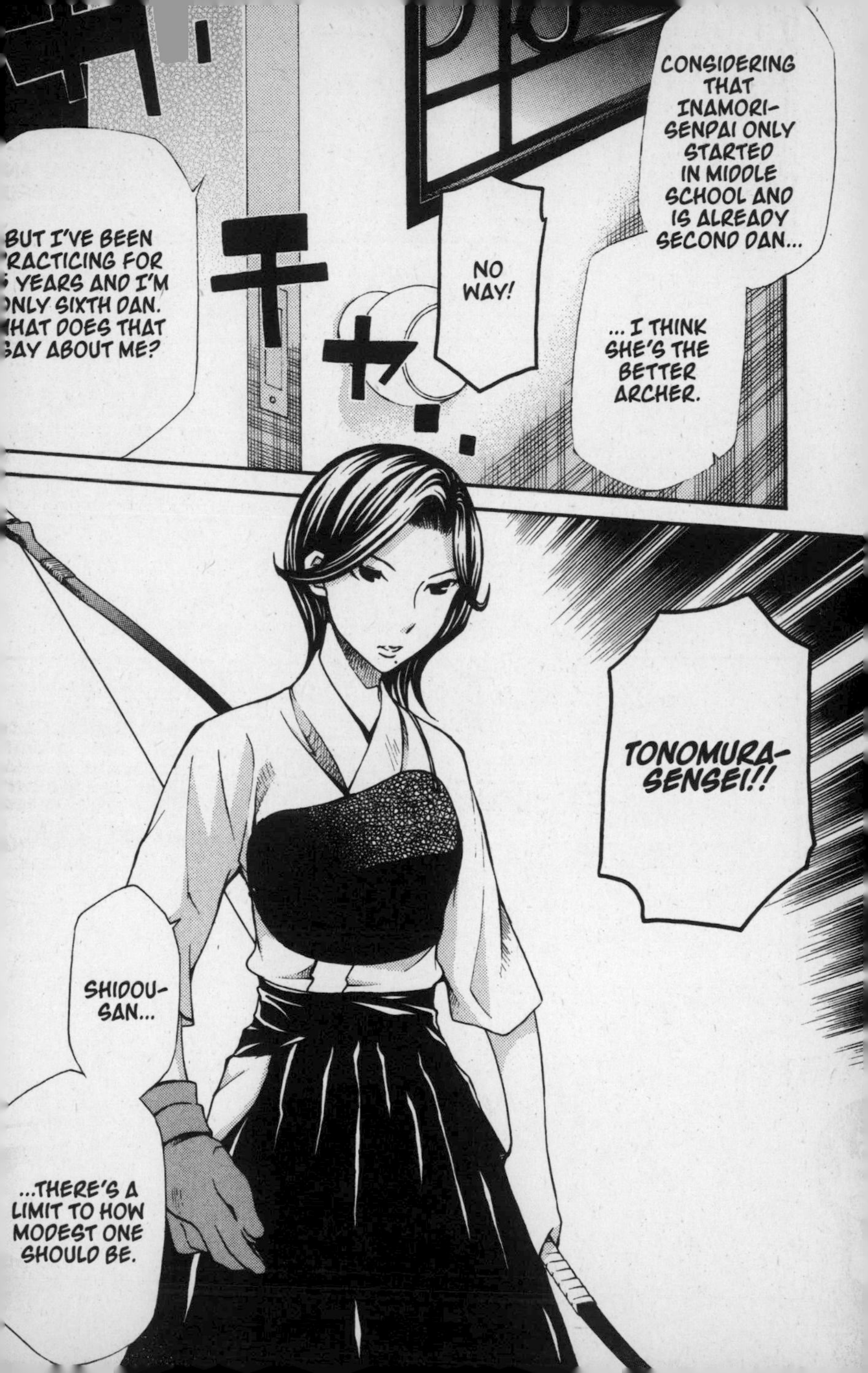
CONSIDERING THAT INAMORI-SENPAI ONLY STARTED IN MIDDLE SCHOOL AND IS ALREADY SECOND DAN...
... I THINK SHE'S THE BETTER ARCHER.
NO WAY!
BUT I'VE BEEN RACTICING FOR YEARS AND I'M NLY SIXTH DAN. HAT DOES THAT AY ABOUT ME?
TONOMURA-SENSEI!!
SHIDOU-SAN...
...THERE'S A LIMIT TO HOW MODEST ONE SHOULD BE.

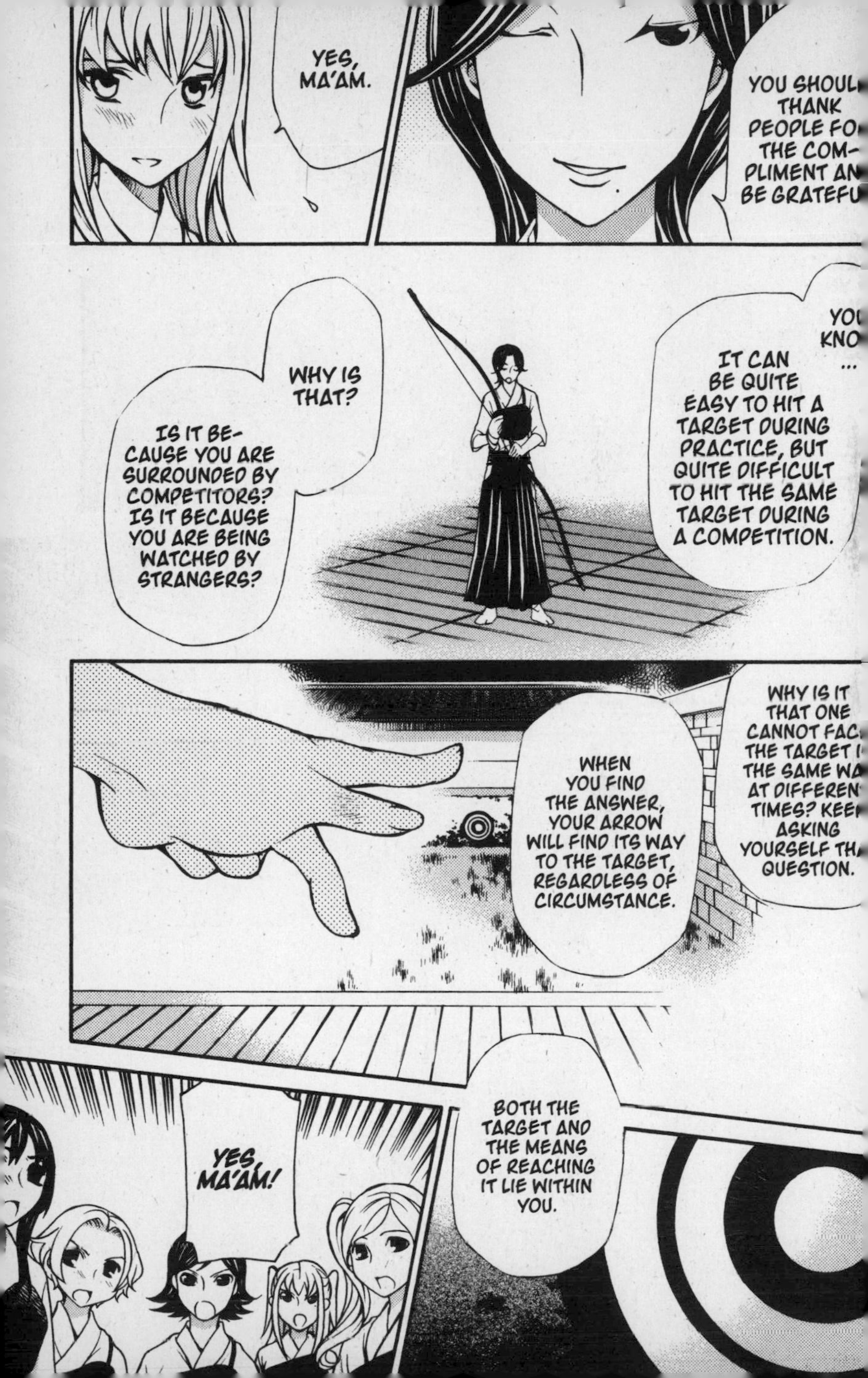
YOU SHOUL THANK PEOPLE FO THE COMPLIMENT AN BE GRATEFU
YES, MA'AM.
YOU KNO ...
IT CAN BE QUITE EASY TO HIT A TARGET DURING PRACTICE, BUT QUITE DIFFICULT TO HIT THE SAME TARGET DURING A COMPETITION.
WHY IS THAT?
IS IT BECAUSE YOU ARE SURROUNDED BY COMPETITORS? IS IT BECAUSE YOU ARE BEING WATCHED BY STRANGERS?
WHY IS IT THAT ONE CANNOT FAC THE TARGET I THE SAME WA AT DIFFEREN TIMES? KEE ASKING YOURSELF TH QUESTION.
WHEN YOU FIND THE ANSWER, YOUR ARROW WILL FIND ITS WAY TO THE TARGET, REGARDLESS OF CIRCUMSTANCE.
BOTH THE TARGET AND THE MEANS OF REACHING IT LIE WITHIN YOU.
YES, MA'AM!

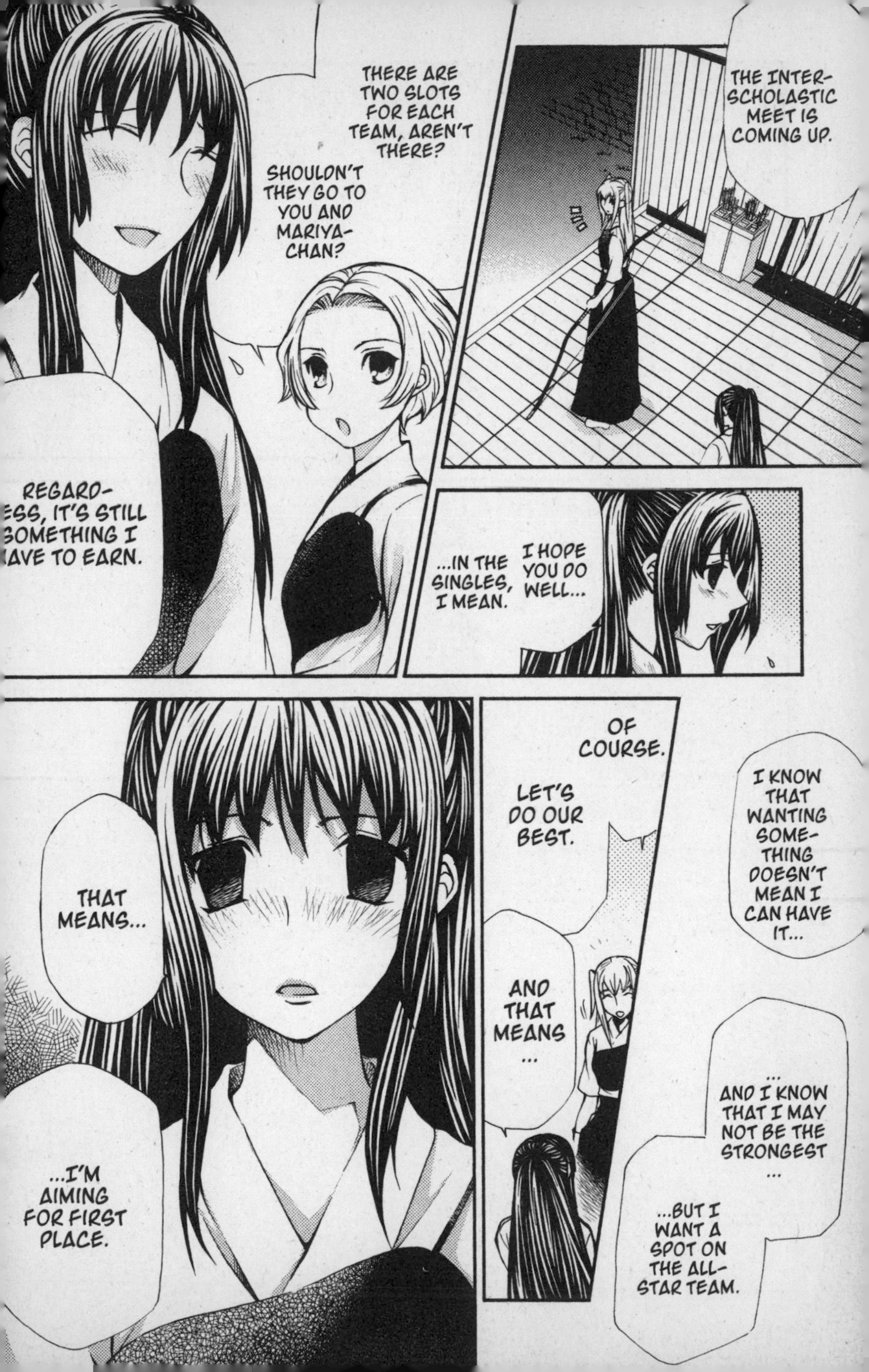
THE INTER-SCHOLASTIC MEET IS COMING UP.
I HOPE YOU DO WELL...
...IN THE SINGLES, I MEAN.
THERE ARE TWO SLOTS FOR EACH TEAM, AREN'T THERE?
SHOULDN'T THEY GO TO YOU AND MARIYA-CHAN?
REGARD-ESS, IT'S STILL SOMETHING I AVE TO EARN.
I KNOW THAT WANTING SOME-THING DOESN'T MEAN I CAN HAVE IT...
...AND I KNOW THAT I MAY NOT BE THE STRONGEST...
...BUT I WANT A SPOT ON THE ALL-STAR TEAM.
OF COURSE.
LET'S DO OUR BEST.
AND THAT MEANS...
THAT MEANS...
...I'M AIMING FOR FIRST PLACE.

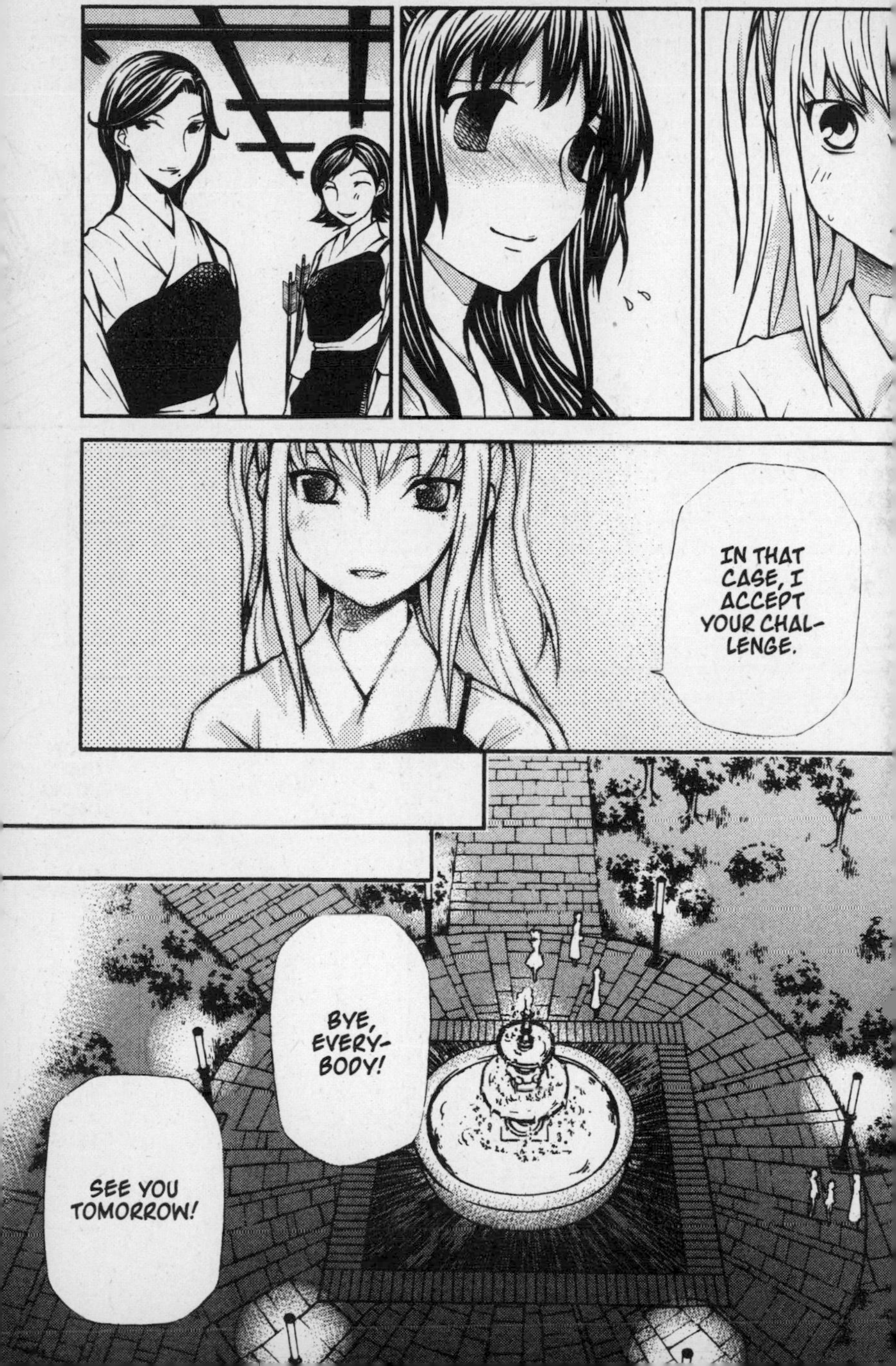
IN THAT CASE, I ACCEPT YOUR CHALLENGE.
BYE, EVERYBODY!
SEE YOU TOMORROW!

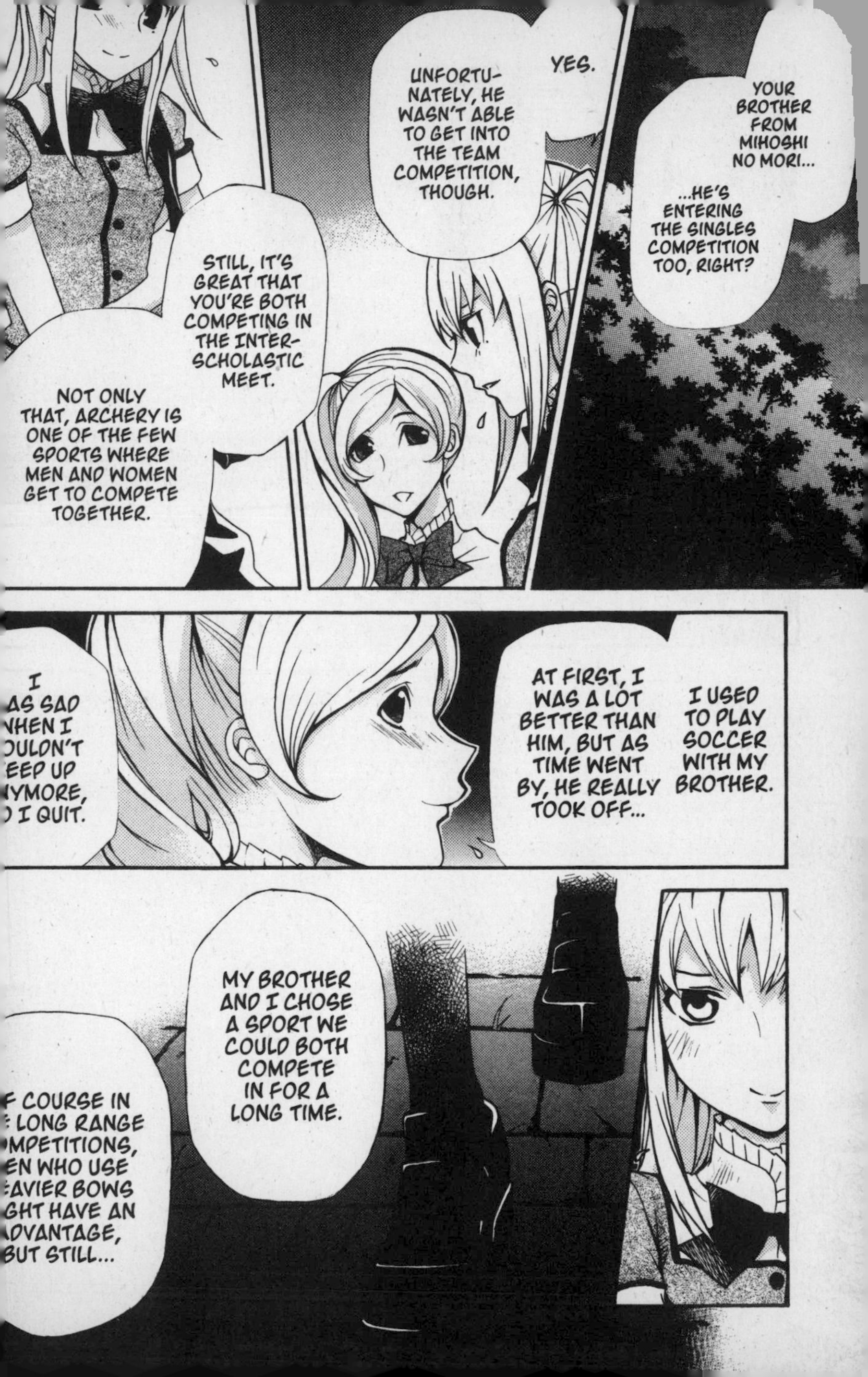
YOUR BROTHER FROM MIHOSHI NO MORI...
...HE'S ENTERING THE SINGLES COMPETITION TOO, RIGHT?
YES.
UNFORTUNATELY, HE WASN'T ABLE TO GET INTO THE TEAM COMPETITION, THOUGH.
STILL, IT'S GREAT THAT YOU'RE BOTH COMPETING IN THE INTER-SCHOLASTIC MEET.
NOT ONLY THAT, ARCHERY IS ONE OF THE FEW SPORTS WHERE MEN AND WOMEN GET TO COMPETE TOGETHER.
I USED TO PLAY SOCCER WITH MY BROTHER.
AT FIRST, I WAS A LOT BETTER THAN HIM, BUT AS TIME WENT BY, HE REALLY TOOK OFF...
I AS SAD HEN I OULDN'T EEP UP NYMORE, I QUIT.
MY BROTHER AND I CHOSE A SPORT WE COULD BOTH COMPETE IN FOR A LONG TIME.
F COURSE IN E LONG RANGE MPETITIONS, EN WHO USE EAVIER BOWS GHT HAVE AN DVANTAGE, BUT STILL...

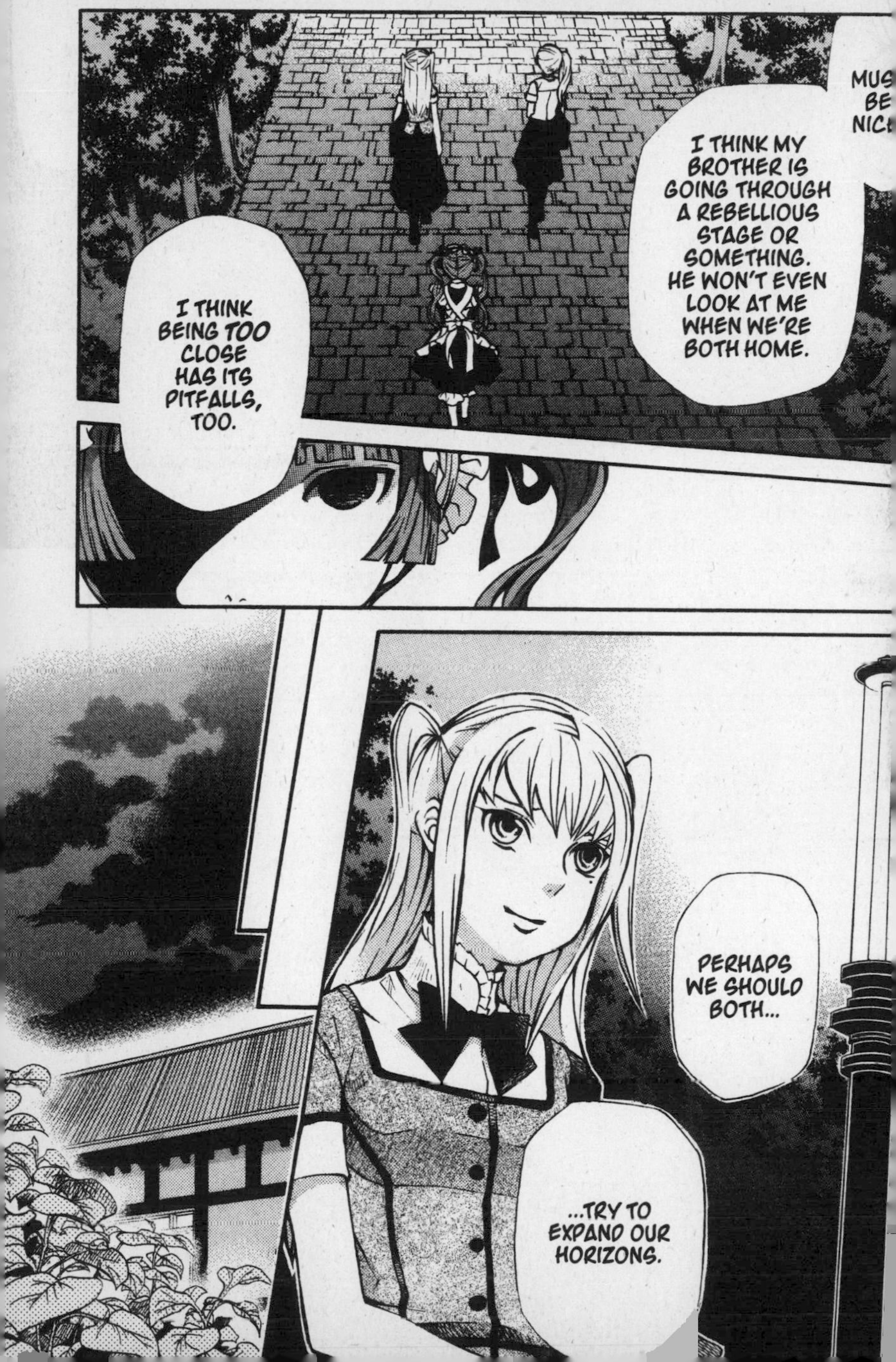
MUS BE NIC
I THINK MY BROTHER IS GOING THROUGH A REBELLIOUS STAGE OR SOMETHING. HE WON'T EVEN LOOK AT ME WHEN WE'RE BOTH HOME.
I THINK BEING TOO CLOSE HAS ITS PITFALLS, TOO.
PERHAPS WE SHOULD BOTH...
...TRY TO EXPAND OUR HORIZONS.

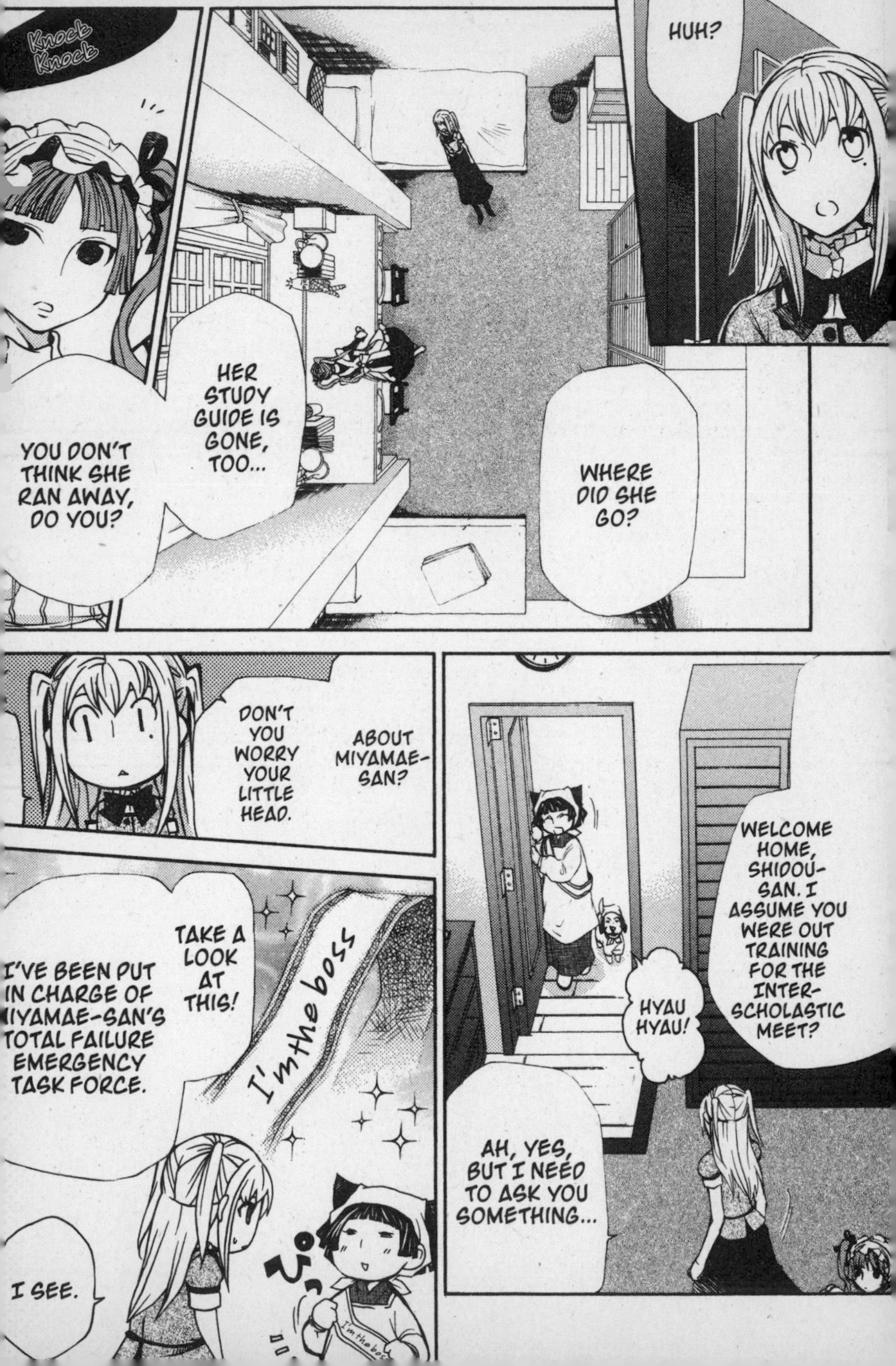
HUH?
WHERE DID SHE GO?
HER STUDY GUIDE IS GONE, TOO...
Knock Knock
YOU DON'T THINK SHE RAN AWAY, DO YOU?
WELCOME HOME, SHIDOU-SAN. I ASSUME YOU WERE OUT TRAINING FOR THE INTER-SCHOLASTIC MEET?
HYAU HYAU!
AH, YES, BUT I NEED TO ASK YOU SOMETHING...
ABOUT MIYAMAE-SAN?
DON'T YOU WORRY YOUR LITTLE HEAD.
TAKE A LOOK AT THIS!
I'VE BEEN PUT IN CHARGE OF MIYAMAE-SAN'S TOTAL FAILURE EMERGENCY TASK FORCE.
I'm the boss
I SEE.

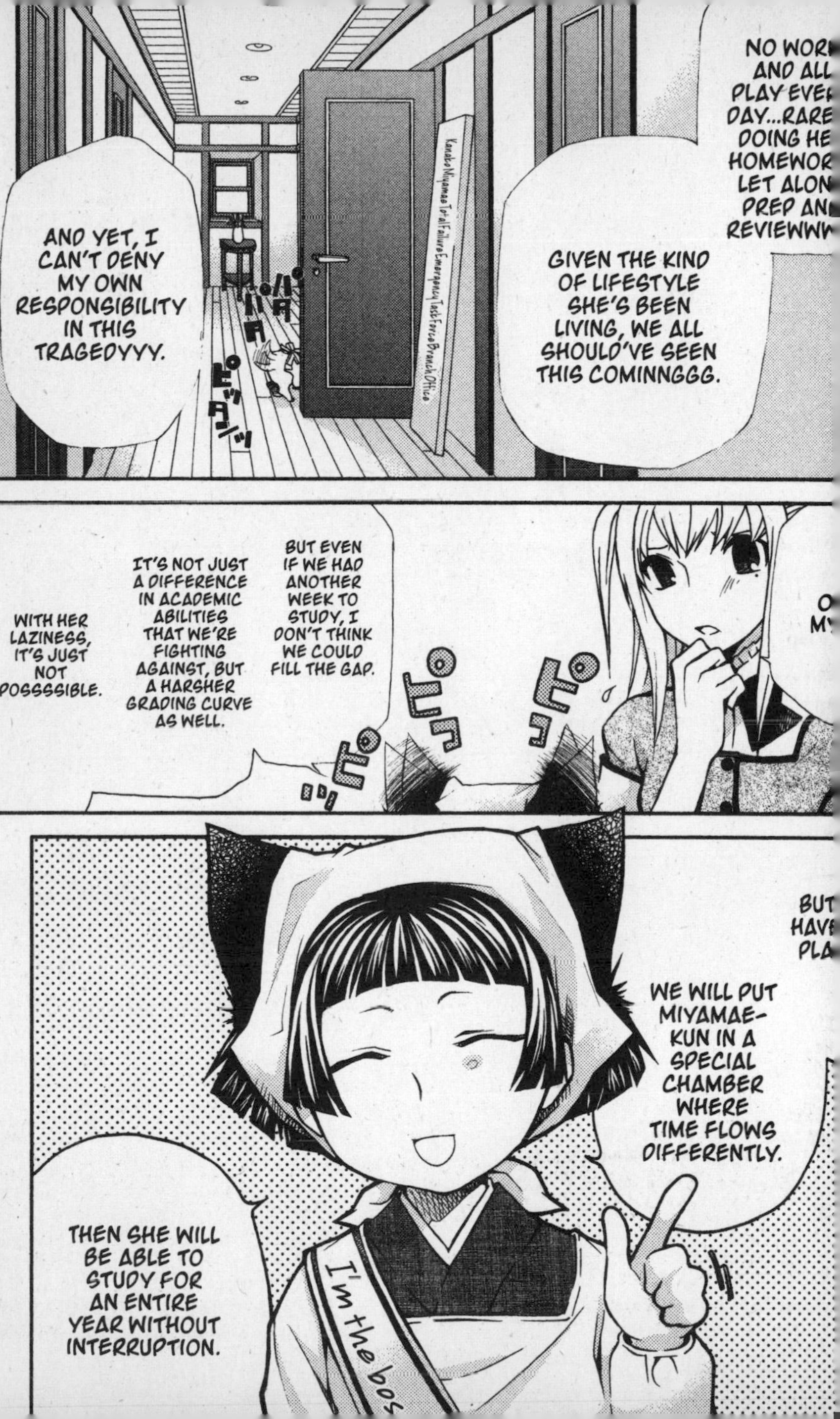
NO WOR AND ALL PLAY EVE DAY...RARE DOING HE HOMEWOR LET ALON PREP AN REVIEWNW
GIVEN THE KIND OF LIFESTYLE SHE'S BEEN LIVING, WE ALL SHOULD'VE SEEN THIS COMINNGGG.
Kanako Miyamae Total Failure Emergency Task Force Branch Office
AND YET, I CAN'T DENY MY OWN RESPONSIBILITY IN THIS TRAGEDYYY.
O MY
BUT EVEN IF WE HAD ANOTHER WEEK TO STUDY, I DON'T THINK WE COULD FILL THE GAP.
IT'S NOT JUST A DIFFERENCE IN ACADEMIC ABILITIES THAT WE'RE FIGHTING AGAINST, BUT A HARSHER GRADING CURVE AS WELL.
WITH HER LAZINESS, IT'S JUST NOT POSSSSIBLE.
BUT HAVE PLA
WE WILL PUT MIYAMAE-KUN IN A SPECIAL CHAMBER WHERE TIME FLOWS DIFFERENTLY.
I'm the bos
THEN SHE WILL BE ABLE TO STUDY FOR AN ENTIRE YEAR WITHOUT INTERRUPTION.

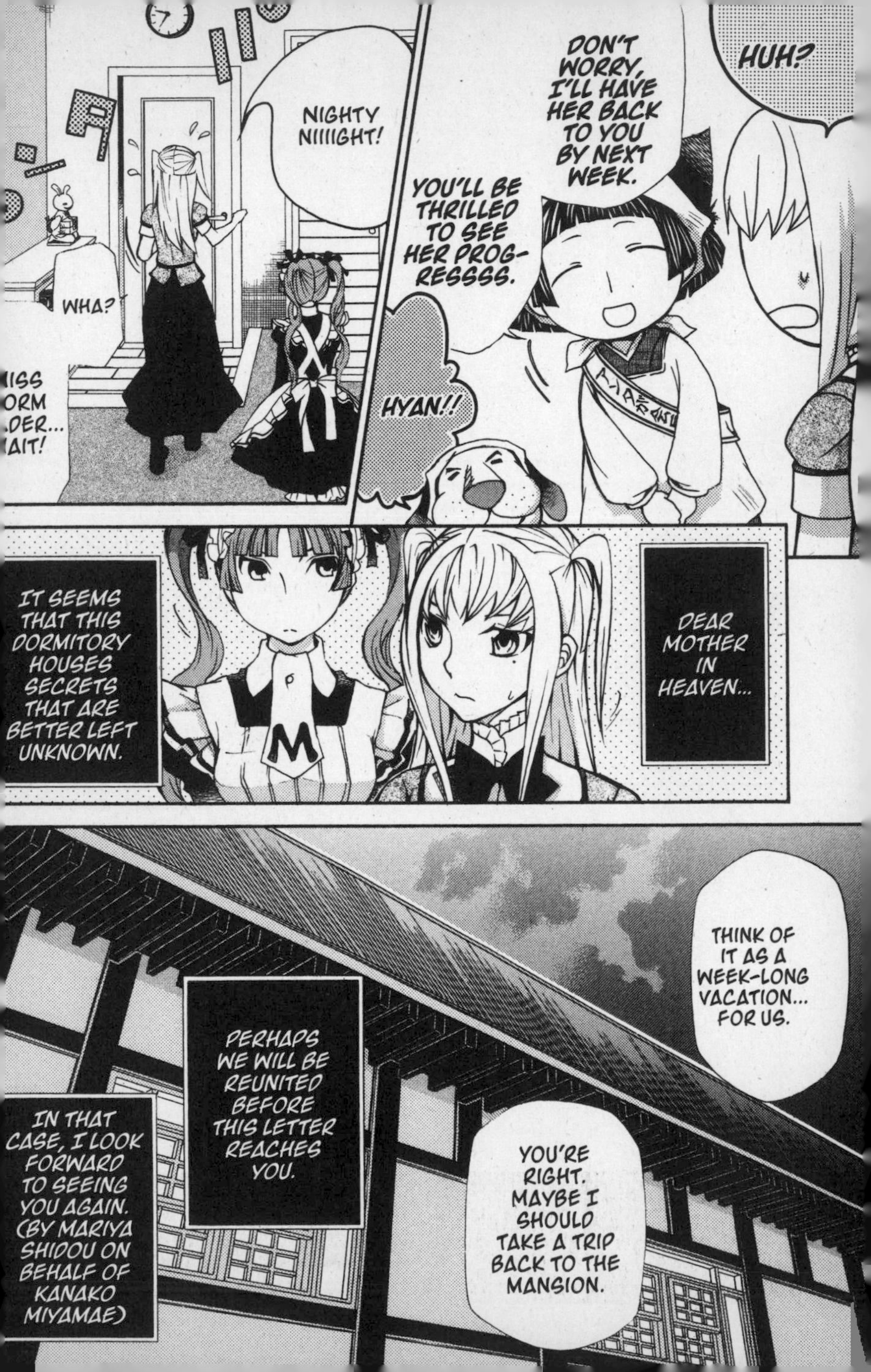
HUH?
DON'T WORRY, I'LL HAVE HER BACK TO YOU BY NEXT WEEK.
YOU'LL BE THRILLED TO SEE HER PROG-RESSSS.
HYAN!!
NIGHTY NIIIIGHT!
WHA?
ISS ORM DER... AIT!
DEAR MOTHER IN HEAVEN...
IT SEEMS THAT THIS DORMITORY HOUSES SECRETS THAT ARE BETTER LEFT UNKNOWN.
THINK OF IT AS A WEEK-LONG VACATION... FOR US.
YOU'RE RIGHT. MAYBE I SHOULD TAKE A TRIP BACK TO THE MANSION.
PERHAPS WE WILL BE REUNITED BEFORE THIS LETTER REACHES YOU.
IN THAT CASE, I LOOK FORWARD TO SEEING YOU AGAIN. (BY MARIYA SHIDOU ON BEHALF OF KANAKO MIYAMAE)

Maria✝Holic

Maria✝Holic

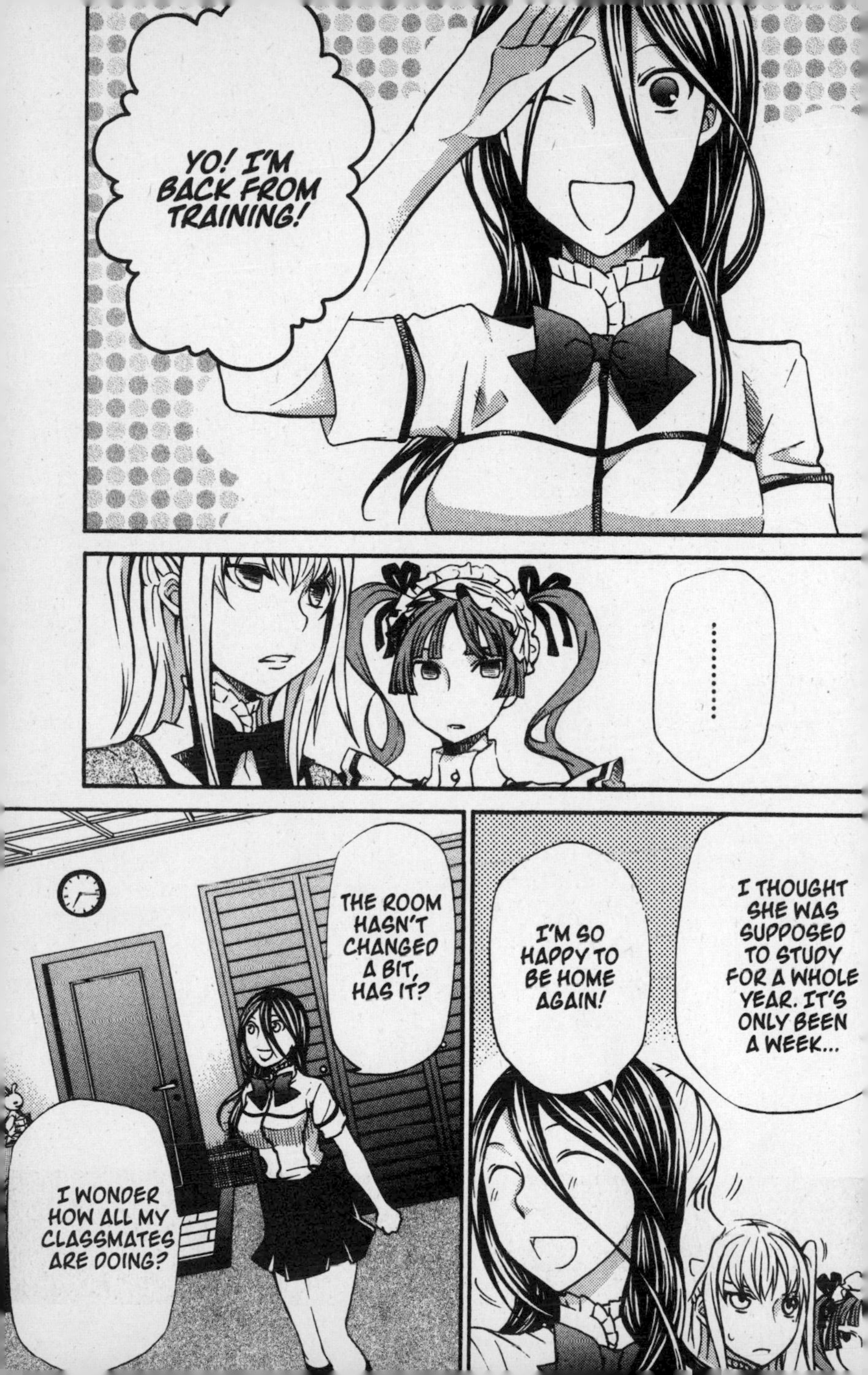
YO! I'M BACK FROM TRAINING!
......
I THOUGHT SHE WAS SUPPOSED TO STUDY FOR A WHOLE YEAR. IT'S ONLY BEEN A WEEK...
I'M SO HAPPY TO BE HOME AGAIN!
THE ROOM HASN'T CHANGED A BIT, HAS IT?
I WONDER HOW ALL MY CLASSMATES ARE DOING?

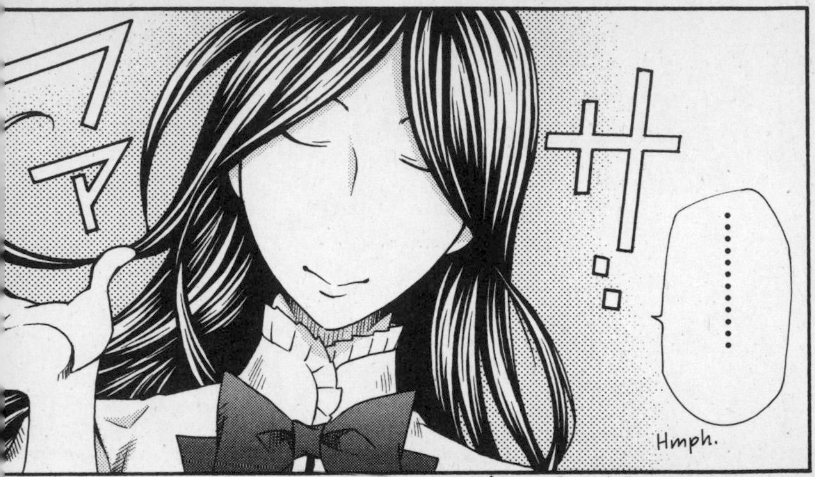
......
Hmph.
PEOPLE OF EARTH, LEND ME YOUR BRAINPOWER!*
SHUT UP!!!

*Quoting Dragonball

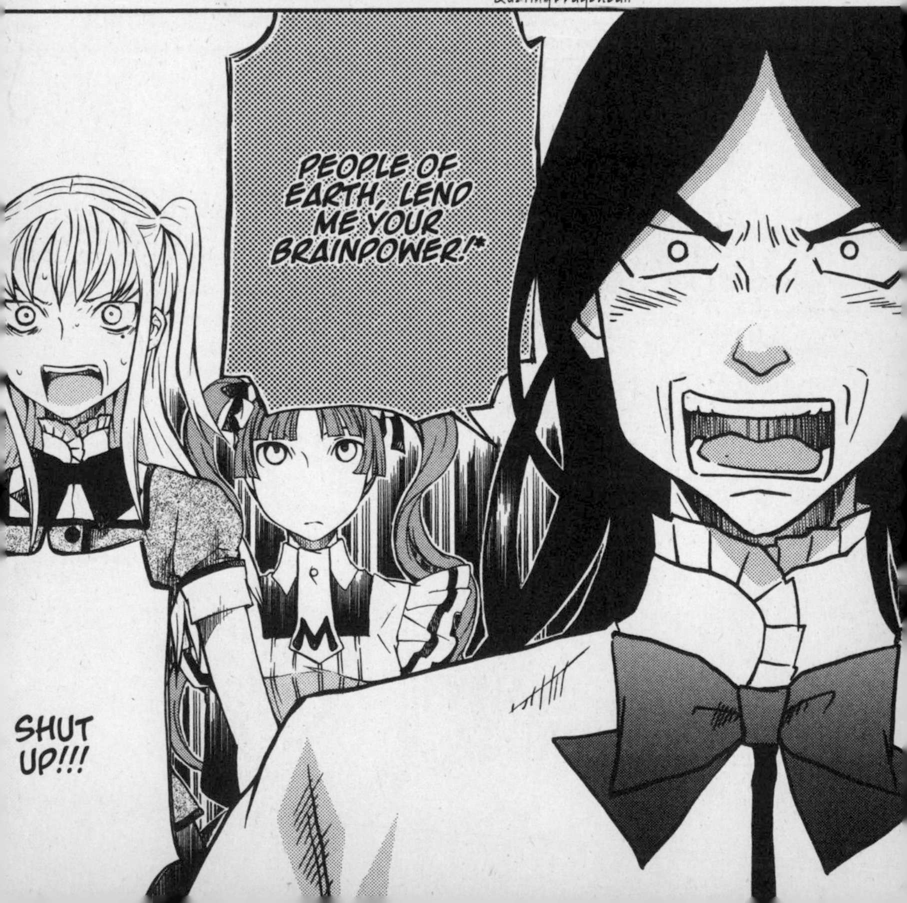

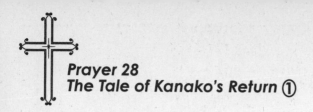

Prayer 28
The Tale of Kanako's Return ①

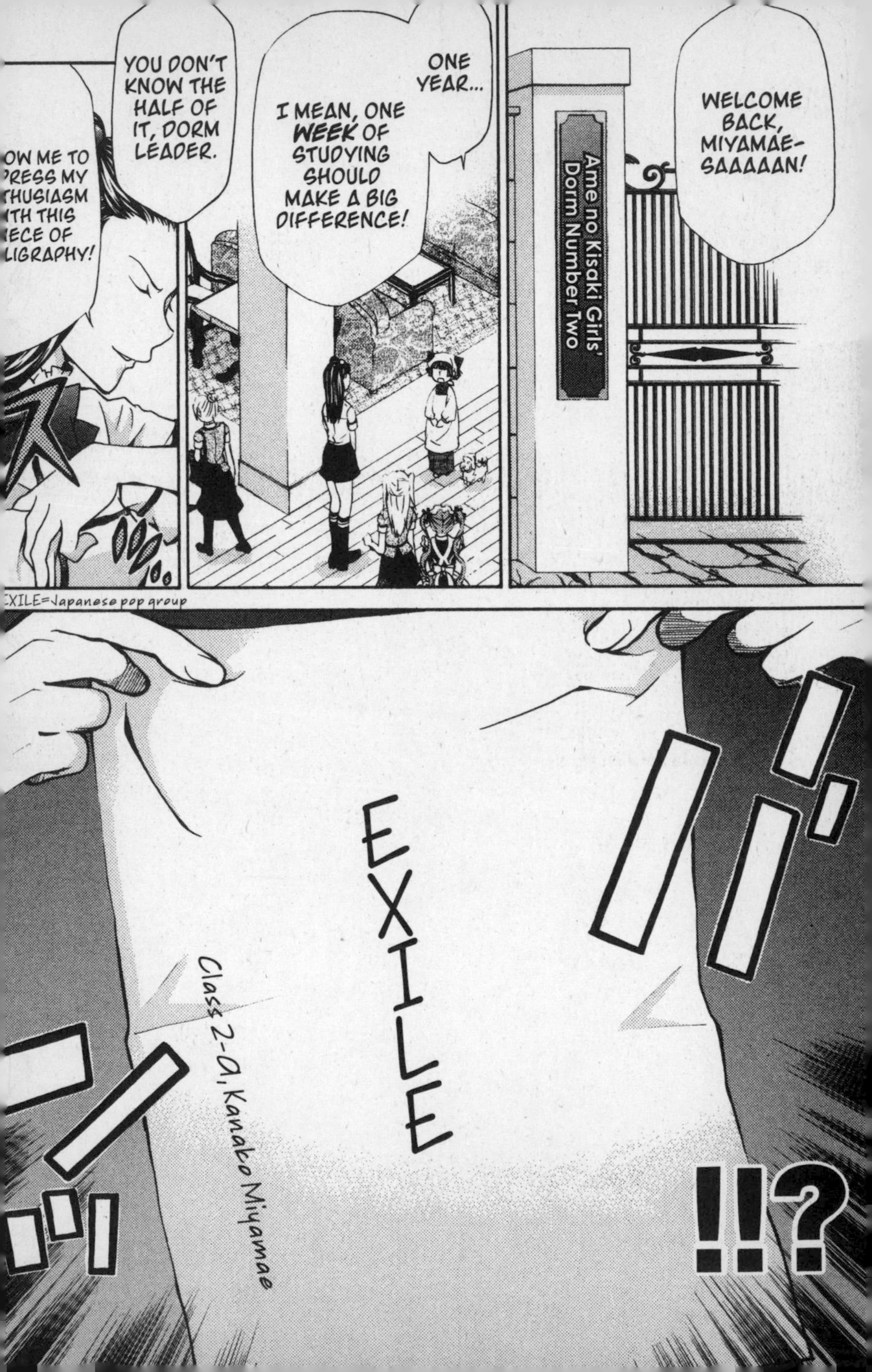
WELCOME BACK, MIYAMAE-SAAAAAN!
Ame no Kisaki Girls' Dorm Number Two
ONE YEAR...
I MEAN, ONE WEEK OF STUDYING SHOULD MAKE A BIG DIFFERENCE!
YOU DON'T KNOW THE HALF OF IT, DORM LEADER.
OW ME TO PRESS MY THUSIASM TH THIS ECE OF LIGRAPHY!
XILE=Japanese pop group
!!?
EXILE
Class 2-A, Kanako Miyamae

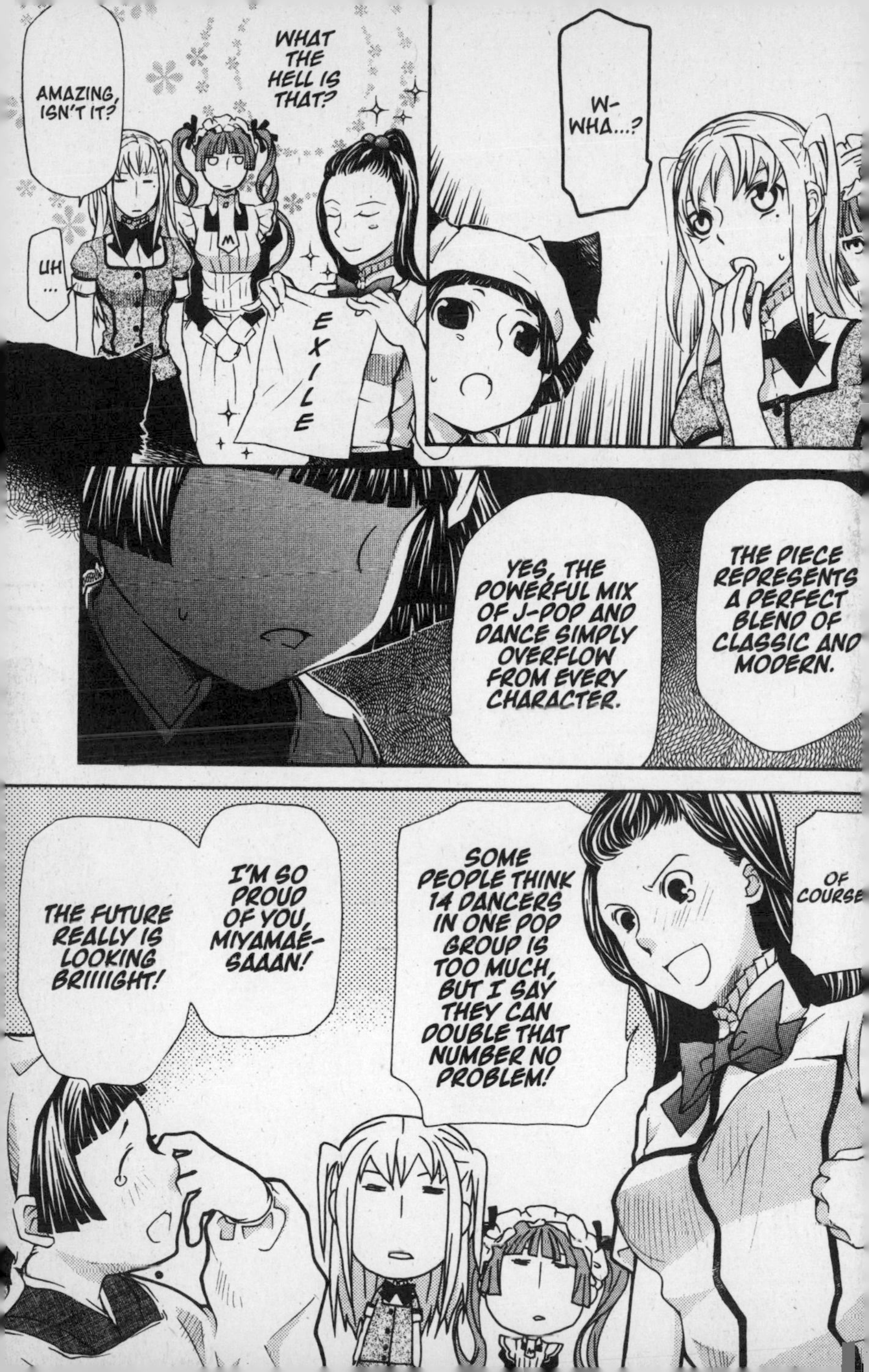
W-WHA...?
WHAT THE HELL IS THAT?
AMAZING, ISN'T IT?
EXILE
UH...
THE PIECE REPRESENTS A PERFECT BLEND OF CLASSIC AND MODERN.
YES, THE POWERFUL MIX OF J-POP AND DANCE SIMPLY OVERFLOW FROM EVERY CHARACTER.
OF COURSE
SOME PEOPLE THINK 14 DANCERS IN ONE POP GROUP IS TOO MUCH, BUT I SAY THEY CAN DOUBLE THAT NUMBER NO PROBLEM!
I'M SO PROUD OF YOU, MIYAMAE-SAAAN!
THE FUTURE REALLY IS LOOKING BRIIIIGHT!

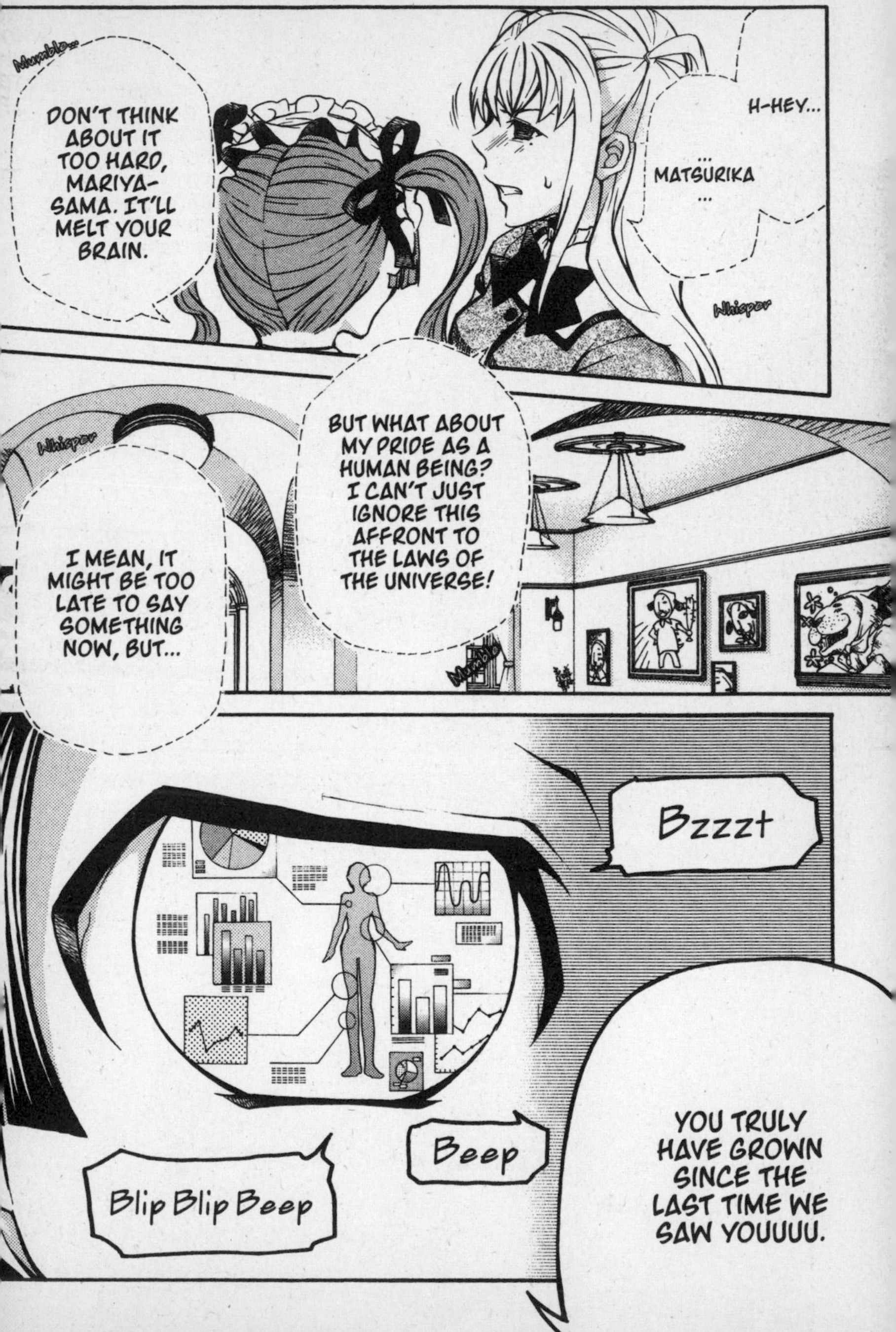
H-HEY...
... MATSURIKA ...
Whisper
Mumble...
DON'T THINK ABOUT IT TOO HARD, MARIYA-SAMA. IT'LL MELT YOUR BRAIN.
BUT WHAT ABOUT MY PRIDE AS A HUMAN BEING? I CAN'T JUST IGNORE THIS AFFRONT TO THE LAWS OF THE UNIVERSE!
Mumble
Whisper
I MEAN, IT MIGHT BE TOO LATE TO SAY SOMETHING NOW, BUT...
Bzzzt
YOU TRULY HAVE GROWN SINCE THE LAST TIME WE SAW YOUUUU.
Beep
Blip Blip Beep

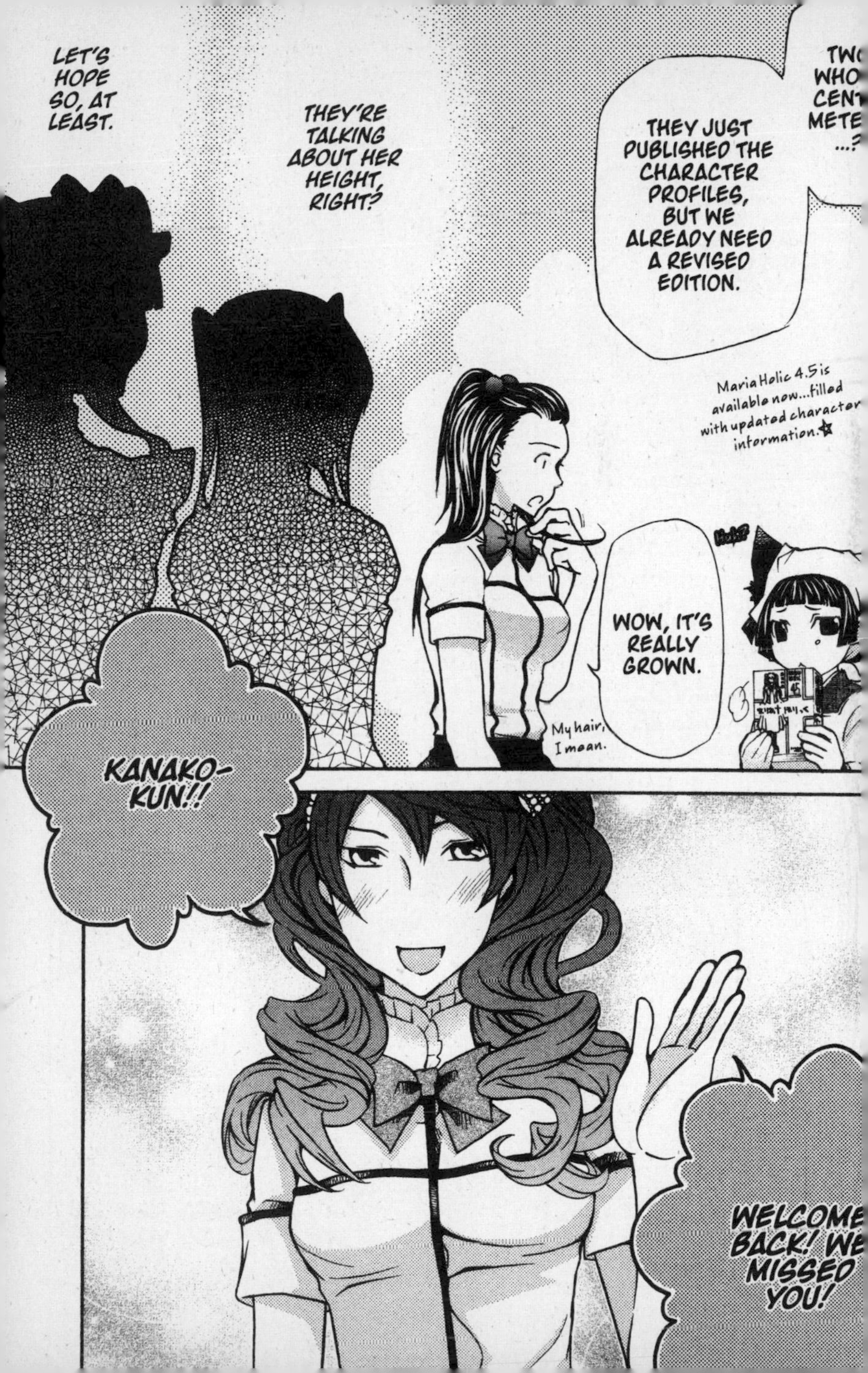
TWO WHO CENT METE ...?
THEY JUST PUBLISHED THE CHARACTER PROFILES, BUT WE ALREADY NEED A REVISED EDITION.
THEY'RE TALKING ABOUT HER HEIGHT, RIGHT?
LET'S HOPE SO, AT LEAST.
Maria Holic 4.5 is available now...filled with updated character information.☆
Huh?
WOW, IT'S REALLY GROWN.
My hair, I mean.
KANAKO-KUN!!
WELCOME BACK! WE MISSED YOU!

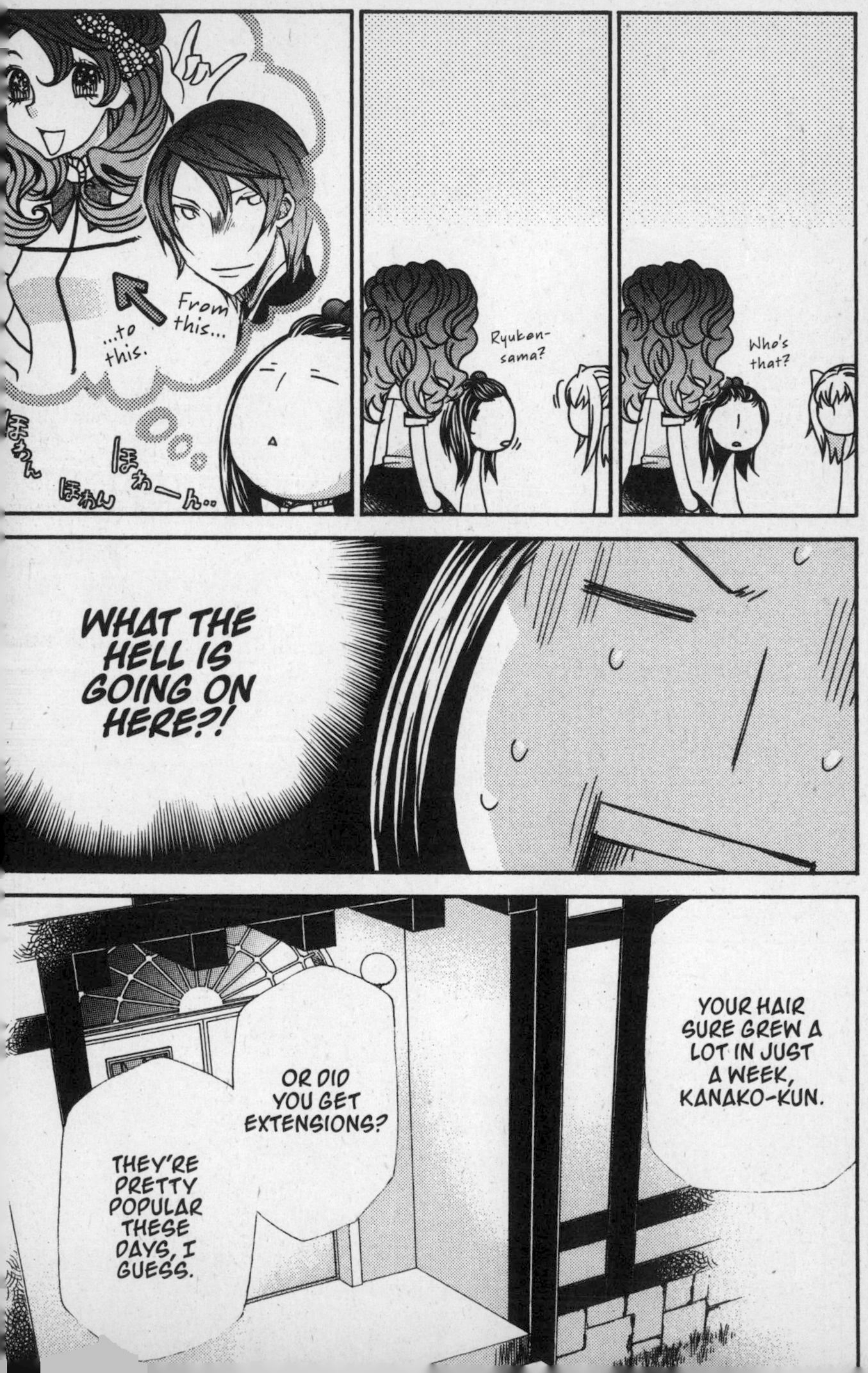
Who's that?
Ryuken-sama?
From this...
...to this.
ほわーん..
ほわん
ほわん
WHAT THE HELL IS GOING ON HERE?!
YOUR HAIR SURE GREW A LOT IN JUST A WEEK, KANAKO-KUN.
OR DID YOU GET EXTENSIONS?
THEY'RE PRETTY POPULAR THESE DAYS, I GUESS.

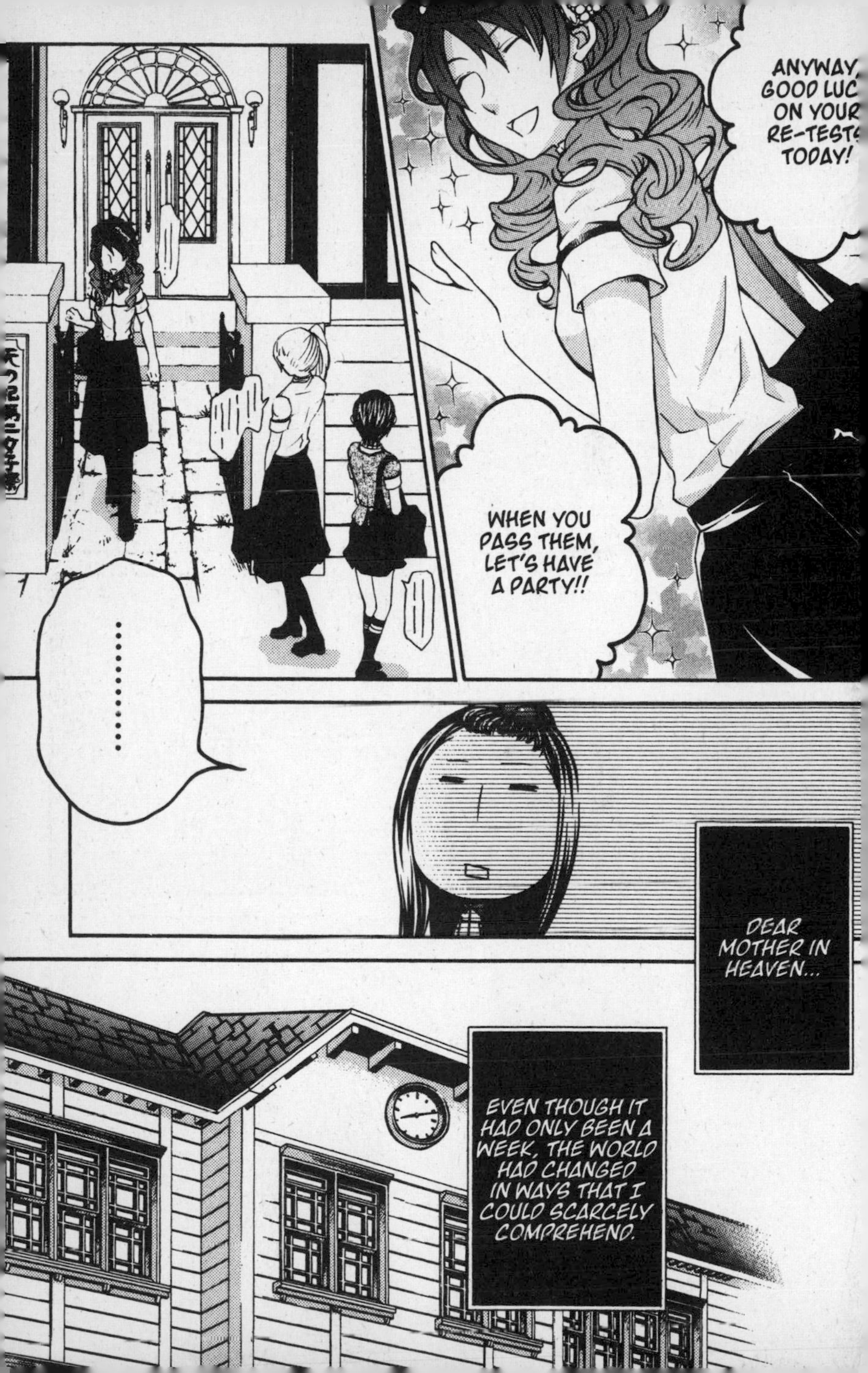
ANYWAY, GOOD LUC ON YOUR RE-TEST TODAY!
WHEN YOU PASS THEM, LET'S HAVE A PARTY!!
......
DEAR MOTHER IN HEAVEN...
EVEN THOUGH IT HAD ONLY BEEN A WEEK, THE WORLD HAD CHANGED IN WAYS THAT I COULD SCARCELY COMPREHEND.

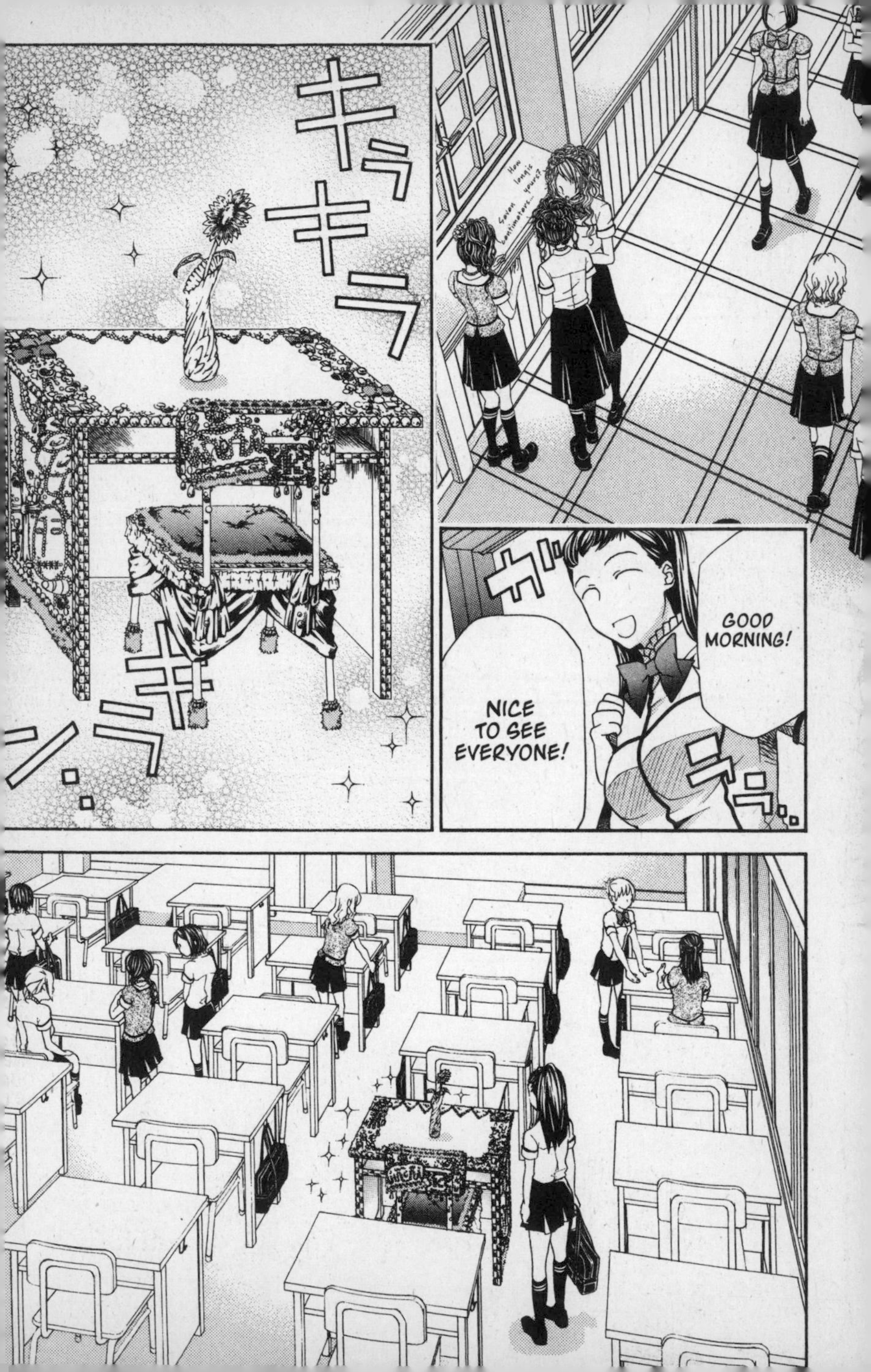
How long is yours?
Seven centimeters...
GOOD MORNING!
NICE TO SEE EVERYONE!
キラキラ

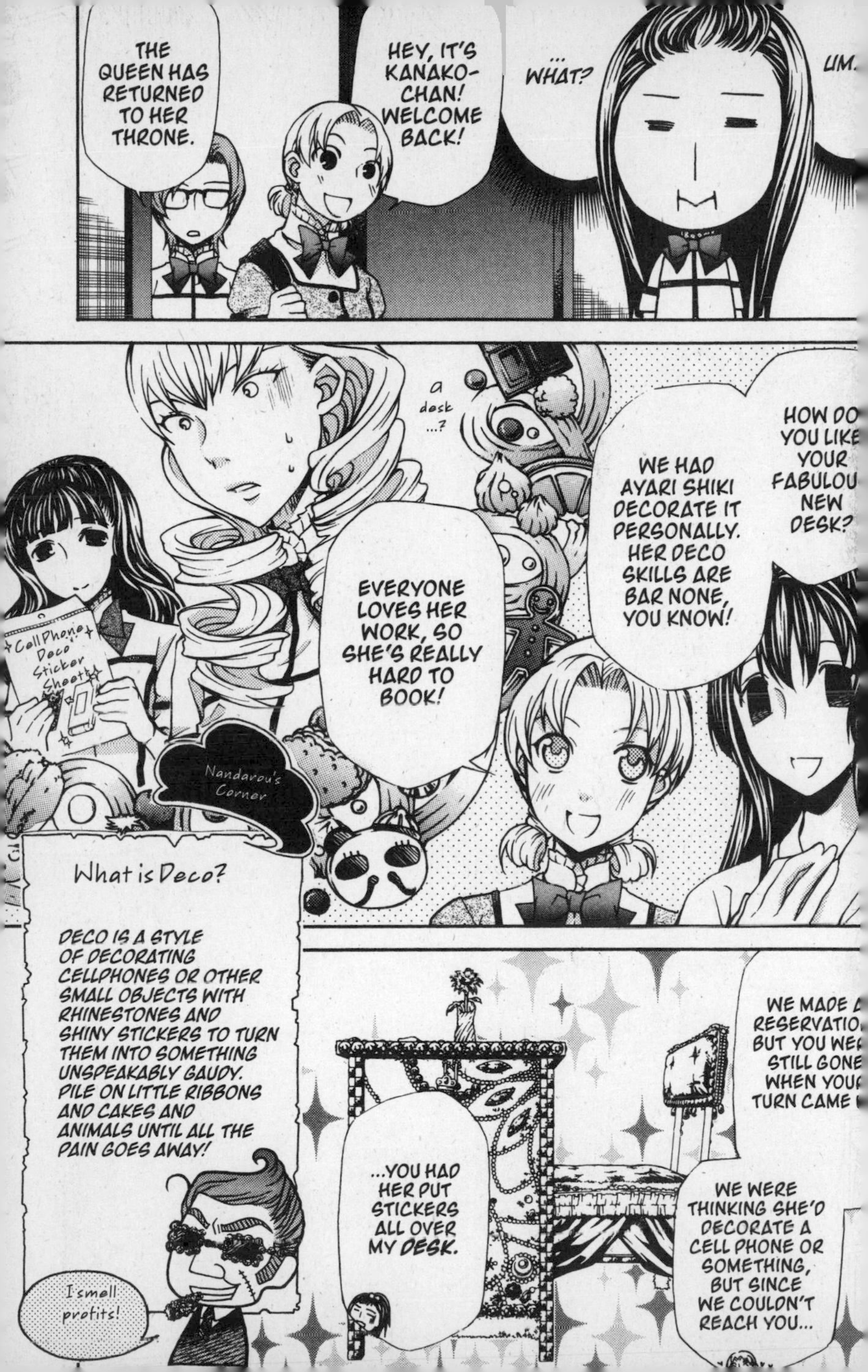
UM.
...WHAT?
HEY, IT'S KANAKO-CHAN! WELCOME BACK!
THE QUEEN HAS RETURNED TO HER THRONE.
HOW DO YOU LIKE YOUR FABULOU NEW DESK?
WE HAD AYARI SHIKI DECORATE IT PERSONALLY. HER DECO SKILLS ARE BAR NONE, YOU KNOW!
EVERYONE LOVES HER WORK, SO SHE'S REALLY HARD TO BOOK!
a desk ...?
CellPhone Deco Sticker Sheet
WE MADE A RESERVATIO BUT YOU WE STILL GONE WHEN YOUR TURN CAME
WE WERE THINKING SHE'D DECORATE A CELL PHONE OR SOMETHING, BUT SINCE WE COULDN'T REACH YOU...
...YOU HAD HER PUT STICKERS ALL OVER MY DESK.
Nandarou's Corner
What is Deco?
DECO IS A STYLE OF DECORATING CELLPHONES OR OTHER SMALL OBJECTS WITH RHINESTONES AND SHINY STICKERS TO TURN THEM INTO SOMETHING UNSPEAKABLY GAUDY. PILE ON LITTLE RIBBONS AND CAKES AND ANIMALS UNTIL ALL THE PAIN GOES AWAY!
I smell profits!

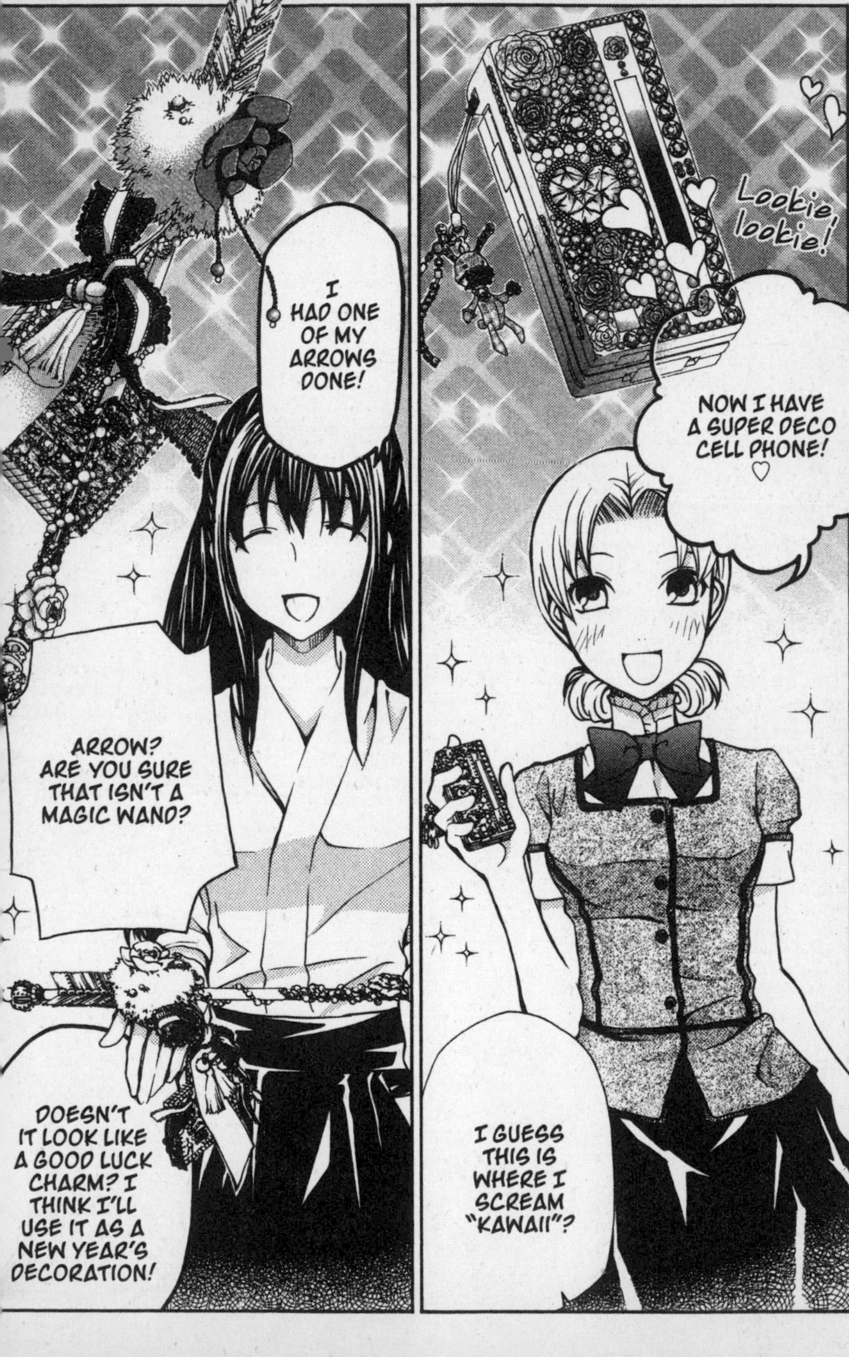
Lookie, lookie!
NOW I HAVE A SUPER DECO CELL PHONE! ♡
I GUESS THIS IS WHERE I SCREAM "KAWAII"?
I HAD ONE OF MY ARROWS DONE!
ARROW? ARE YOU SURE THAT ISN'T A MAGIC WAND?
DOESN'T IT LOOK LIKE A GOOD LUCK CHARM? I THINK I'LL USE IT AS A NEW YEAR'S DECORATION!

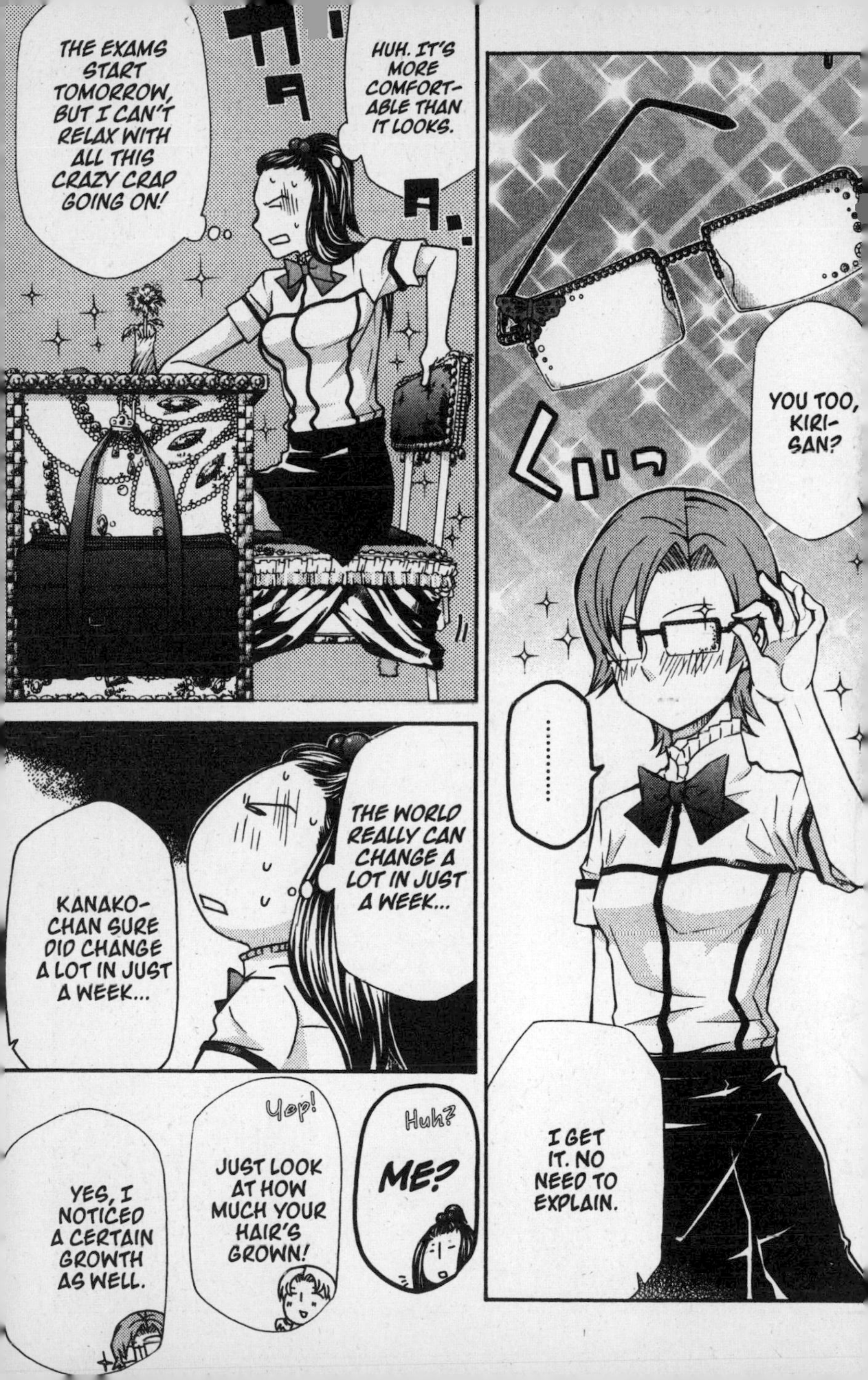
YOU TOO, KIRI-SAN?
くいっ
....
I GET IT. NO NEED TO EXPLAIN.
ガタ
HUH. IT'S MORE COMFORT-ABLE THAN IT LOOKS.
THE EXAMS START TOMORROW, BUT I CAN'T RELAX WITH ALL THIS CRAZY CRAP GOING ON!
THE WORLD REALLY CAN CHANGE A LOT IN JUST A WEEK...
KANAKO-CHAN SURE DID CHANGE A LOT IN JUST A WEEK...
Huh? ME?
Yep! JUST LOOK AT HOW MUCH YOUR HAIR'S GROWN!
YES, I NOTICED A CERTAIN GROWTH AS WELL.

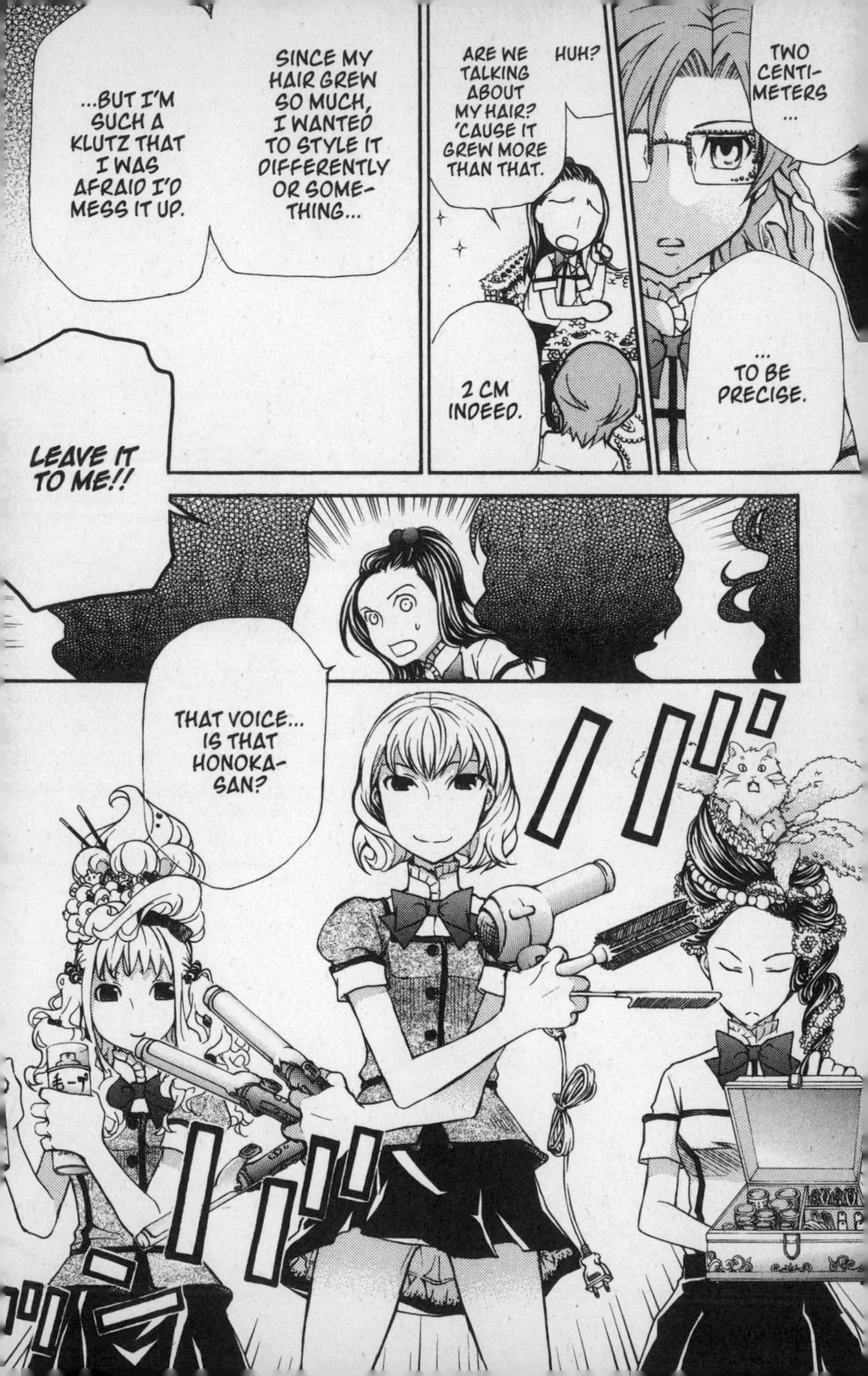
TWO CENTI-METERS ...
... TO BE PRECISE.
HUH?
ARE WE TALKING ABOUT MY HAIR? 'CAUSE IT GREW MORE THAN THAT.
2 CM INDEED.
SINCE MY HAIR GREW SO MUCH, I WANTED TO STYLE IT DIFFERENTLY OR SOME-THING...
...BUT I'M SUCH A KLUTZ THAT I WAS AFRAID I'D MESS IT UP.
LEAVE IT TO ME!!
THAT VOICE... IS THAT HONOKA-SAN?

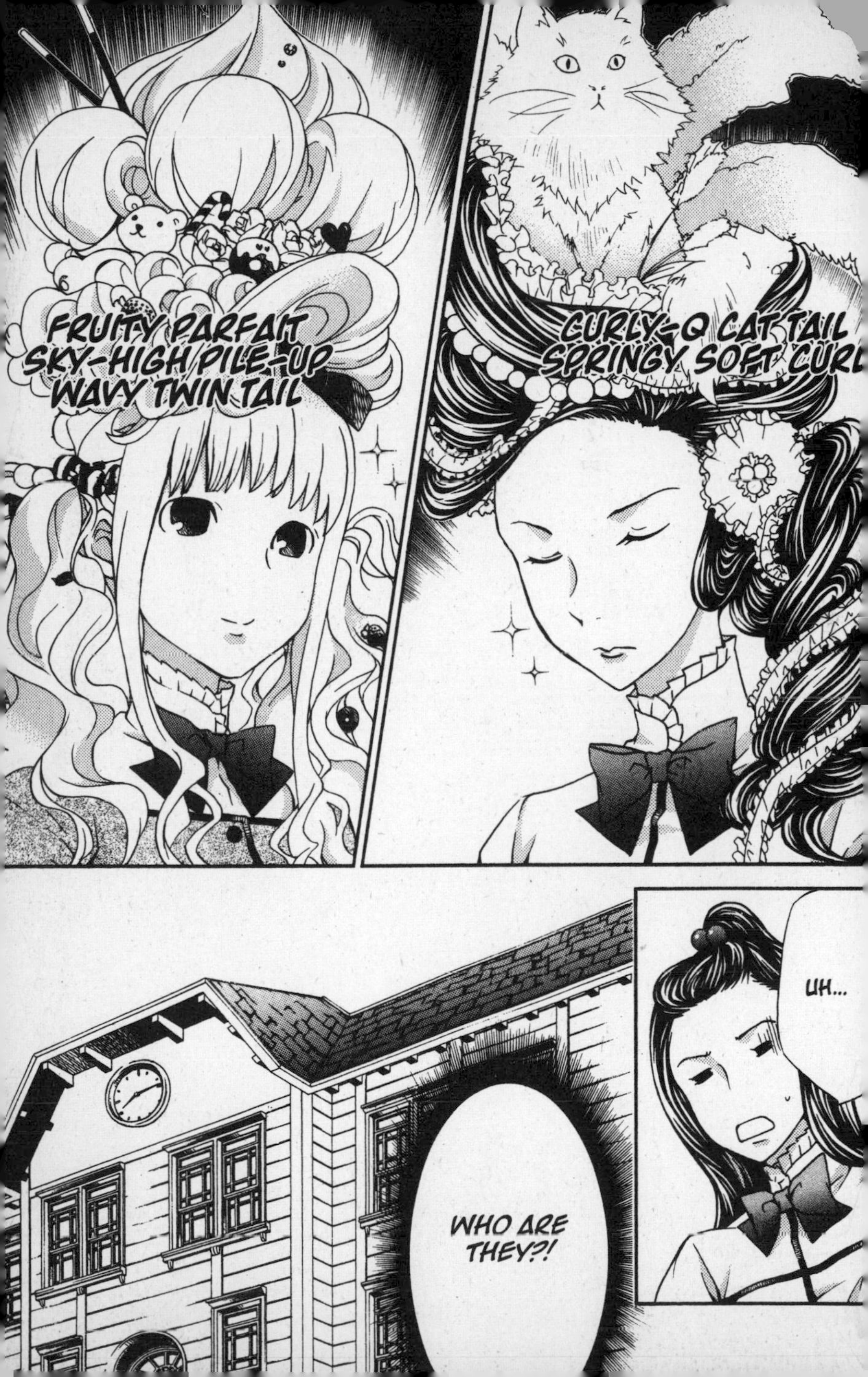
CURLY-Q CAT TAIL
SPRINGY SOFT CURL
FRUITY PARFAIT
SKY-HIGH PILE-UP
WAVY TWIN TAIL
UH...
WHO ARE
THEY?!

A R I A H O L I C

Maria Holic

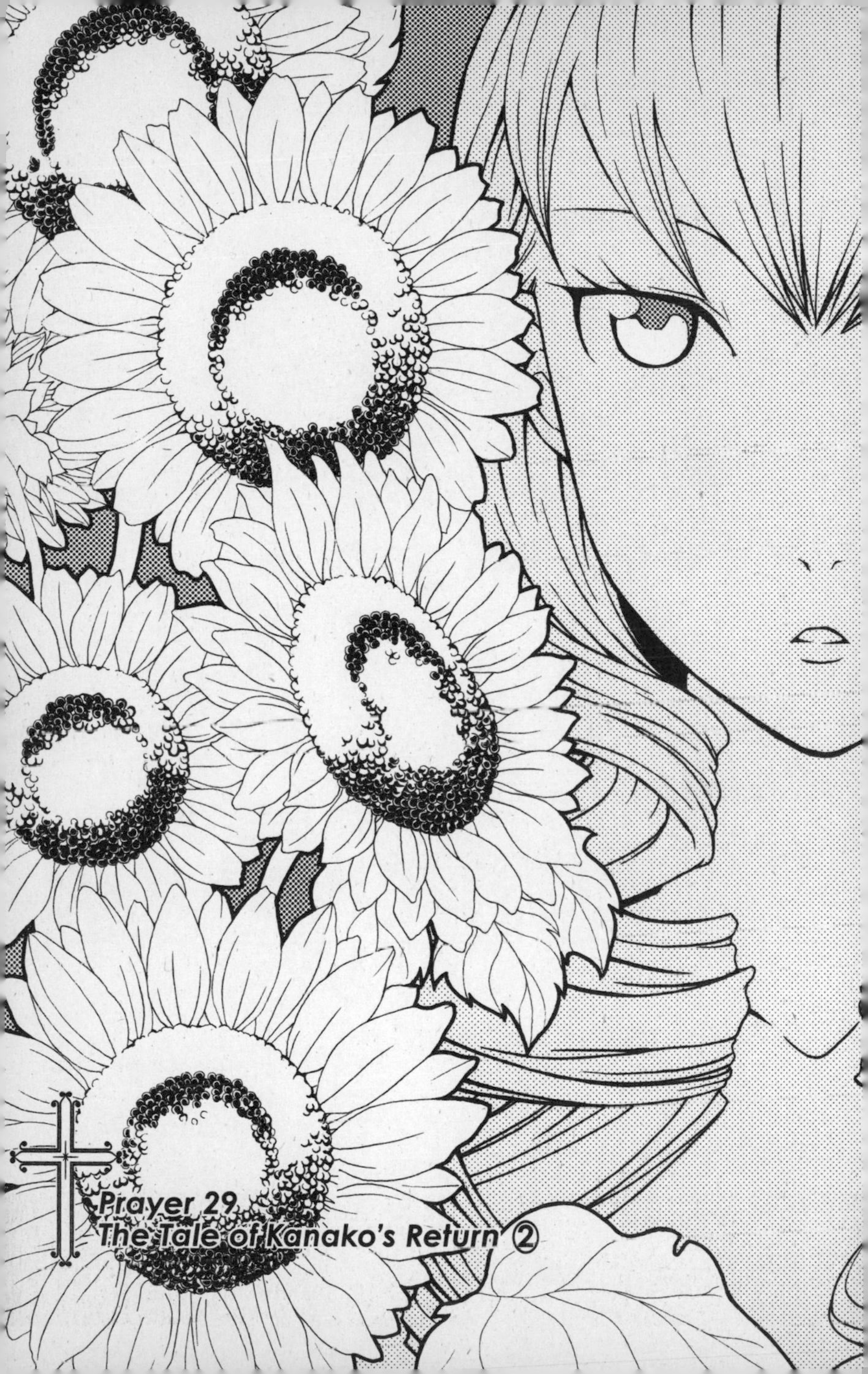
Prayer 29
The Tale of Kanako's Return ②

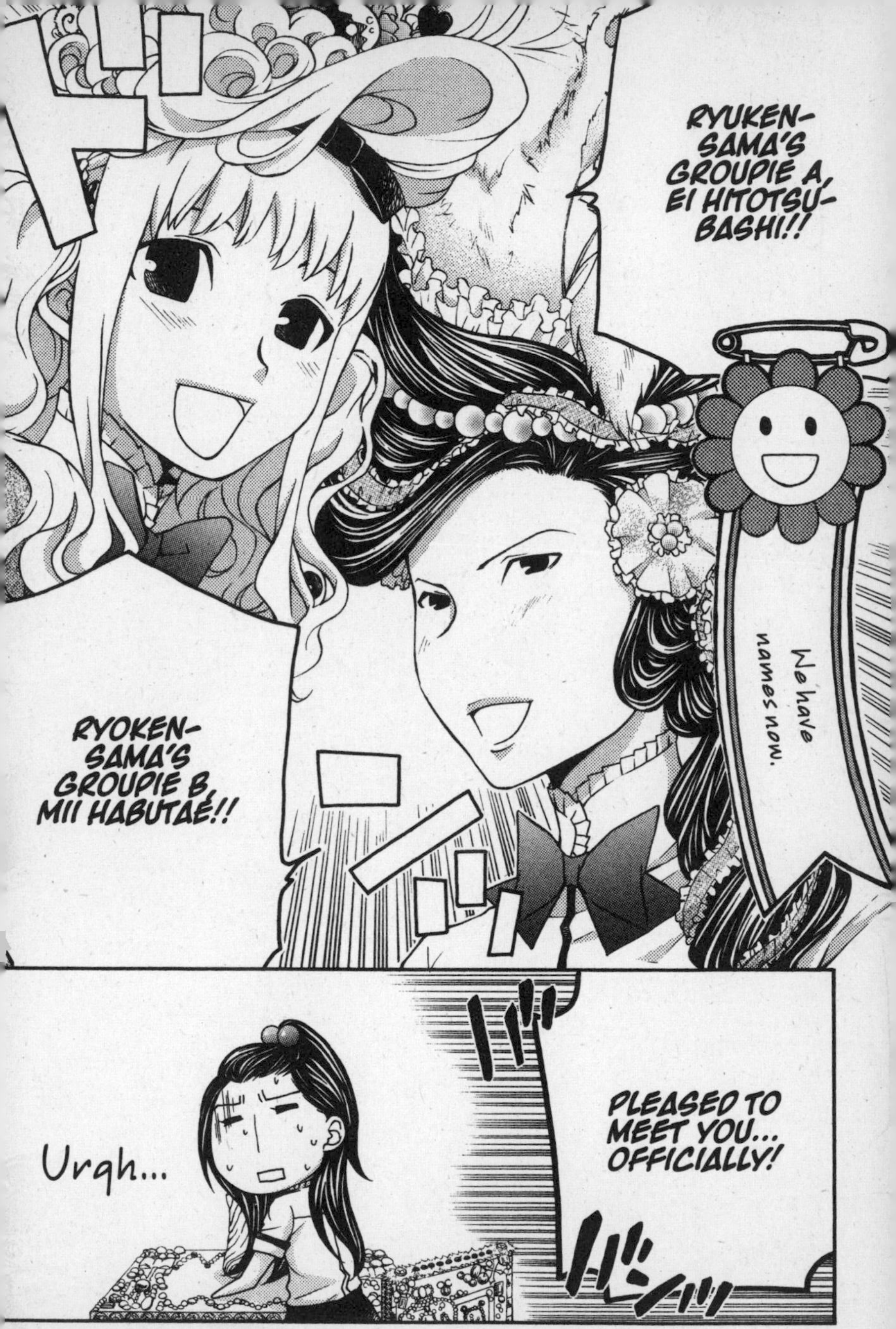
RYUKEN-SAMA'S GROUPIE A, EI HITOTSUBASHI!!
We have names now.
RYOKEN-SAMA'S GROUPIE B, MII HABUTAÉ!!
PLEASED TO MEET YOU... OFFICIALLY!
Urgh...

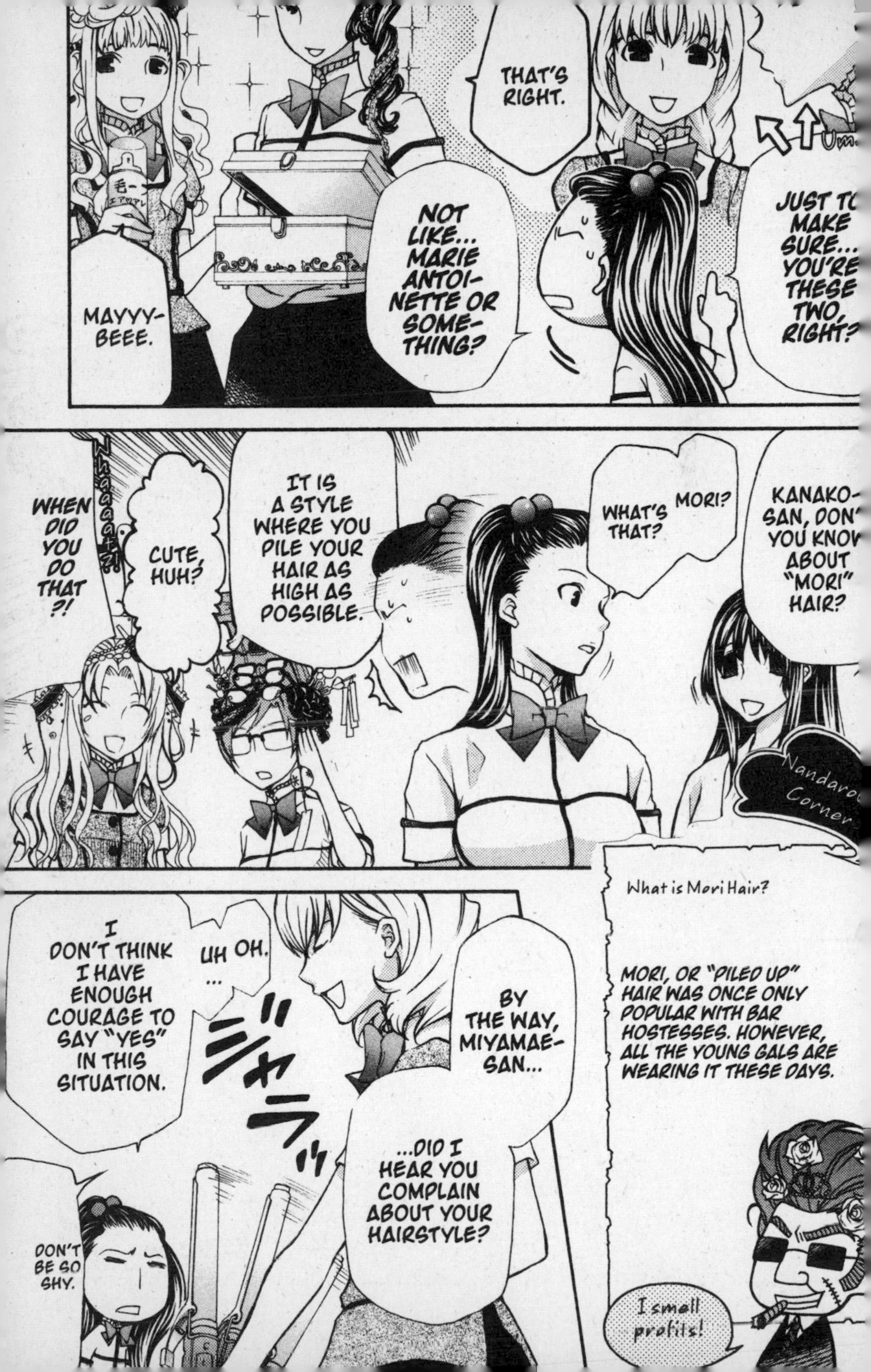
Um.
JUST TO MAKE SURE... YOU'RE THESE TWO, RIGHT?
THAT'S RIGHT.
NOT LIKE... MARIE ANTOI-NETTE OR SOME-THING?
MAYYY-BEEE.
KANAKO-SAN, DON'T YOU KNOW ABOUT "MORI" HAIR?
MORI? WHAT'S THAT?
IT IS A STYLE WHERE YOU PILE YOUR HAIR AS HIGH AS POSSIBLE.
CUTE, HUH?
Whaaaat?!
WHEN DID YOU DO THAT?!
Nandarou Corner
What is Mori Hair?
MORI, OR "PILED UP" HAIR WAS ONCE ONLY POPULAR WITH BAR HOSTESSES. HOWEVER, ALL THE YOUNG GALS ARE WEARING IT THESE DAYS.
I smell profits!
BY THE WAY, MIYAMAE-SAN...
...DID I HEAR YOU COMPLAIN ABOUT YOUR HAIRSTYLE?
ジャラッ
UH OH. ...
I DON'T THINK I HAVE ENOUGH COURAGE TO SAY "YES" IN THIS SITUATION.
DON'T BE SO SHY.

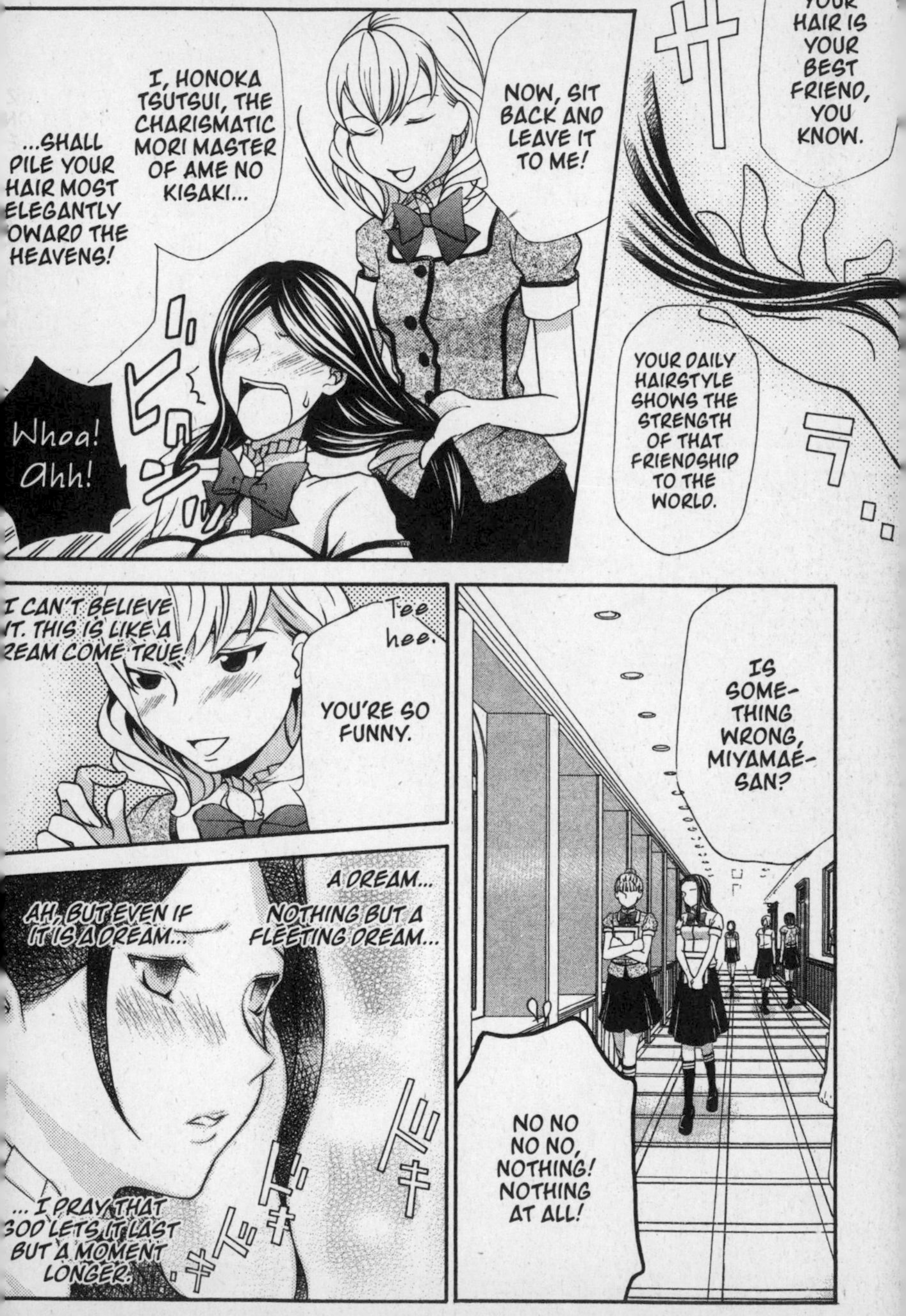
YOUR HAIR IS YOUR BEST FRIEND, YOU KNOW.
YOUR DAILY HAIRSTYLE SHOWS THE STRENGTH OF THAT FRIENDSHIP TO THE WORLD.
NOW, SIT BACK AND LEAVE IT TO ME!
I, HONOKA TSUTSUI, THE CHARISMATIC MORI MASTER OF AME NO KISAKI...
...SHALL PILE YOUR HAIR MOST ELEGANTLY OWARD THE HEAVENS!
Whoa! Ahh!
IS SOMETHING WRONG, MIYAMAE-SAN?
NO NO NO NO, NOTHING! NOTHING AT ALL!
Tee hee.
YOU'RE SO FUNNY.
I CAN'T BELIEVE T. THIS IS LIKE A REAM COME TRUE.
A DREAM... NOTHING BUT A FLEETING DREAM...
AH, BUT EVEN IF IT IS A DREAM...
...I PRAY THAT OD LETS IT LAST BUT A MOMENT LONGER.

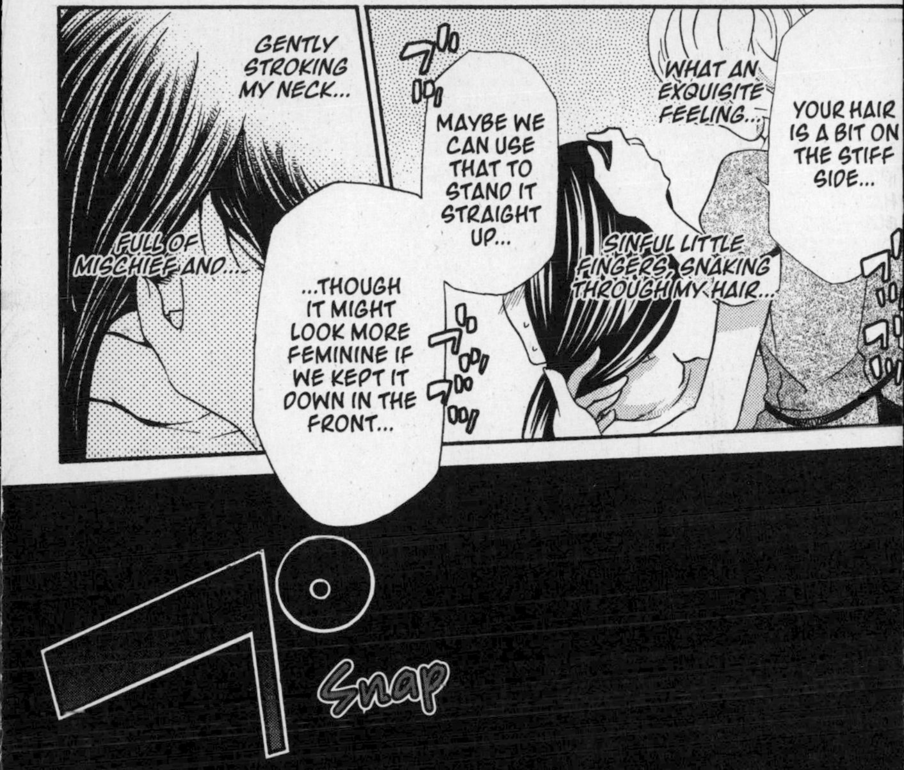
YOUR HAIR IS A BIT ON THE STIFF SIDE...
WHAT AN EXQUISITE FEELING...
SINFUL LITTLE FINGERS, SNAKING THROUGH MY HAIR...
MAYBE WE CAN USE THAT TO STAND IT STRAIGHT UP...
...THOUGH IT MIGHT LOOK MORE FEMININE IF WE KEPT IT DOWN IN THE FRONT...
GENTLY STROKING MY NECK...
FULL OF MISCHIEF AND...
Snap

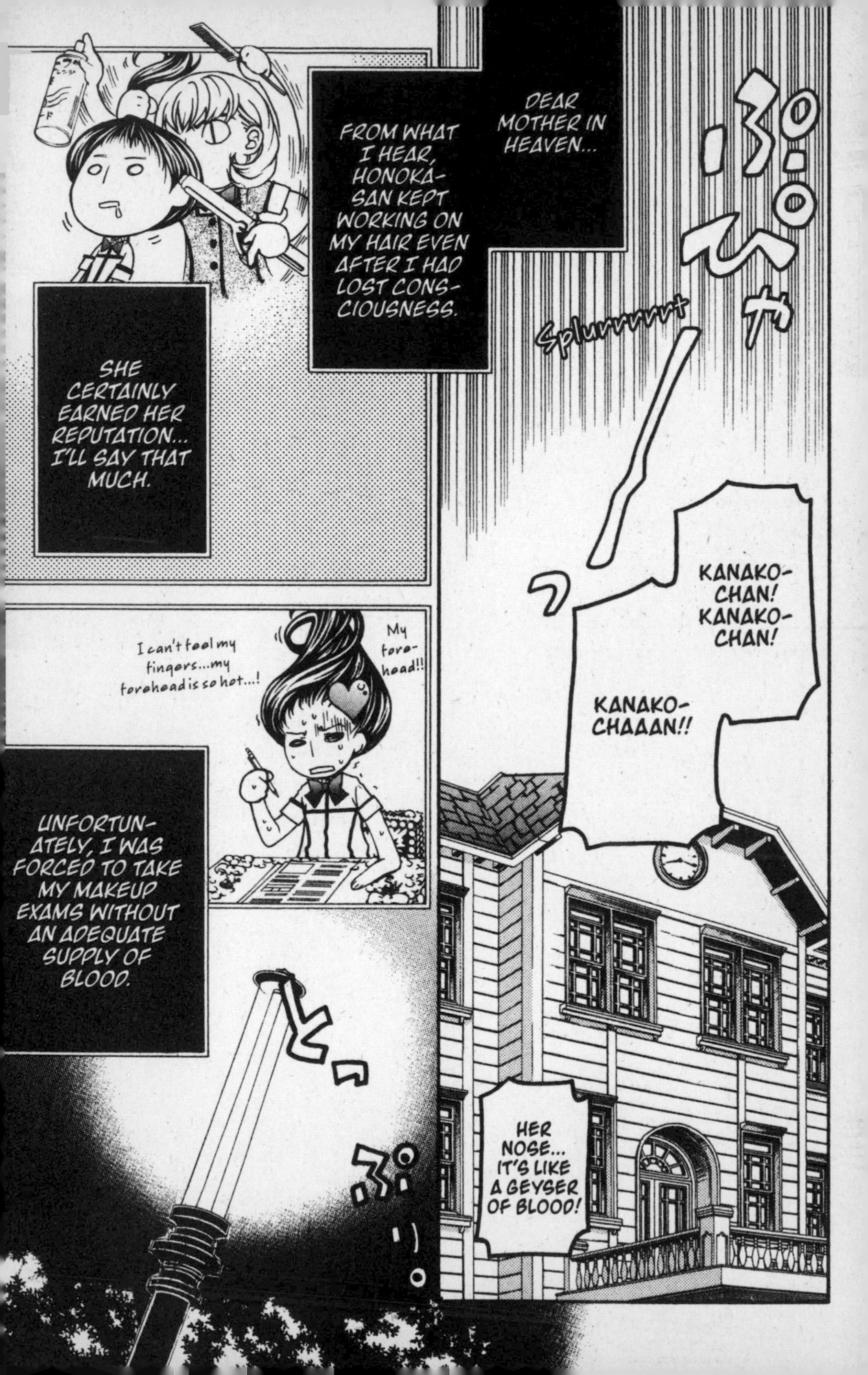

DEAR MOTHER IN HEAVEN...
Splurrrrrrt
KANAKO-CHAN! KANAKO-CHAN!
KANAKO-CHAAAN!!
HER NOSE... IT'S LIKE A GEYSER OF BLOOD!
FROM WHAT I HEAR, HONOKA-SAN KEPT WORKING ON MY HAIR EVEN AFTER I HAD LOST CONSCIOUSNESS.
SHE CERTAINLY EARNED HER REPUTATION... I'LL SAY THAT MUCH.
My forehead!!
I can't feel my fingers...my forehead is so hot...!
UNFORTUNATELY, I WAS FORCED TO TAKE MY MAKEUP EXAMS WITHOUT AN ADEQUATE SUPPLY OF BLOOD.

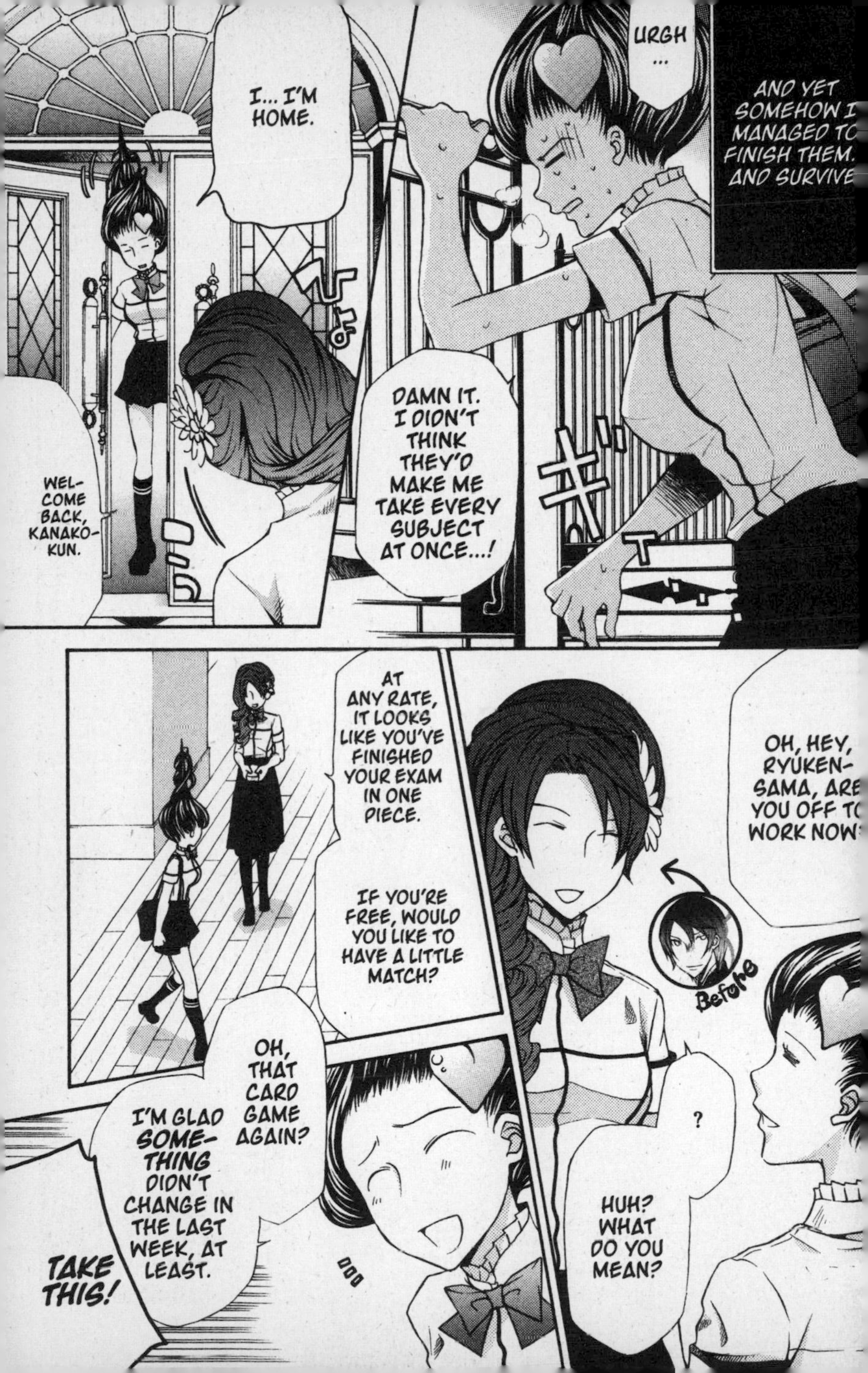
AND YET SOMEHOW I MANAGED TO FINISH THEM. AND SURVIVE
URGH ...
DAMN IT. I DIDN'T THINK THEY'D MAKE ME TAKE EVERY SUBJECT AT ONCE...!
I... I'M HOME.
WEL-COME BACK, KANAKO-KUN.
OH, HEY, RYUKEN-SAMA, ARE YOU OFF TO WORK NOW
Before
?
HUH? WHAT DO YOU MEAN?
AT ANY RATE, IT LOOKS LIKE YOU'VE FINISHED YOUR EXAM IN ONE PIECE.
IF YOU'RE FREE, WOULD YOU LIKE TO HAVE A LITTLE MATCH?
OH, THAT CARD GAME AGAIN?
I'M GLAD SOME-THING DIDN'T CHANGE IN THE LAST WEEK, AT LEAST.
TAKE THIS!

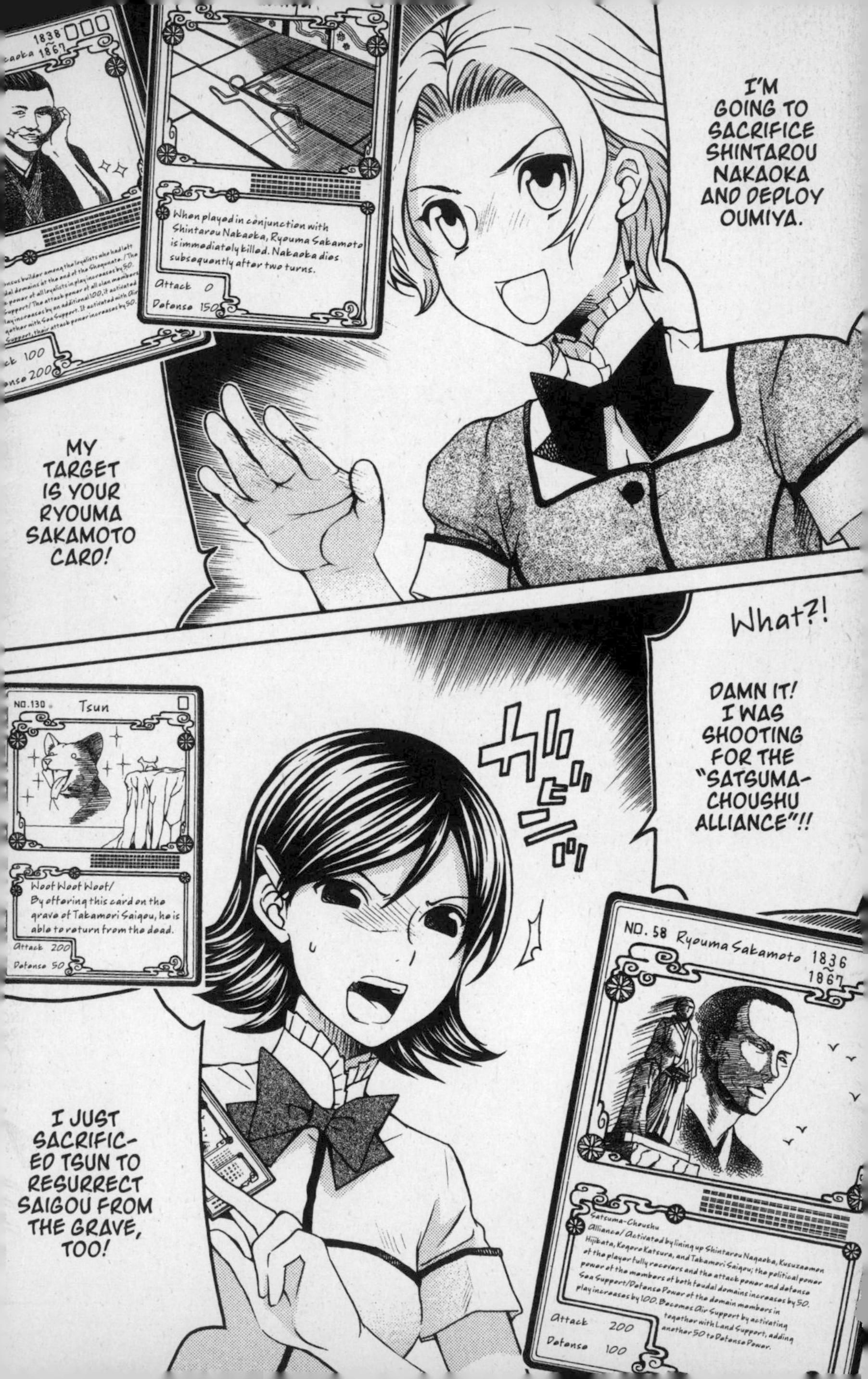
I'M GOING TO SACRIFICE SHINTAROU NAKAOKA AND DEPLOY OUMIYA.
When played in conjunction with Shintarou Nakaoka, Ryouma Sakamoto is immediately killed. Nakaoka dies subsequently after two turns.
Attack 0
Defense 150
MY TARGET IS YOUR RYOUMA SAKAMOTO CARD!
What?!
DAMN IT! I WAS SHOOTING FOR THE "SATSUMA-CHOUSHU ALLIANCE"!!
NO. 58 Ryouma Sakamoto 1836 1867
Satsuma-Choushu Alliance/ Activated by lining up Shintarou Nagaoka, Kusuzaemon Hijikata, Kogoro Katsura, and Takamori Saigou; the player fully recovers and the attack power and defense power of the members of both feudal domains increases by 50. Sea Support/Defense Power of the domain members in play increases by 100. Becomes Air Support by activating together with Land Support, adding another 50 to Defense Power.
Attack 200
Defense 100
NO.130 Tsun
Woot Woot Woot/ By offering this card on the grave of Takamori Saigou, he is able to return from the dead.
Attack 200
Defense 50
I JUST SACRIFICED TSUN TO RESURRECT SAIGOU FROM THE GRAVE, TOO!

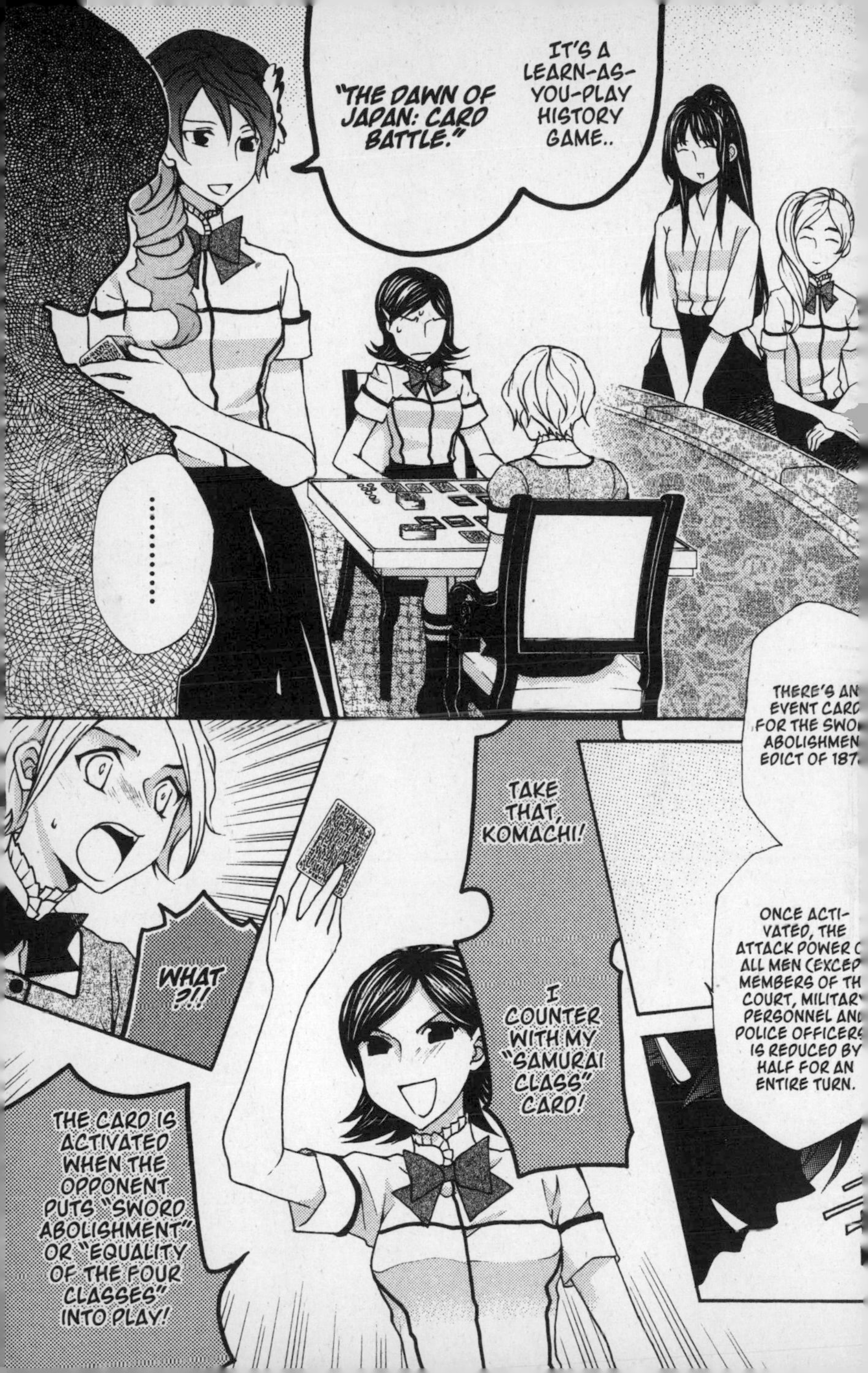
IT'S A LEARN-AS-YOU-PLAY HISTORY GAME..
"THE DAWN OF JAPAN: CARD BATTLE."
......
THERE'S AN EVENT CARD FOR THE SWO ABOLISHMEN EDICT OF 187
ONCE ACTIVATED, THE ATTACK POWER O ALL MEN (EXCEP MEMBERS OF TH COURT, MILITARY PERSONNEL AND POLICE OFFICERS IS REDUCED BY HALF FOR AN ENTIRE TURN.
TAKE THAT, KOMACHI!
I COUNTER WITH MY "SAMURAI CLASS" CARD!
WHAT ?!!
THE CARD IS ACTIVATED WHEN THE OPPONENT PUTS "SWORD ABOLISHMENT" OR "EQUALITY OF THE FOUR CLASSES" INTO PLAY!

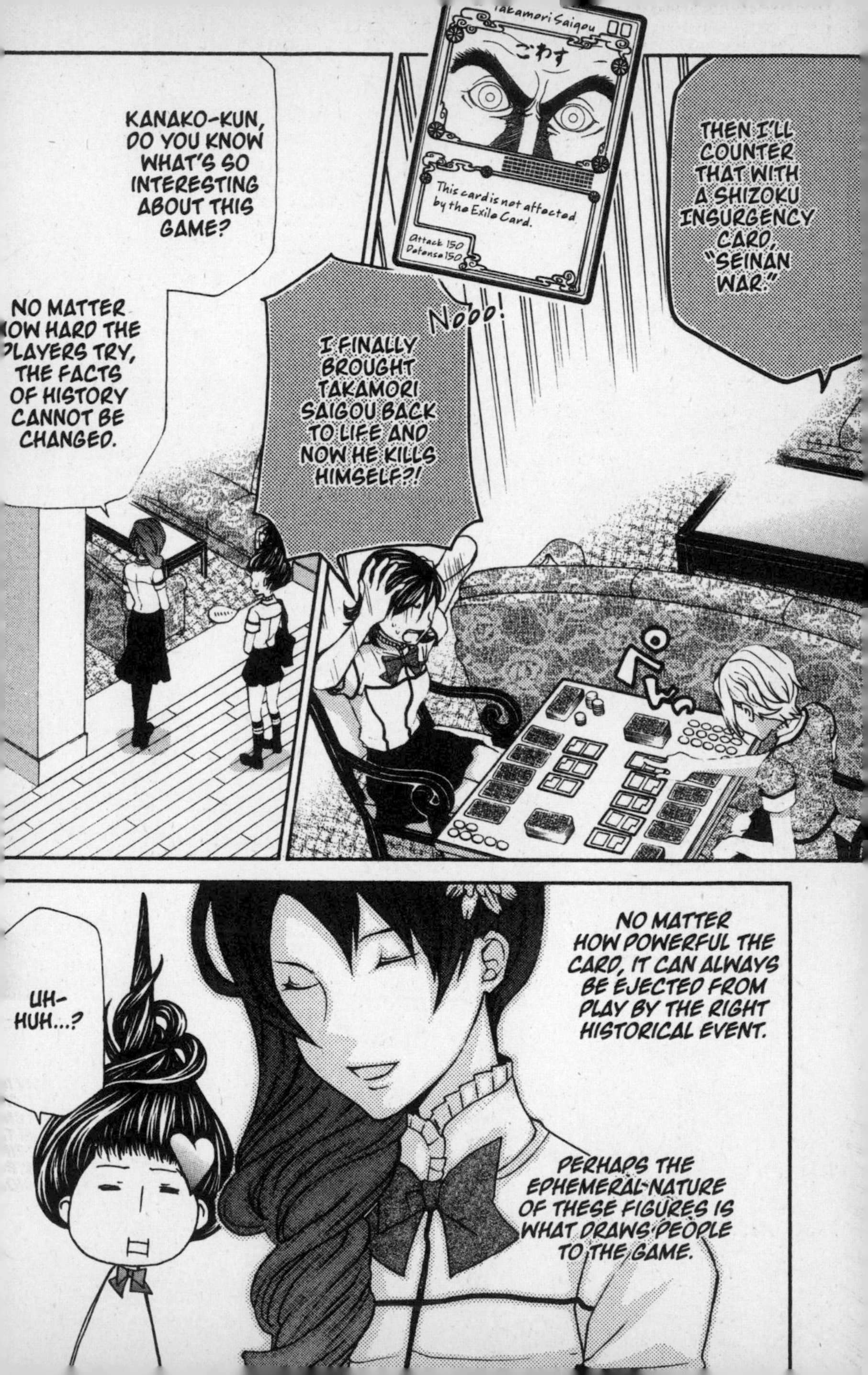
THEN I'LL COUNTER THAT WITH A SHIZOKU INSURGENCY CARD, "SEINAN WAR."
Takamori Saigou
ごわす
This card is not affected by the Exile Card.
Attack 150 Defense 150
Nooo!
I FINALLY BROUGHT TAKAMORI SAIGOU BACK TO LIFE AND NOW HE KILLS HIMSELF?!
KANAKO-KUN, DO YOU KNOW WHAT'S SO INTERESTING ABOUT THIS GAME?
NO MATTER OW HARD THE LAYERS TRY, THE FACTS OF HISTORY CANNOT BE CHANGED.
.....
NO MATTER HOW POWERFUL THE CARD, IT CAN ALWAYS BE EJECTED FROM PLAY BY THE RIGHT HISTORICAL EVENT.
PERHAPS THE EPHEMERAL NATURE OF THESE FIGURES IS WHAT DRAWS PEOPLE TO THE GAME.
UH-HUH...?

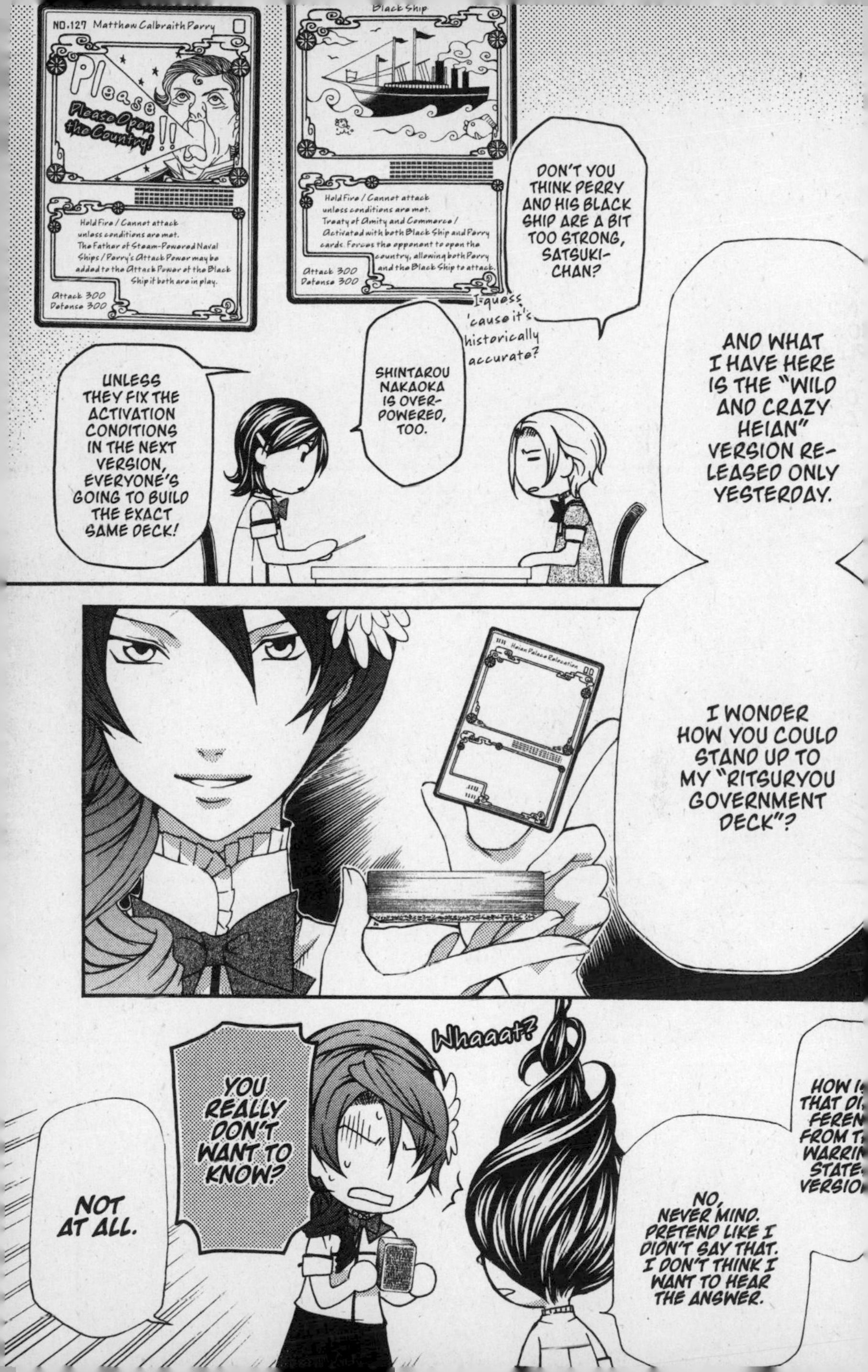
Black Ship
Hold Fire / Cannot attack unless conditions are met. Treaty of Amity and Commerce / Activated with both Black Ship and Perry cards. Forces the opponent to open the country, allowing both Perry and the Black Ship to attack.
Attack 300 Defense 300
NO.127 Matthew Calbraith Perry
Please
Please Open the Country!!
Hold Fire / Cannot attack unless conditions are met. The Father of Steam-Powered Naval Ships / Perry's Attack Power may be added to the Attack Power of the Black Ship if both are in play.
Attack 300 Defense 300
DON'T YOU THINK PERRY AND HIS BLACK SHIP ARE A BIT TOO STRONG, SATSUKI-CHAN?
I guess 'cause it's historically accurate?
SHINTAROU NAKAOKA IS OVER-POWERED, TOO.
UNLESS THEY FIX THE ACTIVATION CONDITIONS IN THE NEXT VERSION, EVERYONE'S GOING TO BUILD THE EXACT SAME DECK!
AND WHAT I HAVE HERE IS THE "WILD AND CRAZY HEIAN" VERSION RE-LEASED ONLY YESTERDAY.
I WONDER HOW YOU COULD STAND UP TO MY "RITSURYOU GOVERNMENT DECK"?
Heian Palace Relocation
HOW I THAT DI- FEREN FROM T WARRIN STATE VERSIO
Whaaat?
NO, NEVER MIND. PRETEND LIKE I DIDN'T SAY THAT. I DON'T THINK I WANT TO HEAR THE ANSWER.
YOU REALLY DON'T WANT TO KNOW?
NOT AT ALL.

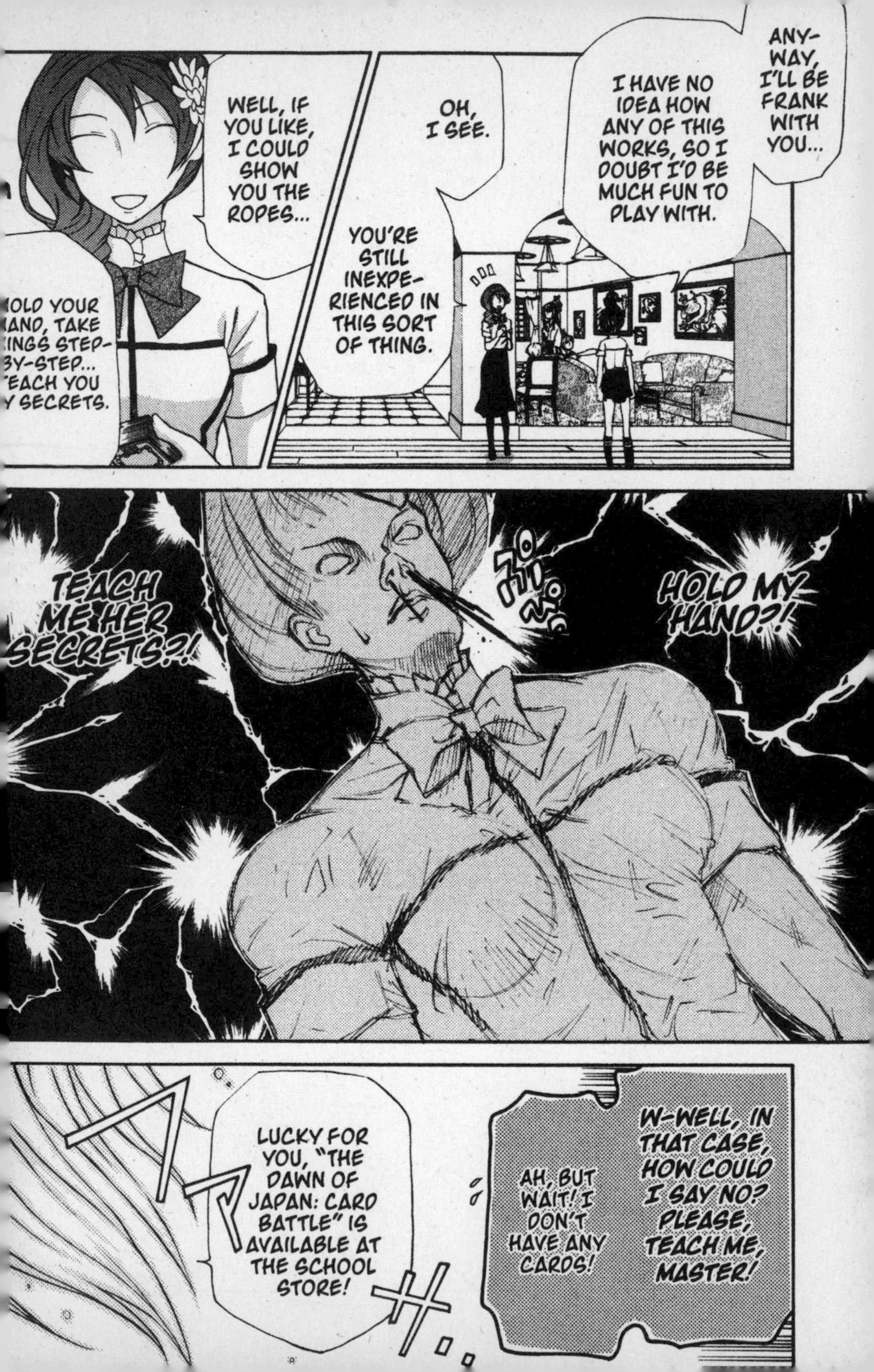
ANY-WAY, I'LL BE FRANK WITH YOU...
I HAVE NO IDEA HOW ANY OF THIS WORKS, SO I DOUBT I'D BE MUCH FUN TO PLAY WITH.
OH, I SEE.
YOU'RE STILL INEXPERIENCED IN THIS SORT OF THING.
WELL, IF YOU LIKE, I COULD SHOW YOU THE ROPES...
OLD YOUR AND, TAKE INGS STEP-BY-STEP... EACH YOU Y SECRETS.
HOLD MY HAND?!
TEACH ME HER SECRETS?!
W-WELL, IN THAT CASE, HOW COULD I SAY NO? PLEASE, TEACH ME, MASTER!
AH, BUT WAIT! I DON'T HAVE ANY CARDS!
LUCKY FOR YOU, "THE DAWN OF JAPAN: CARD BATTLE" IS AVAILABLE AT THE SCHOOL STORE!

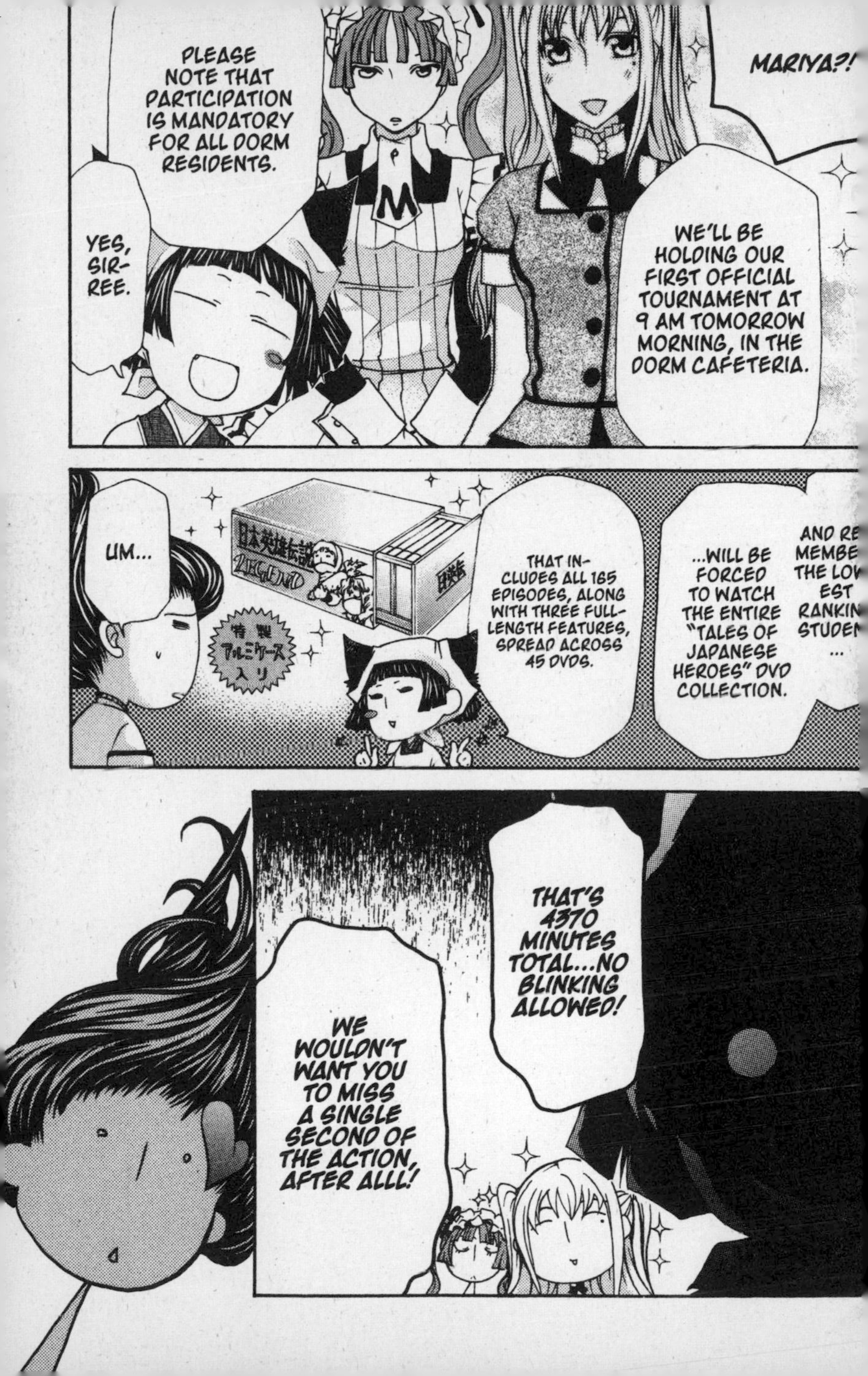
MARIYA?!
WE'LL BE HOLDING OUR FIRST OFFICIAL TOURNAMENT AT 9 AM TOMORROW MORNING, IN THE DORM CAFETERIA.
PLEASE NOTE THAT PARTICIPATION IS MANDATORY FOR ALL DORM RESIDENTS.
YES, SIR-REE.
AND RE MEMBE THE LOW EST RANKIN STUDEN ...
...WILL BE FORCED TO WATCH THE ENTIRE "TALES OF JAPANESE HEROES" DVD COLLECTION.
THAT IN-CLUDES ALL 165 EPISODES, ALONG WITH THREE FULL-LENGTH FEATURES, SPREAD ACROSS 45 DVDS.
日本英雄伝説
特製アルミケース入り
UM...
THAT'S 4370 MINUTES TOTAL...NO BLINKING ALLOWED!
WE WOULDN'T WANT YOU TO MISS A SINGLE SECOND OF THE ACTION, AFTER ALL!

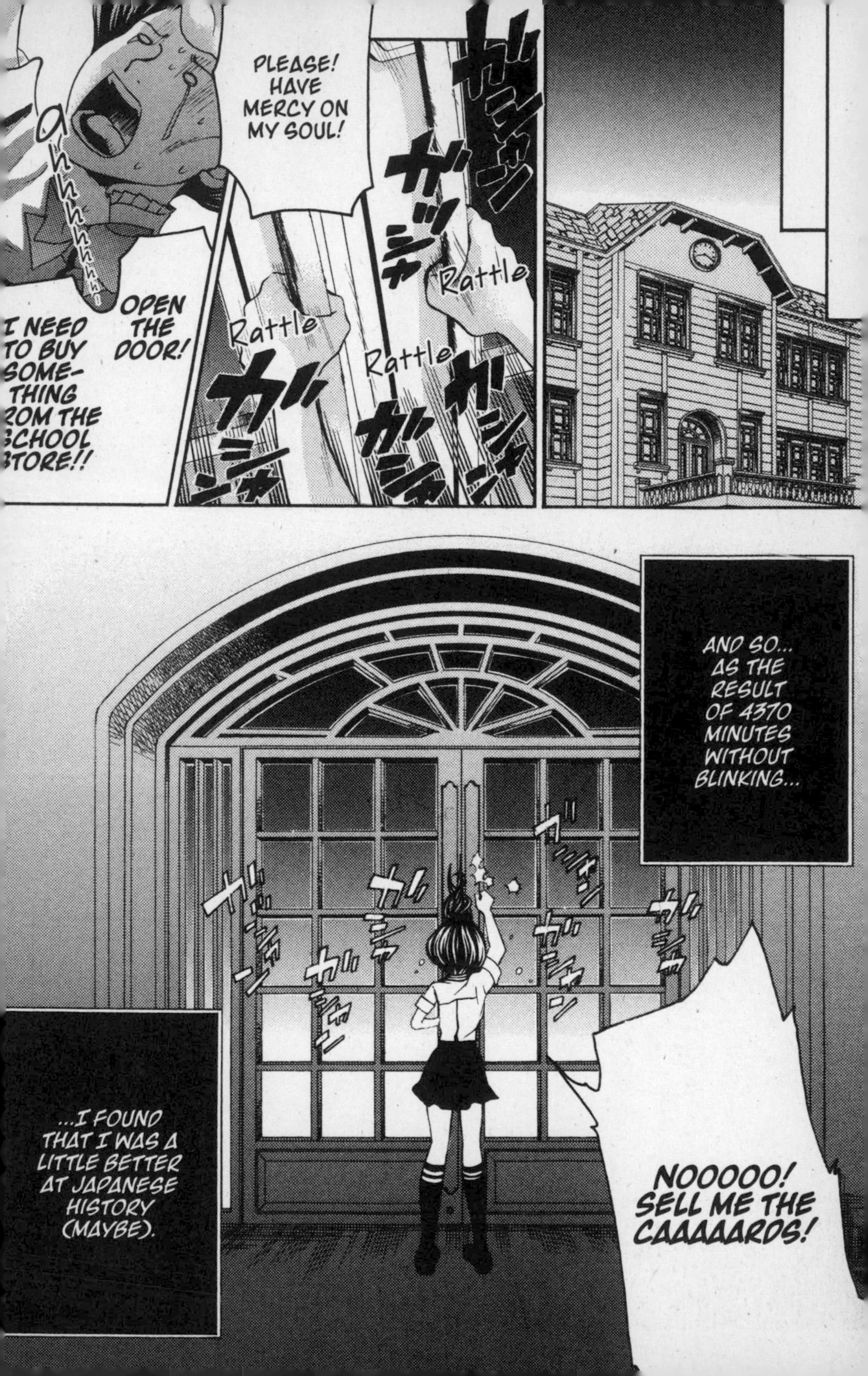
PLEASE! HAVE MERCY ON MY SOUL!
Rattle
Rattle
Rattle
Ahhhhhhhhh!
OPEN THE DOOR!
I NEED TO BUY SOME-THING ROM THE SCHOOL TORE!!
AND SO... AS THE RESULT OF 4370 MINUTES WITHOUT BLINKING...
NOOOOO! SELL ME THE CAAAAARDS!
...I FOUND THAT I WAS A LITTLE BETTER AT JAPANESE HISTORY (MAYBE).

M A R I A H O L I

Maria Holic

A R I A H O L I C

Maria†Holic

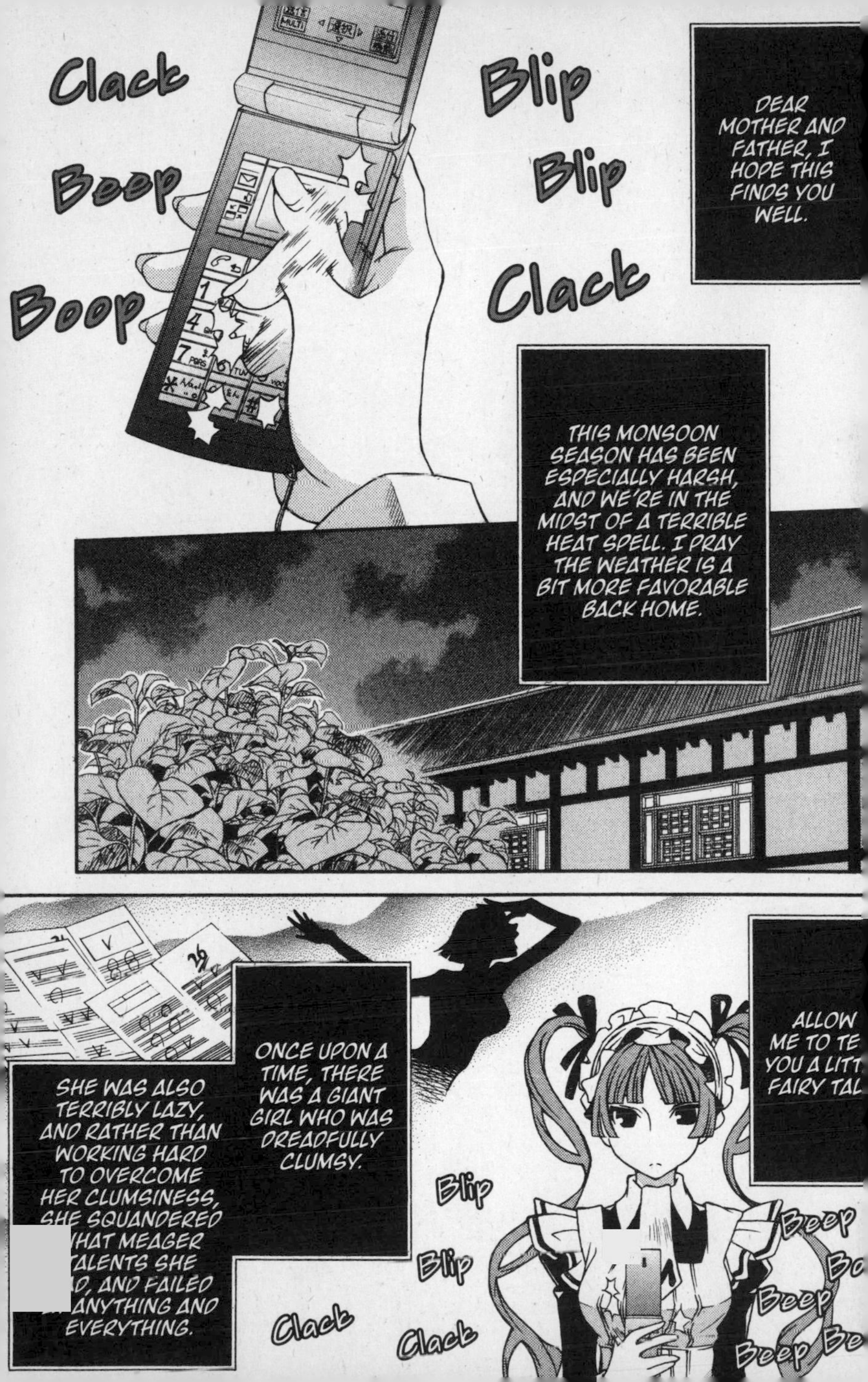
DEAR MOTHER AND FATHER, I HOPE THIS FINDS YOU WELL.
Blip
Blip
Clack
Clack
Beep
Boop
THIS MONSOON SEASON HAS BEEN ESPECIALLY HARSH, AND WE'RE IN THE MIDST OF A TERRIBLE HEAT SPELL. I PRAY THE WEATHER IS A BIT MORE FAVORABLE BACK HOME.
ALLOW ME TO TE YOU A LITT FAIRY TAL
Beep
Beep
Beep
Blip
Blip
Clack
Clack
ONCE UPON A TIME, THERE WAS A GIANT GIRL WHO WAS DREADFULLY CLUMSY.
SHE WAS ALSO TERRIBLY LAZY, AND RATHER THAN WORKING HARD TO OVERCOME HER CLUMSINESS, SHE SQUANDERED WHAT MEAGER TALENTS SHE HAD, AND FAILED AT ANYTHING AND EVERYTHING.

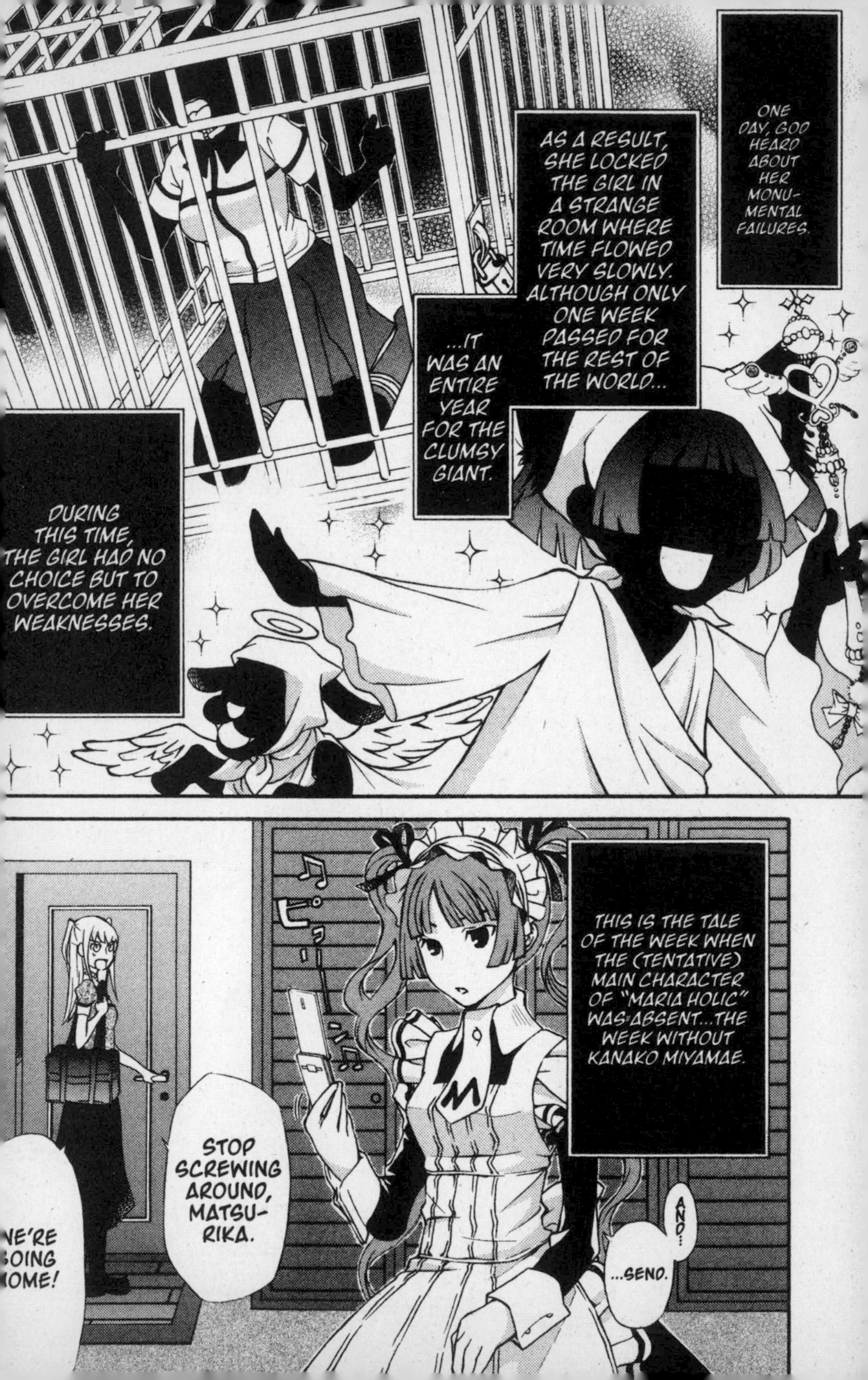
ONE DAY, GOD HEARD ABOUT HER MONUMENTAL FAILURES.
AS A RESULT, SHE LOCKED THE GIRL IN A STRANGE ROOM WHERE TIME FLOWED VERY SLOWLY. ALTHOUGH ONLY ONE WEEK PASSED FOR THE REST OF THE WORLD...
...IT WAS AN ENTIRE YEAR FOR THE CLUMSY GIANT.
DURING THIS TIME, THE GIRL HAD NO CHOICE BUT TO OVERCOME HER WEAKNESSES.
THIS IS THE TALE OF THE WEEK WHEN THE (TENTATIVE) MAIN CHARACTER OF "MARIA HOLIC" WAS ABSENT...THE WEEK WITHOUT KANAKO MIYAMAE.
AND...
...SEND.
STOP SCREWING AROUND, MATSURIKA.
E'RE OING OME!

Prayer 30
The Tale of the Week without Kanako ①

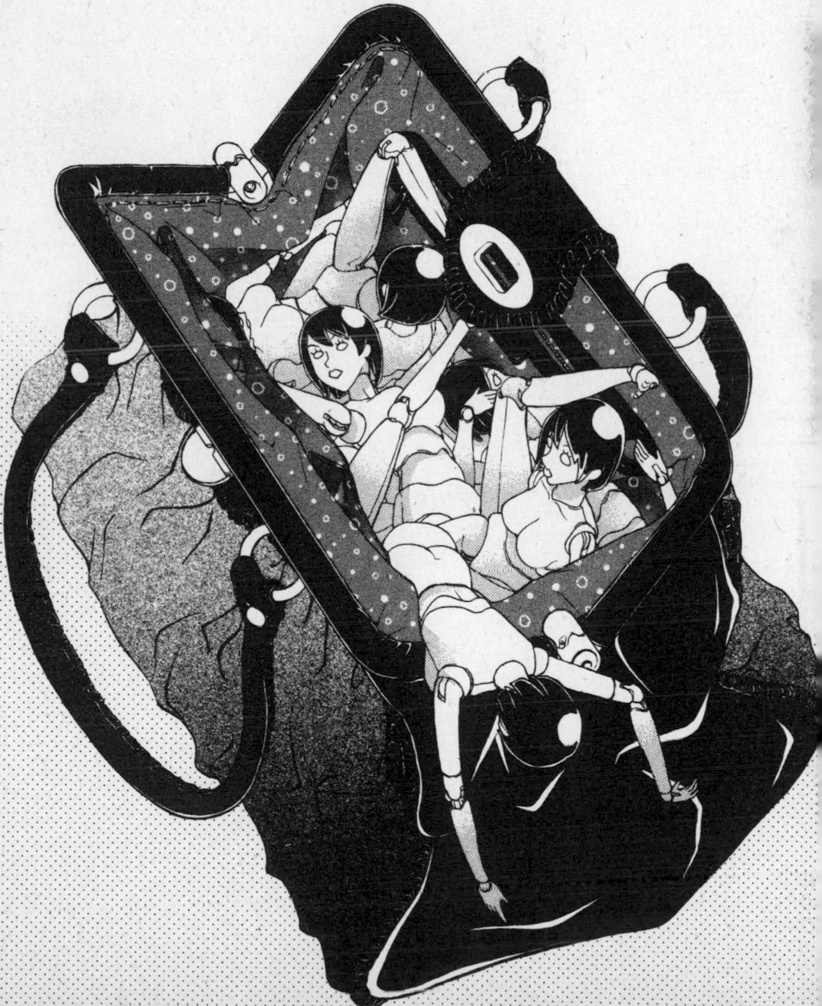

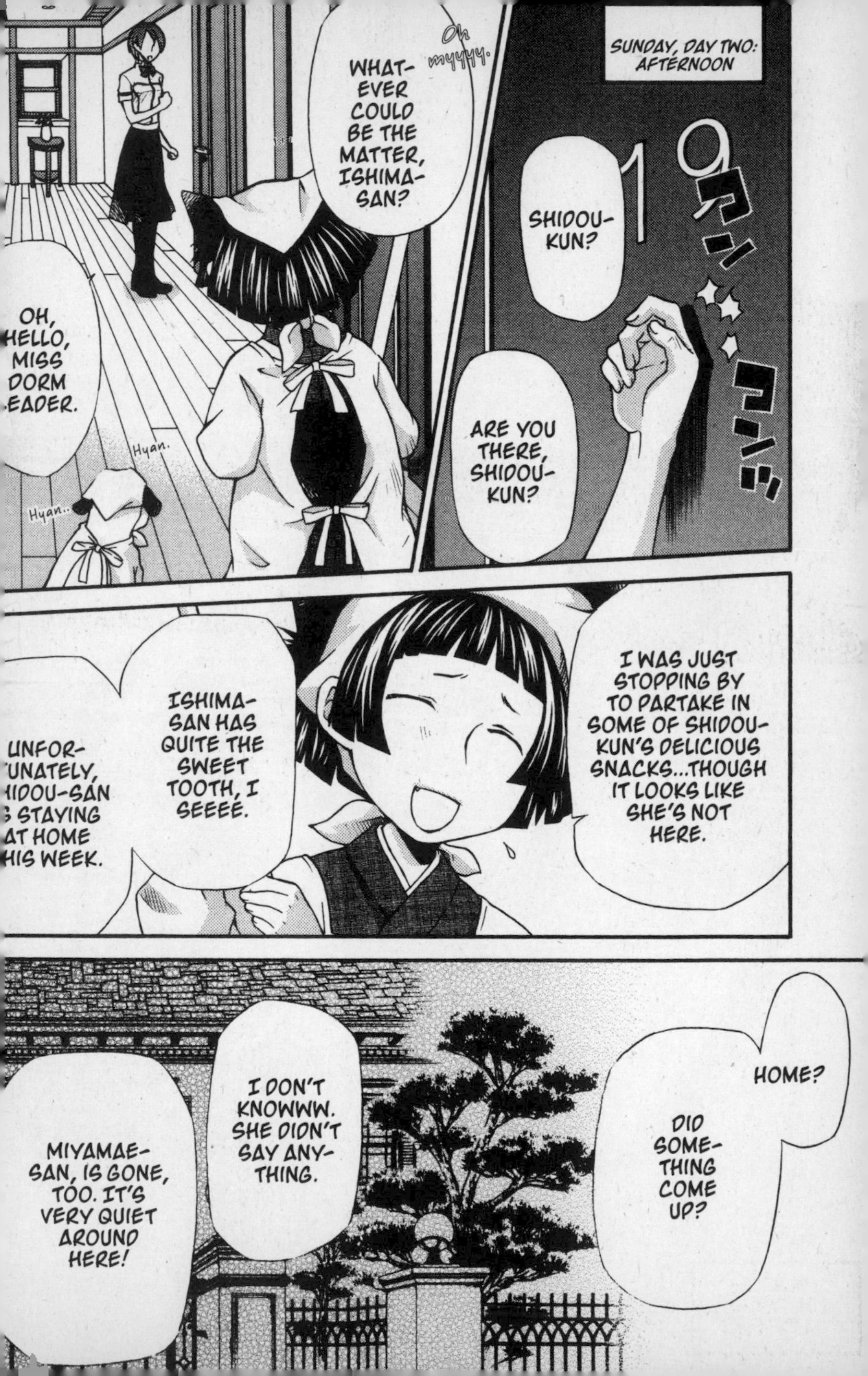
SUNDAY, DAY TWO: AFTERNOON
SHIDOU-KUN?
ARE YOU THERE, SHIDOU-KUN?
WHAT-EVER COULD BE THE MATTER, ISHIMA-SAN?
Oh myyyy.
OH, HELLO, MISS DORM EADER.
Hyan.
Hyan..
I WAS JUST STOPPING BY TO PARTAKE IN SOME OF SHIDOU-KUN'S DELICIOUS SNACKS...THOUGH IT LOOKS LIKE SHE'S NOT HERE.
ISHIMA-SAN HAS QUITE THE SWEET TOOTH, I SEEEE.
UNFOR-TUNATELY, HIDOU-SAN S STAYING AT HOME HIS WEEK.
HOME?
DID SOME-THING COME UP?
I DON'T KNOWWW. SHE DIDN'T SAY ANY-THING.
MIYAMAE-SAN, IS GONE, TOO. IT'S VERY QUIET AROUND HERE!

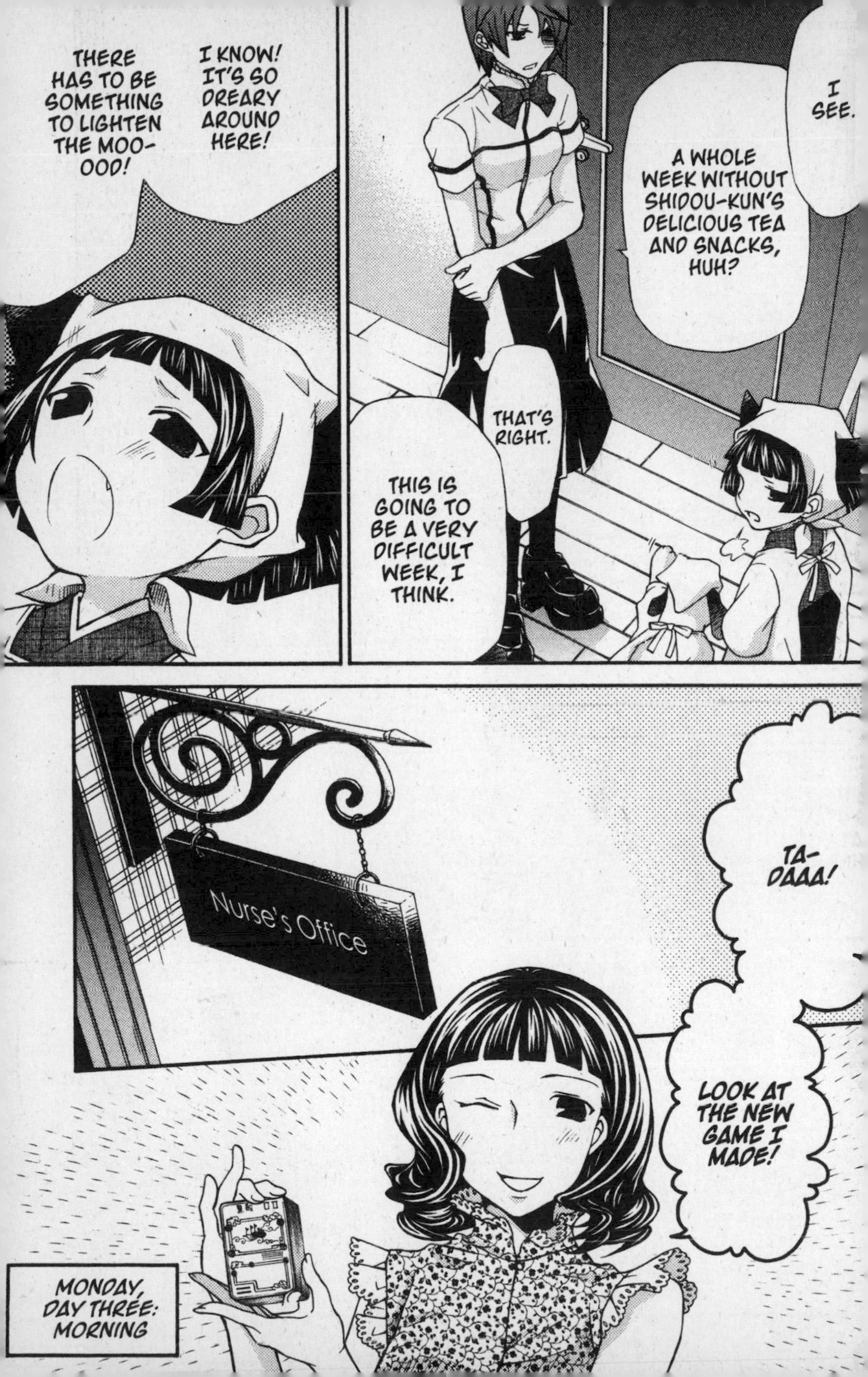
I SEE.
A WHOLE WEEK WITHOUT SHIDOU-KUN'S DELICIOUS TEA AND SNACKS, HUH?
THAT'S RIGHT.
THIS IS GOING TO BE A VERY DIFFICULT WEEK, I THINK.
I KNOW! IT'S SO DREARY AROUND HERE!
THERE HAS TO BE SOMETHING TO LIGHTEN THE MOO-OOD!
TA-DAAA!
Nurse's Office
LOOK AT THE NEW GAME I MADE!
MONDAY, DAY THREE: MORNING

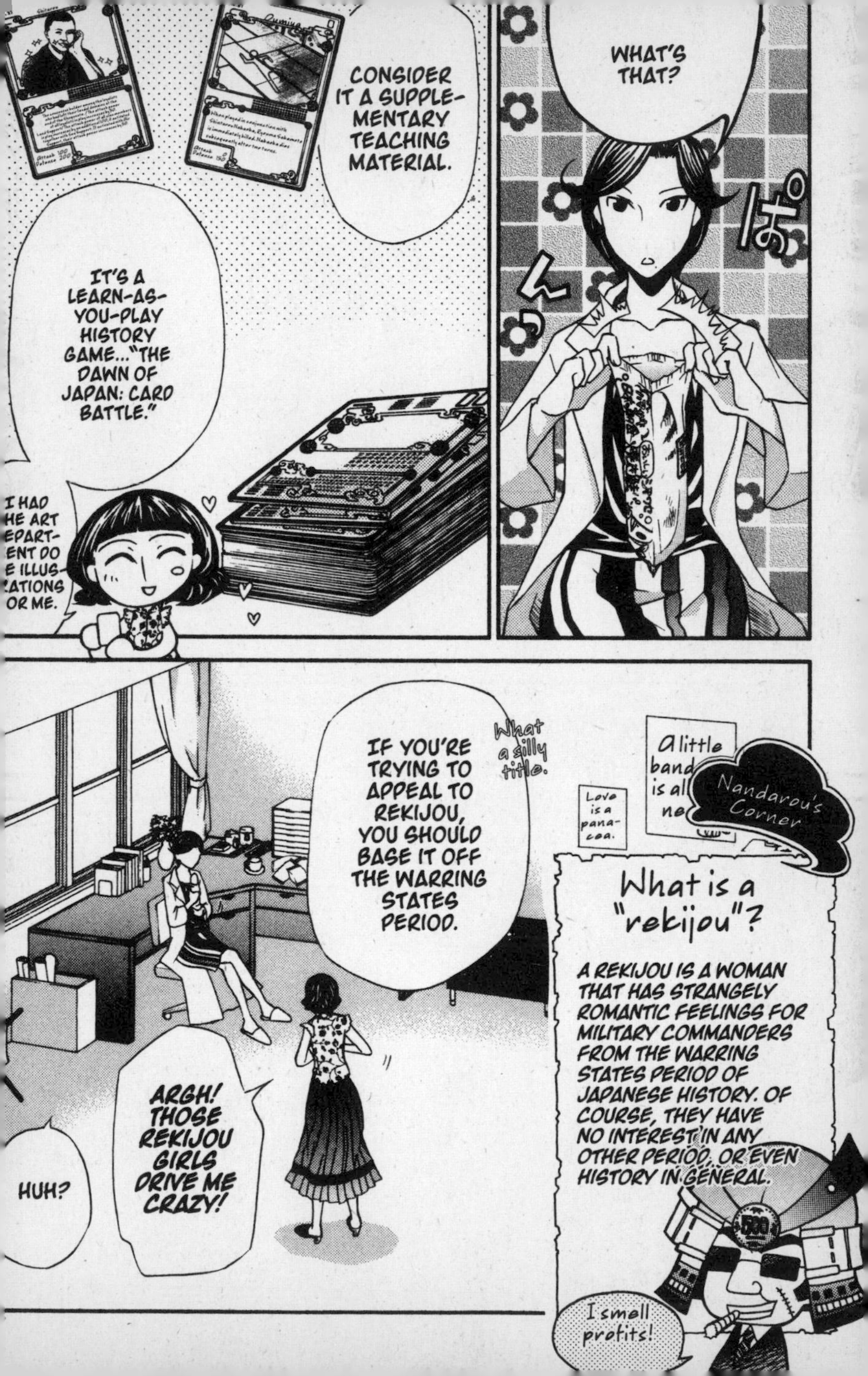
WHAT'S THAT?
CONSIDER IT A SUPPLEMENTARY TEACHING MATERIAL.
IT'S A LEARN-AS-YOU-PLAY HISTORY GAME..."THE DAWN OF JAPAN: CARD BATTLE."
I HAD HE ART EPART- ENT DO E ILLUS- ATIONS OR ME.
IF YOU'RE TRYING TO APPEAL TO REKIJOU, YOU SHOULD BASE IT OFF THE WARRING STATES PERIOD.
What a silly title.
HUH?
ARGH! THOSE REKIJOU GIRLS DRIVE ME CRAZY!
Love is a panacea.
Nandarou's Corner
What is a "rekijou"?
A REKIJOU IS A WOMAN THAT HAS STRANGELY ROMANTIC FEELINGS FOR MILITARY COMMANDERS FROM THE WARRING STATES PERIOD OF JAPANESE HISTORY. OF COURSE, THEY HAVE NO INTEREST IN ANY OTHER PERIOD, OR EVEN HISTORY IN GENERAL.
I smell profits!

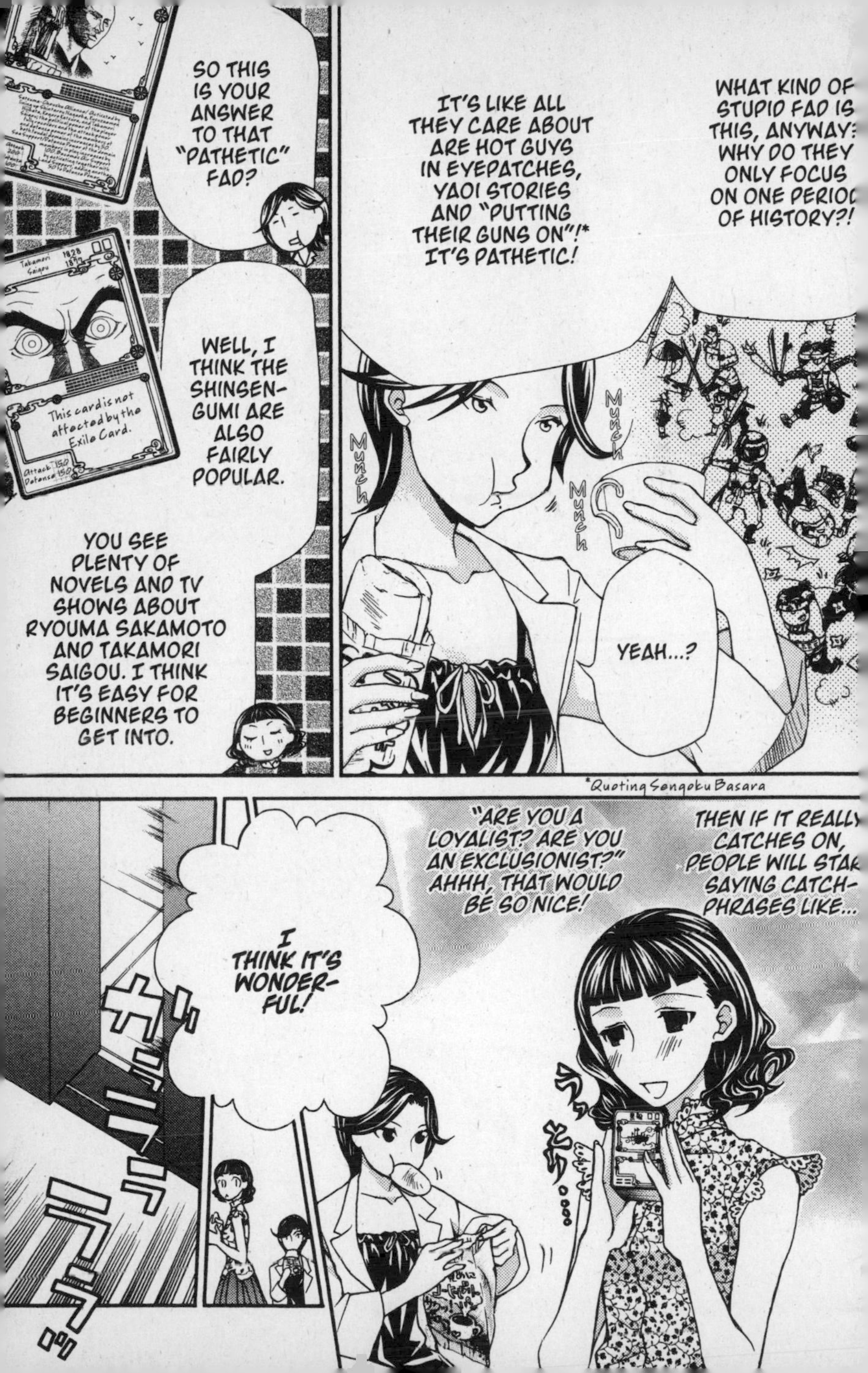
WHAT KIND OF STUPID FAD IS THIS, ANYWAY? WHY DO THEY ONLY FOCUS ON ONE PERIO OF HISTORY?!
IT'S LIKE ALL THEY CARE ABOUT ARE HOT GUYS IN EYEPATCHES, YAOI STORIES AND "PUTTING THEIR GUNS ON"!* IT'S PATHETIC!
Munch Munch
Munch Munch
YEAH...?
SO THIS IS YOUR ANSWER TO THAT "PATHETIC" FAD?
Takamori Saigou 1828 1877
This card is not affected by the Exile Card.
Attack 150 Defense 150
WELL, I THINK THE SHINSEN-GUMI ARE ALSO FAIRLY POPULAR.
YOU SEE PLENTY OF NOVELS AND TV SHOWS ABOUT RYOUMA SAKAMOTO AND TAKAMORI SAIGOU. I THINK IT'S EASY FOR BEGINNERS TO GET INTO.
THEN IF IT REALLY CATCHES ON, PEOPLE WILL STAR SAYING CATCH-PHRASES LIKE...
"ARE YOU A LOYALIST? ARE YOU AN EXCLUSIONIST?" AHHH, THAT WOULD BE SO NICE!
I THINK IT'S WONDERFUL!

*Quoting Sengoku Basara

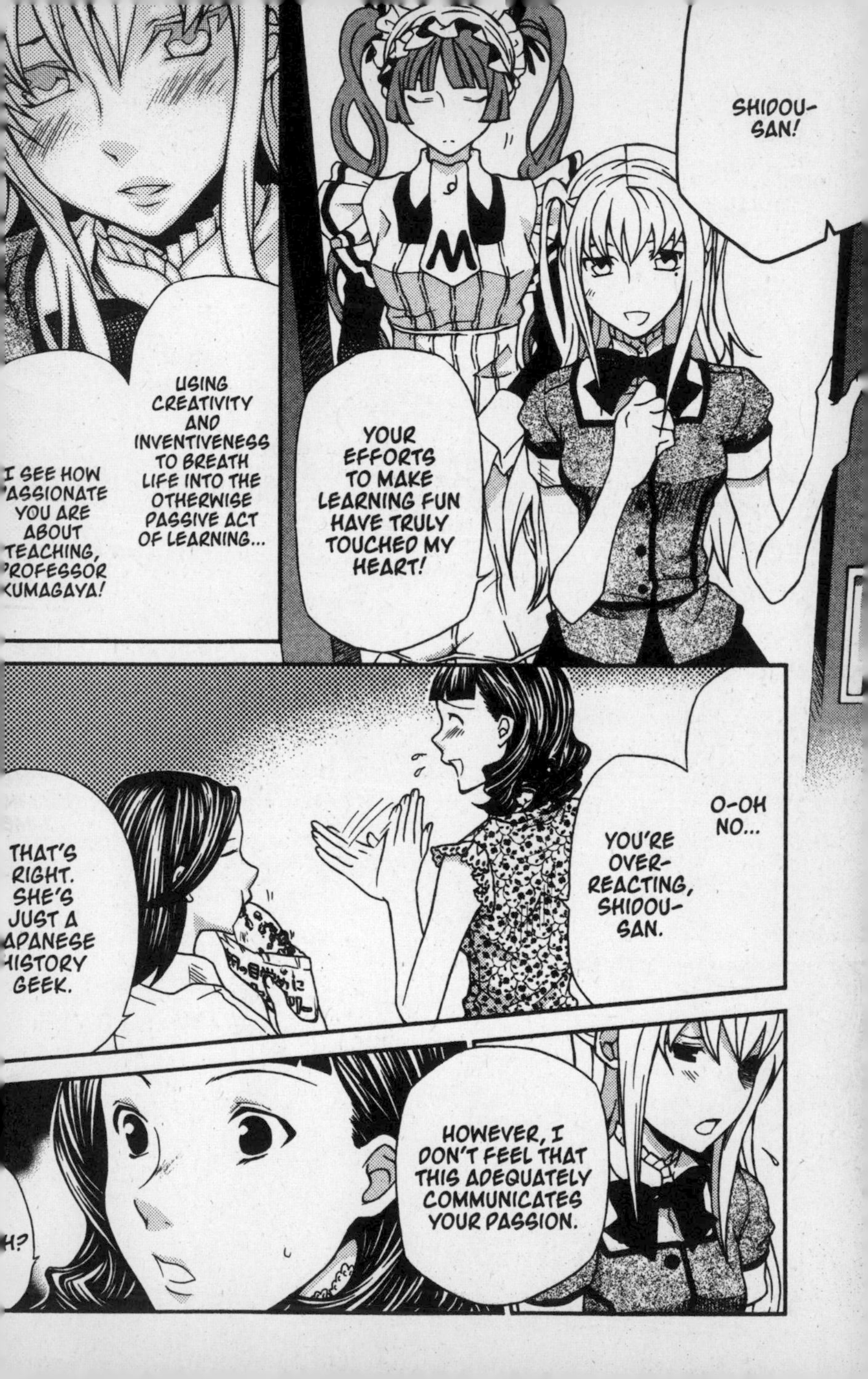
SHIDOU-SAN!
YOUR EFFORTS TO MAKE LEARNING FUN HAVE TRULY TOUCHED MY HEART!
USING CREATIVITY AND INVENTIVENESS TO BREATH LIFE INTO THE OTHERWISE PASSIVE ACT OF LEARNING...
I SEE HOW PASSIONATE YOU ARE ABOUT TEACHING, PROFESSOR KUMAGAYA!
O-OH NO...
YOU'RE OVER-REACTING, SHIDOU-SAN.
THAT'S RIGHT. SHE'S JUST A JAPANESE HISTORY GEEK.
HOWEVER, I DON'T FEEL THAT THIS ADEQUATELY COMMUNICATES YOUR PASSION.
H?

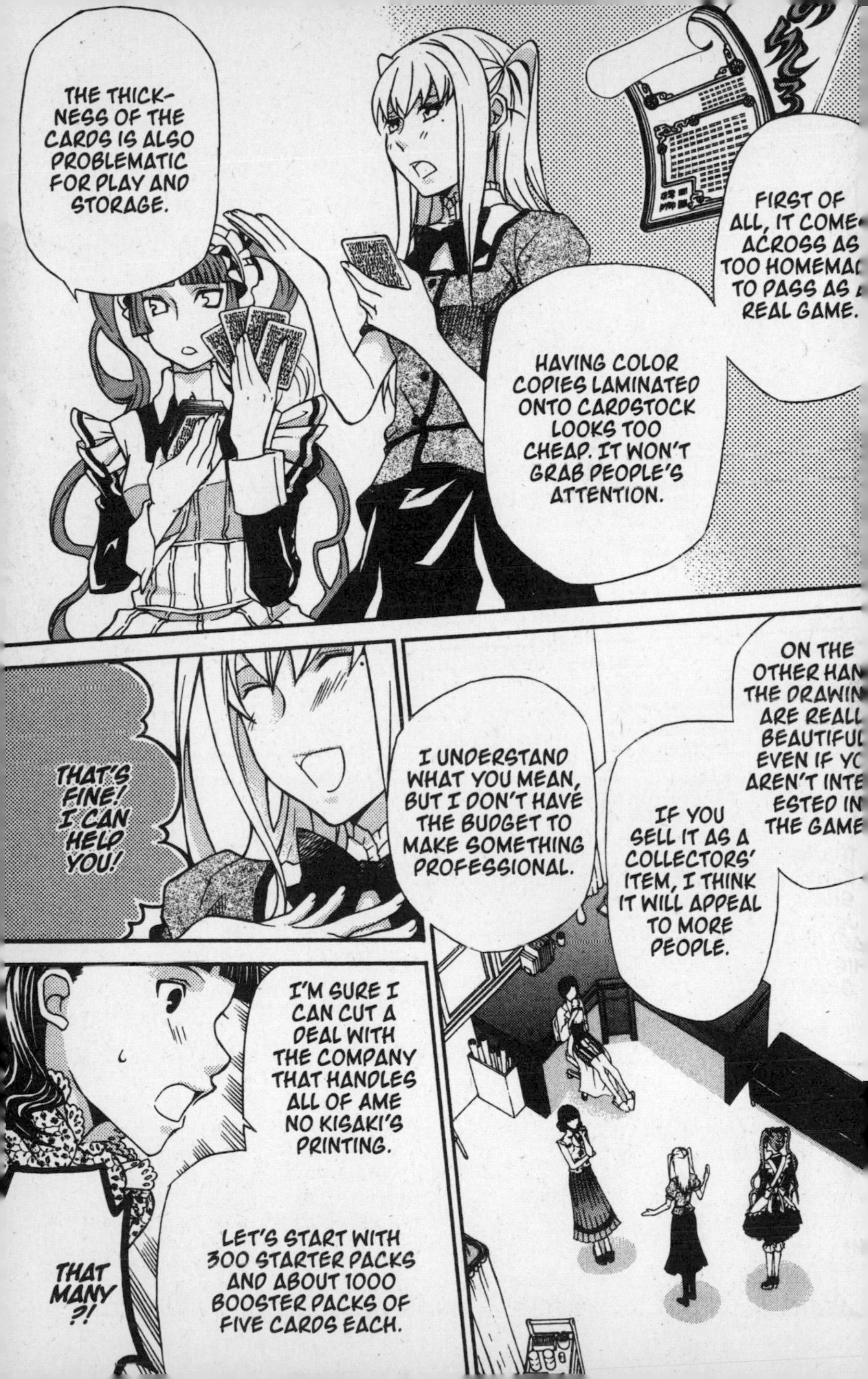
FIRST OF ALL, IT COME ACROSS AS TOO HOMEMA TO PASS AS REAL GAME.
HAVING COLOR COPIES LAMINATED ONTO CARDSTOCK LOOKS TOO CHEAP. IT WON'T GRAB PEOPLE'S ATTENTION.
THE THICKNESS OF THE CARDS IS ALSO PROBLEMATIC FOR PLAY AND STORAGE.
ON THE OTHER HAN THE DRAWIN ARE REALL BEAUTIFUL EVEN IF YO AREN'T INTE ESTED IN THE GAME
IF YOU SELL IT AS A COLLECTORS' ITEM, I THINK IT WILL APPEAL TO MORE PEOPLE.
I UNDERSTAND WHAT YOU MEAN, BUT I DON'T HAVE THE BUDGET TO MAKE SOMETHING PROFESSIONAL.
THAT'S FINE! I CAN HELP YOU!
I'M SURE I CAN CUT A DEAL WITH THE COMPANY THAT HANDLES ALL OF AME NO KISAKI'S PRINTING.
LET'S START WITH 300 STARTER PACKS AND ABOUT 1000 BOOSTER PACKS OF FIVE CARDS EACH.
THAT MANY?!

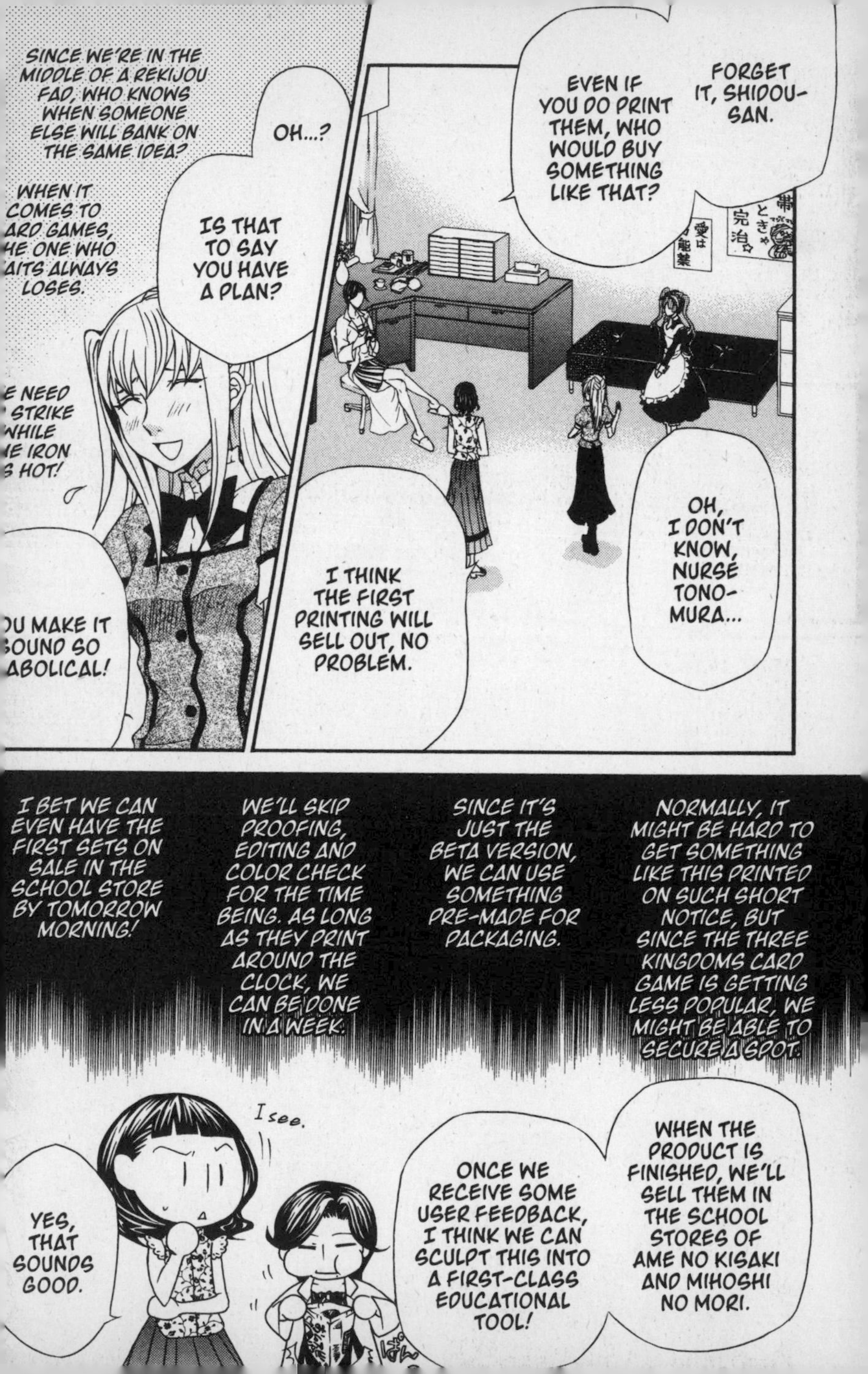
FORGET IT, SHIDOU-SAN.
EVEN IF YOU DO PRINT THEM, WHO WOULD BUY SOMETHING LIKE THAT?
OH, I DON'T KNOW, NURSE TONOMURA...
I THINK THE FIRST PRINTING WILL SELL OUT, NO PROBLEM.
OH...?
IS THAT TO SAY YOU HAVE A PLAN?
SINCE WE'RE IN THE MIDDLE OF A REKIJOU FAD, WHO KNOWS WHEN SOMEONE ELSE WILL BANK ON THE SAME IDEA?
WHEN IT COMES TO ARD GAMES, HE ONE WHO AITS ALWAYS LOSES.
E NEED STRIKE WHILE IE IRON S HOT!
OU MAKE IT SOUND SO ABOLICAL!
NORMALLY, IT MIGHT BE HARD TO GET SOMETHING LIKE THIS PRINTED ON SUCH SHORT NOTICE, BUT SINCE THE THREE KINGDOMS CARD GAME IS GETTING LESS POPULAR, WE MIGHT BE ABLE TO SECURE A SPOT.
SINCE IT'S JUST THE BETA VERSION, WE CAN USE SOMETHING PRE-MADE FOR PACKAGING.
WE'LL SKIP PROOFING, EDITING AND COLOR CHECK FOR THE TIME BEING. AS LONG AS THEY PRINT AROUND THE CLOCK, WE CAN BE DONE IN A WEEK.
I BET WE CAN EVEN HAVE THE FIRST SETS ON SALE IN THE SCHOOL STORE BY TOMORROW MORNING!
WHEN THE PRODUCT IS FINISHED, WE'LL SELL THEM IN THE SCHOOL STORES OF AME NO KISAKI AND MIHOSHI NO MORI.
ONCE WE RECEIVE SOME USER FEEDBACK, I THINK WE CAN SCULPT THIS INTO A FIRST-CLASS EDUCATIONAL TOOL!
I see.
YES, THAT SOUNDS GOOD.

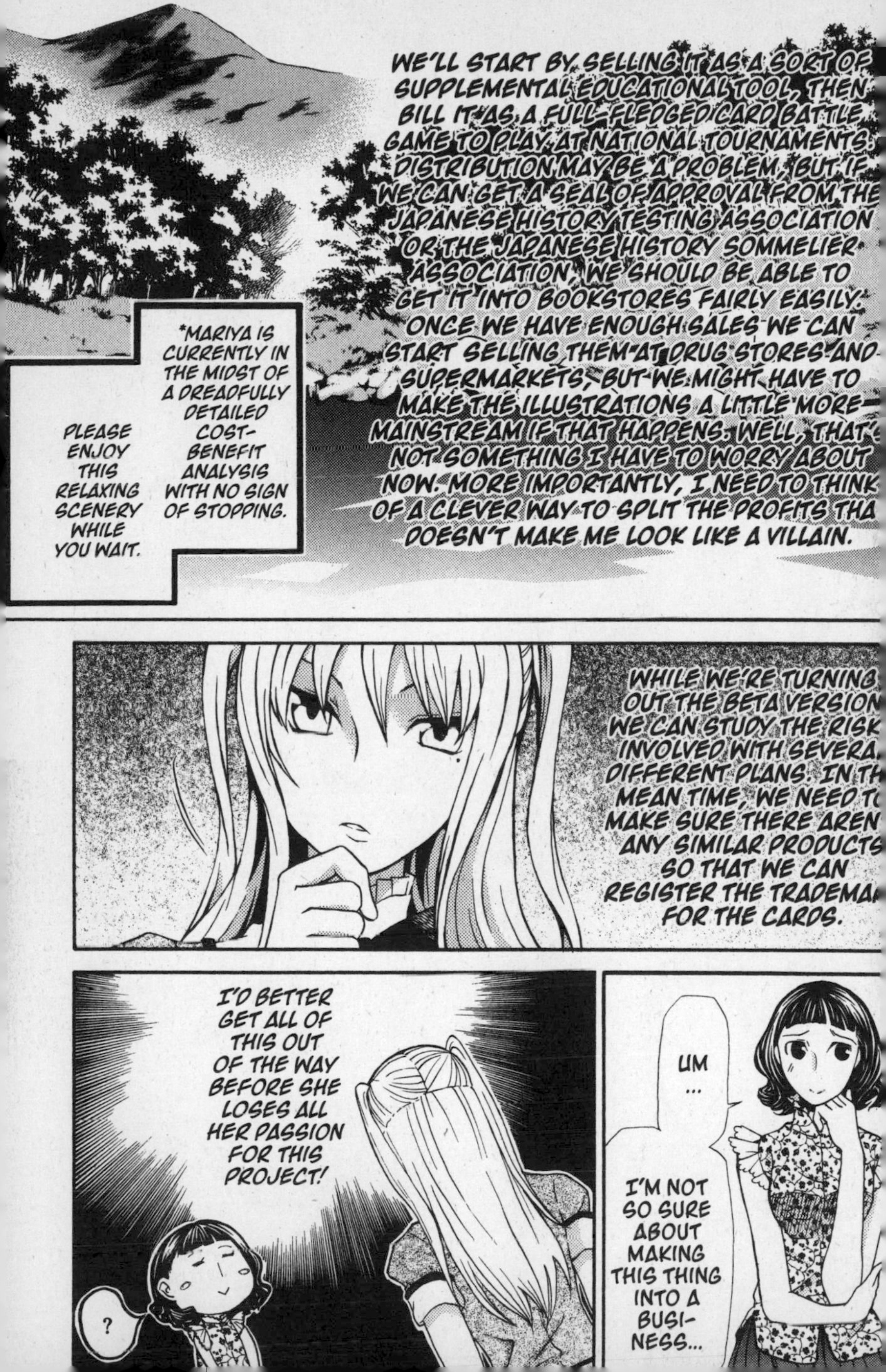
WE'LL START BY SELLING IT AS A SORT OF SUPPLEMENTAL EDUCATIONAL TOOL, THEN BILL IT AS A FULL-FLEDGED CARD BATTLE GAME TO PLAY AT NATIONAL TOURNAMENTS. DISTRIBUTION MAY BE A PROBLEM, BUT IF WE CAN GET A SEAL OF APPROVAL FROM THE JAPANESE HISTORY TESTING ASSOCIATION OR THE JAPANESE HISTORY SOMMELIER ASSOCIATION, WE SHOULD BE ABLE TO GET IT INTO BOOKSTORES FAIRLY EASILY. ONCE WE HAVE ENOUGH SALES WE CAN START SELLING THEM AT DRUG STORES AND SUPERMARKETS, BUT WE MIGHT HAVE TO MAKE THE ILLUSTRATIONS A LITTLE MORE MAINSTREAM IF THAT HAPPENS. WELL, THAT'S NOT SOMETHING I HAVE TO WORRY ABOUT NOW. MORE IMPORTANTLY, I NEED TO THINK OF A CLEVER WAY TO SPLIT THE PROFITS THA DOESN'T MAKE ME LOOK LIKE A VILLAIN.
*MARIYA IS CURRENTLY IN THE MIDST OF A DREADFULLY DETAILED COST-BENEFIT ANALYSIS WITH NO SIGN OF STOPPING.
PLEASE ENJOY THIS RELAXING SCENERY WHILE YOU WAIT.
WHILE WE'RE TURNING OUT THE BETA VERSION WE CAN STUDY THE RISK INVOLVED WITH SEVERA DIFFERENT PLANS. IN TH MEAN TIME, WE NEED T MAKE SURE THERE AREN ANY SIMILAR PRODUCTS SO THAT WE CAN REGISTER THE TRADEMA FOR THE CARDS.
UM ...
I'M NOT SO SURE ABOUT MAKING THIS THING INTO A BUSI-NESS...
I'D BETTER GET ALL OF THIS OUT OF THE WAY BEFORE SHE LOSES ALL HER PASSION FOR THIS PROJECT!
?

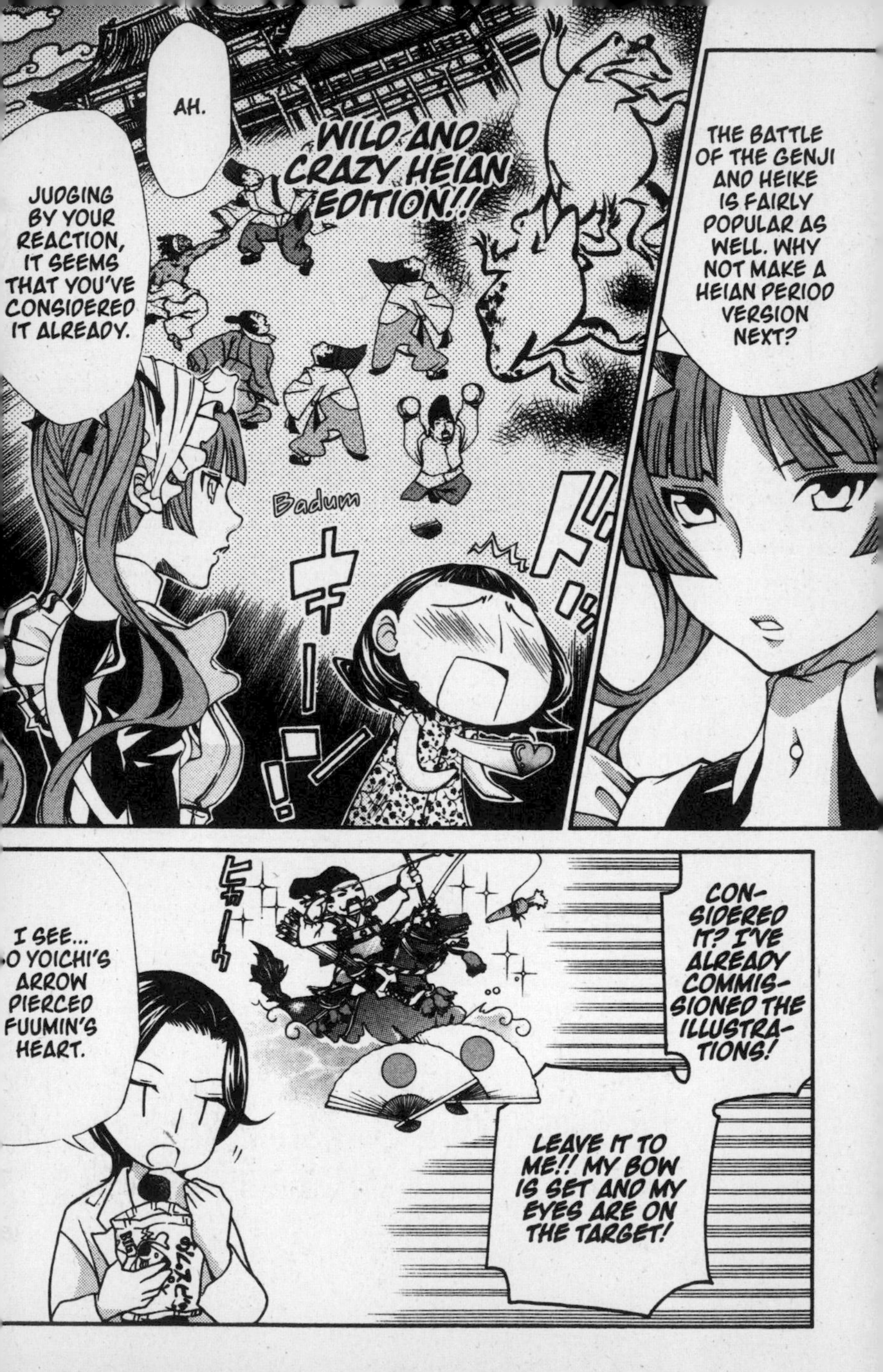

THE BATTLE OF THE GENJI AND HEIKE IS FAIRLY POPULAR AS WELL. WHY NOT MAKE A HEIAN PERIOD VERSION NEXT?
AH.
JUDGING BY YOUR REACTION, IT SEEMS THAT YOU'VE CONSIDERED IT ALREADY.
WILD AND CRAZY HEIAN EDITION!!
Badum
CON-SIDERED IT? I'VE ALREADY COMMIS-SIONED THE ILLUSTRA-TIONS!
LEAVE IT TO ME!! MY BOW IS SET AND MY EYES ARE ON THE TARGET!
I SEE... O YOICHI'S ARROW PIERCED FUUMIN'S HEART.

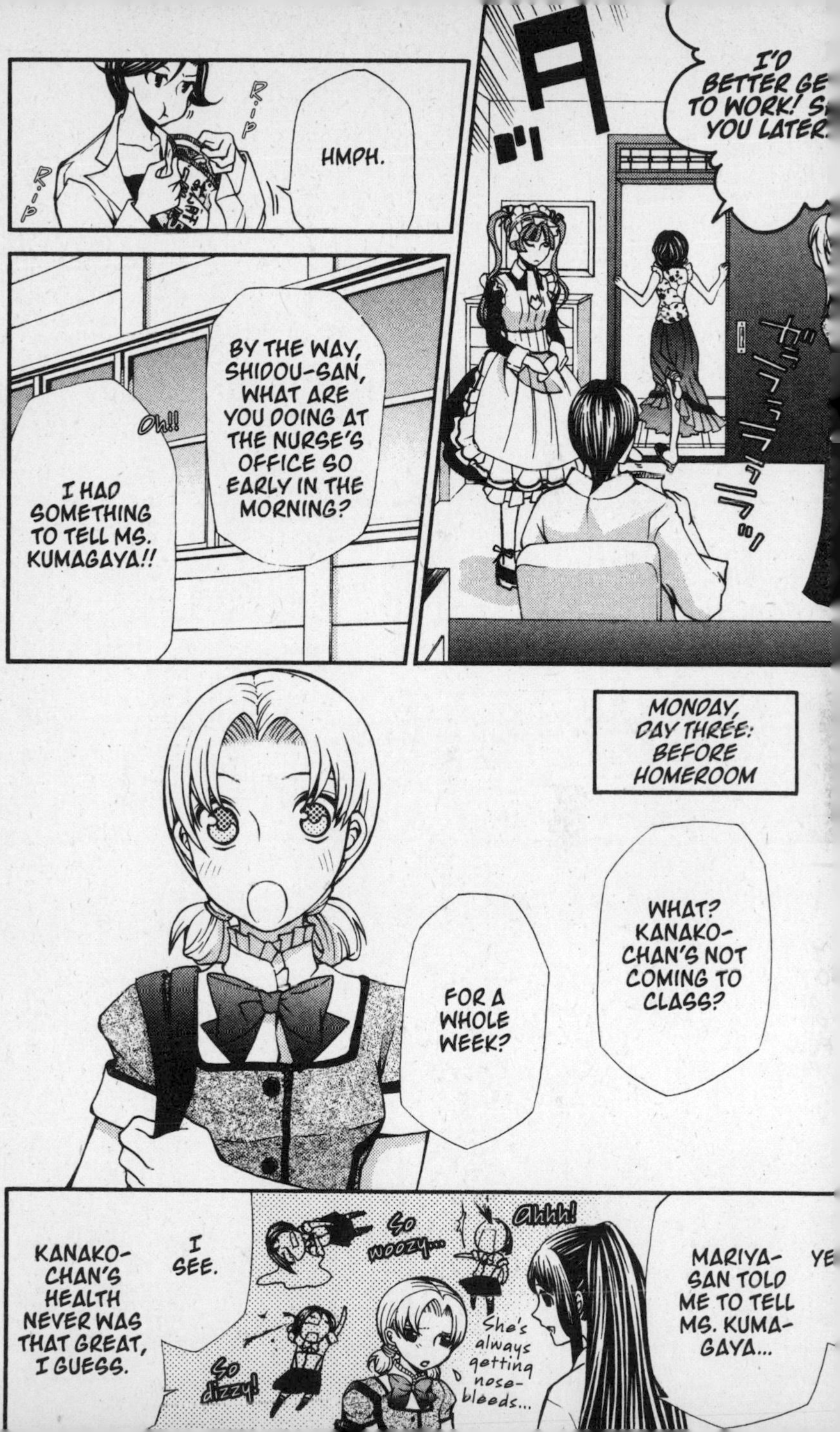
I'D BETTER GE TO WORK! S YOU LATER.
HMPH.
R-ip
R-ip
BY THE WAY, SHIDOU-SAN, WHAT ARE YOU DOING AT THE NURSE'S OFFICE SO EARLY IN THE MORNING?
Oh!!
I HAD SOMETHING TO TELL MS. KUMAGAYA!!
MONDAY, DAY THREE: BEFORE HOMEROOM
WHAT? KANAKO-CHAN'S NOT COMING TO CLASS?
FOR A WHOLE WEEK?
YE
MARIYA-SAN TOLD ME TO TELL MS. KUMAGAYA...
Ahhh!
So woozy...
She's always getting nose-bleeds...
So dizzy!
I SEE.
KANAKO-CHAN'S HEALTH NEVER WAS THAT GREAT, I GUESS.

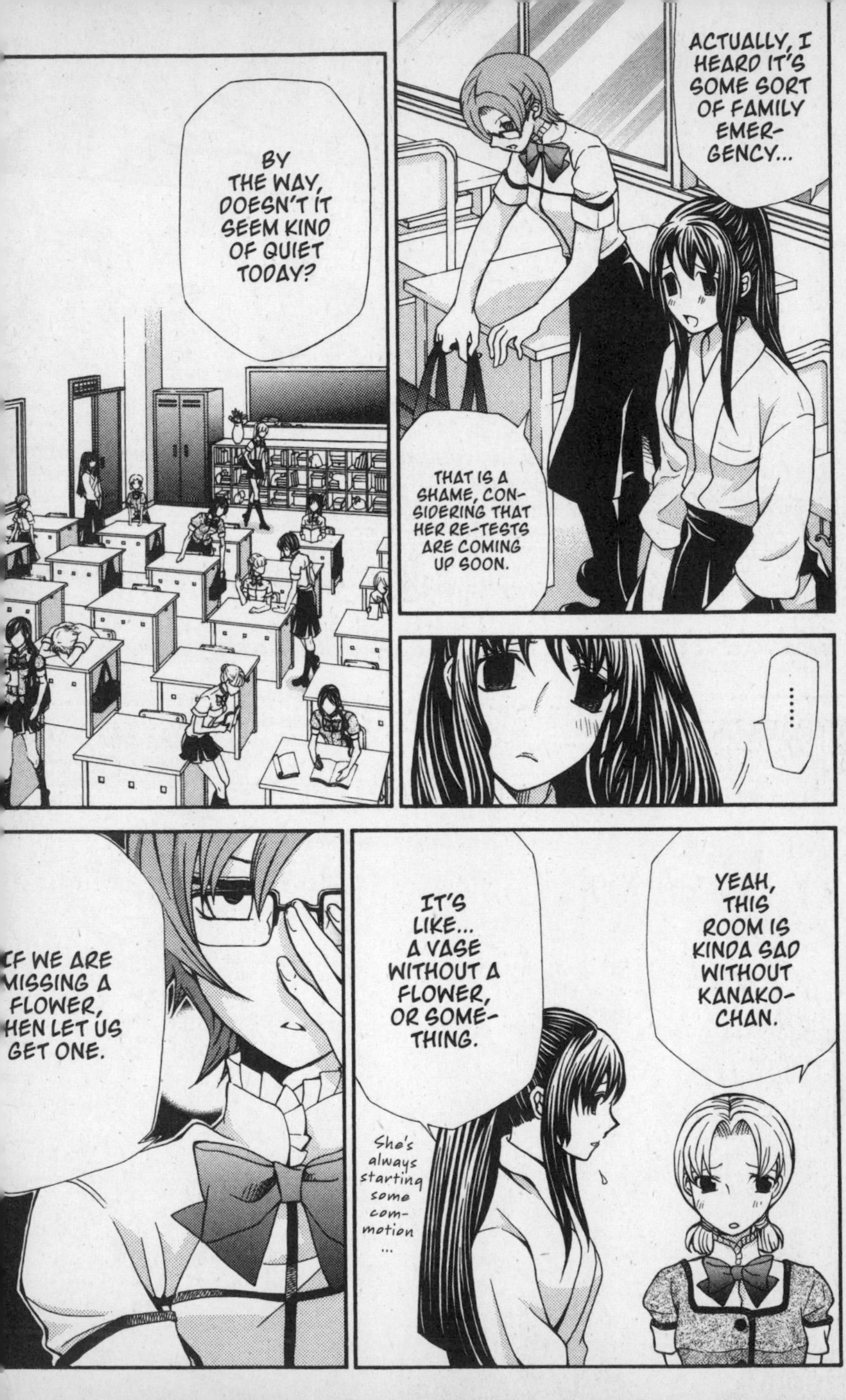
ACTUALLY, I HEARD IT'S SOME SORT OF FAMILY EMER-GENCY...
THAT IS A SHAME, CON-SIDERING THAT HER RE-TESTS ARE COMING UP SOON.
......
BY THE WAY, DOESN'T IT SEEM KIND OF QUIET TODAY?
YEAH, THIS ROOM IS KINDA SAD WITHOUT KANAKO-CHAN.
IT'S LIKE... A VASE WITHOUT A FLOWER, OR SOME-THING.
She's always starting some com-motion ...
IF WE ARE MISSING A FLOWER, THEN LET US GET ONE.

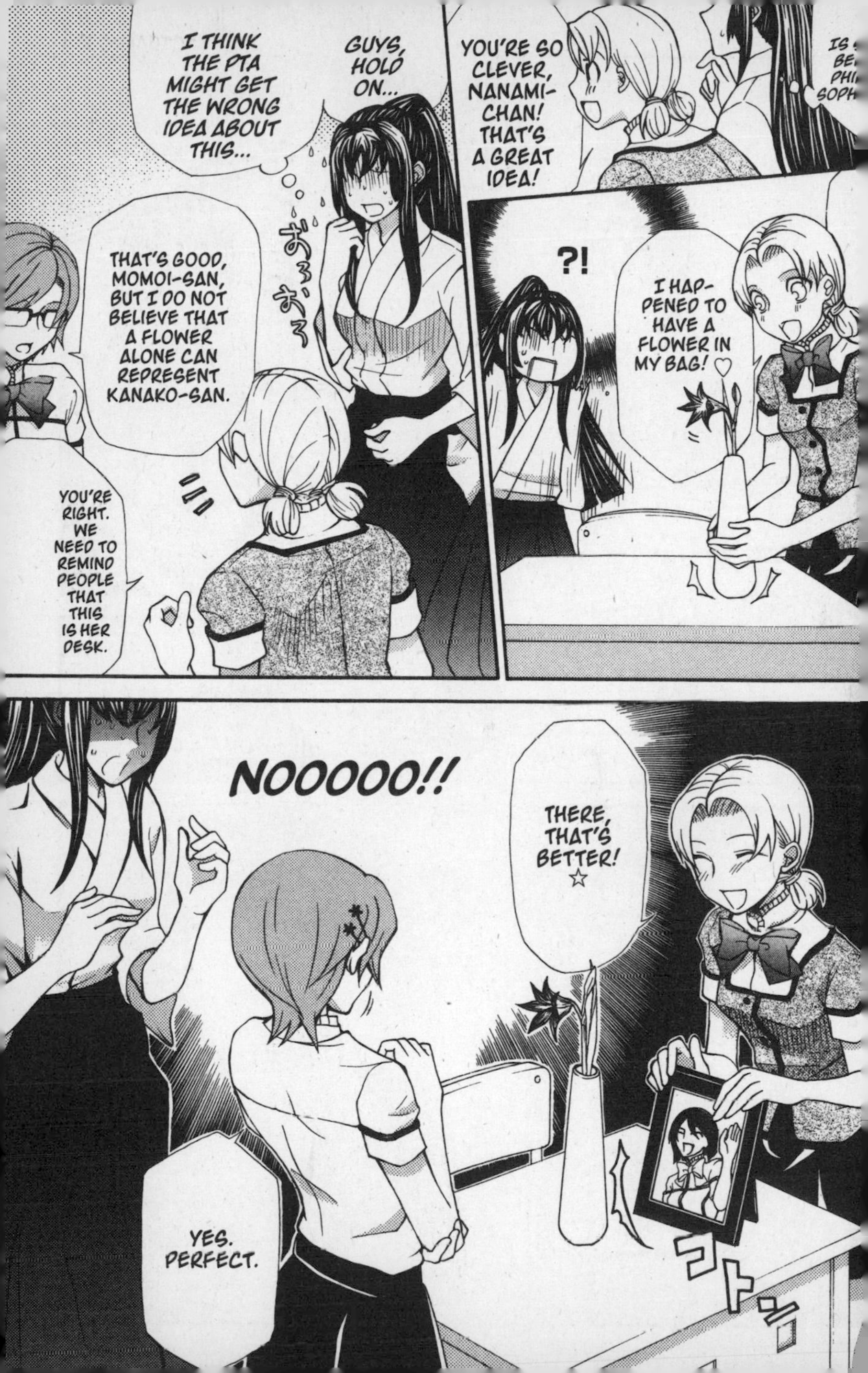
YOU'RE SO CLEVER, NANAMI-CHAN! THAT'S A GREAT IDEA!
I HAP-PENED TO HAVE A FLOWER IN MY BAG! ♡
?!
GUYS, HOLD ON...
I THINK THE PTA MIGHT GET THE WRONG IDEA ABOUT THIS...
おろおろ
THAT'S GOOD, MOMOI-SAN, BUT I DO NOT BELIEVE THAT A FLOWER ALONE CAN REPRESENT KANAKO-SAN.
YOU'RE RIGHT. WE NEED TO REMIND PEOPLE THAT THIS IS HER DESK.
THERE, THAT'S BETTER! ☆
NOOOOO!!
YES. PERFECT.

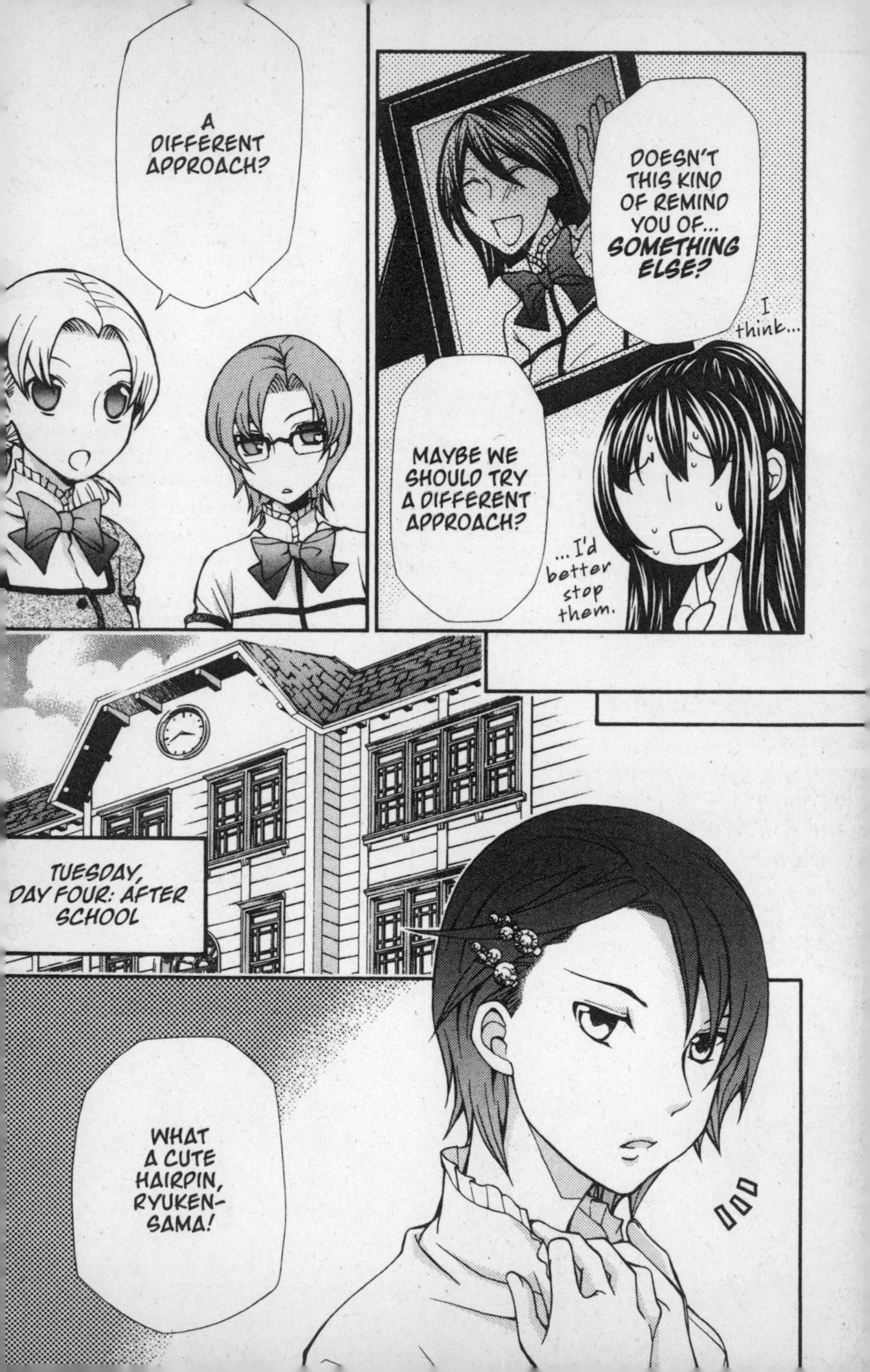
DOESN'T THIS KIND OF REMIND YOU OF... SOMETHING ELSE?
I think...
MAYBE WE SHOULD TRY A DIFFERENT APPROACH?
... I'd better stop them.
A DIFFERENT APPROACH?
TUESDAY, DAY FOUR: AFTER SCHOOL
WHAT A CUTE HAIRPIN, RYUKEN-SAMA!

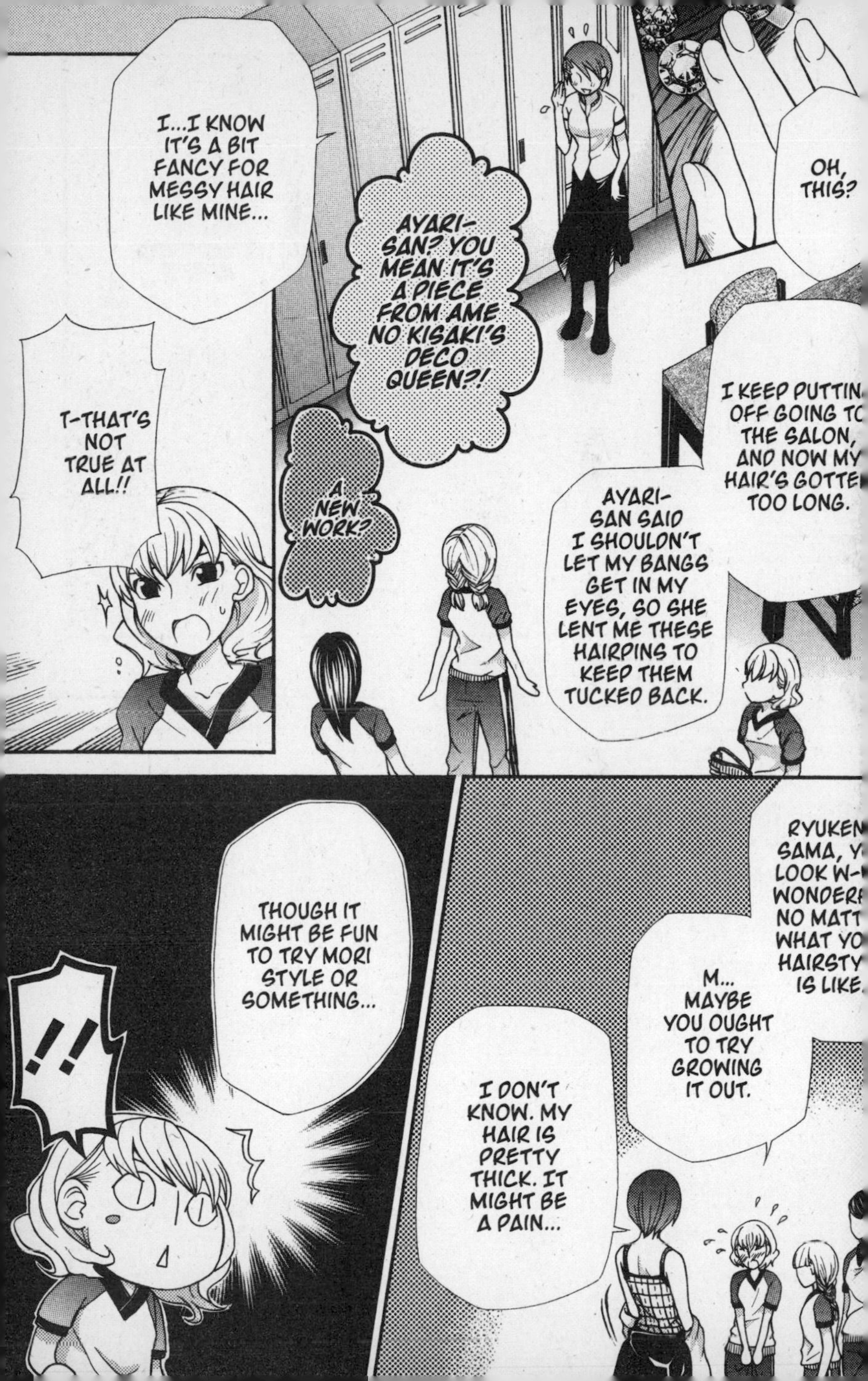
OH, THIS?
I KEEP PUTTIN OFF GOING TO THE SALON, AND NOW MY HAIR'S GOTTE TOO LONG.
AYARI-SAN SAID I SHOULDN'T LET MY BANGS GET IN MY EYES, SO SHE LENT ME THESE HAIRPINS TO KEEP THEM TUCKED BACK.
AYARI-SAN? YOU MEAN IT'S A PIECE FROM AME NO KISAKI'S DECO QUEEN?!
A NEW WORK?
I...I KNOW IT'S A BIT FANCY FOR MESSY HAIR LIKE MINE...
T-THAT'S NOT TRUE AT ALL!!
RYUKEN SAMA, Y LOOK W- WONDERF NO MATT WHAT YO HAIRSTY IS LIKE.
M... MAYBE YOU OUGHT TO TRY GROWING IT OUT.
I DON'T KNOW. MY HAIR IS PRETTY THICK. IT MIGHT BE A PAIN...
THOUGH IT MIGHT BE FUN TO TRY MORI STYLE OR SOMETHING...
!!

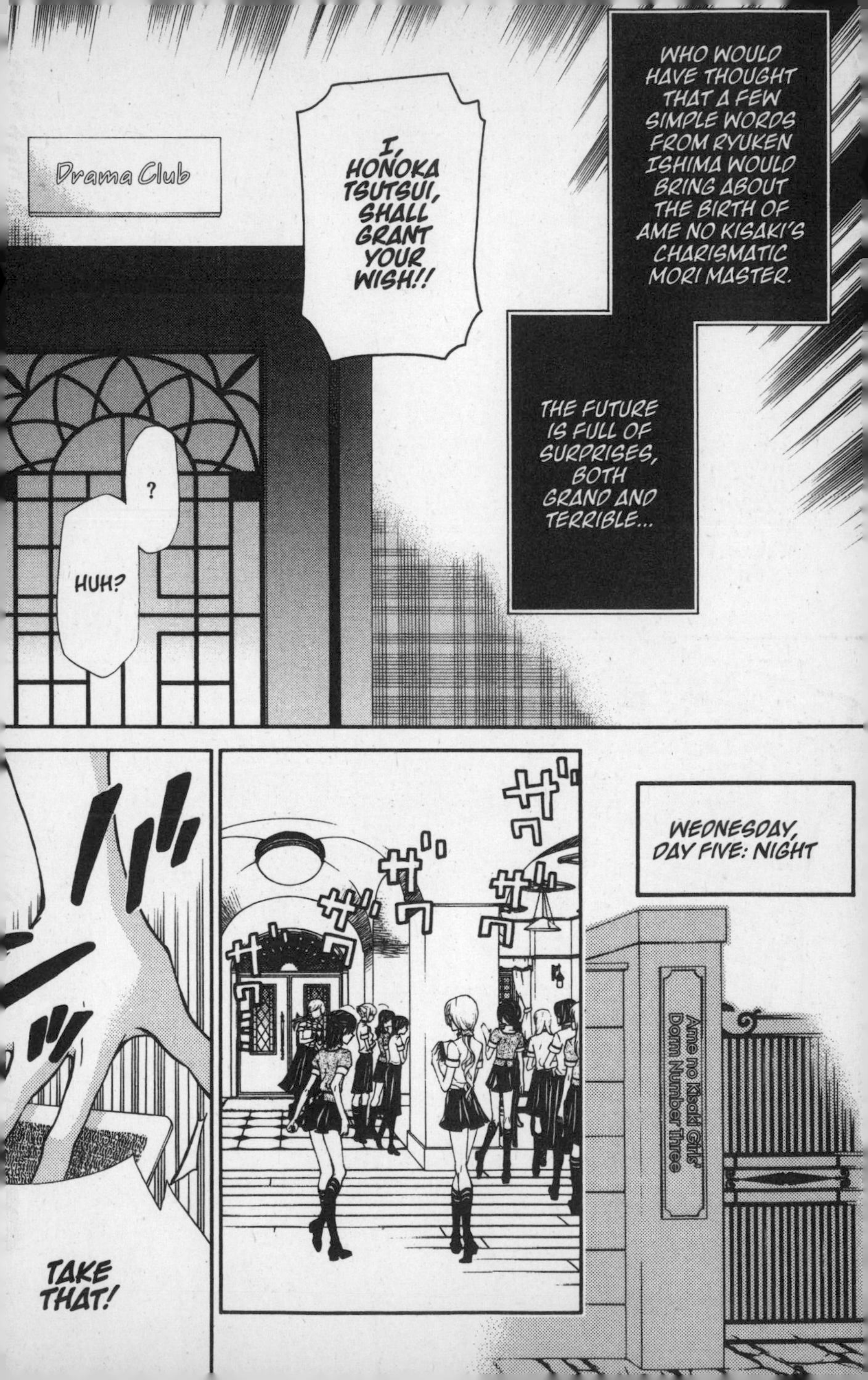
WHO WOULD HAVE THOUGHT THAT A FEW SIMPLE WORDS FROM RYUKEN ISHIMA WOULD BRING ABOUT THE BIRTH OF AME NO KISAKI'S CHARISMATIC MORI MASTER.
I, HONOKA TSUTSUI, SHALL GRANT YOUR WISH!!
Drama Club
?
HUH?
THE FUTURE IS FULL OF SURPRISES, BOTH GRAND AND TERRIBLE...
WEDNESDAY, DAY FIVE: NIGHT
Ame no Kisaki Girls' Dorm Number Three
TAKE THAT!

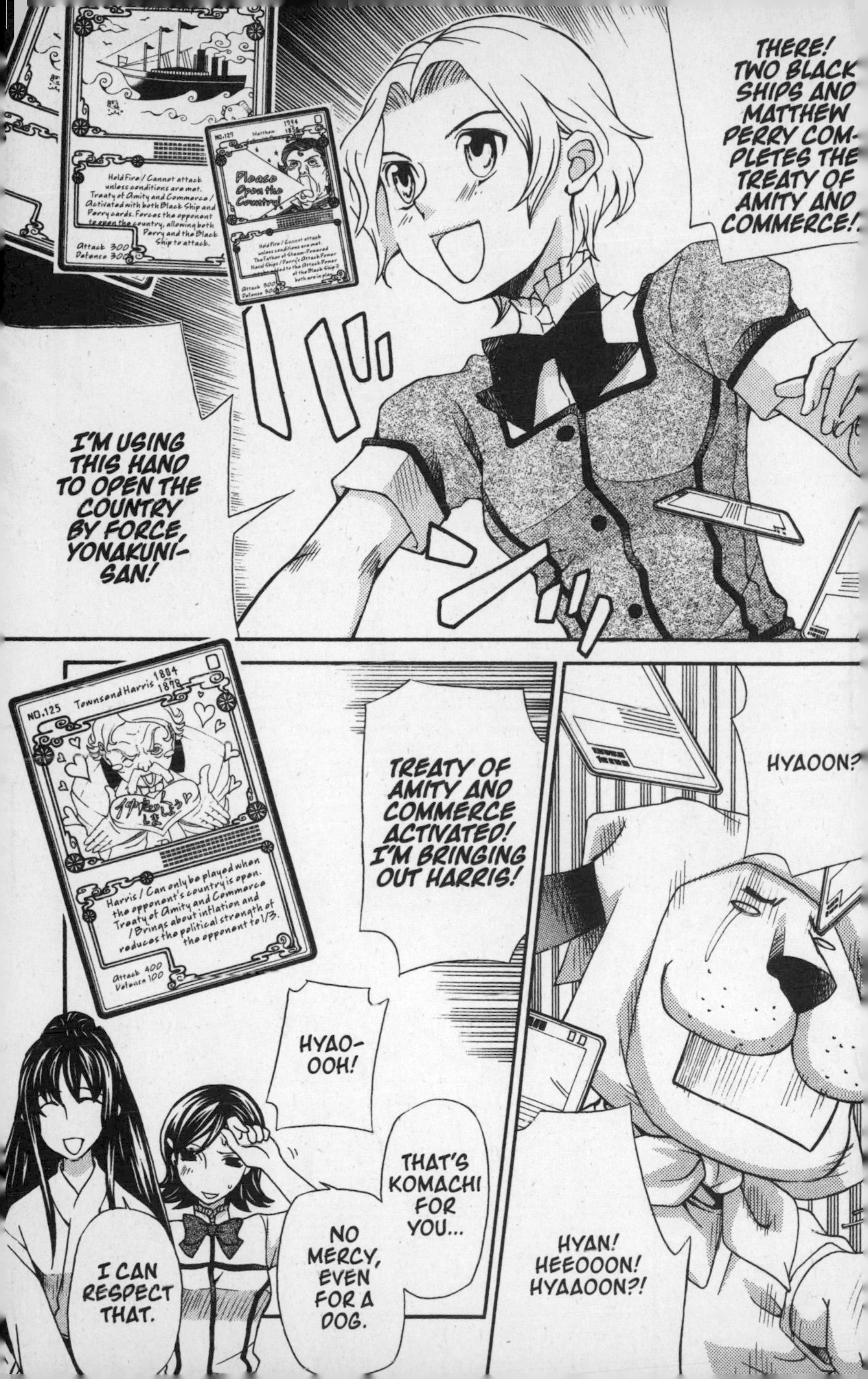
THERE! TWO BLACK SHIPS AND MATTHEW PERRY COMPLETES THE TREATY OF AMITY AND COMMERCE!
I'M USING THIS HAND TO OPEN THE COUNTRY BY FORCE, YONAKUNI-SAN!
Hold Fire / Cannot attack unless conditions are met. Treaty of Amity and Commerce / Activated with both Black Ship and Perry cards. Forces the opponent to open the country, allowing both Perry and the Black Ship to attack.
Attack 300
Defense 300
NO.127
Matthew
1794
1858
Please Open the Country!
Hold Fire / Cannot attack unless conditions are met. The Father of Steam-Powered Naval Ships / Perry's Attack Power
added to the Attack Power of the Black Ship if both are in play.
Attack 300
Defense 300
HYAOON?
HYAN! HEEOOON! HYAAOON?!
NO.125
Townsend Harris
1804
1878
Harris / Can only be played when the opponent's country is open. Treaty of Amity and Commerce / Brings about inflation and reduces the political strength of the opponent to 1/3.
Attack 400
Defense 100
TREATY OF AMITY AND COMMERCE ACTIVATED! I'M BRINGING OUT HARRIS!
HYAO-OOH!
THAT'S KOMACHI FOR YOU...
NO MERCY, EVEN FOR A DOG.
I CAN RESPECT THAT.

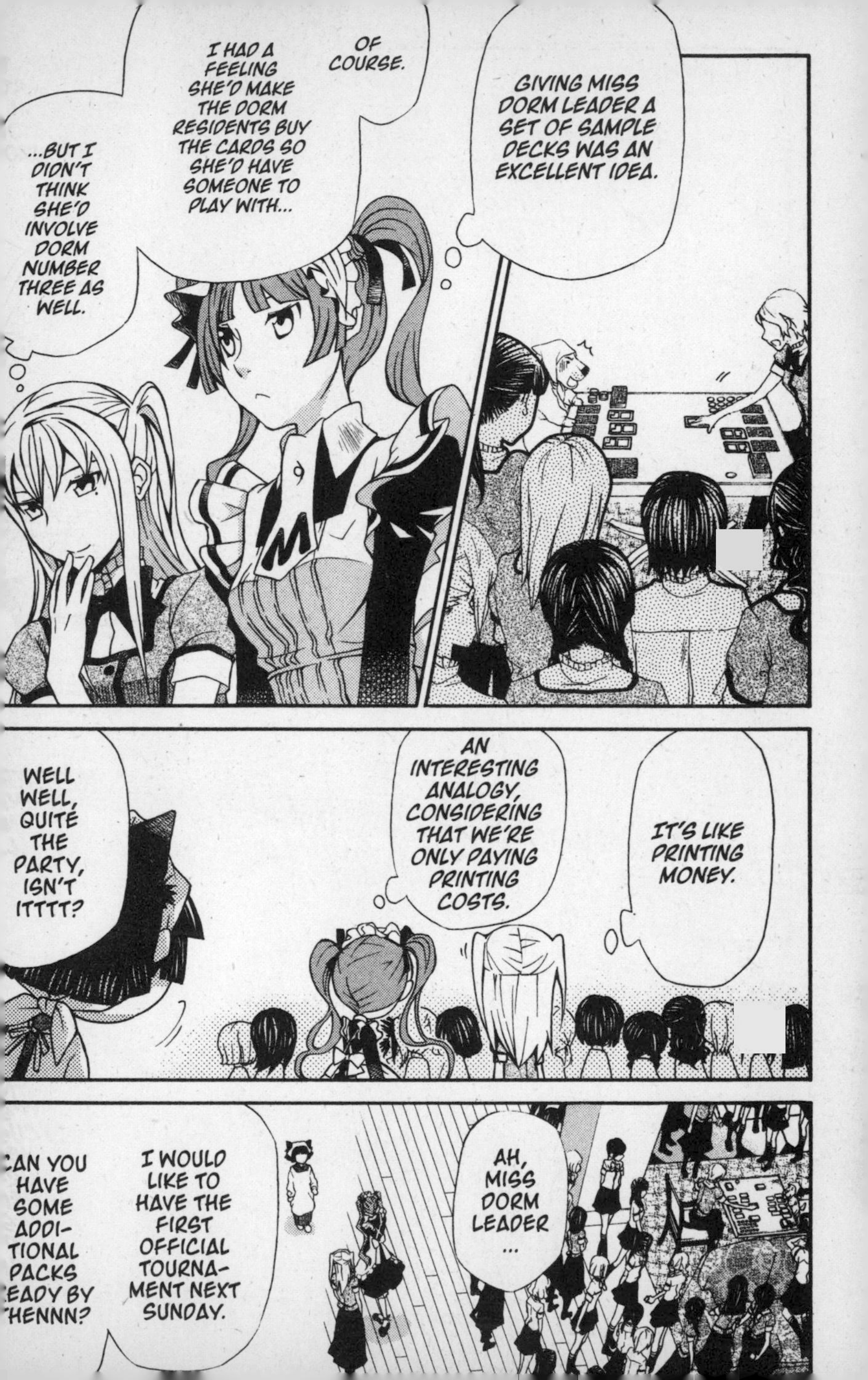
GIVING MISS DORM LEADER A SET OF SAMPLE DECKS WAS AN EXCELLENT IDEA.
OF COURSE.
I HAD A FEELING SHE'D MAKE THE DORM RESIDENTS BUY THE CARDS SO SHE'D HAVE SOMEONE TO PLAY WITH...
...BUT I DIDN'T THINK SHE'D INVOLVE DORM NUMBER THREE AS WELL.
IT'S LIKE PRINTING MONEY.
AN INTERESTING ANALOGY, CONSIDERING THAT WE'RE ONLY PAYING PRINTING COSTS.
WELL WELL, QUITE THE PARTY, ISN'T ITTTT?
AH, MISS DORM LEADER ...
I WOULD LIKE TO HAVE THE FIRST OFFICIAL TOURNAMENT NEXT SUNDAY.
CAN YOU HAVE SOME ADDITIONAL PACKS EADY BY HENNN?

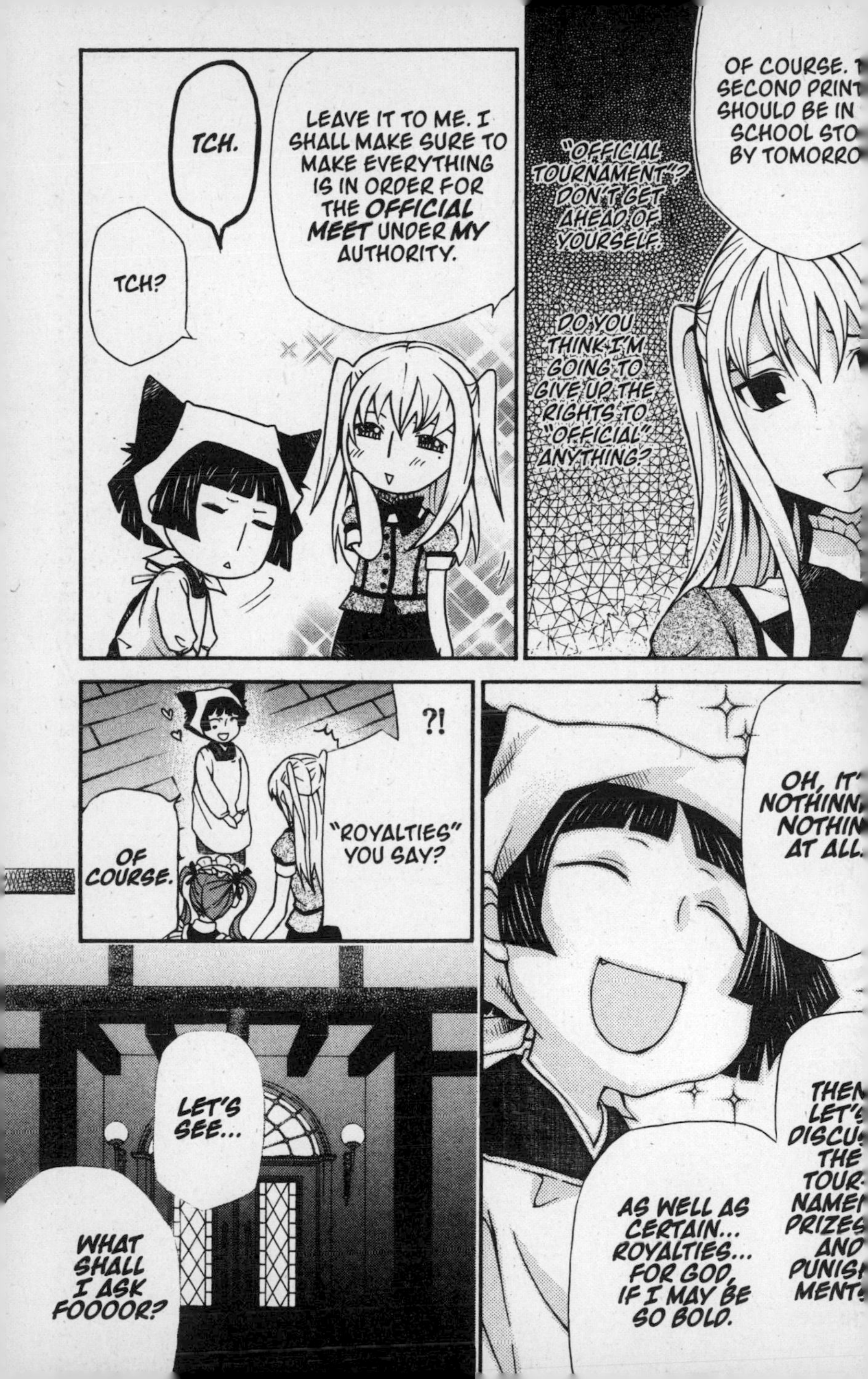
OF COURSE. T SECOND PRINT SHOULD BE IN SCHOOL STO BY TOMORRO
"OFFICIAL TOURNAMENT"? DON'T GET AHEAD OF YOURSELF.
DO YOU THINK I'M GOING TO GIVE UP THE RIGHTS TO "OFFICIAL" ANYTHING?
LEAVE IT TO ME. I SHALL MAKE SURE TO MAKE EVERYTHING IS IN ORDER FOR THE OFFICIAL MEET UNDER MY AUTHORITY.
TCH.
TCH?
OH, IT' NOTHINN NOTHIN AT ALL.
THEN LET'S DISCU THE TOUR- NAMEN PRIZES AND PUNIS MENTS
AS WELL AS CERTAIN... ROYALTIES... FOR GOD, IF I MAY BE SO BOLD.
?!
"ROYALTIES" YOU SAY?
OF COURSE.
LET'S SEE...
WHAT SHALL I ASK FOOOOR?

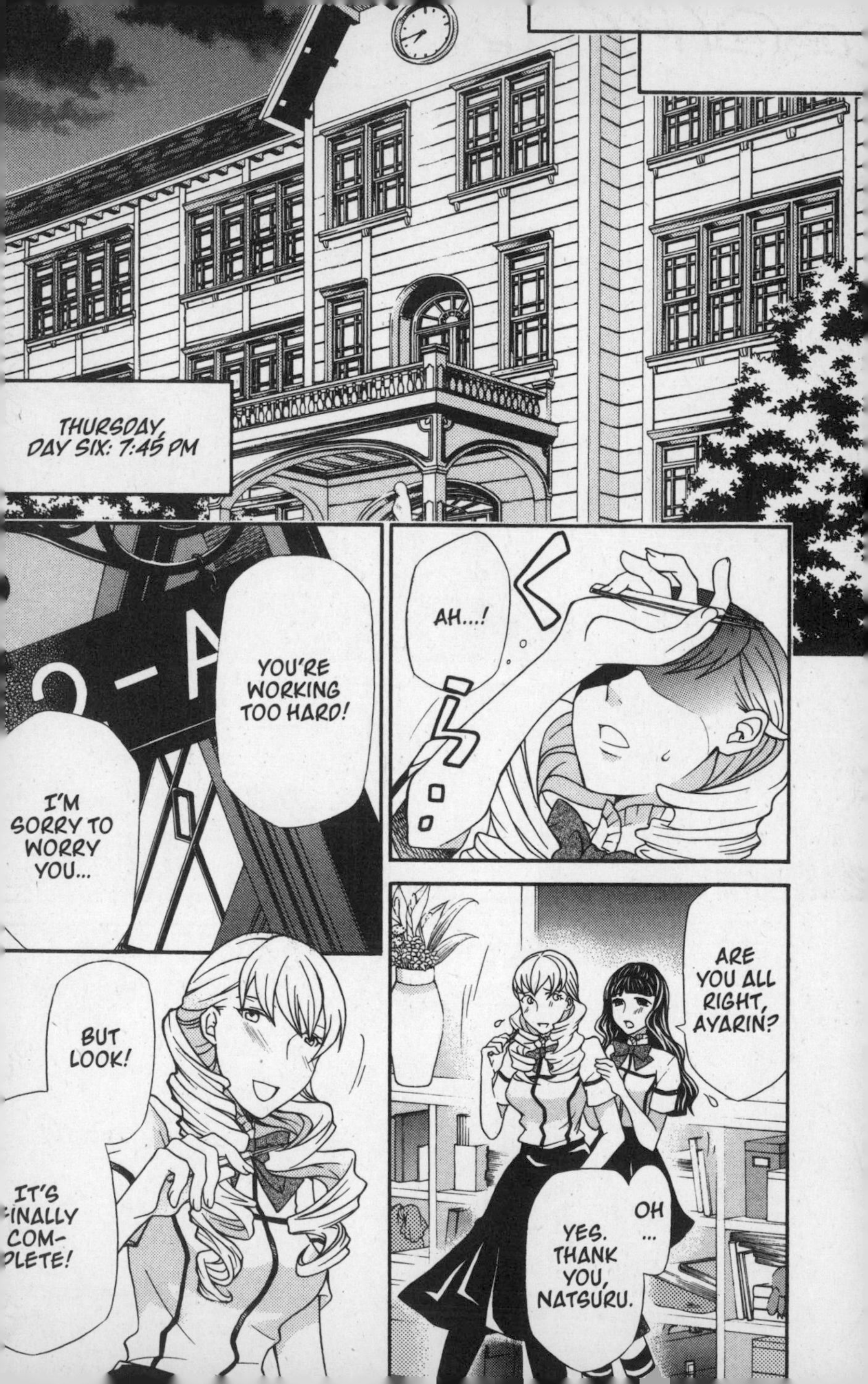
THURSDAY, DAY SIX: 7:45 PM
AH...!
ARE YOU ALL RIGHT, AYARIN?
OH...
YES. THANK YOU, NATSURU.
YOU'RE WORKING TOO HARD!
I'M SORRY TO WORRY YOU...
BUT LOOK!
IT'S INALLY COM-LETE!

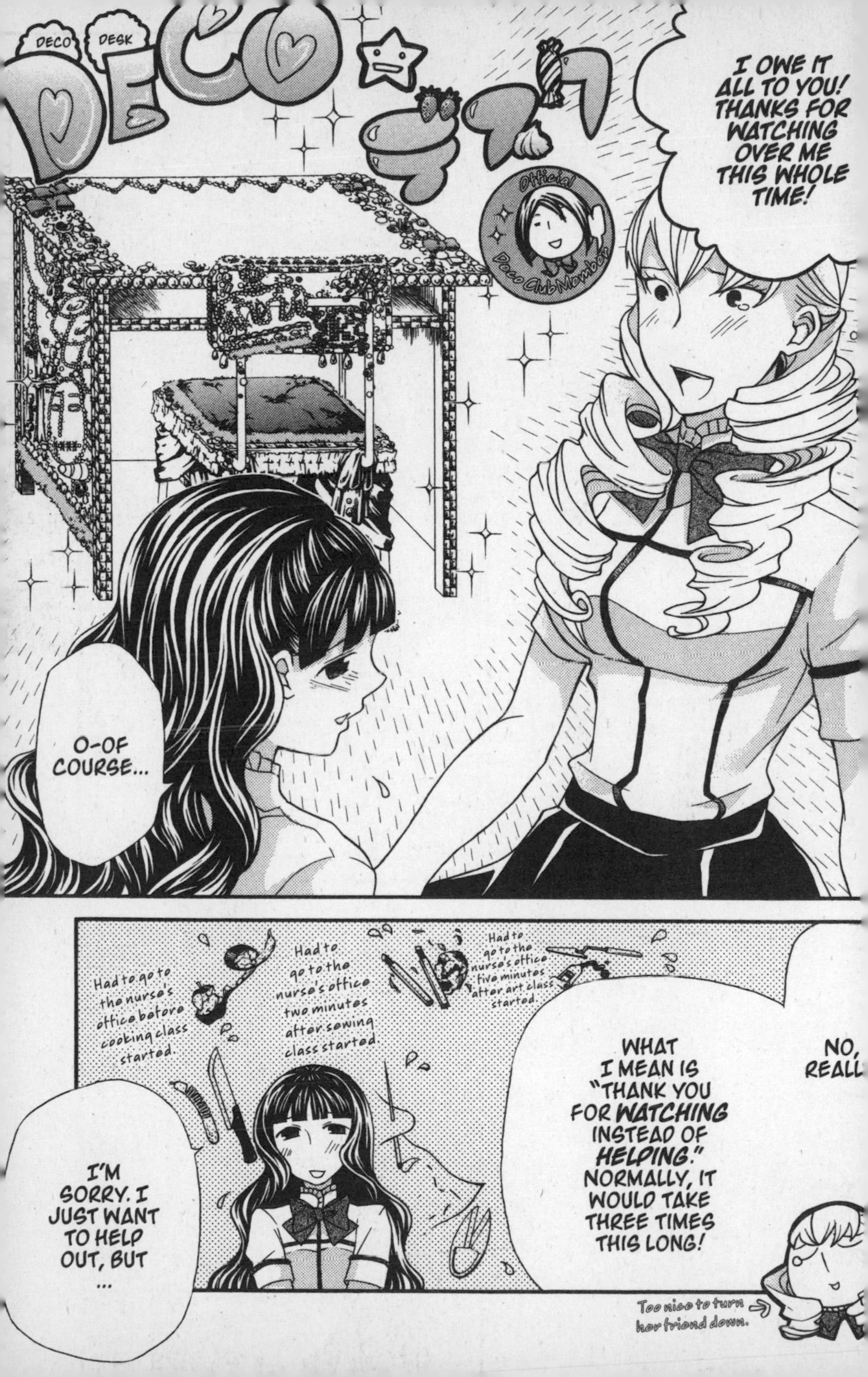
I OWE IT ALL TO YOU! THANKS FOR WATCHING OVER ME THIS WHOLE TIME!
DECO DESK
DECO
Official Deco Club Member
O-OF COURSE...
NO, REALL
WHAT I MEAN IS "THANK YOU FOR WATCHING INSTEAD OF HELPING." NORMALLY, IT WOULD TAKE THREE TIMES THIS LONG!
Had to go to the nurse's office five minutes after art class started.
Had to go to the nurse's office two minutes after sewing class started.
Had to go to the nurse's office before cooking class started.
I'M SORRY. I JUST WANT TO HELP OUT, BUT ...
Too nice to turn her friend down.

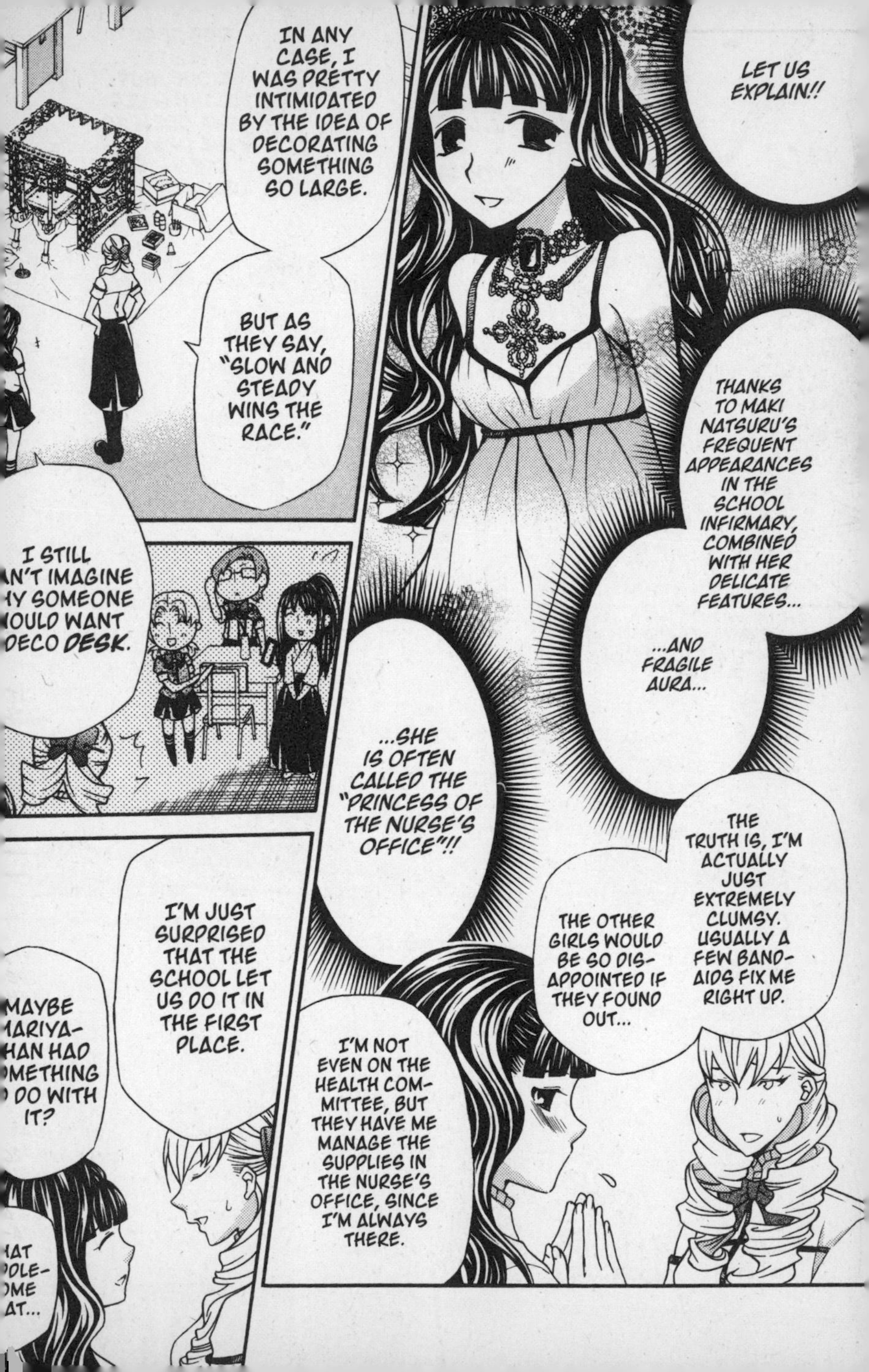
IN ANY CASE, I WAS PRETTY INTIMIDATED BY THE IDEA OF DECORATING SOMETHING SO LARGE.
BUT AS THEY SAY, "SLOW AND STEADY WINS THE RACE."
I STILL AN'T IMAGINE HY SOMEONE OULD WANT DECO DESK.
I'M JUST SURPRISED THAT THE SCHOOL LET US DO IT IN THE FIRST PLACE.
MAYBE MARIYA-HAN HAD METHING DO WITH IT?
HAT POLE-OME AT...
LET US EXPLAIN!!
THANKS TO MAKI NATSURU'S FREQUENT APPEARANCES IN THE SCHOOL INFIRMARY, COMBINED WITH HER DELICATE FEATURES...
...AND FRAGILE AURA...
...SHE IS OFTEN CALLED THE "PRINCESS OF THE NURSE'S OFFICE"!!
THE TRUTH IS, I'M ACTUALLY JUST EXTREMELY CLUMSY. USUALLY A FEW BAND-AIDS FIX ME RIGHT UP.
THE OTHER GIRLS WOULD BE SO DIS-APPOINTED IF THEY FOUND OUT...
I'M NOT EVEN ON THE HEALTH COM-MITTEE, BUT THEY HAVE ME MANAGE THE SUPPLIES IN THE NURSE'S OFFICE, SINCE I'M ALWAYS THERE.

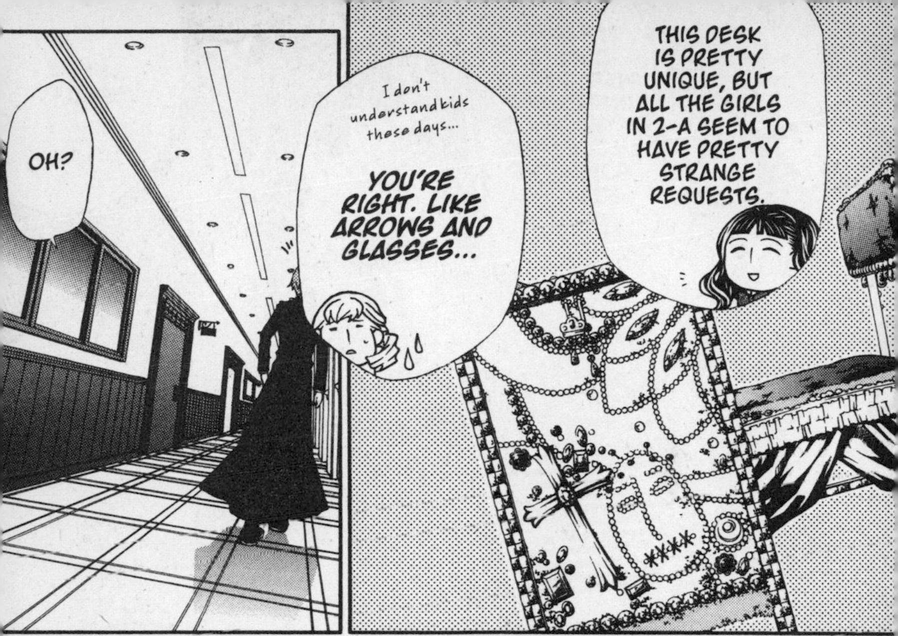
THIS DESK IS PRETTY UNIQUE, BUT ALL THE GIRLS IN 2-A SEEM TO HAVE PRETTY STRANGE REQUESTS.
I don't understand kids these days...
YOU'RE RIGHT. LIKE ARROWS AND GLASSES...
OH?

※ A four character saying that expresses how the inner beauty of someone shines through to the exterior.

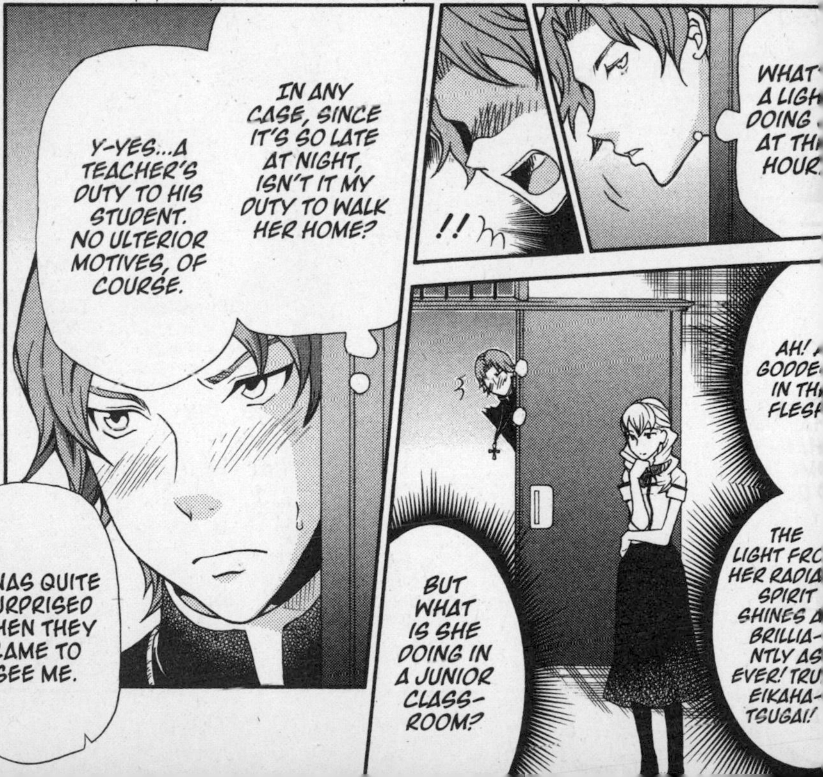
WHAT' A LIGH DOING AT TH HOUR.
!!
AH! A GODDE IN TH FLESH
THE LIGHT FRO HER RADIA SPIRIT SHINES A BRILLIA-NTLY AS EVER! TRU EIKAHA-TSUGAI!
BUT WHAT IS SHE DOING IN A JUNIOR CLASS-ROOM?
IN ANY CASE, SINCE IT'S SO LATE AT NIGHT, ISN'T IT MY DUTY TO WALK HER HOME?
Y-YES...A TEACHER'S DUTY TO HIS STUDENT. NO ULTERIOR MOTIVES, OF COURSE.
I WAS QUITE SURPRISED WHEN THEY CAME TO SEE ME.

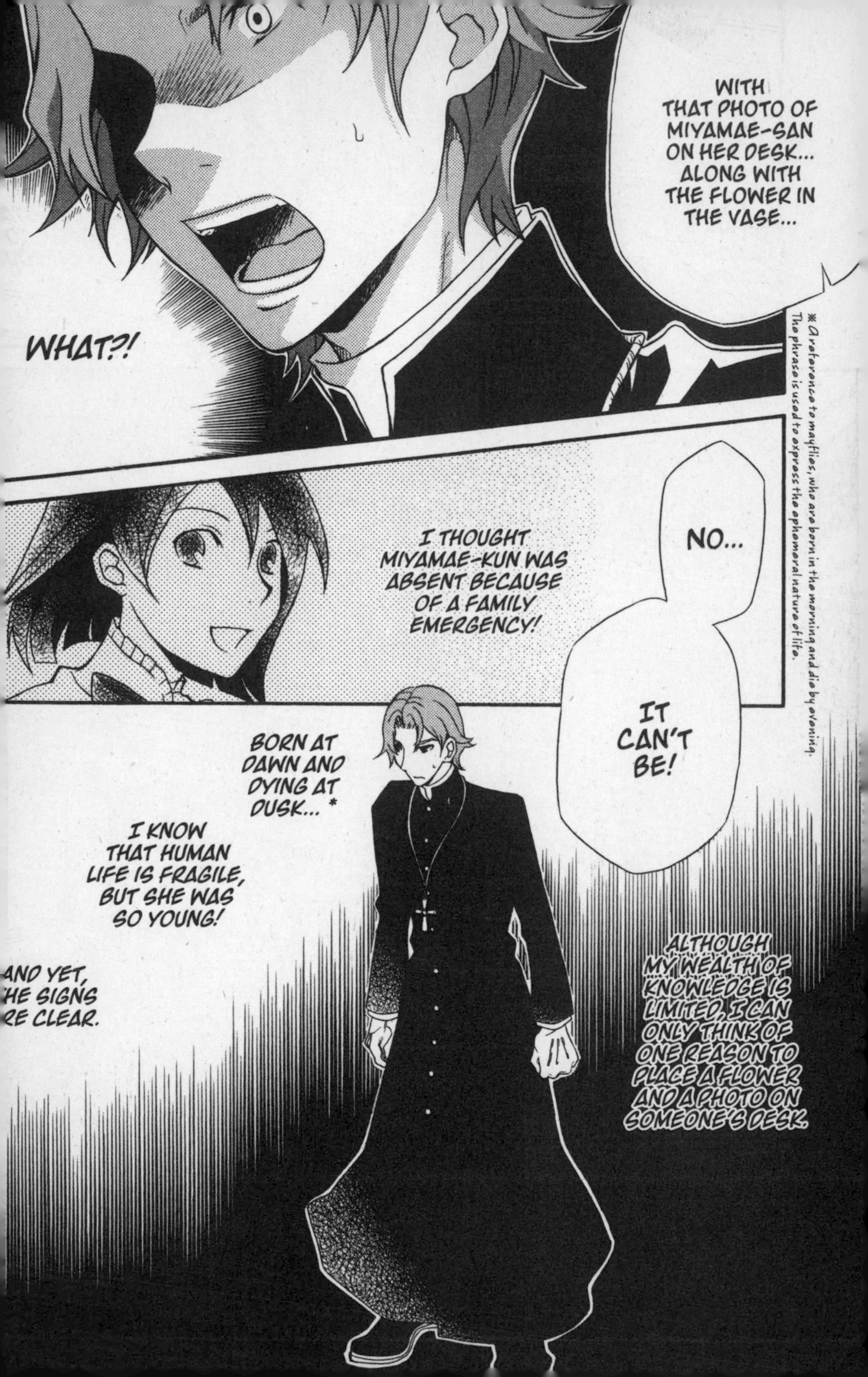
WITH THAT PHOTO OF MIYAMAE-SAN ON HER DESK... ALONG WITH THE FLOWER IN THE VASE...
WHAT?!
NO...
I THOUGHT MIYAMAE-KUN WAS ABSENT BECAUSE OF A FAMILY EMERGENCY!
IT CAN'T BE!
BORN AT DAWN AND DYING AT DUSK... *
I KNOW THAT HUMAN LIFE IS FRAGILE, BUT SHE WAS SO YOUNG!
ALTHOUGH MY WEALTH OF KNOWLEDGE IS LIMITED, I CAN ONLY THINK OF ONE REASON TO PLACE A FLOWER AND A PHOTO ON SOMEONE'S DESK.
AND YET,
HE SIGNS
RE CLEAR.

※ A reference to mayflies, who are born in the morning and die by evening. The phrase is used to express the ephemeral nature of life.

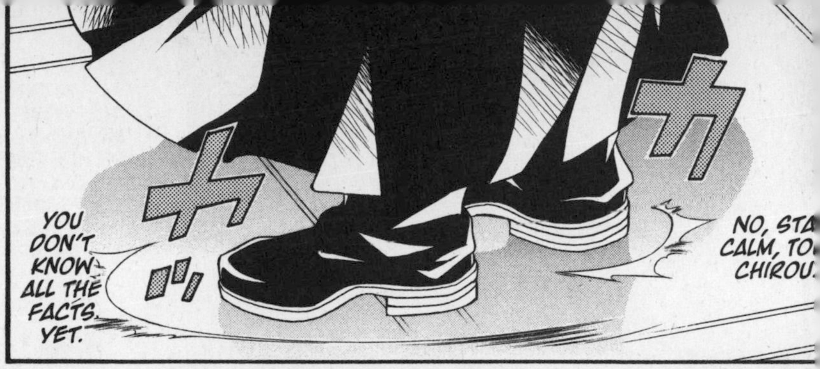
NO, STA
CALM, TO
CHIROU.
YOU DON'T KNOW ALL THE FACTS YET.

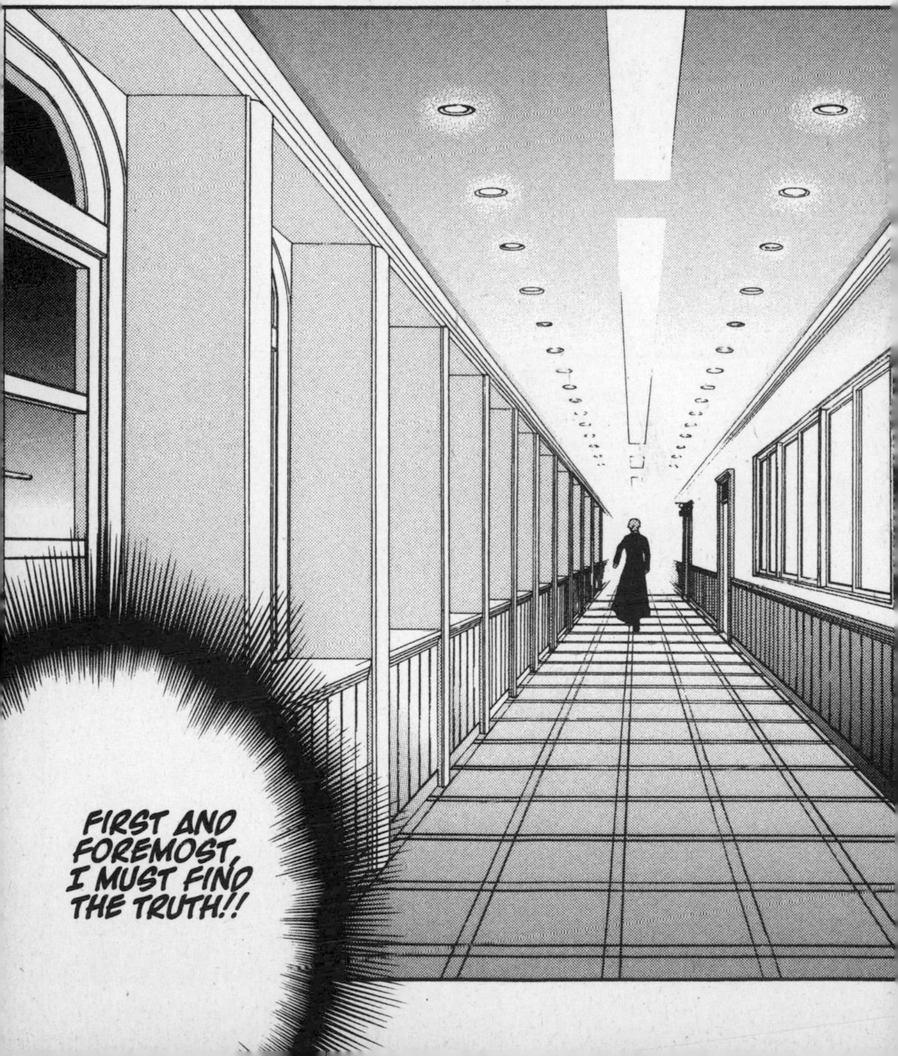
FIRST AND FOREMOST, I MUST FIND THE TRUTH!!

A R I A H O L I C

Maria Holic

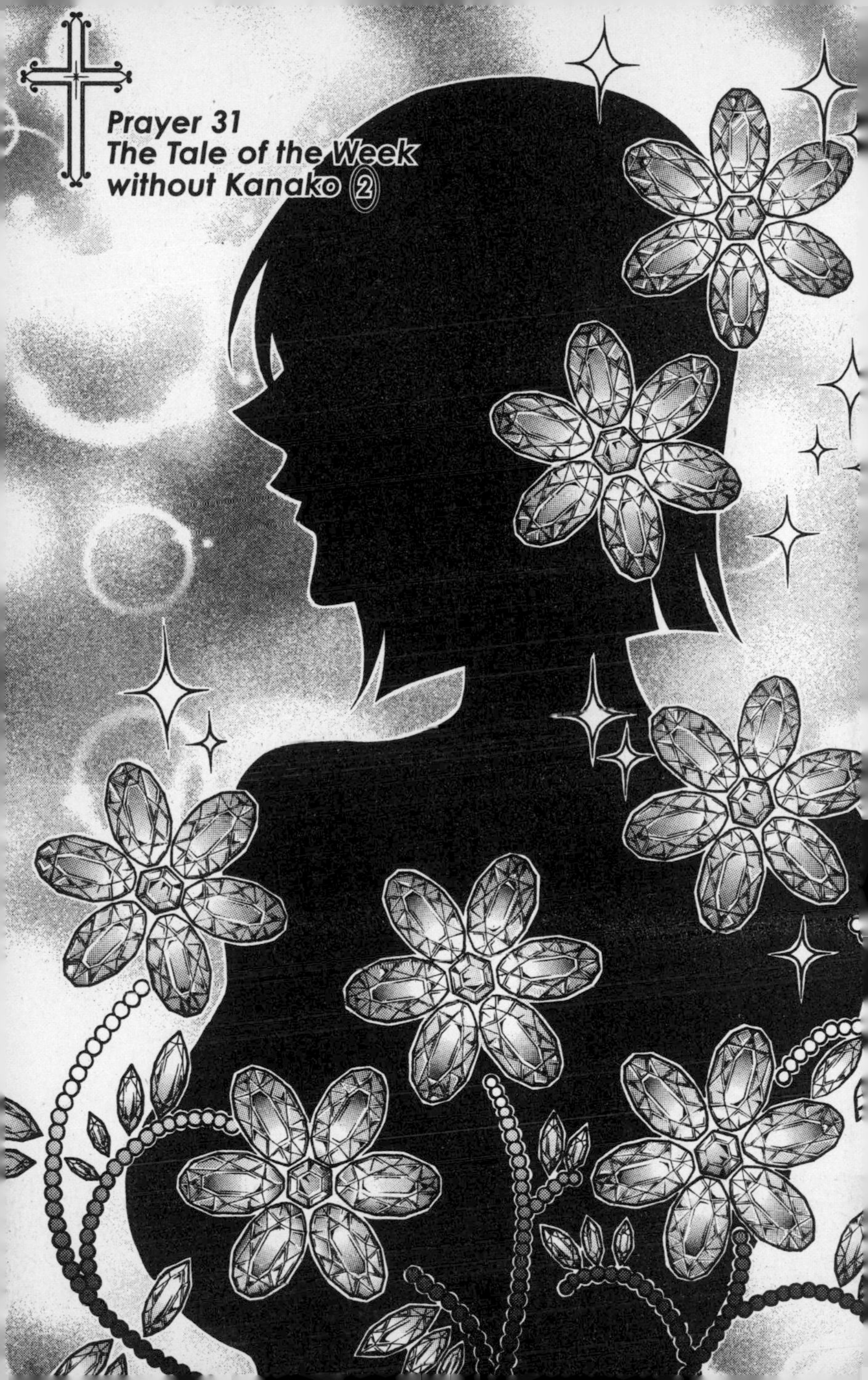
Prayer 31
The Tale of the Week
without Kanako 2

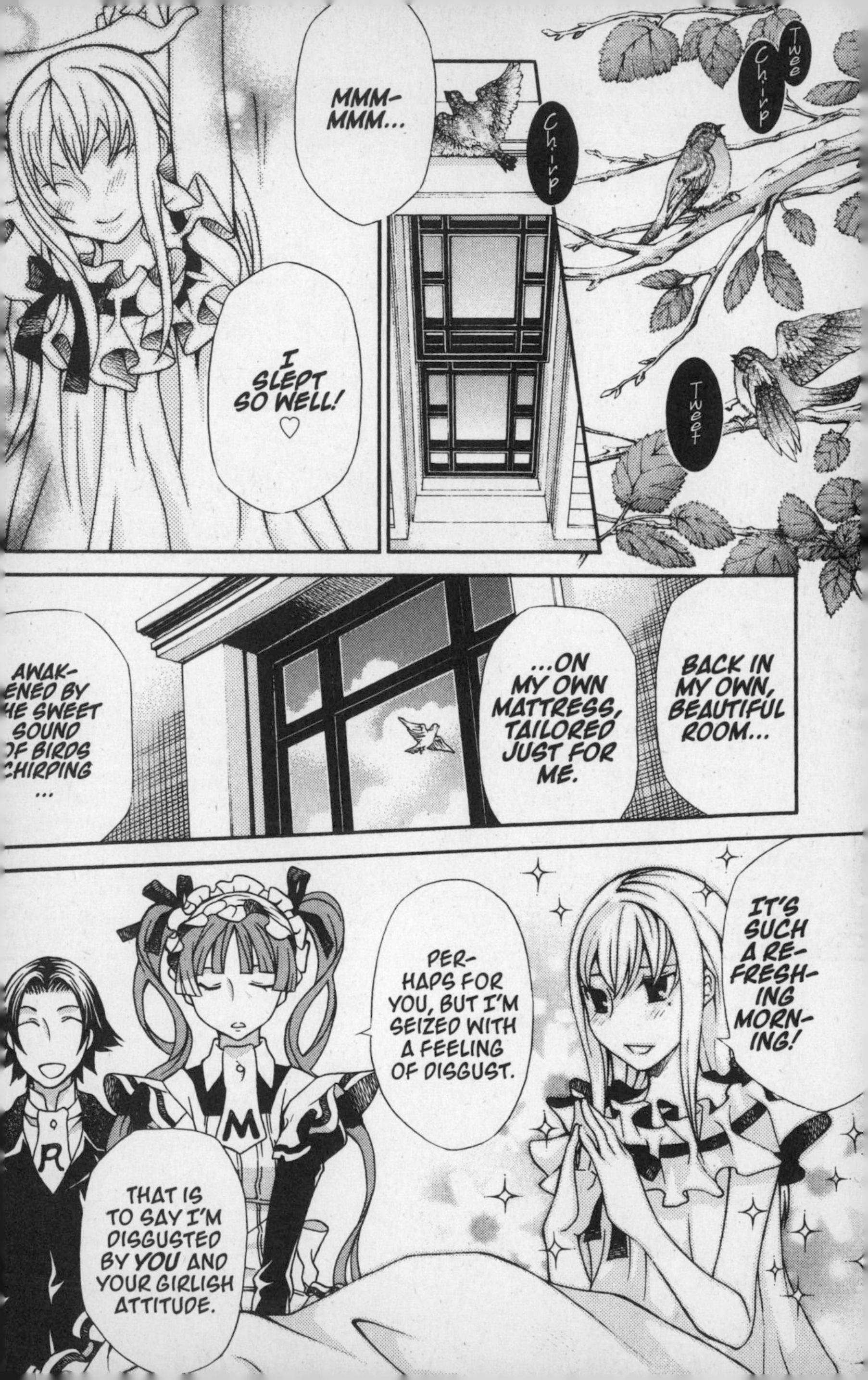
Twee
Chirp
Chirp
Tweet
MMM-MMM...
I SLEPT SO WELL! ♡
BACK IN MY OWN, BEAUTIFUL ROOM...
...ON MY OWN MATTRESS, TAILORED JUST FOR ME.
AWAK-ENED BY HE SWEET SOUND OF BIRDS CHIRPING ...
IT'S SUCH A RE-FRESH-ING MORN-ING!
PER-HAPS FOR YOU, BUT I'M SEIZED WITH A FEELING OF DISGUST.
THAT IS TO SAY I'M DISGUSTED BY *YOU* AND YOUR GIRLISH ATTITUDE.

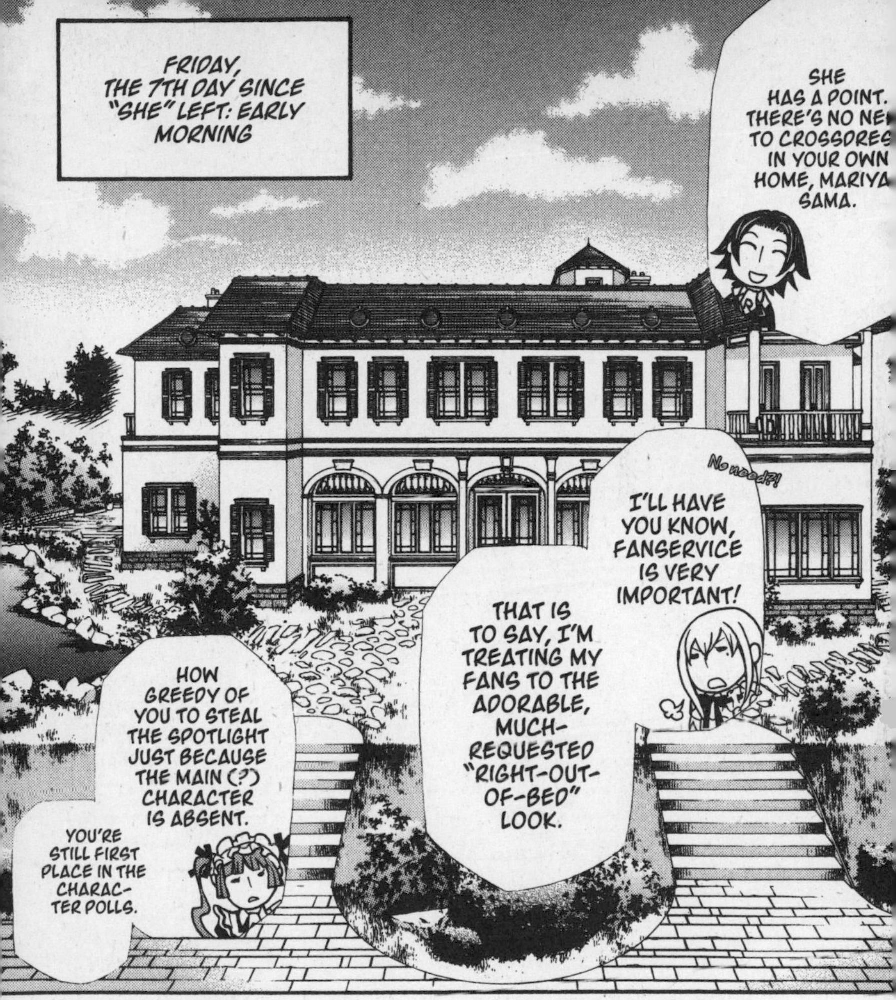
FRIDAY, THE 7TH DAY SINCE "SHE" LEFT: EARLY MORNING
SHE HAS A POINT. THERE'S NO NE TO CROSSDRES IN YOUR OWN HOME, MARIYA SAMA.
No need?!
I'LL HAVE YOU KNOW, FANSERVICE IS VERY IMPORTANT!
THAT IS TO SAY, I'M TREATING MY FANS TO THE ADORABLE, MUCH-REQUESTED "RIGHT-OUT-OF-BED" LOOK.
HOW GREEDY OF YOU TO STEAL THE SPOTLIGHT JUST BECAUSE THE MAIN (?) CHARACTER IS ABSENT.
YOU'RE STILL FIRST PLACE IN THE CHARACTER POLLS.
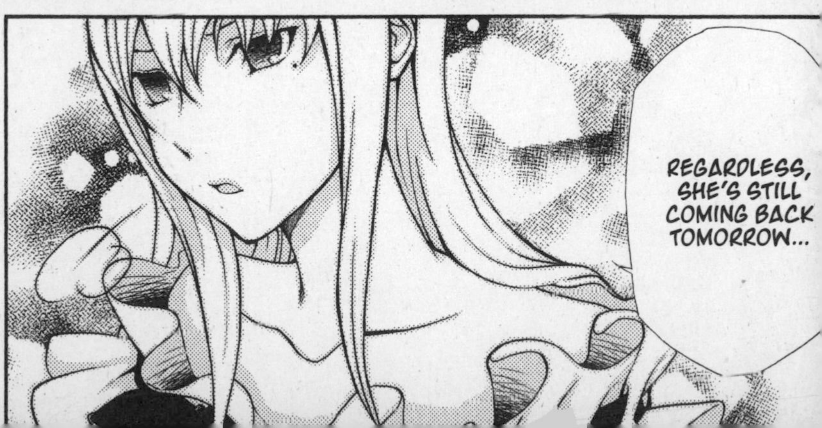
REGARDLESS, SHE'S STILL COMING BACK TOMORROW...

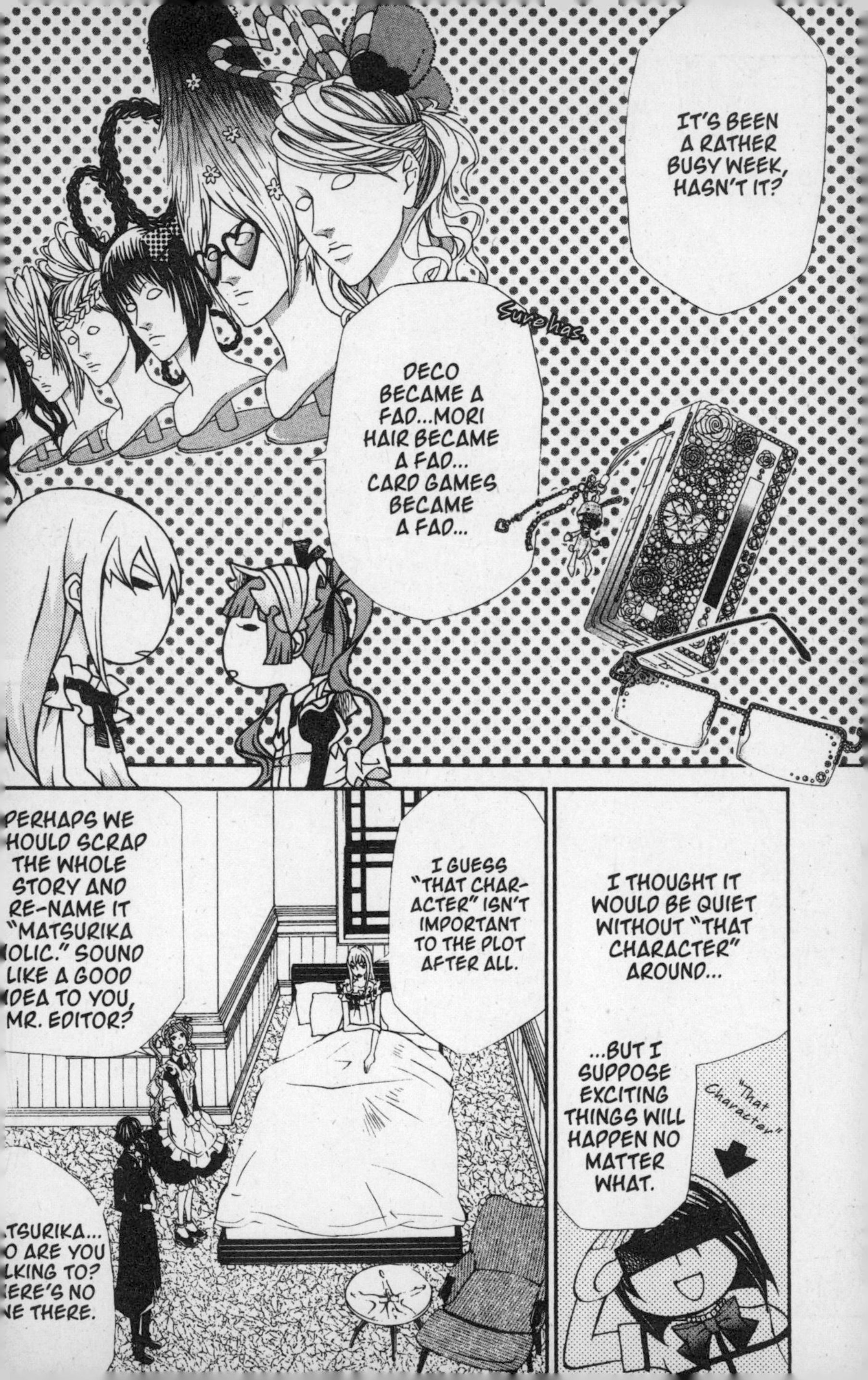
IT'S BEEN A RATHER BUSY WEEK, HASN'T IT?
Sure has.
DECO BECAME A FAD...MORI HAIR BECAME A FAD... CARD GAMES BECAME A FAD...
I THOUGHT IT WOULD BE QUIET WITHOUT "THAT CHARACTER" AROUND...
...BUT I SUPPOSE EXCITING THINGS WILL HAPPEN NO MATTER WHAT.
"That Character"
I GUESS "THAT CHAR-ACTER" ISN'T IMPORTANT TO THE PLOT AFTER ALL.
PERHAPS WE HOULD SCRAP THE WHOLE STORY AND RE-NAME IT "MATSURIKA OLIC." SOUND LIKE A GOOD DEA TO YOU, MR. EDITOR?
TSURIKA... O ARE YOU LKING TO? ERE'S NO NE THERE.

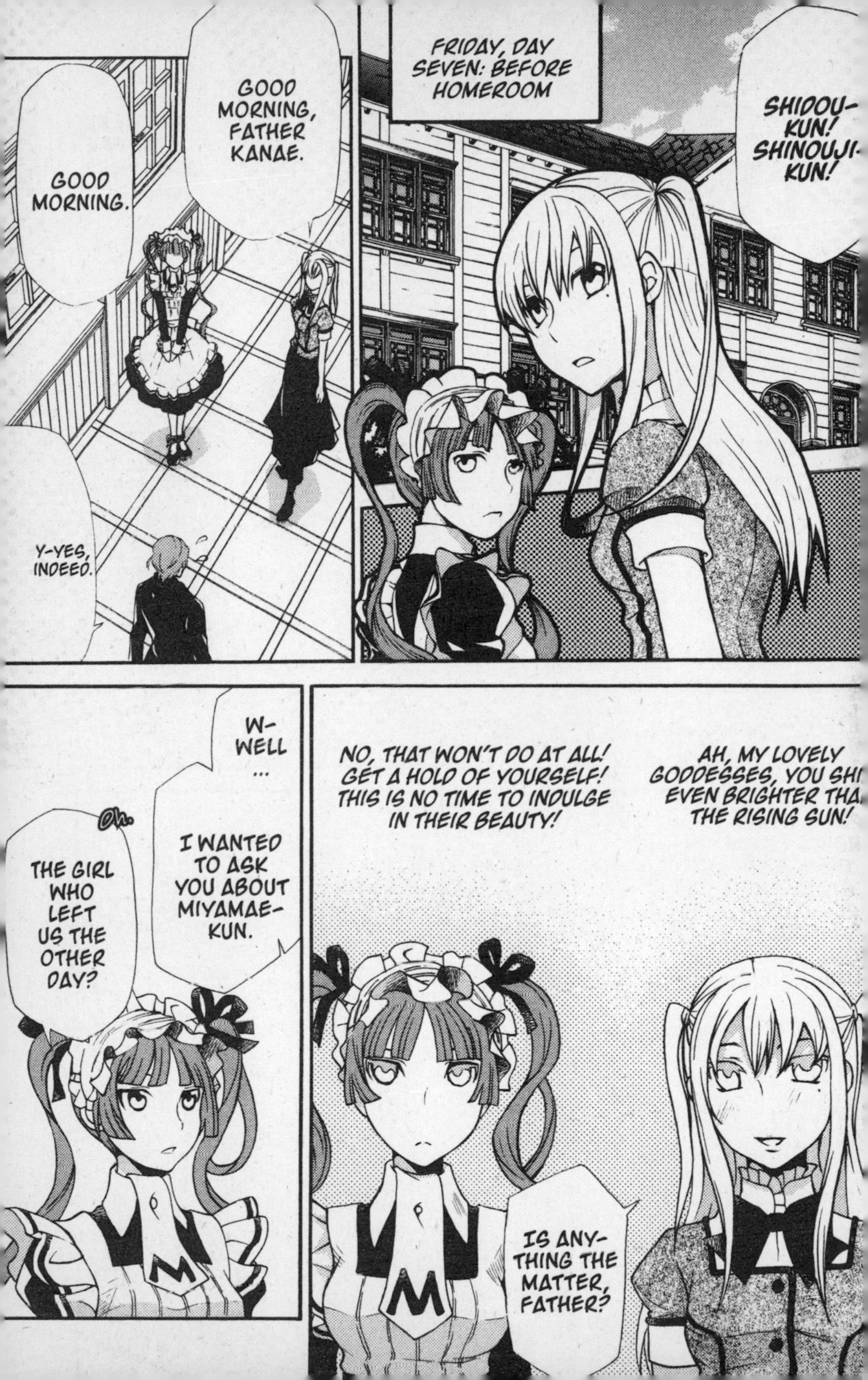
FRIDAY, DAY SEVEN: BEFORE HOMEROOM
SHIDOU-KUN! SHINOUJI-KUN!
GOOD MORNING, FATHER KANAE.
GOOD MORNING.
Y-YES, INDEED.
AH, MY LOVELY GODDESSES, YOU SHI EVEN BRIGHTER THA THE RISING SUN!
NO, THAT WON'T DO AT ALL! GET A HOLD OF YOURSELF! THIS IS NO TIME TO INDULGE IN THEIR BEAUTY!
IS ANYTHING THE MATTER, FATHER?
W-WELL ...
I WANTED TO ASK YOU ABOUT MIYAMAE-KUN.
Oh.
THE GIRL WHO LEFT US THE OTHER DAY?

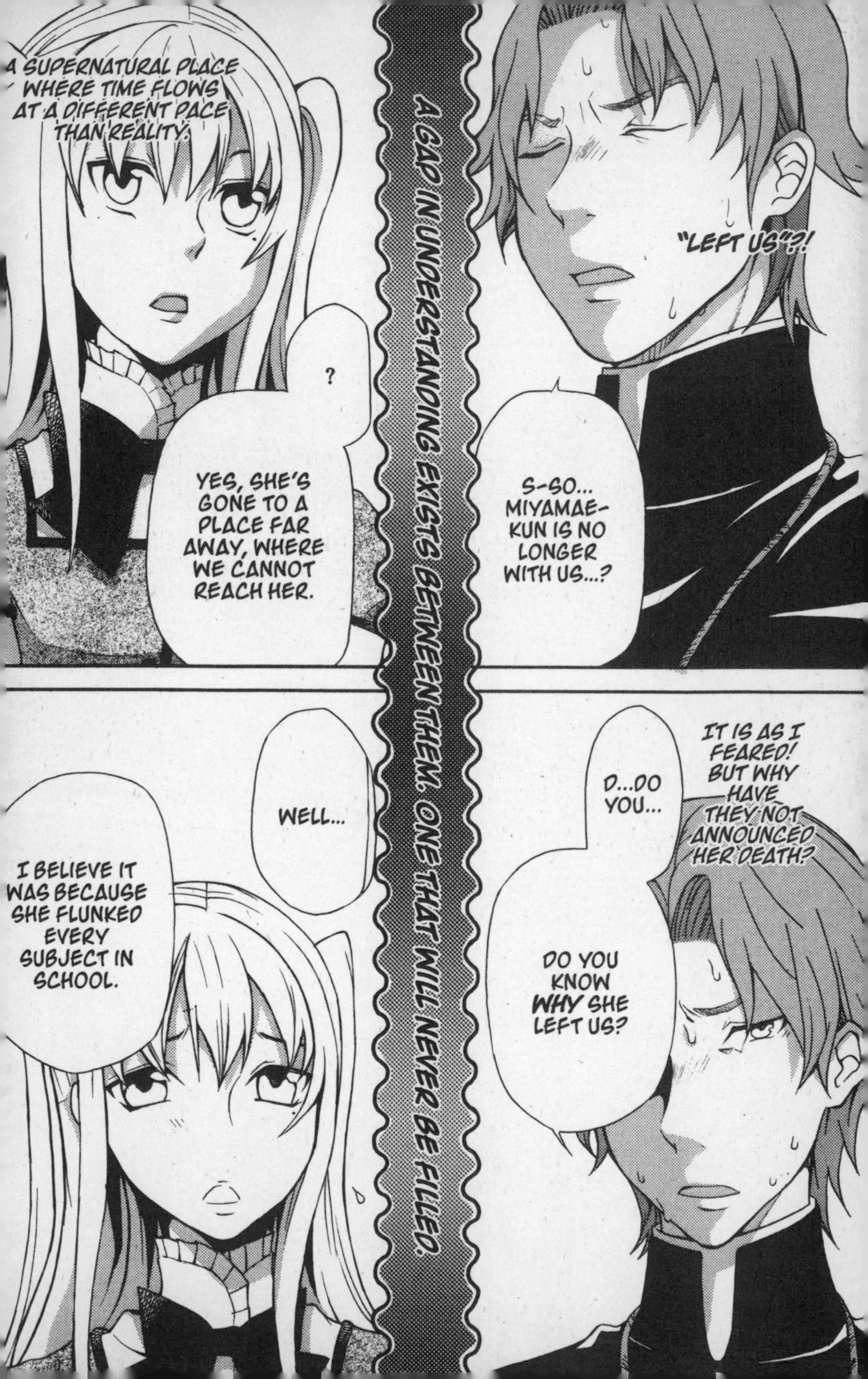
"LEFT US"?!
S-SO... MIYAMAE-KUN IS NO LONGER WITH US...?
?
YES, SHE'S GONE TO A PLACE FAR AWAY, WHERE WE CANNOT REACH HER.
A SUPERNATURAL PLACE WHERE TIME FLOWS AT A DIFFERENT PACE THAN REALITY.
IT IS AS I FEARED! BUT WHY HAVE THEY NOT ANNOUNCED HER DEATH?
D...DO YOU...
DO YOU KNOW WHY SHE LEFT US?
WELL...
I BELIEVE IT WAS BECAUSE SHE FLUNKED EVERY SUBJECT IN SCHOOL.
A GAP IN UNDERSTANDING EXISTS BETWEEN THEM. ONE THAT WILL NEVER BE FILLED.

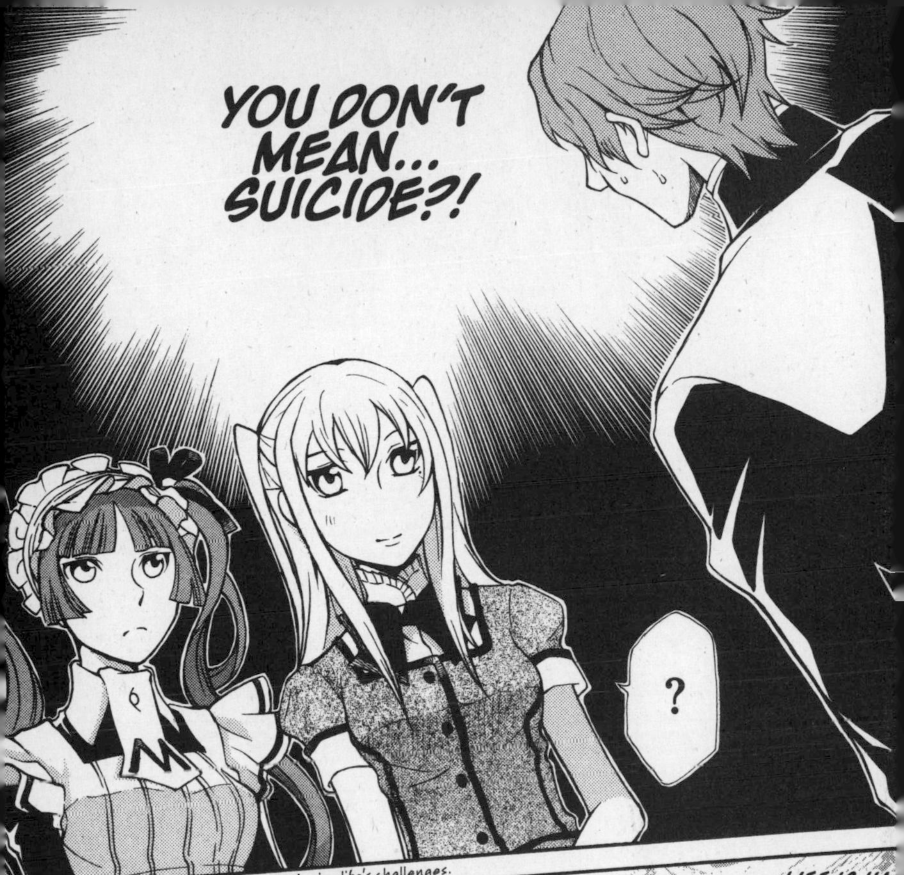
YOU DON'T MEAN... SUICIDE?!
?

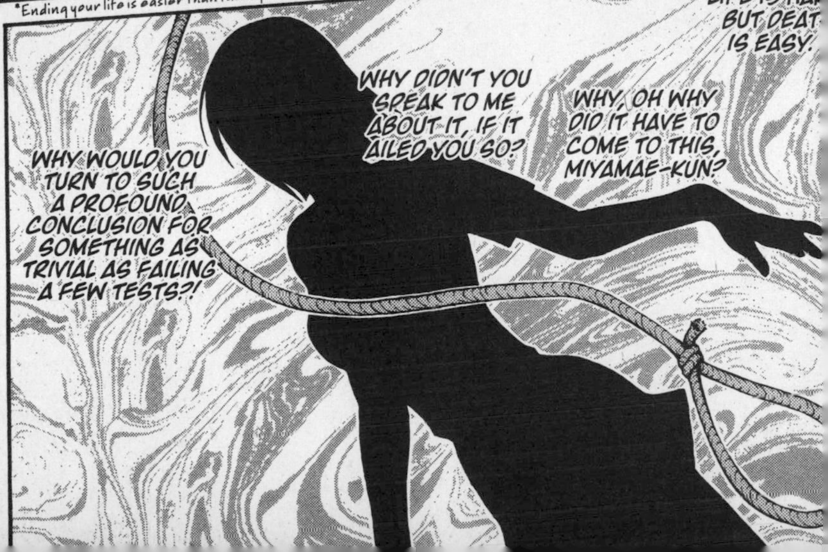
LIFE IS HA
BUT DEAT
IS EASY.
WHY, OH WHY DID IT HAVE TO COME TO THIS, MIYAMAE-KUN?
WHY DIDN'T YOU SPEAK TO ME ABOUT IT, IF IT AILED YOU SO?
WHY WOULD YOU TURN TO SUCH A PROFOUND CONCLUSION FOR SOMETHING AS TRIVIAL AS FAILING A FEW TESTS?!

*Ending your life is easier than facing life's challenges.

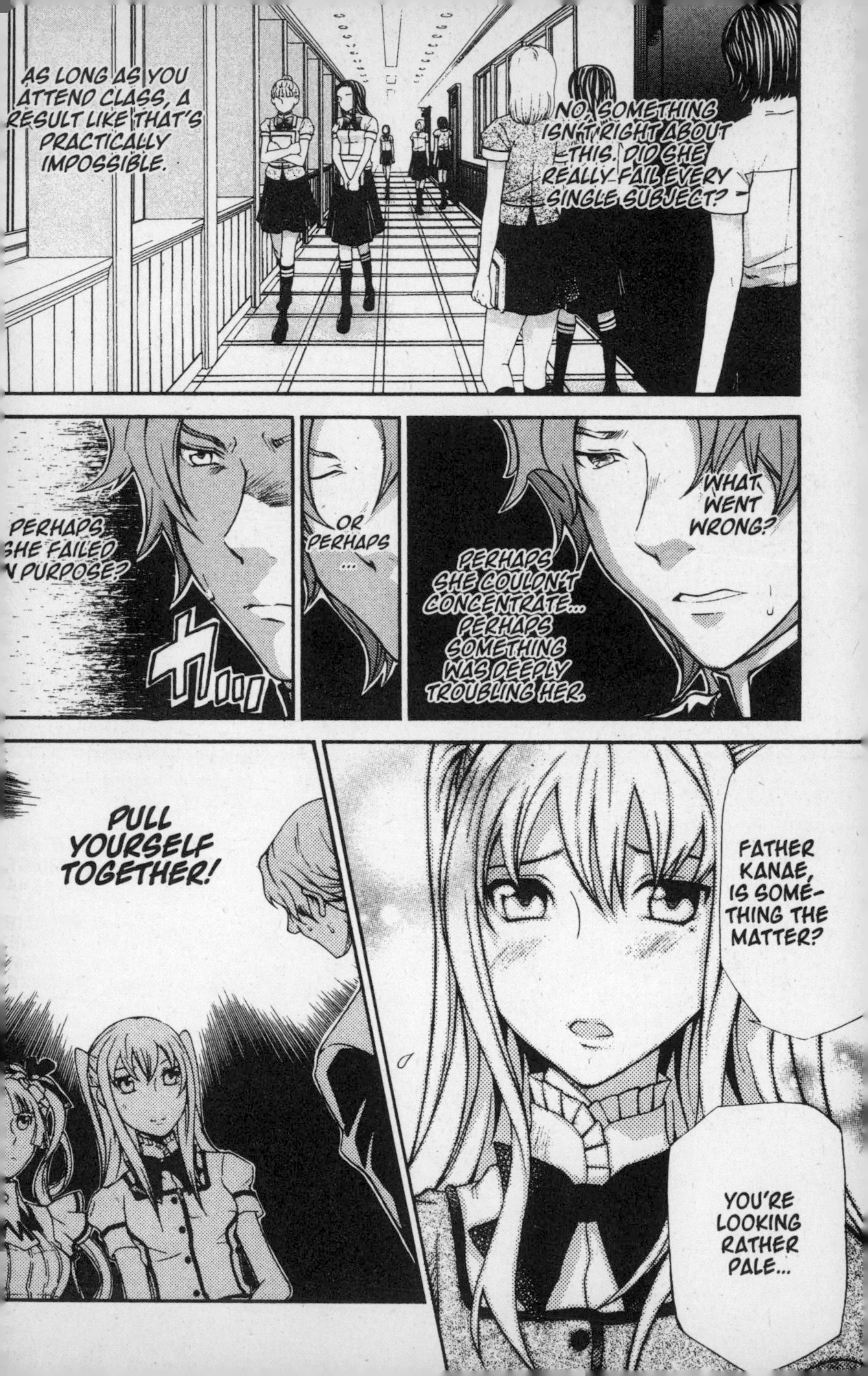
NO, SOMETHING ISN'T RIGHT ABOUT THIS. DID SHE REALLY FAIL EVERY SINGLE SUBJECT?
AS LONG AS YOU ATTEND CLASS, A RESULT LIKE THAT'S PRACTICALLY IMPOSSIBLE.
WHAT WENT WRONG?
PERHAPS SHE COULDN'T CONCENTRATE... PERHAPS SOMETHING WAS DEEPLY TROUBLING HER.
OR PERHAPS ...
PERHAPS SHE FAILED N PURPOSE?
FATHER KANAE, IS SOME-THING THE MATTER?
YOU'RE LOOKING RATHER PALE...
PULL YOURSELF TOGETHER!

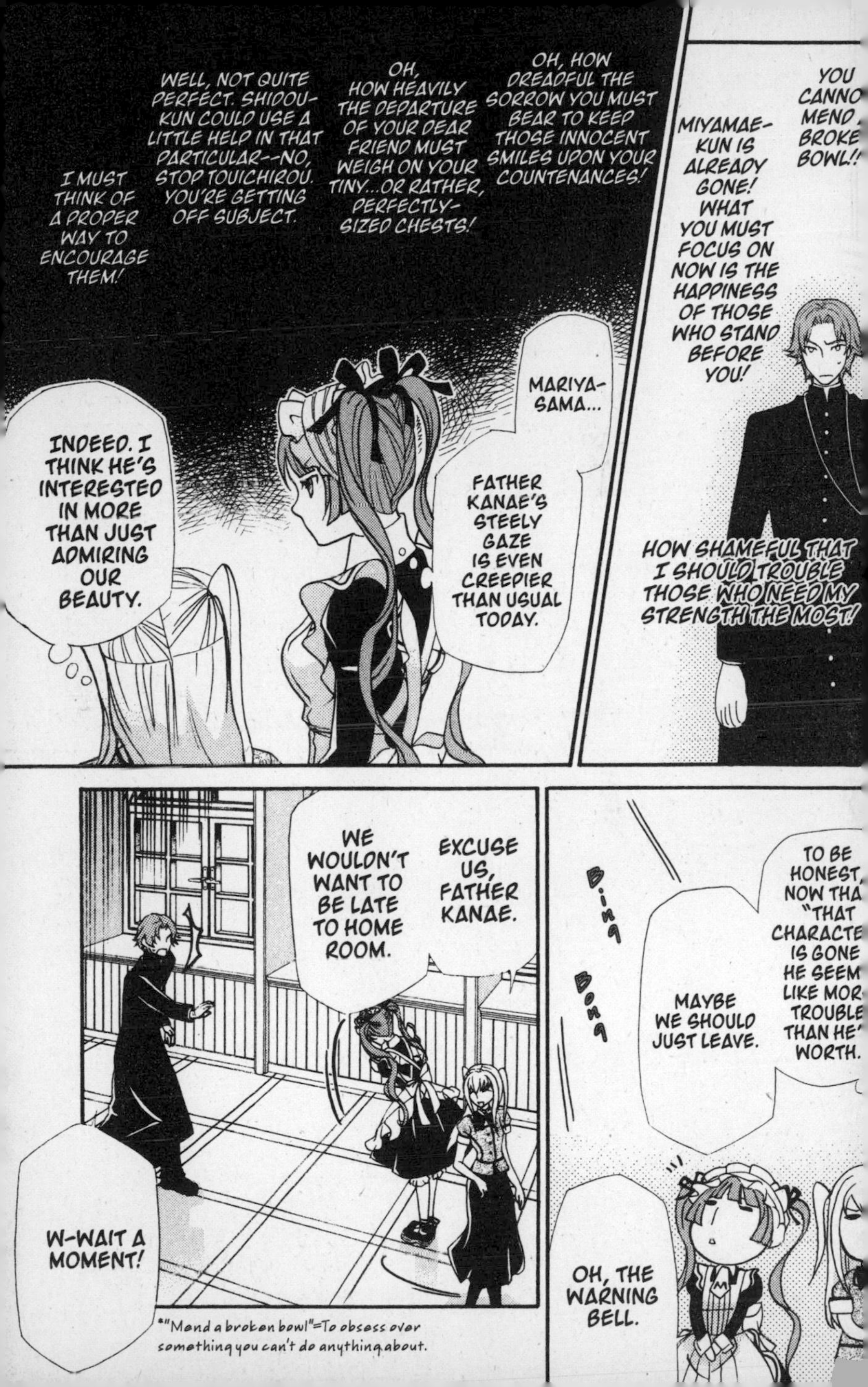
YOU CANNO MEND BROKE BOWL!!
MIYAMAE-KUN IS ALREADY GONE! WHAT YOU MUST FOCUS ON NOW IS THE HAPPINESS OF THOSE WHO STAND BEFORE YOU!
HOW SHAMEFUL THAT I SHOULD TROUBLE THOSE WHO NEED MY STRENGTH THE MOST!
OH, HOW DREADFUL THE SORROW YOU MUST BEAR TO KEEP THOSE INNOCENT SMILES UPON YOUR COUNTENANCES!
OH, HOW HEAVILY THE DEPARTURE OF YOUR DEAR FRIEND MUST WEIGH ON YOUR TINY...OR RATHER, PERFECTLY-SIZED CHESTS!
WELL, NOT QUITE PERFECT. SHIDOU-KUN COULD USE A LITTLE HELP IN THAT PARTICULAR--NO, STOP TOUICHIROU. YOU'RE GETTING OFF SUBJECT.
I MUST THINK OF A PROPER WAY TO ENCOURAGE THEM!
MARIYA-SAMA...
FATHER KANAE'S STEELY GAZE IS EVEN CREEPIER THAN USUAL TODAY.
INDEED. I THINK HE'S INTERESTED IN MORE THAN JUST ADMIRING OUR BEAUTY.
TO BE HONEST, NOW THA "THAT CHARACTE IS GONE HE SEEM LIKE MOR TROUBLE THAN HE' WORTH.
MAYBE WE SHOULD JUST LEAVE.
Bing
Bong
OH, THE WARNING BELL.
EXCUSE US, FATHER KANAE.
WE WOULDN'T WANT TO BE LATE TO HOME ROOM.
W-WAIT A MOMENT!
*"Mend a broken bowl"=To obsess over something you can't do anything about.

"Stone on the roadside"=Indicating something boring, ordinary and generally not worth noticing.

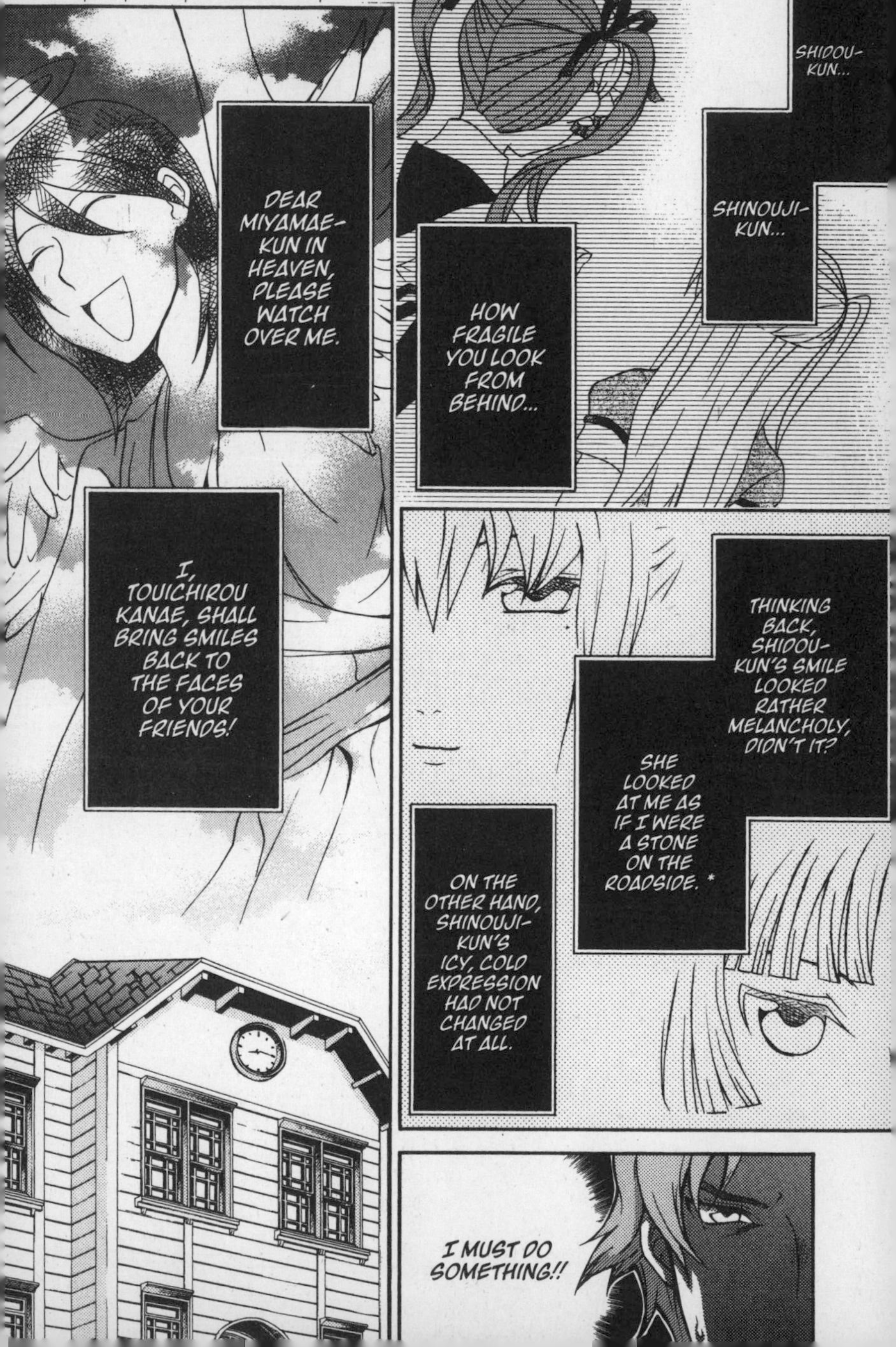
SHIDOU-KUN...
SHINOUJI-KUN...
HOW FRAGILE YOU LOOK FROM BEHIND...
DEAR MIYAMAE-KUN IN HEAVEN, PLEASE WATCH OVER ME.
I, TOUICHIROU KANAE, SHALL BRING SMILES BACK TO THE FACES OF YOUR FRIENDS!
THINKING BACK, SHIDOU-KUN'S SMILE LOOKED RATHER MELANCHOLY, DIDN'T IT?
SHE LOOKED AT ME AS IF I WERE A STONE ON THE ROADSIDE. *
ON THE OTHER HAND, SHINOUJI-KUN'S ICY, COLD EXPRESSION HAD NOT CHANGED AT ALL.
I MUST DO SOMETHING!!

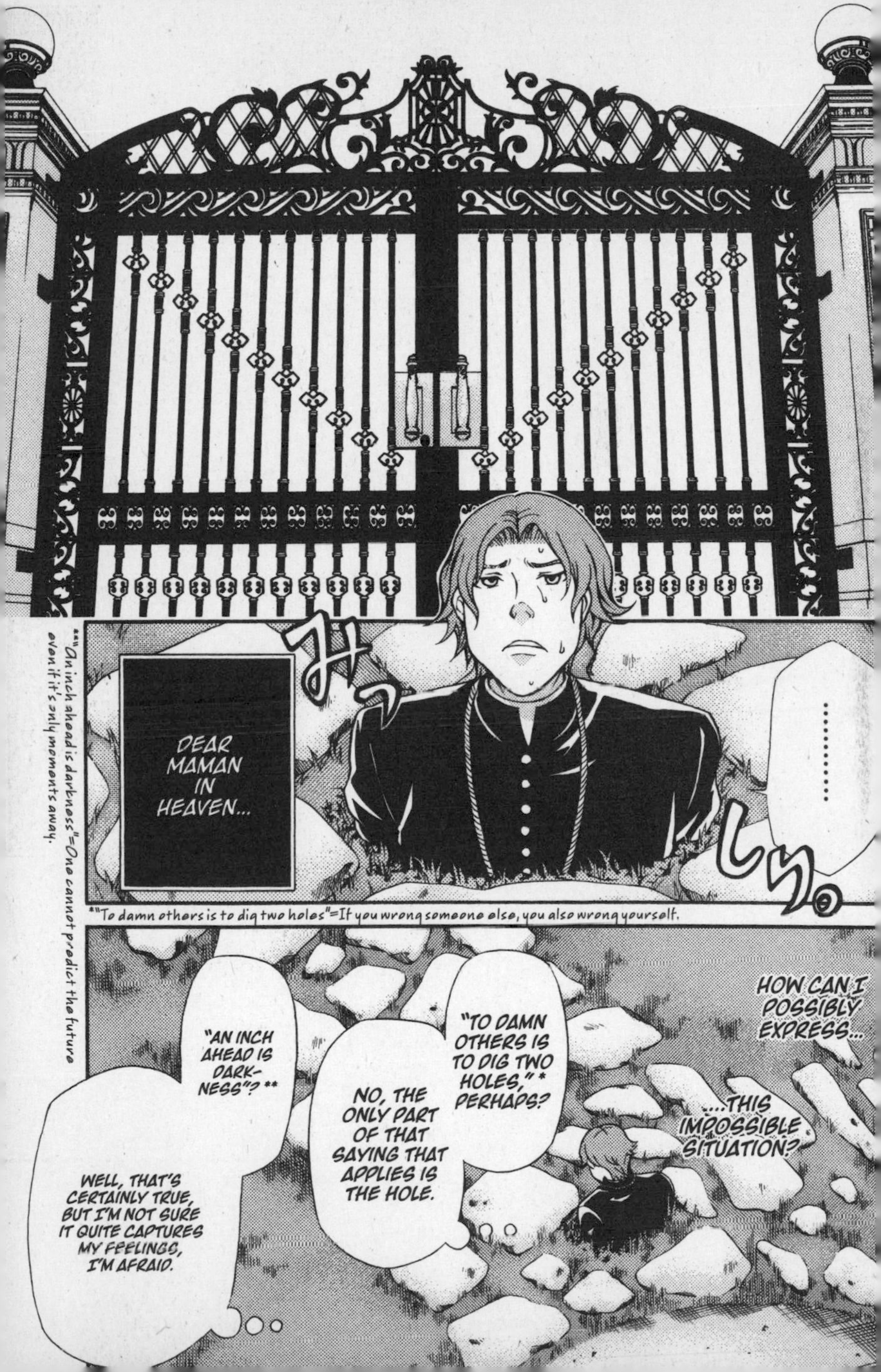

......
DEAR MAMAN IN HEAVEN...
HOW CAN I POSSIBLY EXPRESS...
...THIS IMPOSSIBLE SITUATION?
"TO DAMN OTHERS IS TO DIG TWO HOLES," * PERHAPS?
NO, THE ONLY PART OF THAT SAYING THAT APPLIES IS THE HOLE.
"AN INCH AHEAD IS DARKNESS"? **
WELL, THAT'S CERTAINLY TRUE, BUT I'M NOT SURE IT QUITE CAPTURES MY FEELINGS, I'M AFRAID.

*"To damn others is to dig two holes"=If you wrong someone else, you also wrong yourself.

**"An inch ahead is darkness"=One cannot predict the future even if it's only moments away.

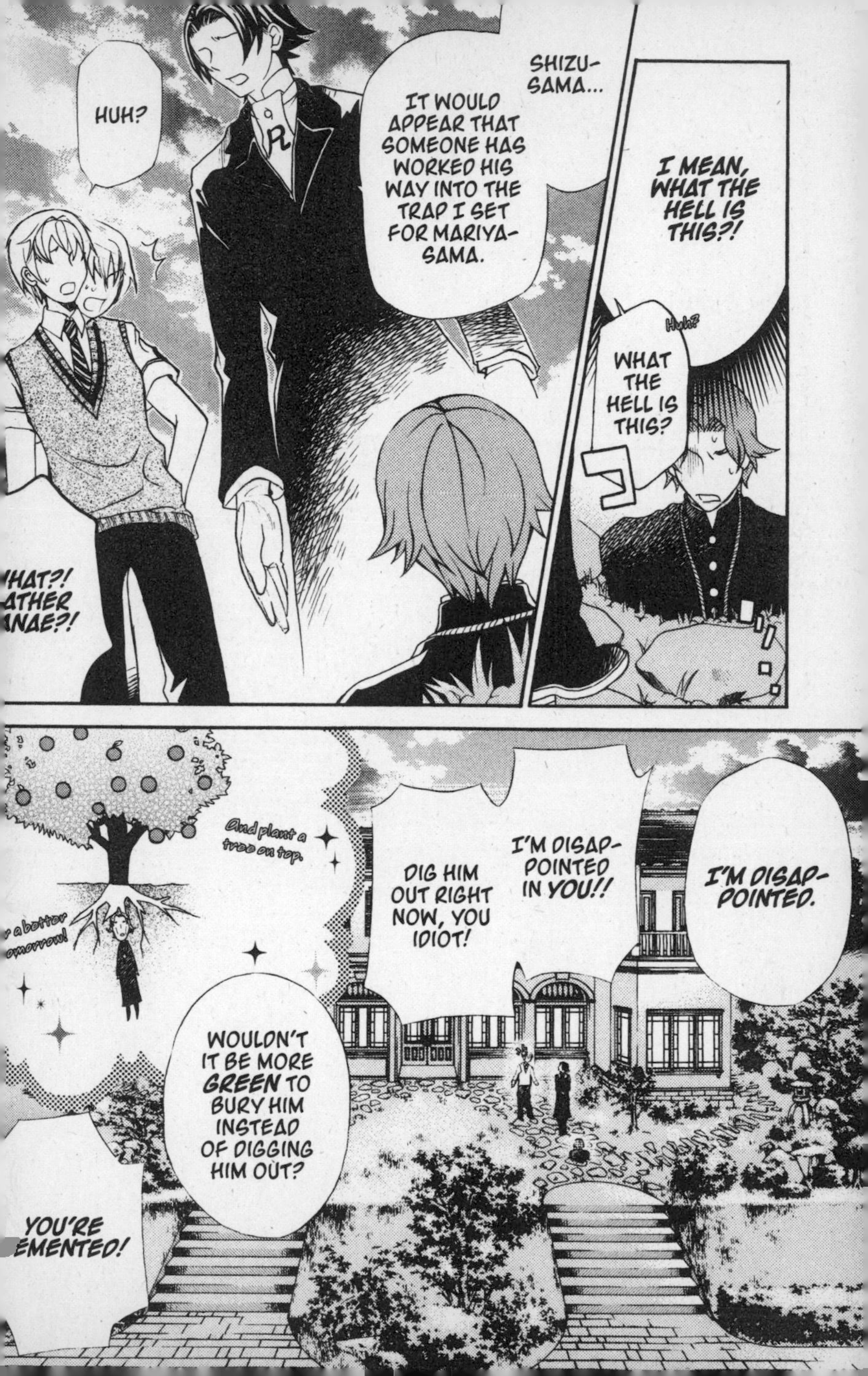
I MEAN, WHAT THE HELL IS THIS?!
Huh?
WHAT THE HELL IS THIS?
SHIZU-SAMA...
IT WOULD APPEAR THAT SOMEONE HAS WORKED HIS WAY INTO THE TRAP I SET FOR MARIYA-SAMA.
HUH?
HAT?! ATHER ANAE?!
I'M DISAP-POINTED.
I'M DISAP-POINTED IN YOU!!
DIG HIM OUT RIGHT NOW, YOU IDIOT!
WOULDN'T IT BE MORE GREEN TO BURY HIM INSTEAD OF DIGGING HIM OUT?
And plant a tree on top.
a better tomorrow!
YOU'RE EMENTED!

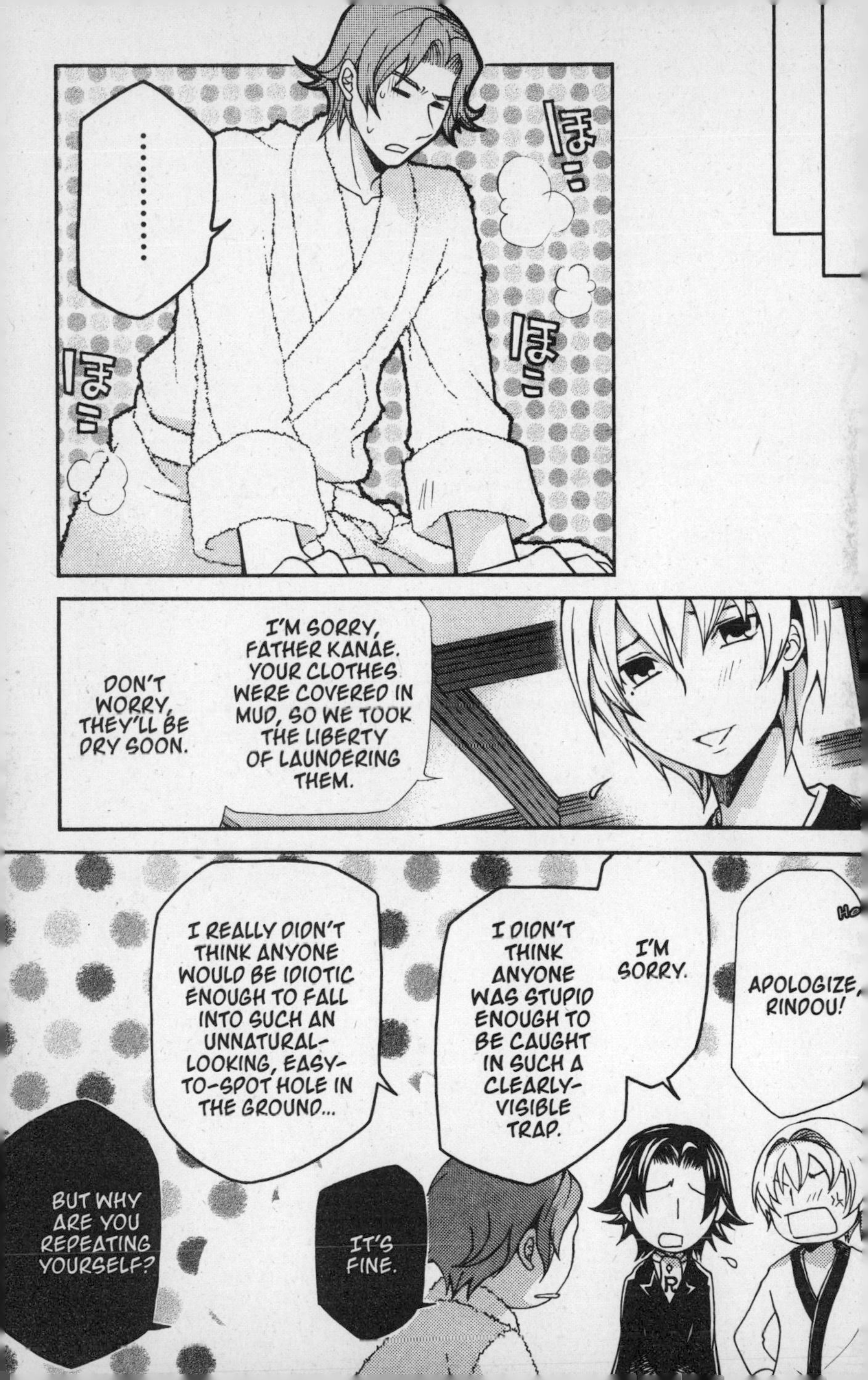
ほっ
ほっ
……
ほっ
I'M SORRY, FATHER KANAE. YOUR CLOTHES WERE COVERED IN MUD, SO WE TOOK THE LIBERTY OF LAUNDERING THEM.
DON'T WORRY, THEY'LL BE DRY SOON.
APOLOGIZE, RINDOU!
I'M SORRY.
I DIDN'T THINK ANYONE WAS STUPID ENOUGH TO BE CAUGHT IN SUCH A CLEARLY-VISIBLE TRAP.
I REALLY DIDN'T THINK ANYONE WOULD BE IDIOTIC ENOUGH TO FALL INTO SUCH AN UNNATURAL-LOOKING, EASY-TO-SPOT HOLE IN THE GROUND...
IT'S FINE.
BUT WHY ARE YOU REPEATING YOURSELF?

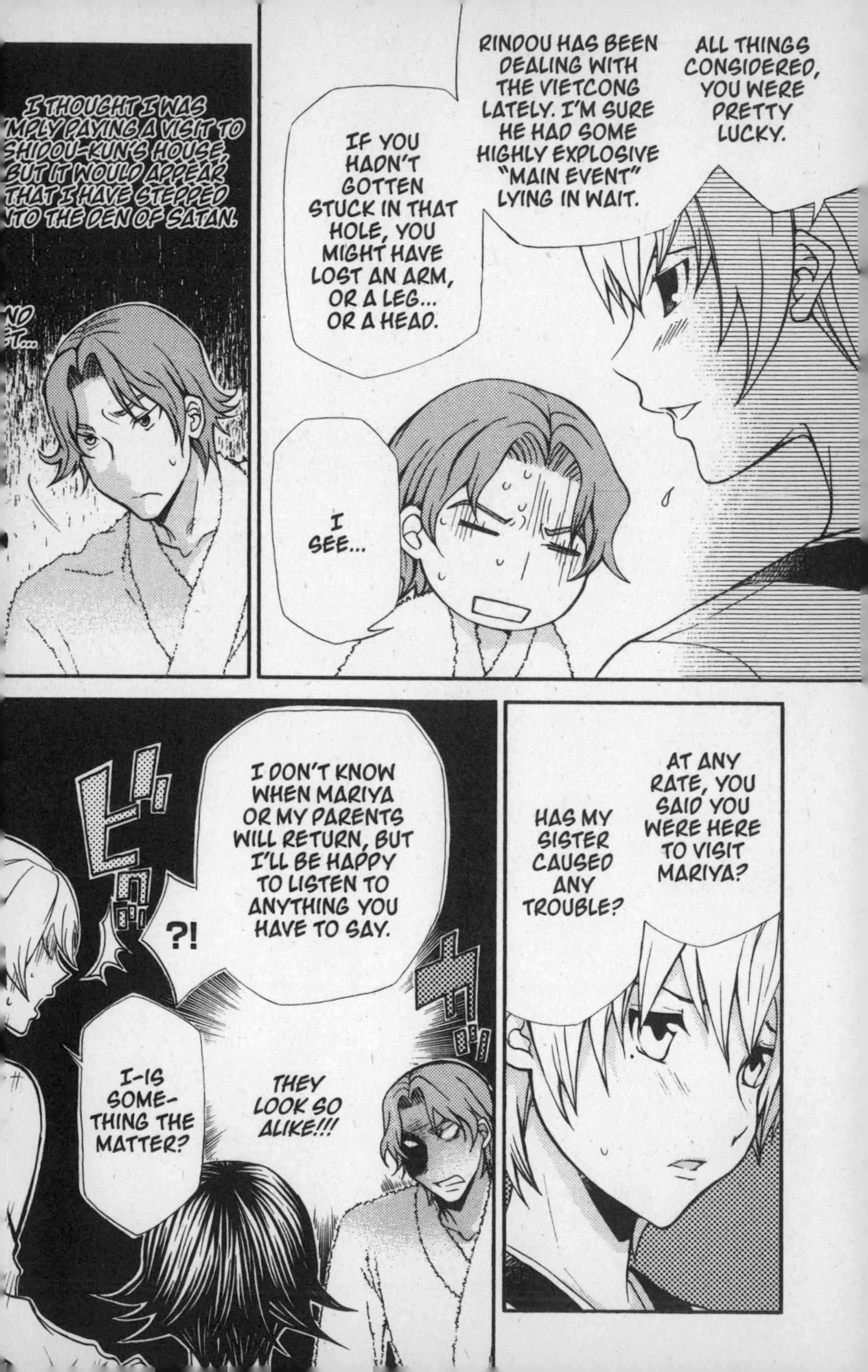
ALL THINGS CONSIDERED, YOU WERE PRETTY LUCKY.
RINDOU HAS BEEN DEALING WITH THE VIETCONG LATELY. I'M SURE HE HAD SOME HIGHLY EXPLOSIVE "MAIN EVENT" LYING IN WAIT.
IF YOU HADN'T GOTTEN STUCK IN THAT HOLE, YOU MIGHT HAVE LOST AN ARM, OR A LEG... OR A HEAD.
I SEE...
I THOUGHT I WAS MPLY PAYING A VISIT TO SHIDOU-KUN'S HOUSE, BUT IT WOULD APPEAR THAT I HAVE STEPPED NTO THE DEN OF SATAN.
AT ANY RATE, YOU SAID YOU WERE HERE TO VISIT MARIYA?
HAS MY SISTER CAUSED ANY TROUBLE?
I DON'T KNOW WHEN MARIYA OR MY PARENTS WILL RETURN, BUT I'LL BE HAPPY TO LISTEN TO ANYTHING YOU HAVE TO SAY.
?!
THEY LOOK SO ALIKE!!!
I-IS SOMETHING THE MATTER?

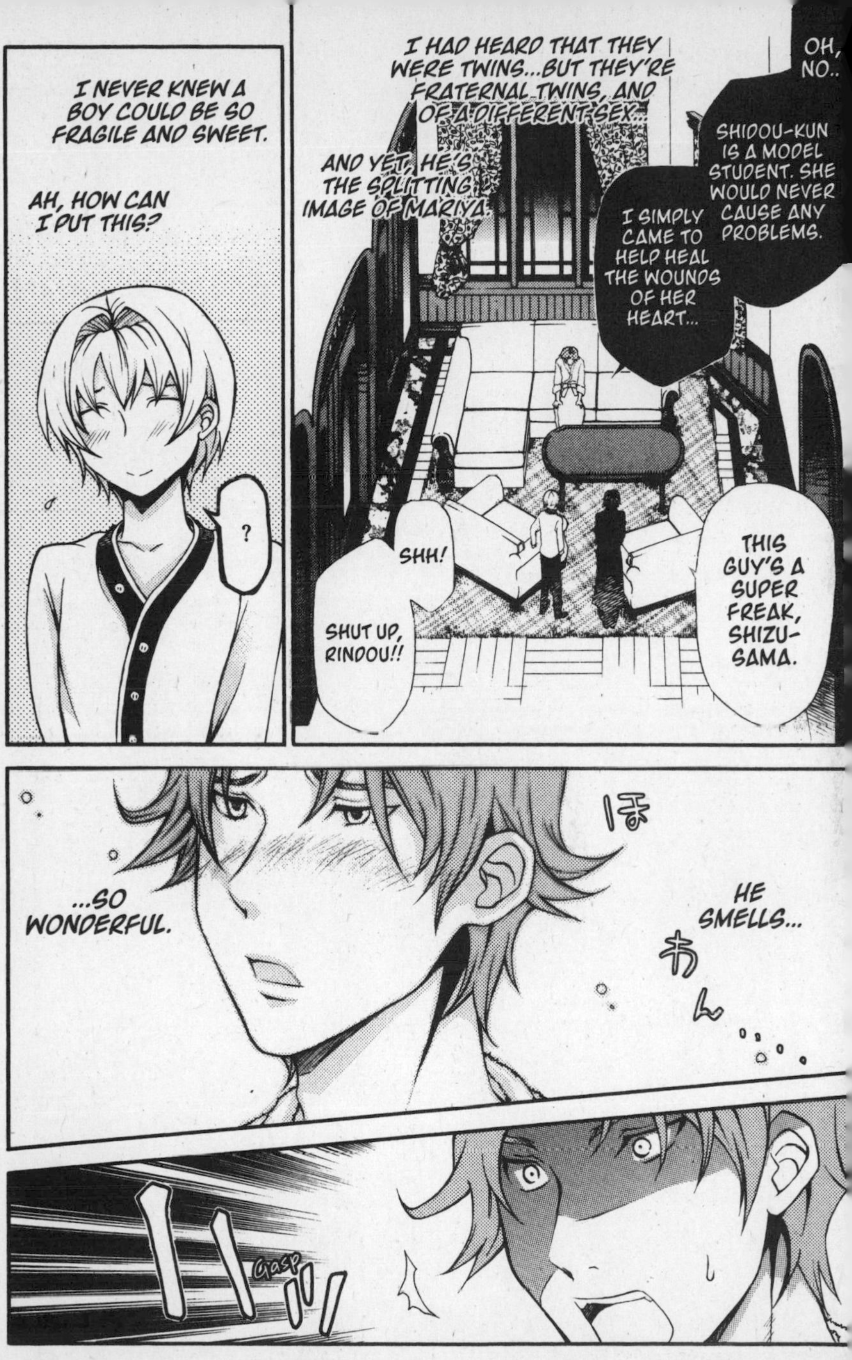

OH, NO..
SHIDOU-KUN IS A MODEL STUDENT. SHE WOULD NEVER CAUSE ANY PROBLEMS.
I SIMPLY CAME TO HELP HEAL THE WOUNDS OF HER HEART...
I HAD HEARD THAT THEY WERE TWINS...BUT THEY'RE FRATERNAL TWINS, AND OF A DIFFERENT SEX...
AND YET, HE'S THE SPLITTING IMAGE OF MARIYA.
THIS GUY'S A SUPER FREAK, SHIZU-SAMA.
SHH!
SHUT UP, RINDOU!!
I NEVER KNEW A BOY COULD BE SO FRAGILE AND SWEET.
AH, HOW CAN I PUT THIS?
?
ほわん
HE SMELLS...
...SO WONDERFUL.
Gasp

"Boys be ambitious"="See ya, mate. Good luck," in a William S. Clark kind of way.

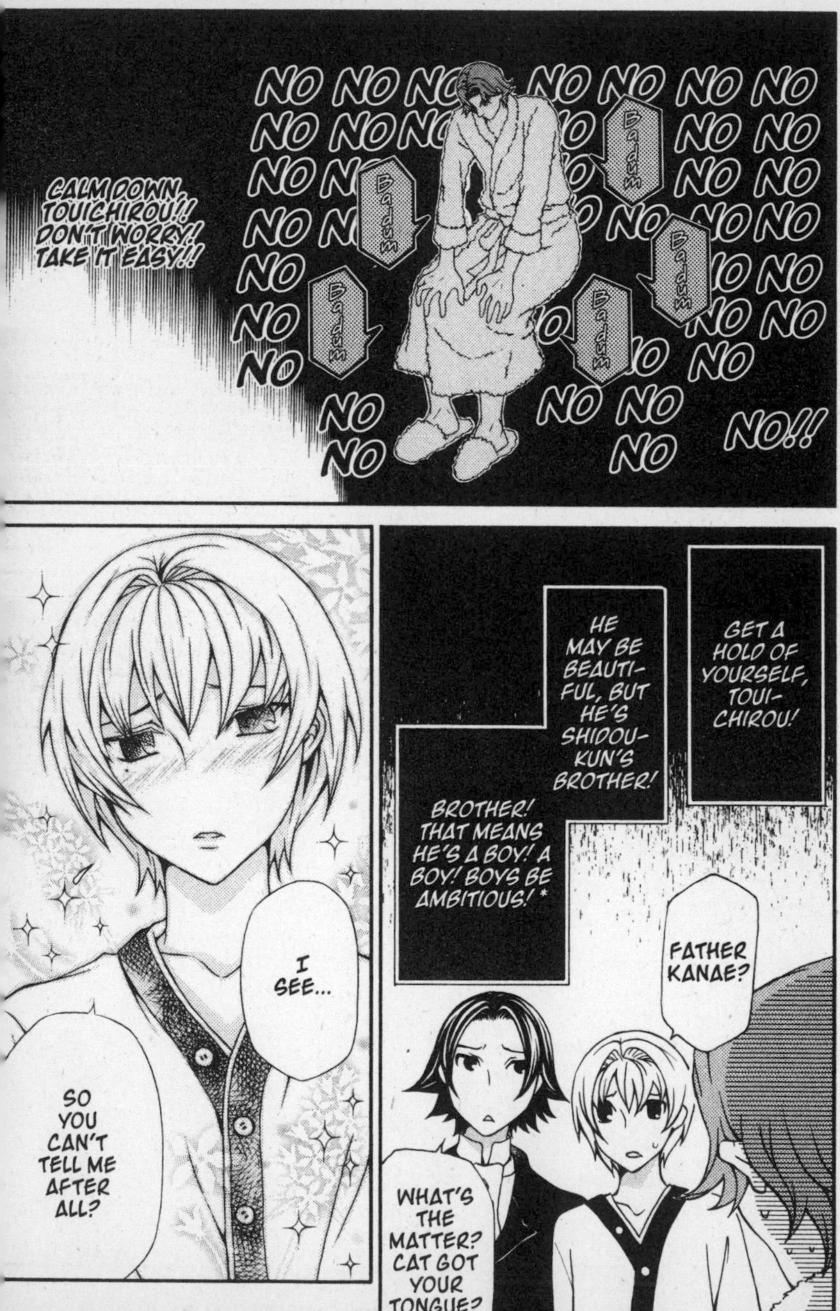
NO NO NO NO NO NO NO
NO NO NO NO NO
Badum
Badum
Badum
Badum
Badum
NO NO
NO NO NO
NO!!
CALM DOWN, TOUICHIROU!! DON'T WORRY! TAKE IT EASY!!
GET A HOLD OF YOURSELF, TOUI-CHIROU!
HE MAY BE BEAUTI-FUL, BUT HE'S SHIDOU-KUN'S BROTHER!
BROTHER! THAT MEANS HE'S A BOY! A BOY! BOYS BE AMBITIOUS! *
FATHER KANAE?
WHAT'S THE MATTER? CAT GOT YOUR TONGUE?
I SEE...
SO YOU CAN'T TELL ME AFTER ALL?

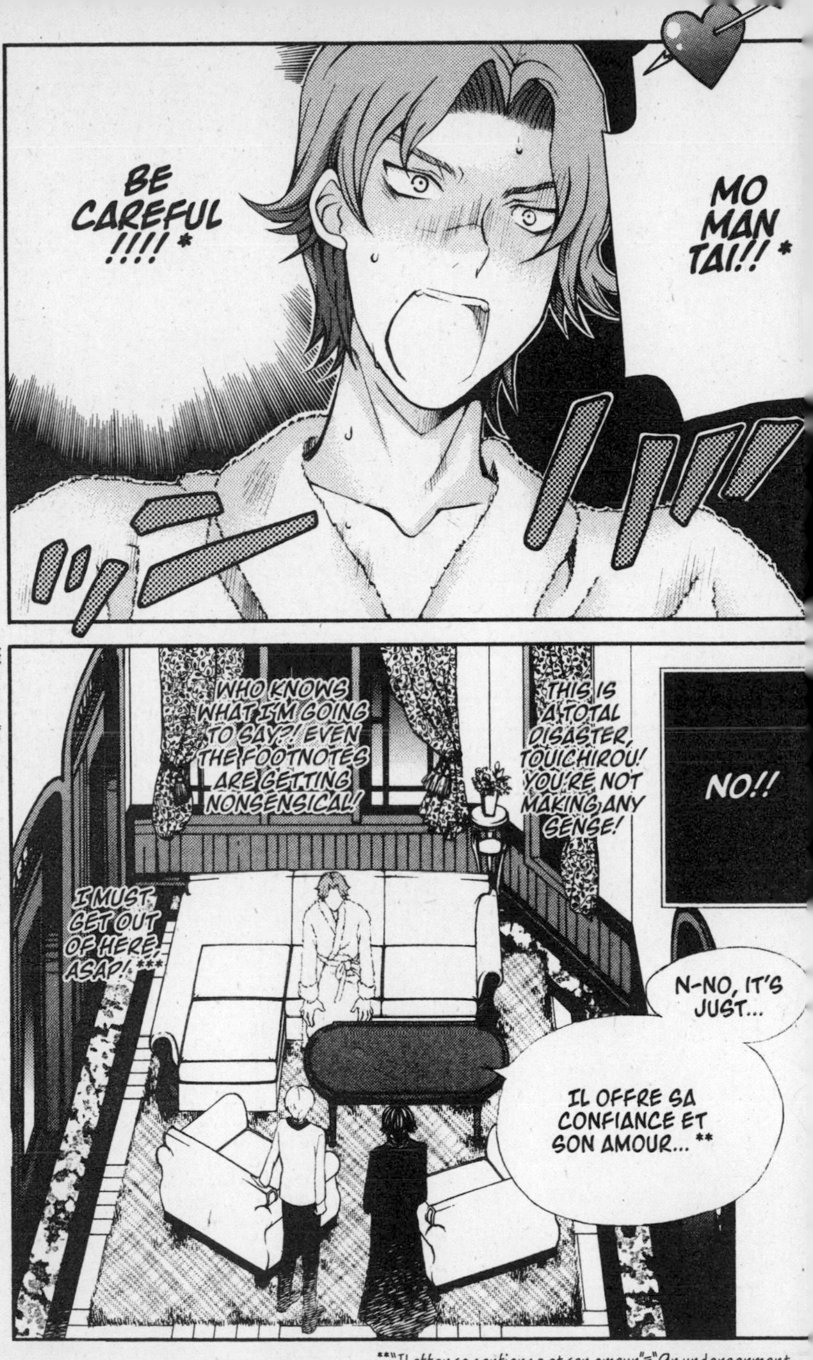
MO MAN TAI!! *
BE CAREFUL!!!! *
NO!!
THIS IS A TOTAL DISASTER, TOUICHIROU! YOU'RE NOT MAKING ANY SENSE!
WHO KNOWS WHAT I'M GOING TO SAY?! EVEN THE FOOTNOTES ARE GETTING NONSENSICAL!
I MUST GET OUT OF HERE, ASAP! ***
N-NO, IT'S JUST...
IL OFFRE SA CONFIANCE ET SON AMOUR... **

*"Be careful!!!!!"="In Cantonese; in English. As in "Beep Beep Beep Beep! Emergency, emergency! (in a robotic voice)"

***"ASAP"="I want some steaming hot yakisoba on the count of three!"

**"Il offer sa confiance et son amour"="An undergarment manufacturer that brings you trust and love."

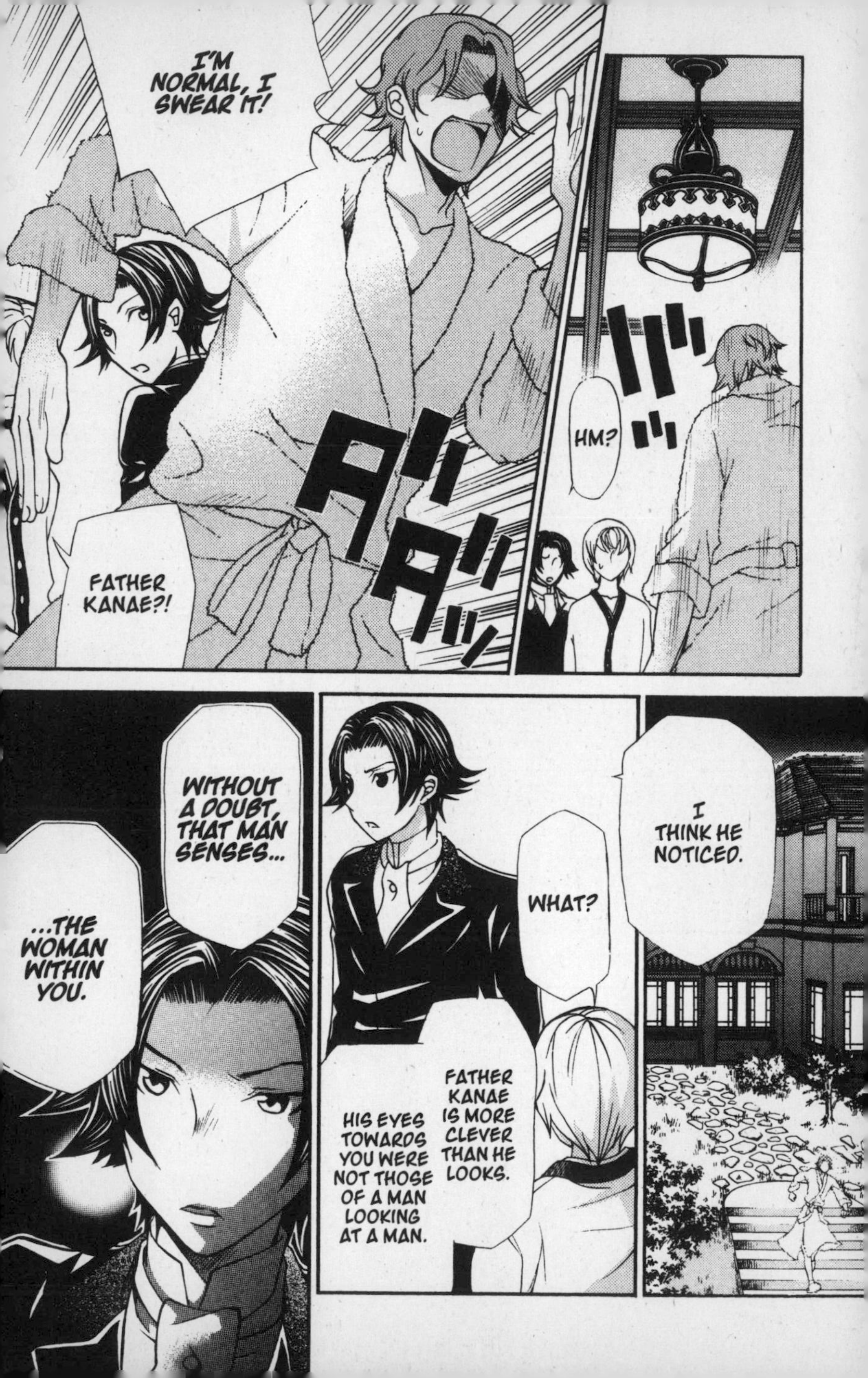
HM?
I'M NORMAL, I SWEAR IT!
FATHER KANAE?!
I THINK HE NOTICED.
WHAT?
FATHER KANAE IS MORE CLEVER THAN HE LOOKS.
HIS EYES TOWARDS YOU WERE NOT THOSE OF A MAN LOOKING AT A MAN.
WITHOUT A DOUBT, THAT MAN SENSES...
...THE WOMAN WITHIN YOU.

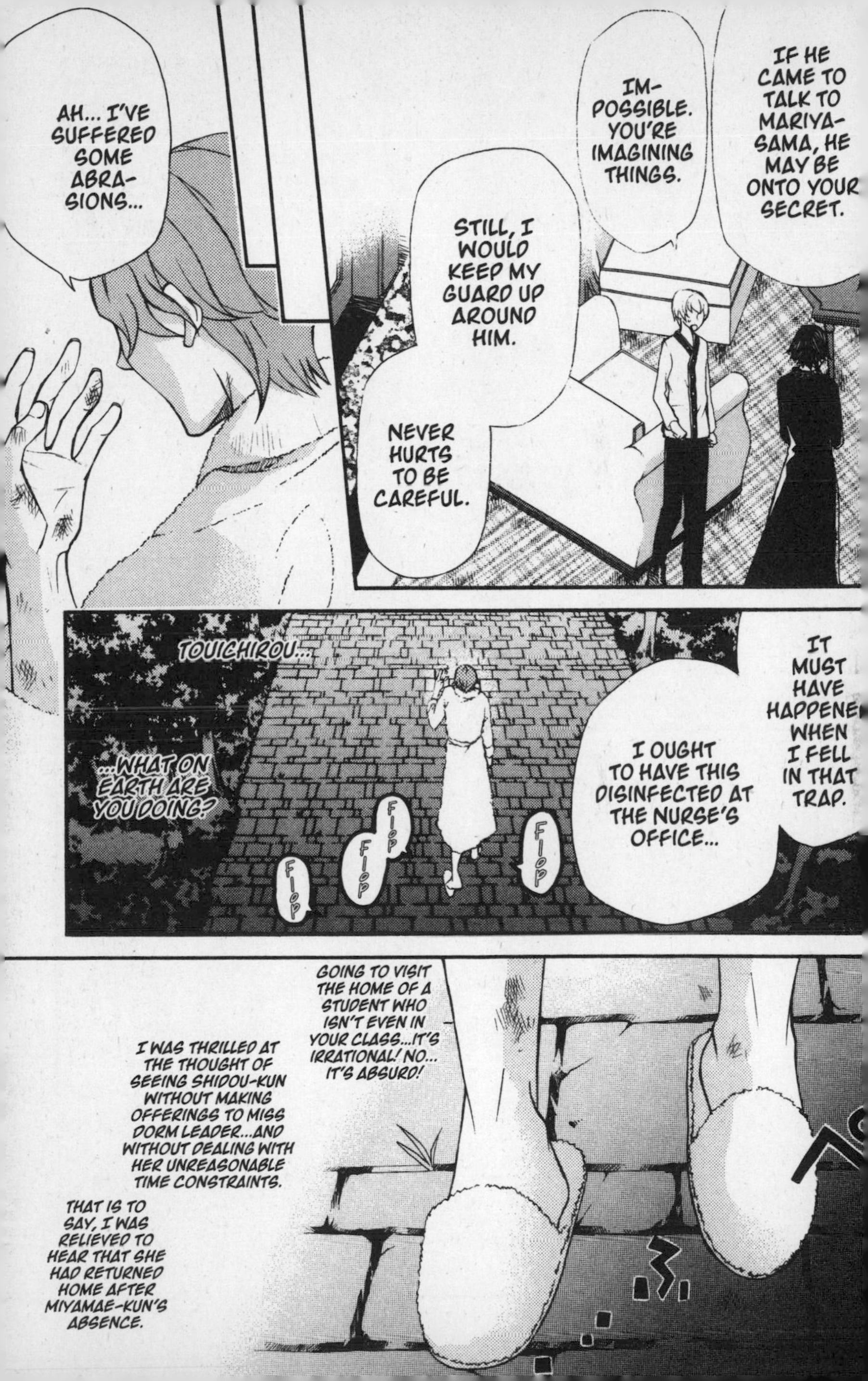
IF HE CAME TO TALK TO MARIYA-SAMA, HE MAY BE ONTO YOUR SECRET.
IM-POSSIBLE. YOU'RE IMAGINING THINGS.
STILL, I WOULD KEEP MY GUARD UP AROUND HIM.
NEVER HURTS TO BE CAREFUL.
AH... I'VE SUFFERED SOME ABRA-SIONS...
IT MUST HAVE HAPPENE WHEN I FELL IN THAT TRAP.
I OUGHT TO HAVE THIS DISINFECTED AT THE NURSE'S OFFICE...
TOUICHIROU...
...WHAT ON EARTH ARE YOU DOING?
Flop
Flop
Flop
Flop
GOING TO VISIT THE HOME OF A STUDENT WHO ISN'T EVEN IN YOUR CLASS...IT'S IRRATIONAL! NO... IT'S ABSURD!
I WAS THRILLED AT THE THOUGHT OF SEEING SHIDOU-KUN WITHOUT MAKING OFFERINGS TO MISS DORM LEADER...AND WITHOUT DEALING WITH HER UNREASONABLE TIME CONSTRAINTS.
THAT IS TO SAY, I WAS RELIEVED TO HEAR THAT SHE HAD RETURNED HOME AFTER MIYAMAE-KUN'S ABSENCE.

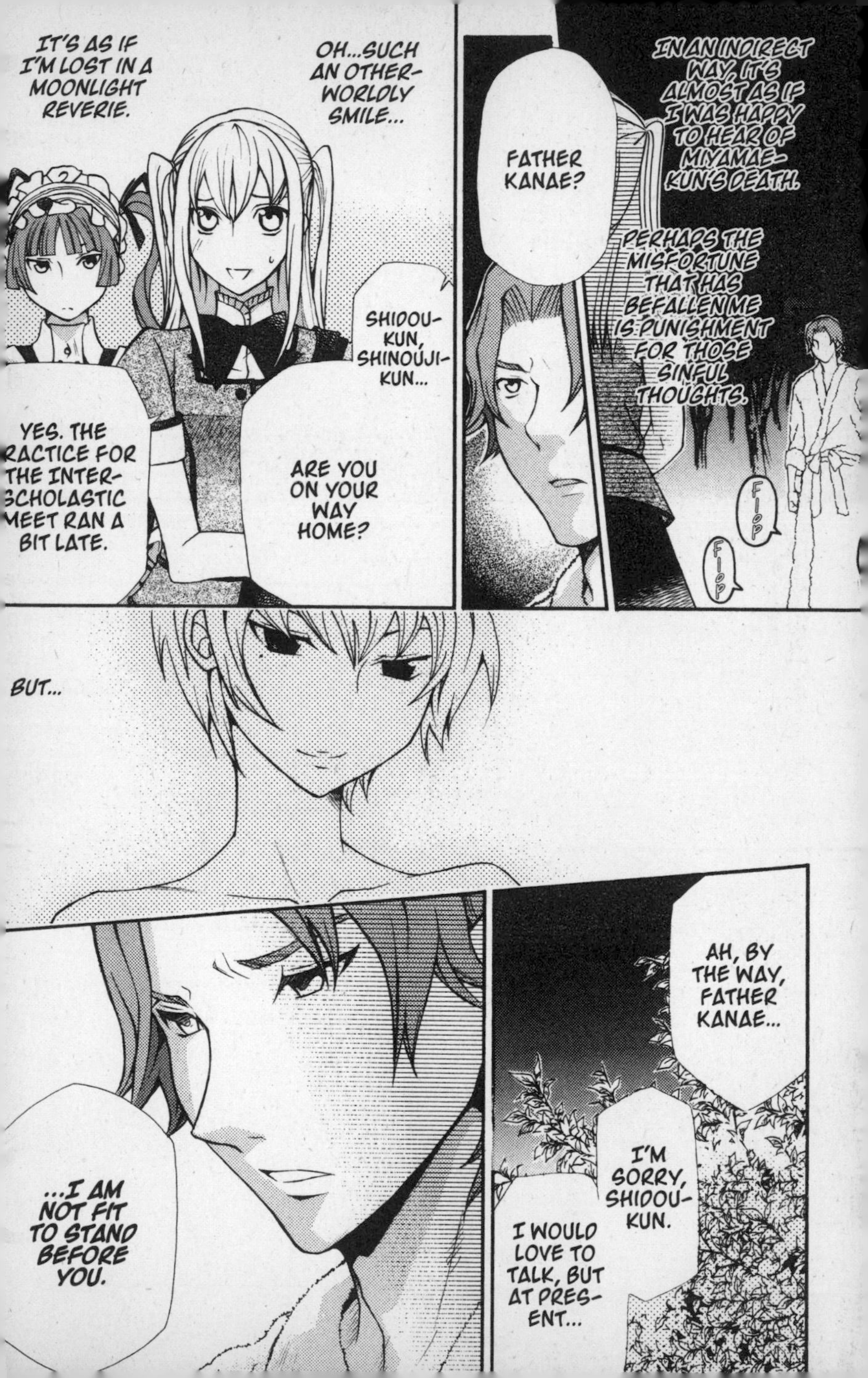
IN AN INDIRECT WAY, IT'S ALMOST AS IF I WAS HAPPY TO HEAR OF MIYAMAE-KUN'S DEATH.
FATHER KANAE?
PERHAPS THE MISFORTUNE THAT HAS BEFALLEN ME IS PUNISHMENT FOR THOSE SINFUL THOUGHTS.
Flop
Flop
OH...SUCH AN OTHER-WORLDLY SMILE...
IT'S AS IF I'M LOST IN A MOONLIGHT REVERIE.
SHIDOU-KUN, SHINOUJI-KUN...
ARE YOU ON YOUR WAY HOME?
YES. THE RACTICE FOR THE INTER-SCHOLASTIC MEET RAN A BIT LATE.
BUT...
AH, BY THE WAY, FATHER KANAE...
I'M SORRY, SHIDOU-KUN.
I WOULD LOVE TO TALK, BUT AT PRES-ENT...
...I AM NOT FIT TO STAND BEFORE YOU.

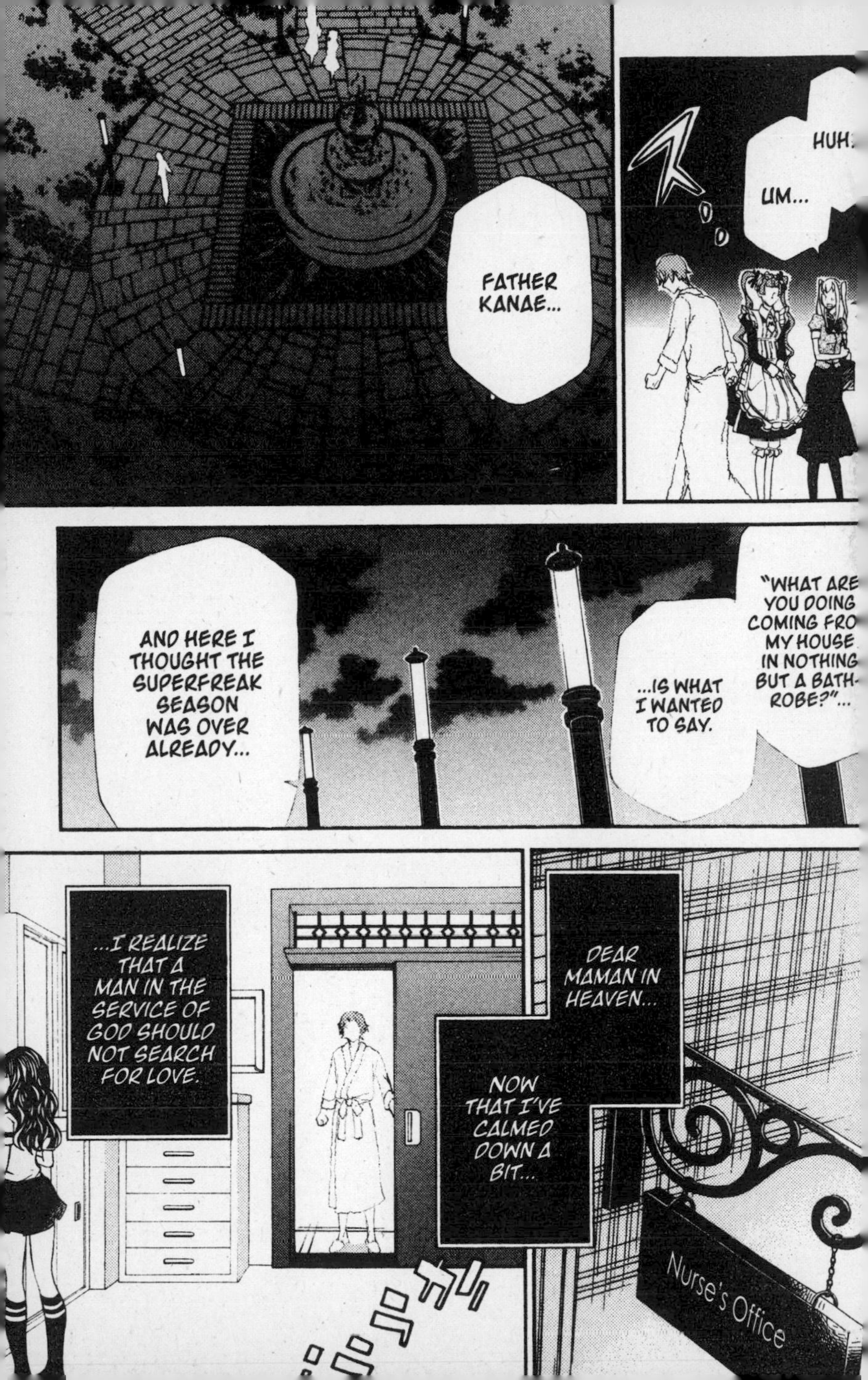
HUH
UM...
FATHER KANAE...
"WHAT ARE YOU DOING COMING FRO MY HOUSE IN NOTHING BUT A BATH-ROBE?"...
...IS WHAT I WANTED TO SAY.
AND HERE I THOUGHT THE SUPERFREAK SEASON WAS OVER ALREADY...
DEAR MAMAN IN HEAVEN...
NOW THAT I'VE CALMED DOWN A BIT...
Nurse's Office
...I REALIZE THAT A MAN IN THE SERVICE OF GOD SHOULD NOT SEARCH FOR LOVE.

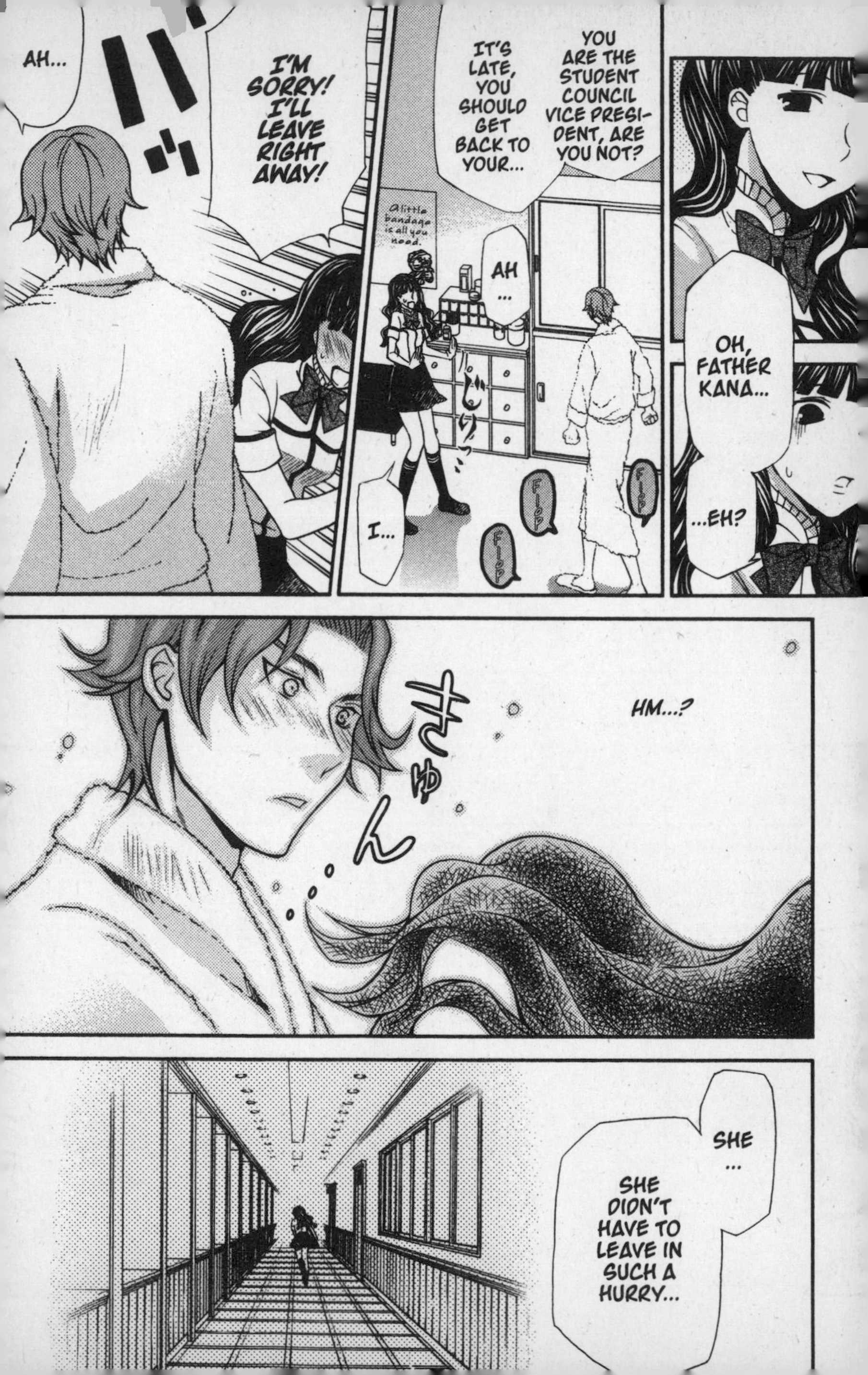
OH, FATHER KANA...
...EH?
YOU ARE THE STUDENT COUNCIL VICE PRESIDENT, ARE YOU NOT?
IT'S LATE, YOU SHOULD GET BACK TO YOUR...
AH ...
A little bandage is all you need.
Flop
Flop
Flop
I...
I'M SORRY! I'LL LEAVE RIGHT AWAY!
AH...
HM...?
きゅん
SHE ...
SHE DIDN'T HAVE TO LEAVE IN SUCH A HURRY...

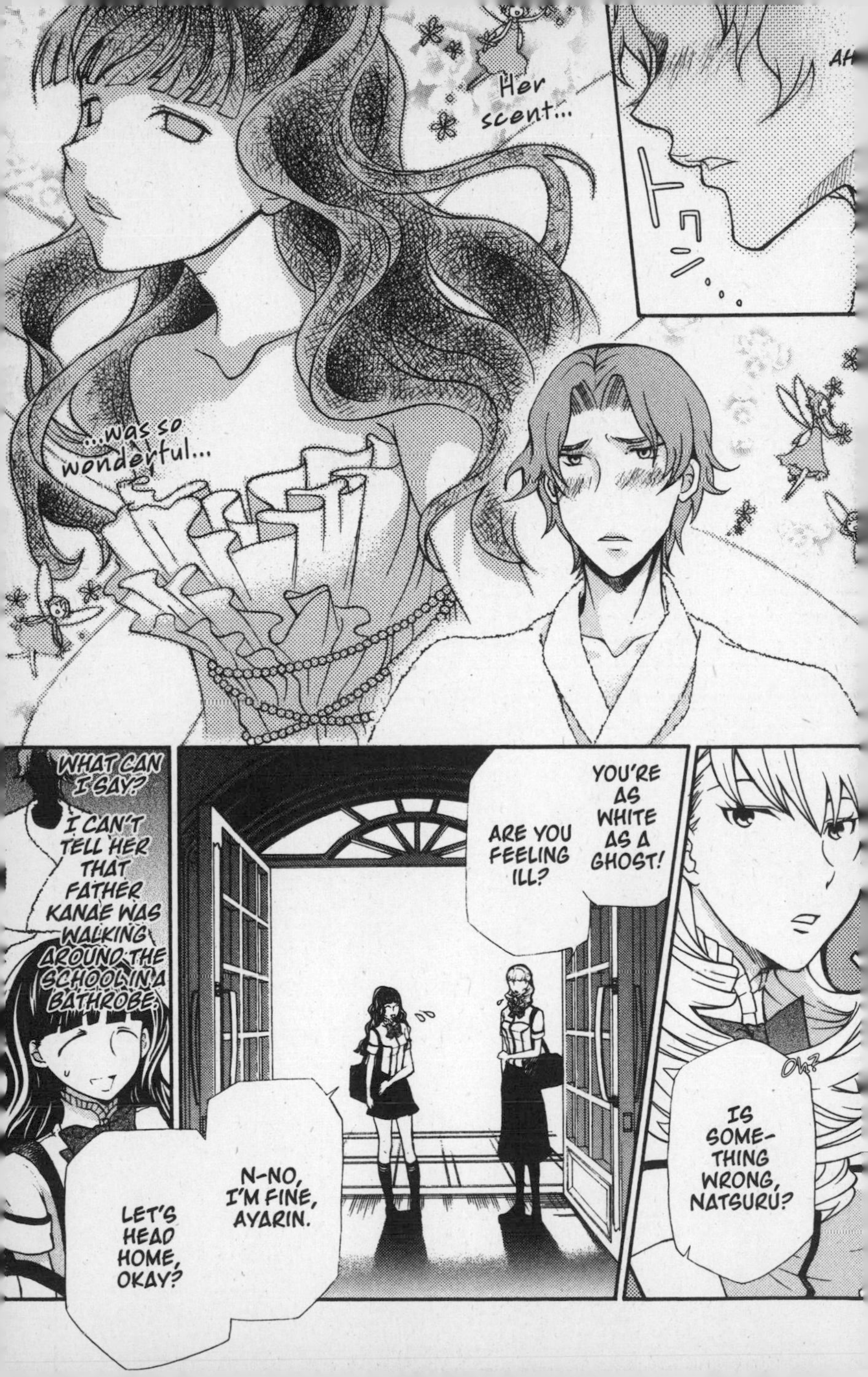

AH
トクン…
Her scent...
...was so wonderful...
Oh?
IS SOME-THING WRONG, NATSURU?
YOU'RE AS WHITE AS A GHOST!
ARE YOU FEELING ILL?
N-NO, I'M FINE, AYARIN.
WHAT CAN I SAY? I CAN'T TELL HER THAT FATHER KANAE WAS WALKING AROUND THE SCHOOL IN A BATHROBE.
LET'S HEAD HOME, OKAY?

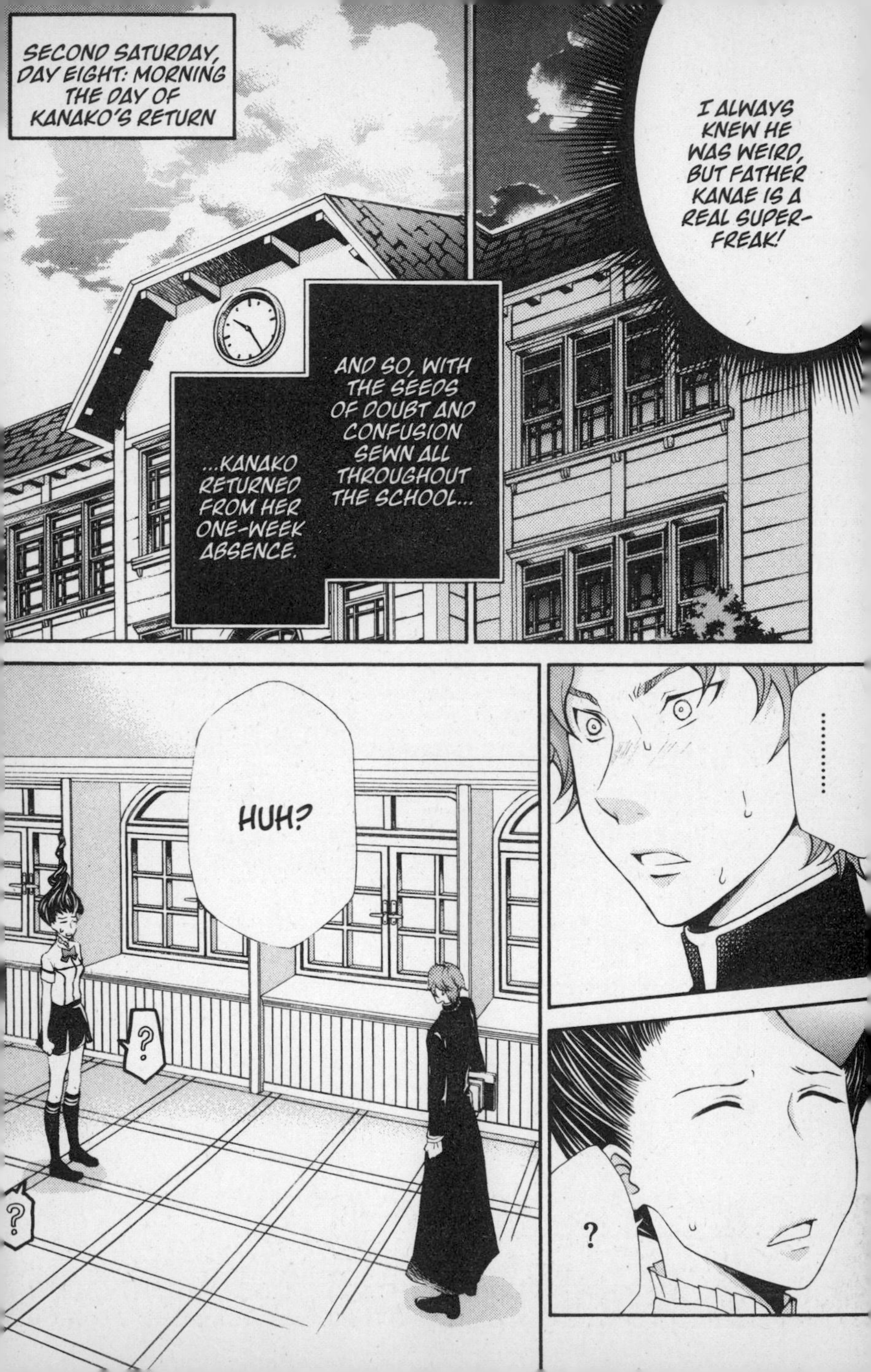
I ALWAYS KNEW HE WAS WEIRD, BUT FATHER KANAE IS A REAL SUPER-FREAK!
SECOND SATURDAY, DAY EIGHT: MORNING
THE DAY OF KANAKO'S RETURN
AND SO, WITH THE SEEDS OF DOUBT AND CONFUSION SEWN ALL THROUGHOUT THE SCHOOL...
...KANAKO RETURNED FROM HER ONE-WEEK ABSENCE.
......
?
HUH?
?
?

Maria Holic

A R I A H O L I C

Maria Holic

AYARI'S CHARMING DECO COLLECTION ①

Rear view

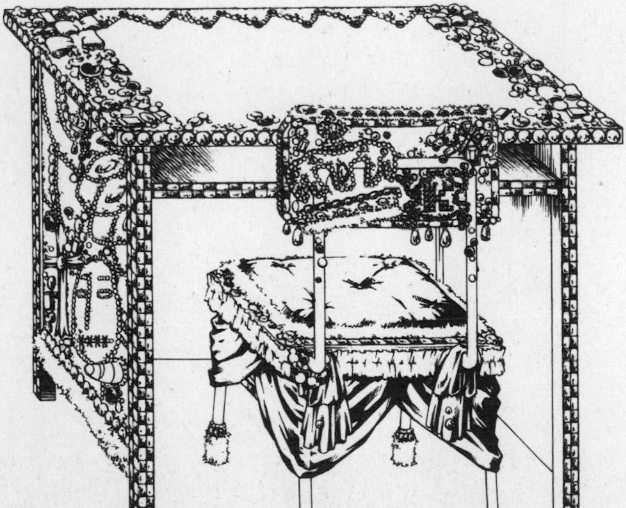

AYARI'S CHARMING DECO COLLECTION ②

Side view

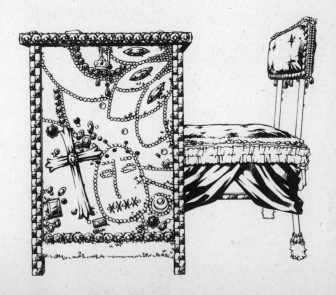

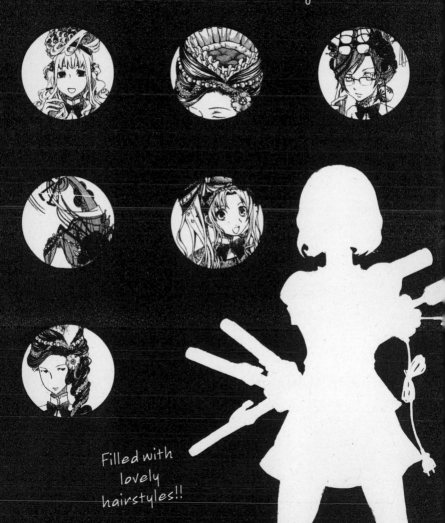

Special End of the Volume Bonus
Mori Master Honoka's

Hair Catalogue

Filled with
lovely
hairstyles!!

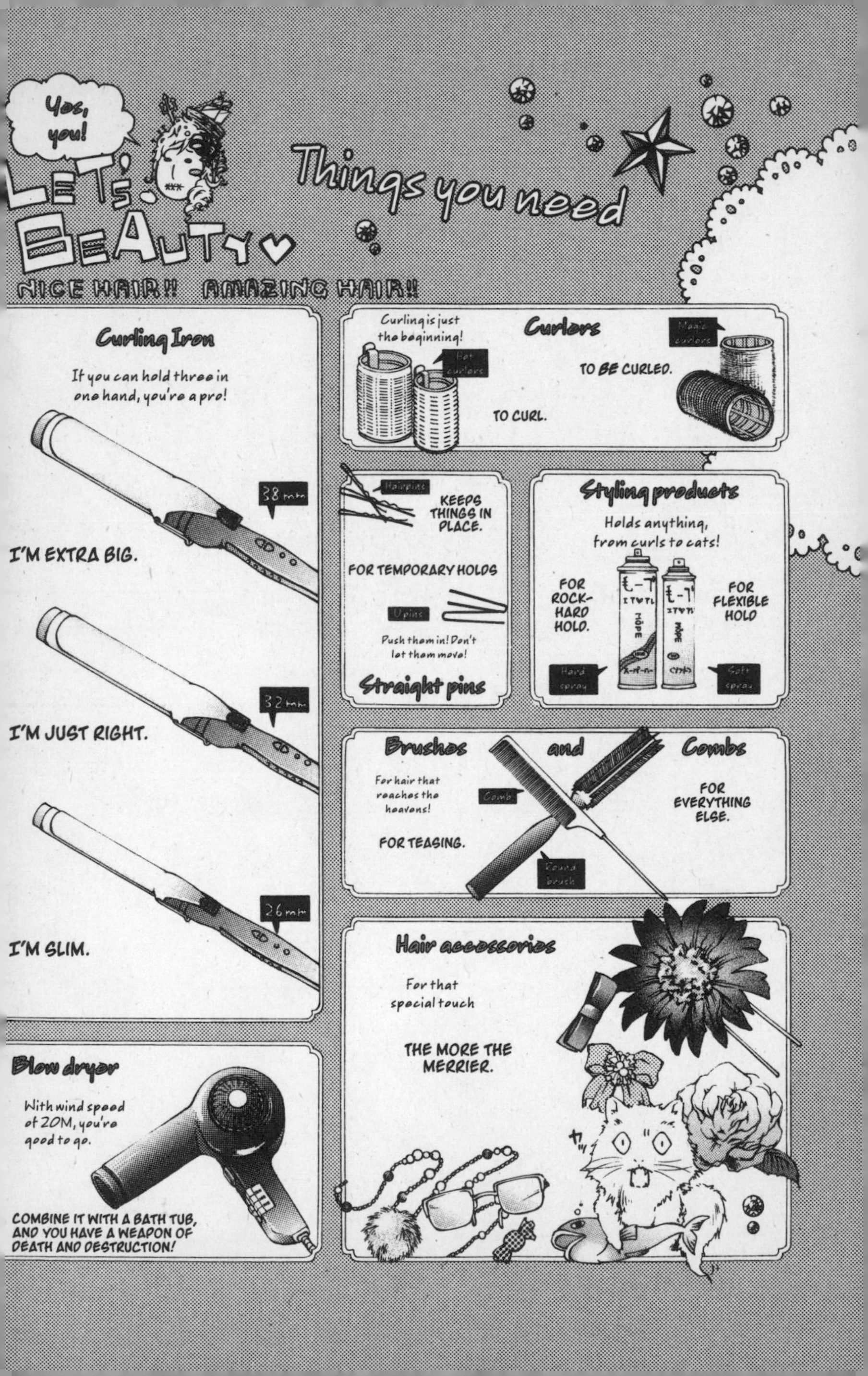

Yes, you!
LET'S BEAUTY♥
NICE HAIR!! AMAZING HAIR!!
Things you need
Curlers
Curling is just the beginning!
Hot curlers
Magic curlers
TO BE CURLED.
TO CURL.
Styling products
Holds anything, from curls to cats!
FOR FLEXIBLE HOLD
FOR ROCK-HARD HOLD.
Hard spray
Soft spray
Hairpins
KEEPS THINGS IN PLACE.
FOR TEMPORARY HOLDS
U-pins
Push them in! Don't let them move!
Straight pins
Brushes and Combs
FOR EVERYTHING ELSE.
Comb
For hair that reaches the heavens!
FOR TEASING.
Round brush
Hair accessories
For that special touch
THE MORE THE MERRIER.
Curling Iron
If you can hold three in one hand, you're a pro!
38mm
I'M EXTRA BIG.
32mm
I'M JUST RIGHT.
26mm
I'M SLIM.
Blow dryer
With wind speed of 20M, you're good to go.
COMBINE IT WITH A BATH TUB, AND YOU HAVE A WEAPON OF DEATH AND DESTRUCTION!

FILE NO.1 FRUITY PARFAIT SKY-HIGH PILE-UP WAVY TWIN TA

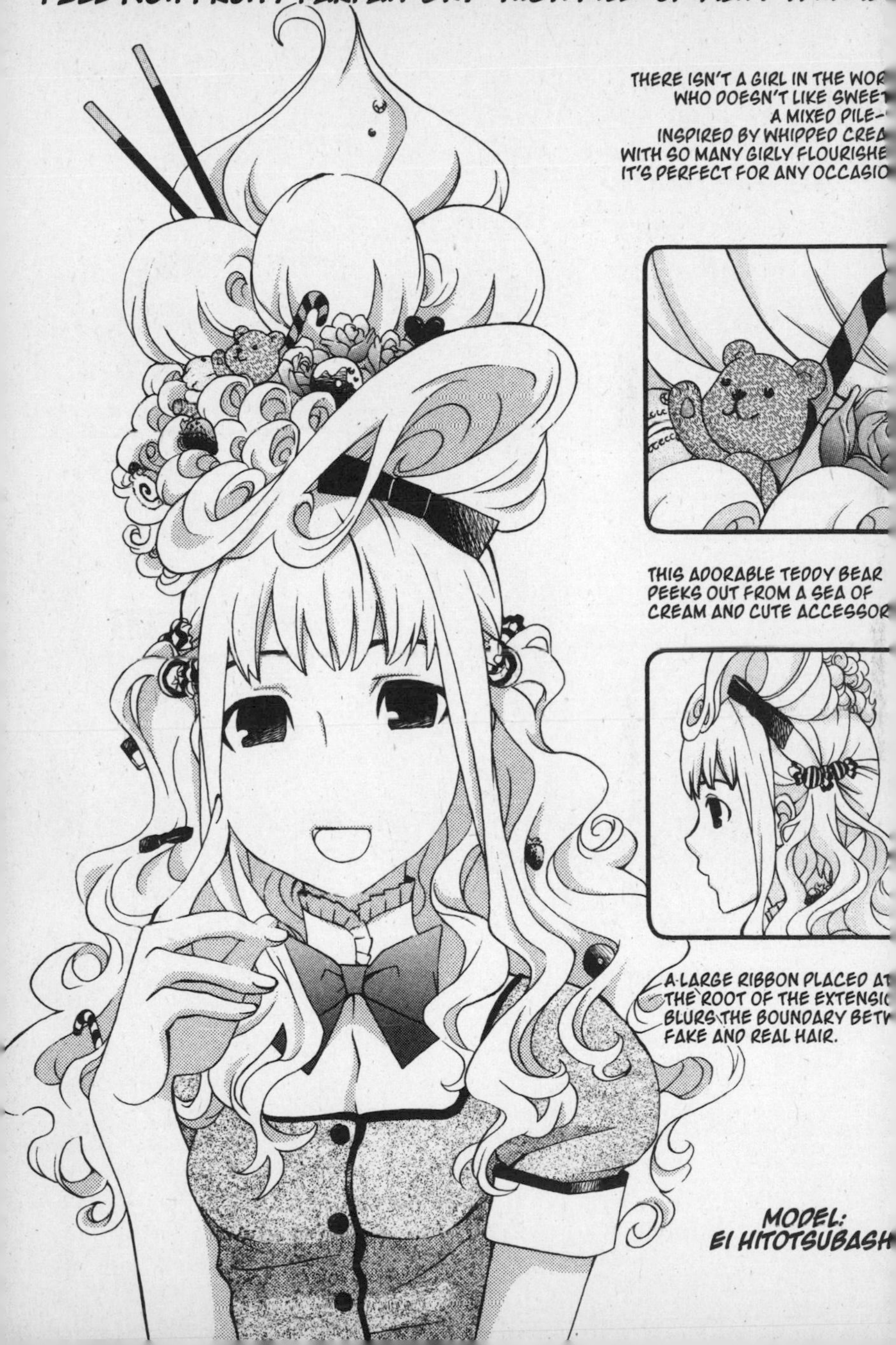
THERE ISN'T A GIRL IN THE WOR
WHO DOESN'T LIKE SWEET
A MIXED PILE-
INSPIRED BY WHIPPED CREA
WITH SO MANY GIRLY FLOURISHE
IT'S PERFECT FOR ANY OCCASIO
THIS ADORABLE TEDDY BEAR
PEEKS OUT FROM A SEA OF
CREAM AND CUTE ACCESSOR
A LARGE RIBBON PLACED AT
THE ROOT OF THE EXTENSIC
BLURS THE BOUNDARY BETV
FAKE AND REAL HAIR.
MODEL:
EI HITOTSUBASH

FILE NO.2 CURLY-Q CAT TAIL SPRINGY SOFT CURL

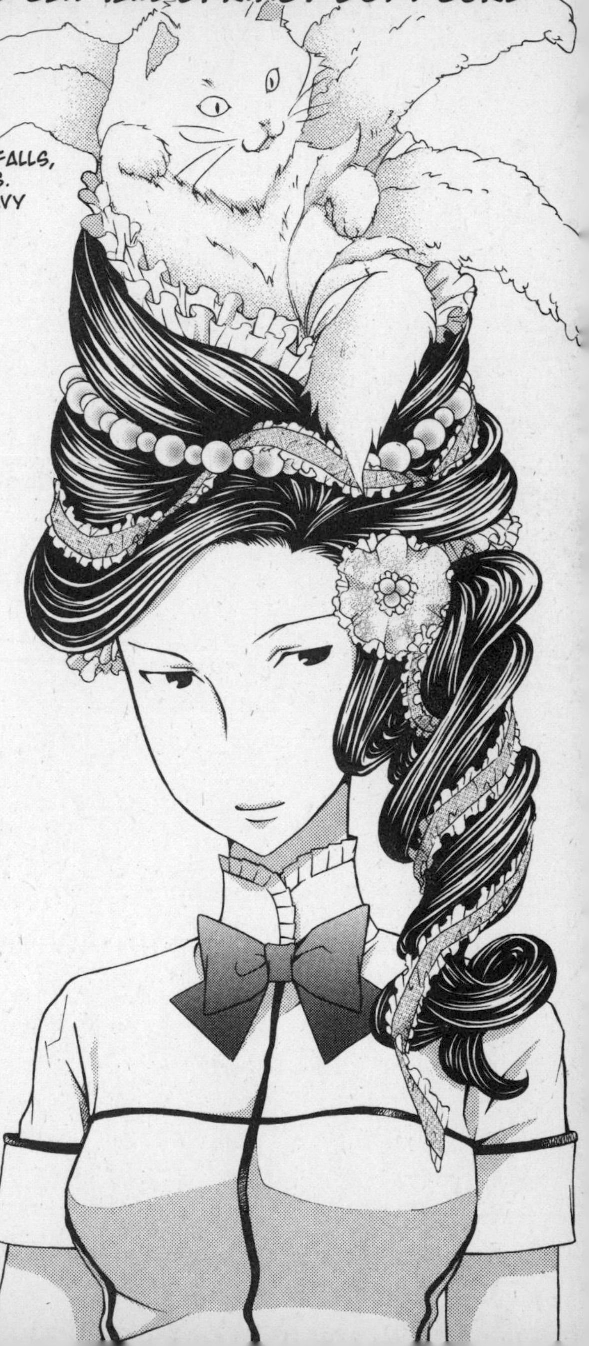

ELEGANT STYLE WITH CASCADING
RLS ON THE SIDE.
N'T WORRY ABOUT THE CAT. IF IT FALLS,
CAN MAKE A PERFECT TEN LANDING.
S STYLE CAN BE A BIT ON THE HEAVY
E, SO TRAIN YOUR NECK WELL!

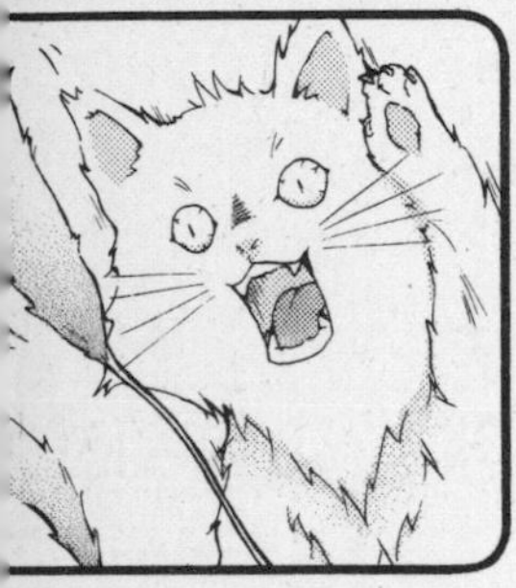

U MUST PLAY WITH THE CAT
TEN, OR IT WILL GET BORED.

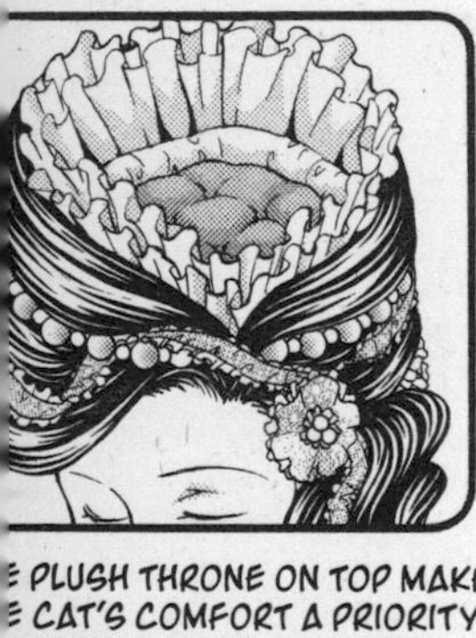

E PLUSH THRONE ON TOP MAKES
E CAT'S COMFORT A PRIORITY.
U MUST ALWAYS CONSIDER
UR PET'S FEELINGS!

ODEL: MII HABUTAE

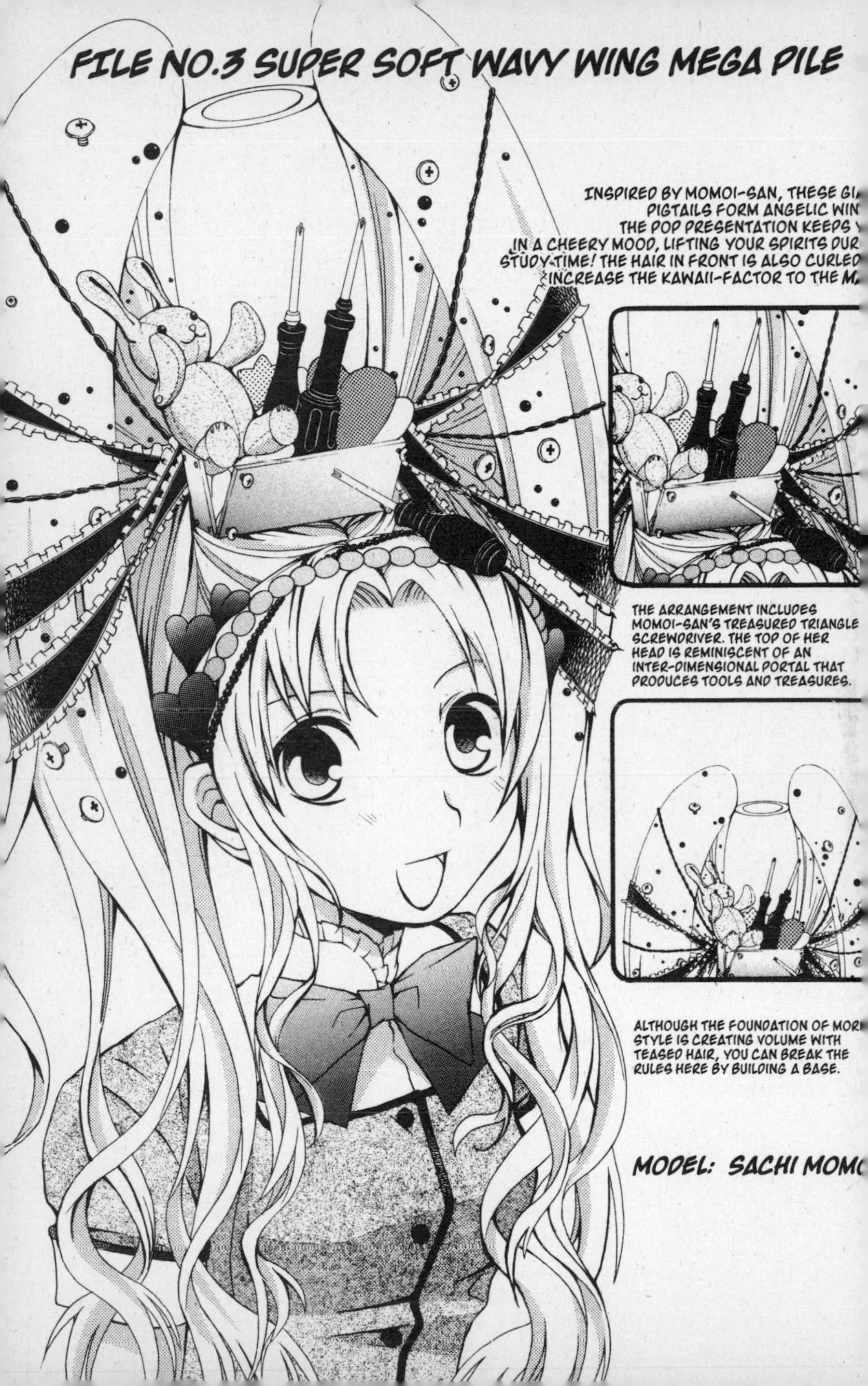
FILE NO.3 SUPER SOFT WAVY WING MEGA PILE
INSPIRED BY MOMOI-SAN, THESE GI
PIGTAILS FORM ANGELIC WIN
THE POP PRESENTATION KEEPS
IN A CHEERY MOOD, LIFTING YOUR SPIRITS DUR
STUDY TIME! THE HAIR IN FRONT IS ALSO CURLED
INCREASE THE KAWAII-FACTOR TO THE M
THE ARRANGEMENT INCLUDES MOMOI-SAN'S TREASURED TRIANGLE SCREWDRIVER. THE TOP OF HER HEAD IS REMINISCENT OF AN INTER-DIMENSIONAL PORTAL THAT PRODUCES TOOLS AND TREASURES.
ALTHOUGH THE FOUNDATION OF MOR
STYLE IS CREATING VOLUME WITH TEASED HAIR, YOU CAN BREAK THE RULES HERE BY BUILDING A BASE.
MODEL: SACHI MOM

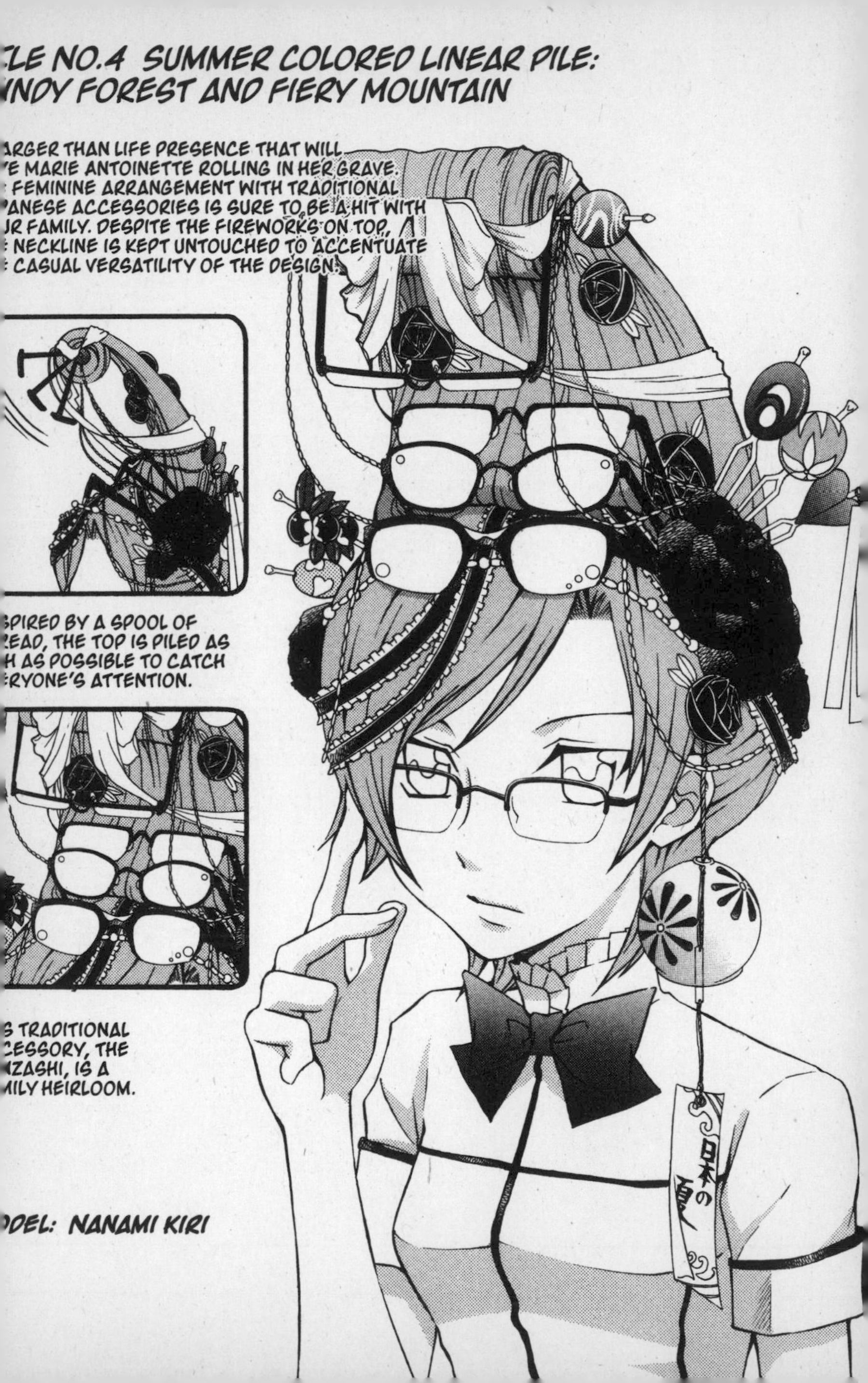
LE NO.4 SUMMER COLORED LINEAR PILE:
NDY FOREST AND FIERY MOUNTAIN
ARGER THAN LIFE PRESENCE THAT WILL
E MARIE ANTOINETTE ROLLING IN HER GRAVE.
FEMININE ARRANGEMENT WITH TRADITIONAL
PANESE ACCESSORIES IS SURE TO BE A HIT WITH
R FAMILY. DESPITE THE FIREWORKS ON TOP,
NECKLINE IS KEPT UNTOUCHED TO ACCENTUATE
CASUAL VERSATILITY OF THE DESIGN.
SPIRED BY A SPOOL OF
EAD, THE TOP IS PILED AS
H AS POSSIBLE TO CATCH
ERYONE'S ATTENTION.
S TRADITIONAL
CESSORY, THE
ZASHI, IS A
ILY HEIRLOOM.
DEL: NANAMI KIRI
日本の夏

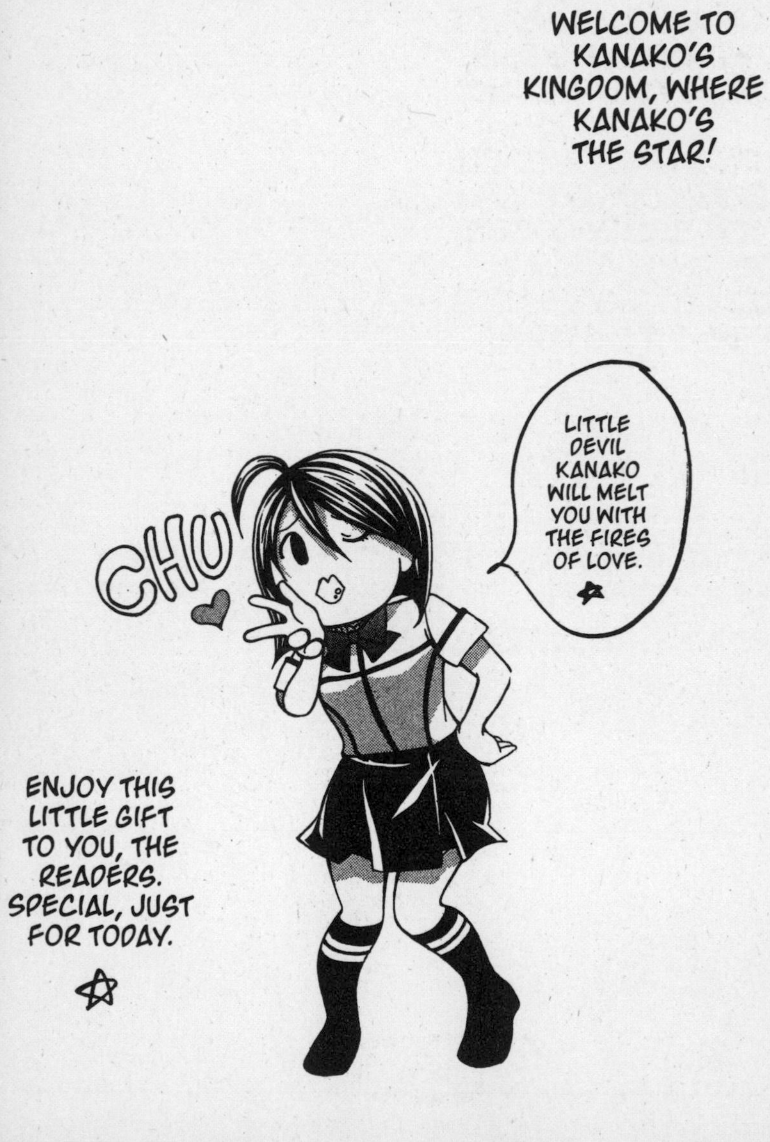
WELCOME TO KANAKO'S KINGDOM, WHERE KANAKO'S THE STAR!
LITTLE DEVIL KANAKO WILL MELT YOU WITH THE FIRES OF LOVE. ☆
CHU ♥
ENJOY THIS LITTLE GIFT TO YOU, THE READERS. SPECIAL, JUST FOR TODAY. ☆

OH! STOP, PLEASE!
I'M REALLY SORRY! I
WON'T DO IT AGAIN.
STOP TOUCHING ME!

I'LL BREAK OUT!! I'LL
BREAK OUT IN HIVES!!
I'M REALLY SORRY!
REALLY I AM!!
I'LL TRY MY BEST TO
BE EVEN SEXIER!!

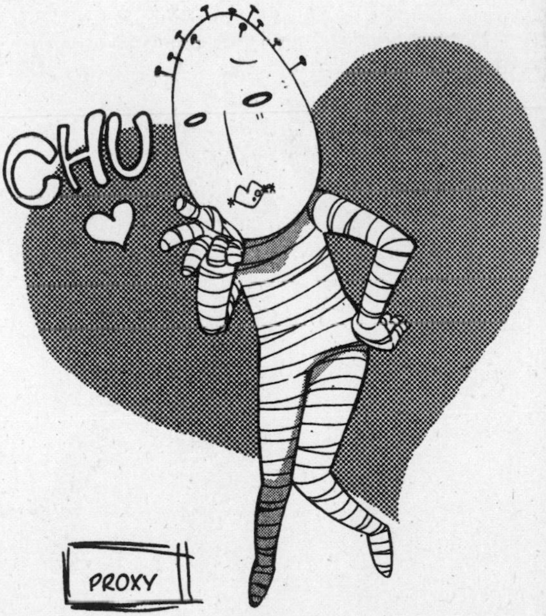
CHU
PROXY

There's more maidenly mischief
to be had in the next volume of...

*Even perverts have friends and family.
First, it's Sachi's birthday, and everyone
has a wonderful birthday present
prepared for Sachi except Kanako.
Thoughtfully, Mariya replaces Kanako's
lame gift with Kanako's secret photo
stash! Later, Kanako's little sister comes
to visit, revealing the real reason
their father left Ame no Kisaki...and it
apparently has something to do with
the creepy crazy funhouse that is the
mysterious Girls' Dormitory No. 1!*

"TEACH ME ALL THE HISTORY YOU WANT, BABY."
–JAPANATOR.COM

SEASON ONE
VAILABLE ON DVD 9/14/10

WATCH THE TRAILER!

SEASON TWO
AVAILABLE ON DVD 10/12/10

SPECIAL **BONUS** BANDANA
IN EACH BOX FOR A LIMITED TIME!

HETALIA
A X I S   P O W E R S

YOU SHOULD BE WATCHING WWW.FUNIMATION.COM/HETALIA
© 2008 HIDEKAZ HIMARUYA,GENTOSHA COMICS/HETALIA PROJECT. Licensed by FUNimation® Productions, Ltd. All Rights Reserved.

FUNIMATION
ENTERTAINMENT

Great Empires,
A Fight to the Finish...and PASTA?

Manga available October 2010!!

Get ready to brush up on world history with these handsome and hysterical personifications of the Axis Powers as they meet, become friends and form one of the most powerful alliances the world has ever seen!

It all begins when tough soldier Germany stumbles upon Italy, who, despite being the descendant of the greatest empire in history, is found hiding in a tomato box. In another twist of fate around a rather lovely kotatsu, Japan hops on board and the Axis Powers are forged! What trials and tribulations will this mighty trio face?

© 2008 HIDEKAZ HIMARUYA, GENTOSHA COMICS

 COMEDY

LIKE US ON FACEBOOK.COM/TOKYOPOP

Love Cats? Love Ramen?

Then,

Kenji Sonishi's

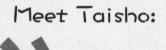

Neko Ramen
猫ラーメン

is for you!

Meet Taisho:

→ 大将 Taisho

Delcious, cute, or just plain weird? You decide.

...And I want your opinian!!

Hey!

I have an idea for a dessert ramen...

Dessert ramen?!

Milk { } Strawberries

Ramen

Woman or man, I doubt this counts as a dessert...

What do you think?! It should be a hit with the ladies, right?!

I think you're missing the point...

Not enough straw- berries, huh?!

www.neko-ramen.com

TOKYOPOP MANGA SUPPLEMENT

Naruto star **Yuri Lowenthal** is
VAN VON HUNTER

Featuring

Shoji Kawamori
- **Anime master**
(Macross, The Vision of Escaflowne)

Stu Levy
- **TOKYOPOP Founder and CEO**
(Princess Ai, Juror 13)

Get ready for a hilarious,
VANtastic adventure
as the out-of-work evil
vanquisher Van Von Hunter
unravels the mysteries of
manga, anime, and
Japanese "pop" culture
in order to save the world.

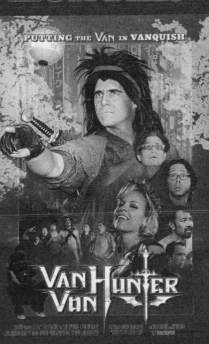

Get your DVD now at
www.createspace.com/283456

f facebook

Van Von Hunter on Facebook

Become a Fan

To watch the trailer,
hear original music from the film,
become a **VAN FAN**, and more, visit
www.facebook.com/vanvonhunter

AVAILABLE FOR PURCHASE ON DVD NOW
AND SCREENING AT FAN CONVENTIONS AROUND THE WORLD!

TOKYOPOP MANGA SUPPLEMENT

4 ♦ Alice IN THE COUNTRY OF Hearts
WONDERFUL WONDER WORLD
™

WHAT KIND OF DEADLY DANCES WILL TAKE PLACE AT THIS STRANGE PARTY?

NEW YORK TIMES BEST SELLER

© SOUMEI HOSHINO / MAG GARDEN CORPORATION
© QUINROSE ALL RIGHTS RESERVED.

ALICE IN THE COUNTRY OF HEARTS VOLUME 4
ON SALE EVERYWHERE SEPTEMBER 2010!

ROMANCE

T TEEN AGE 13+

FOR MORE INFORMATION VISIT: www.TOKYOPOP.com

Let the Banquet Begin

Fruits Basket
Banquet

The #1 selling shojo manga in America!

Natsuki Takaya

Never-before-seen creator interview!

Special short story!

Includes:
- *16 beautifully colored pages of the best Furuba artwork, including a gorgeous two-page spread of Kyo and Tohru!
- *Celebrated scenes from your favorite chapters
- *Furuba-themed zodiac games
- *Odd couple pairings
- *An impressive line-up of Fruits Basket books published all around the world!

© 1998 Natsuki Takaya / HAKUSENSHA, Inc.

FOR MORE INFORMATION VISIT: WWW.TOKYOPOP.COM

NO ONE IS SAFE ANYMORE

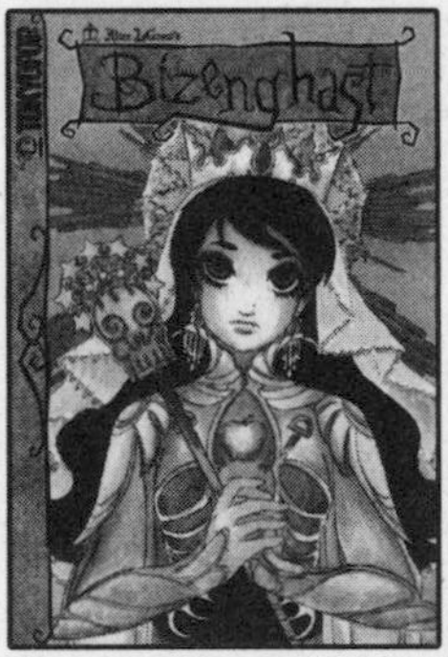
Bizenghast
TOKYOPOP

VOLUME 7

The final battle rages for the lives and souls of the inhabitants of Bizenghast, and no one is safe anymore. Shocking revelations of the town's dark history continue to emerge, and Dinah's struggle will go beyond the borders of the mausoleum...and into some of her worst nightmares...

PREVIEW AT www.TOKYOPOP.com/NoOneIsSafe

Bizenghast

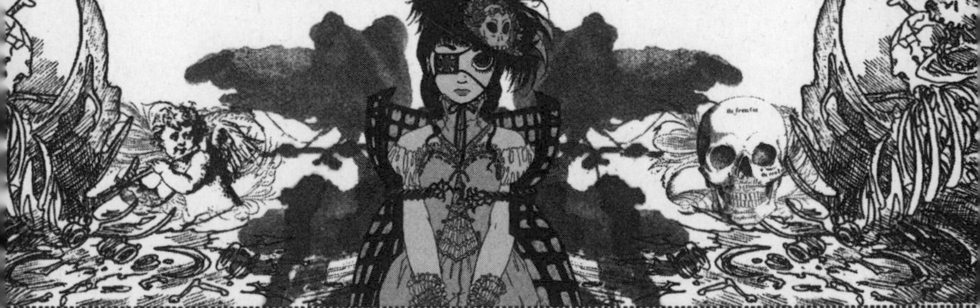

FOR MORE INFORMATION VISIT: www.TOKYOPOP.com

THE SMALLEST HERO!?

RATMAN

ラットマン

THE SMALLEST HERO!?
RATMAN
TOKYOPOP
Story and Art by INUI Sekihiko
2
SECOND VOLUME

Not your typical good versus evil story

Even with a successful caper under his belt, Shuto Katsuragi is still not very comfortable w his role as the dark anti-hero "Ratman" for th evil secret organization "Jackal." Deciding to advantage of Ratman's abilities, he tries his h at some vigilante heroism on his off time fro the organization. The first attempt goes well, he even shows up in the papers as a "myster ous, unnamed hero." The second attempt do not go nearly as well, as he is mistaken for th criminal instead of the guy trying to stop the crime. The misunderstandings continue whe he tries to break up a fight between membe a hero sentai team. He has to knock them ou do it, and a late-coming Ankaiser pounces o the excuse to pick a fight of his own!

the smallest hero?!

Story and Art by INUI Sekihiko

2

ACTION

OT OLDER TEEN AGE 16+

BE SURE TO VISIT WWW.TOKYOPOP.COM/SHOP FOR EVERYTHING YOU COULD EVER WANT!

STOP!

This is the back of the book. You wouldn't want to spoil a great ending!

This book is printed "manga-style," in the authentic Japanese right-to-left format. Since none of the artwork has been flipped or altered, readers get to experience the story just as the creator intended. You've been asking for it, so TOKYOPOP® delivered: authentic, hot-off-the-press, and far more fun!

DIRECTIONS

If this is your first time reading manga-style, here's a quick guide to help you understand how it works.

It's easy... just start in the top right panel and follow the numbers. Have fun, and look for more 100% authentic manga from TOKYOPOP®!